Publisher
MIKE RICHARDSON

Collection Editor
SUZANNE TAYLOR

Collection Designer
JULIE E. GASSAWAY

This volume collects issues 1-6 and stories from issues 7-8
of the Mirage Publishing, Inc. comic-book series *Usagi Yojimbo Volume Two*.

Visit the Usagi Yojimbo Dojo website
www.usagiyojimbo.com

Published by
Dark Horse Comics, Inc.
10956 SE Main Street
Milwaukie, OR 97222

www.darkhorse.com

To find a comics shop in your area,
call the Comic Shop Locator Service toll-free at 1-888-266-4226

First edition: September 1997
ISBN: 1-56971-259-X

5 7 9 10 8 6 4
Printed in Canada

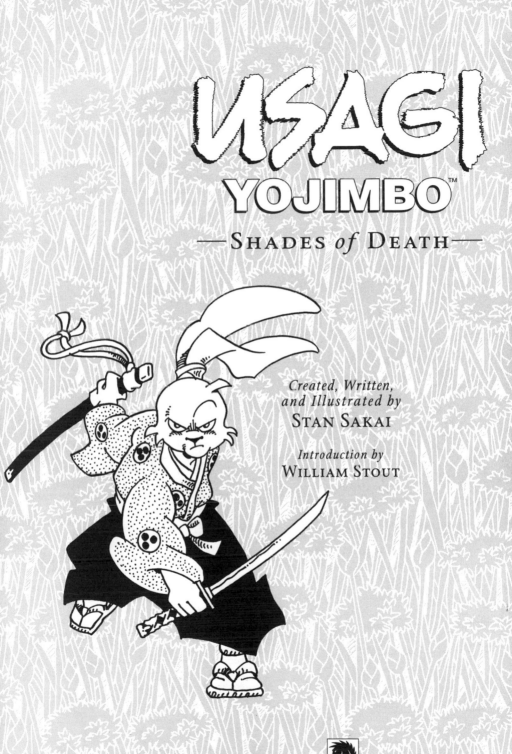

USAGI YOJIMBO™
—SHADES of DEATH—

Created, Written,
and Illustrated by
STAN SAKAI

Introduction by
WILLIAM STOUT

DARK HORSE COMICS®

Usagi Yojimbo

Storytelling from a Master

The entertainment business is a world where concepts need to be condensed into just a few words (typical pitch: "I've got a great story here: it's *Tootsie* meets *Die Hard* — with more nudity"). So for those of you impatient readers and studio executives who are scanning this introduction to find out whether or not to buy (or option) this book, let me put it this way:

Usagi Yojimbo is Carl Barks meets Akira Kurosawa — with more nudity.

Now buy this book, damn it, take it home, and read it.

For the rest of you with patience that extends beyond the MTV attention span, let's savor the exquisite qualities that make *Usagi Yojimbo* so special. Each compendium of *Usagi Yojimbo* is a collection of rarities. No, the comic books from which the particular stories in this volume were collected are not rare (yet). It is the many artistic and literary qualities of *Usagi Yojimbo* that put this particular rabbit on the Endangered Species list.

Stan Sakai is the Akira Kurosawa of comic books. Stan's stories are not the hyper-shriek blasts that seem the norm for most comics nowadays. His stories are not an excuse for a series of pinup pages. Stan does not have to resort to cheap flash and false bravado in order to tell a story. He is a man who is in full literary and artistic control of his medium. Stan's pacing is deliberate, and, like Paul Chadwick, he is not afraid to slow it down a little bit to make a subtle but powerful point. Like Carl Barks, Stan's graphic simplicity reinforces the readability of his storytelling.

Kurosawa has always understood that contrast is the essence of good art. In *Usagi Yojimbo*, a richness of contrasts abounds: gentleness/violence; quiet story pauses/explosions of action; lowbrow guffaws/subtle and sophisticated wit.

Some writers excel at the short form of storytelling; others find their strengths within a more epic form. This volume includes two long stories, one medium-length story, and four short stories from the Mirage editions (volume two, issues one through six, and back-up tales from issues seven and eight). Stan is a master of all of these forms (my own personal favorites are the short and powerfully poetic back-up stories).

The samurai subject matter provokes expectations of heavy violence. The violence is here, but I don't know that I would call it heavy. With masterful restraint, Stan dances a delicate line between fulfilling that required story expectation and resisting the depiction of the overtly graphic consequences of the inevitable.

There is real clarity to Stan's design, a seeming rarity at this time in the history of comics. His art reflects the influence of the best Japanese prints. This influence is also felt in the book's color. Unfortunately, the valuable film containing the color separations for the comics has been lost, so the stories are reprinted here in black and white.

Nevertheless, I would like to briefly discuss the color that graded the first appearance of these stories. Perhaps you'll be inspired to search out the original publications of these stories just to savor them in their intended color form.

I've found that any colorist worth his or her paintbox has been smart enough to study the world's greatest art form in terms of sensually subtle "flat" (as opposed to painted or modeled) color: *ukiyo-e* ("floating world": the Japanese name for their woodblock prints). *Usagi Yojimbo* colorist Tom Luth is no exception. It's easy to argue that no better comic than *Usagi Yojimbo* could be found to exploit this influence on one's retinal memory. Tom has studied those color relationships well. His sensitivity to color is rare to comics.

So sit back in your favorite chair and enjoy a rich classic. Take pleasure and contentment in the knowledge that during your relaxed state a city full of studio executives are frantically trying to outbid each other for the film rights to the book that you are reading.

William Stout

William Stout has worked as a designer on over 25 major feature films (including the Conan films). Acknowledged by Michael Crichton as an inspiration for Jurassic Park, *Stout is the author/illustrator of the best-selling book* The Dinosaurs — A Fantastic New View of a Lost Era. *Stout is the co-creator of the entertainment industry comic-book satire* Mickey at 60 *and the chief designer for Steven Spielberg's* GameWorks. *He is currently working on a book that will be the first visual history of prehistoric and contemporary life in Antarctica.*

CONTENTS

"SHADES OF GREEN"   7

"JIZO"   67

"SHI"   75

"THE LIZARDS' TALE"   131

"USAGI'S GARDEN"   151

"AUTUMN"   159

"BATTLEFIELD"   167

To Ed, Diane,
Kristy, and
Cheryl

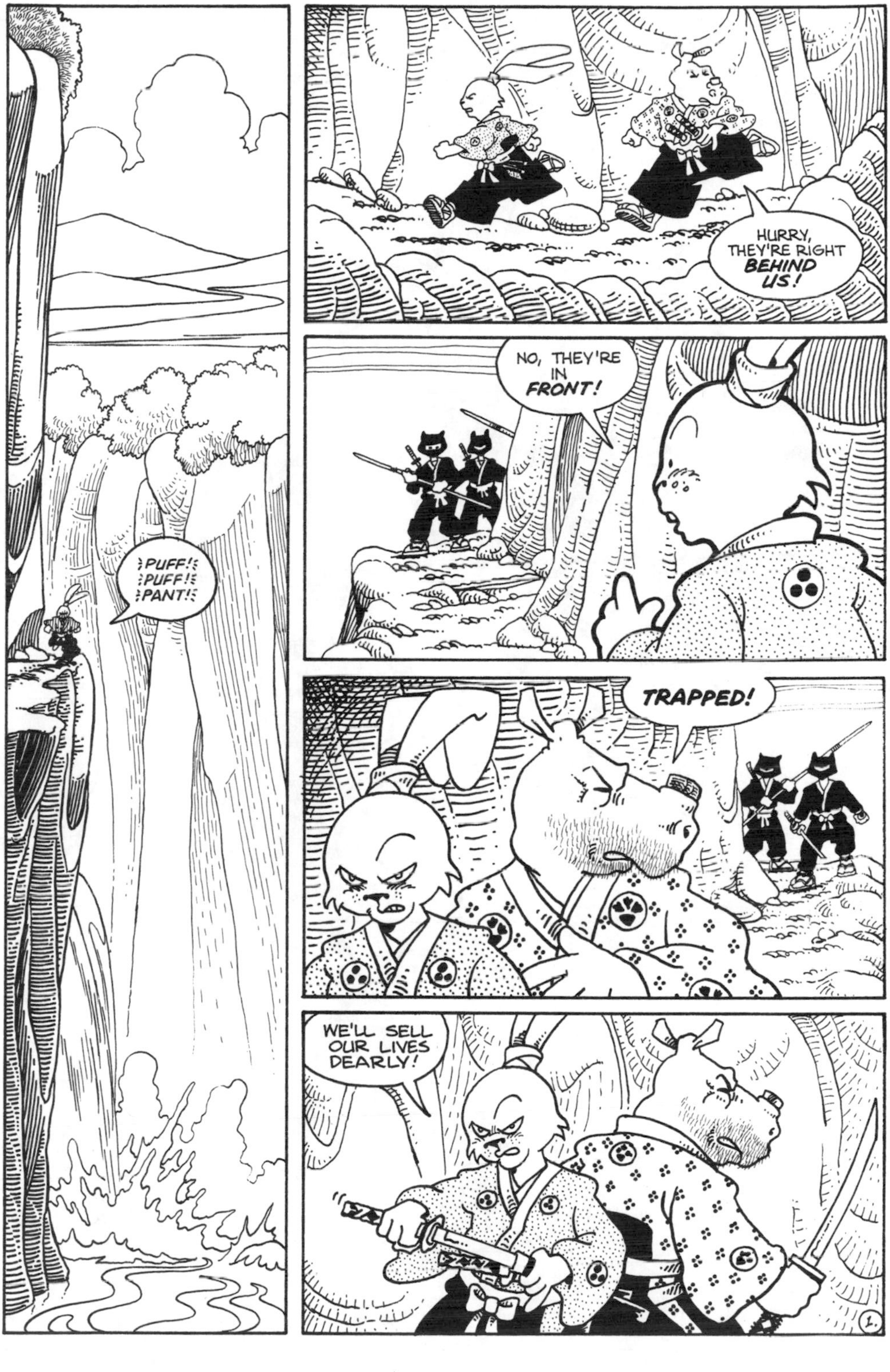
PUFF! PUFF! PANT!
HURRY, THEY'RE RIGHT BEHIND US!
NO, THEY'RE IN FRONT!
TRAPPED!
WE'LL SELL OUR LIVES DEARLY!

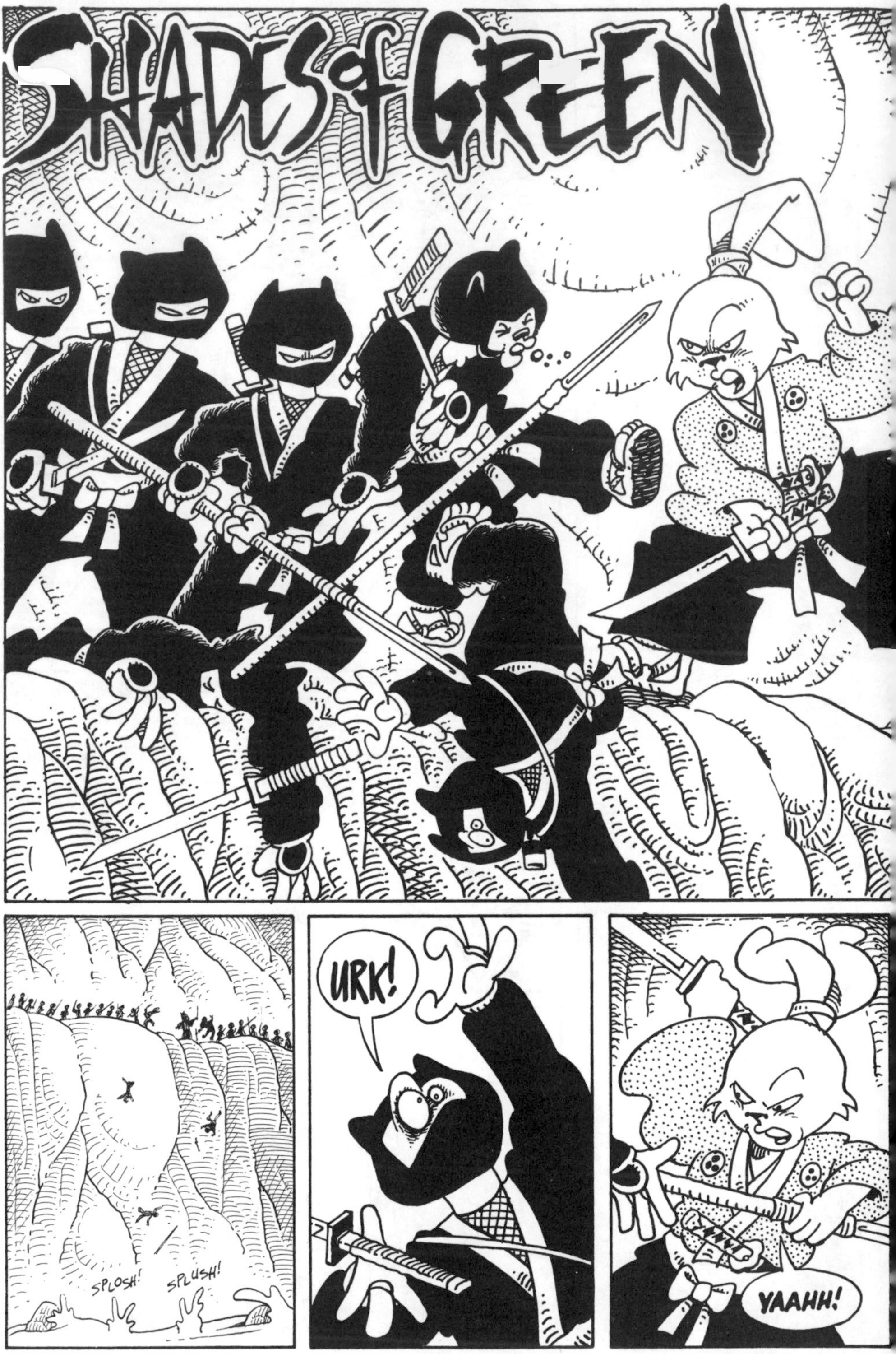
SHADES OF GREEN
SPLOSH!
SPLUSH!
URK!
YAAHH!

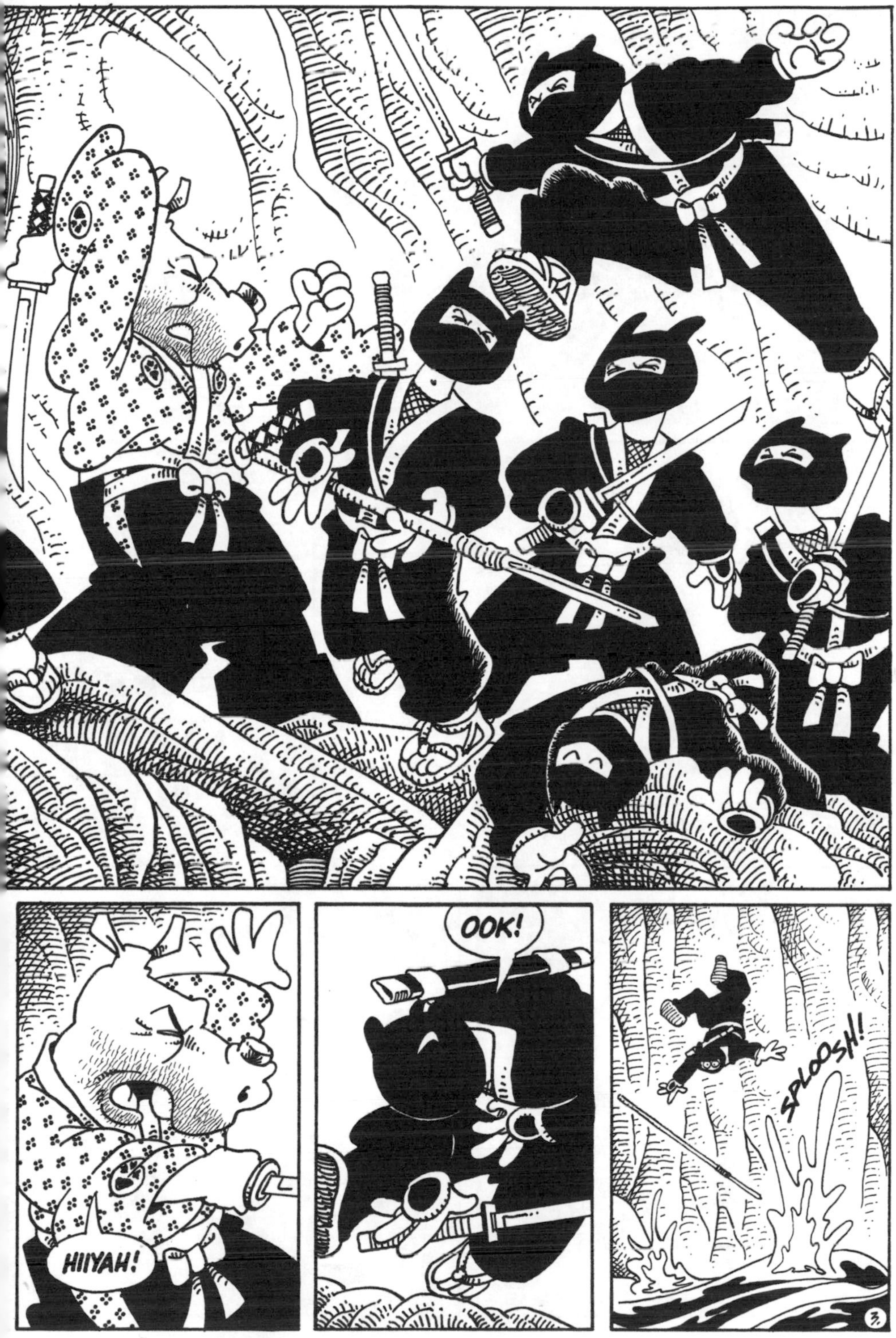
HIIYAH!
OOK!
SPLOOSH!

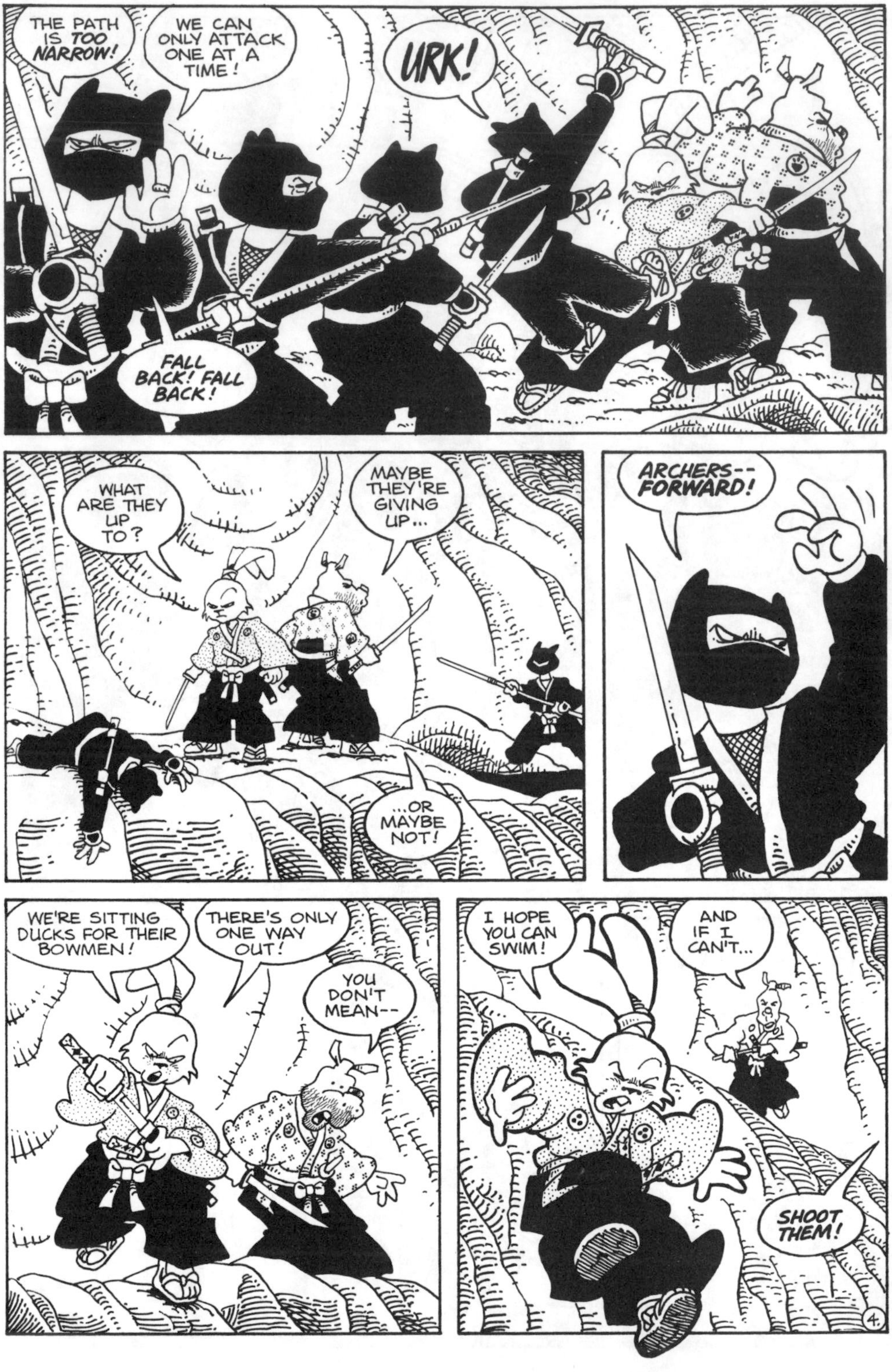
THE PATH IS TOO NARROW!
WE CAN ONLY ATTACK ONE AT A TIME!
URK!
FALL BACK! FALL BACK!
WHAT ARE THEY UP TO?
MAYBE THEY'RE GIVING UP...
...OR MAYBE NOT!
ARCHERS-- FORWARD!
WE'RE SITTING DUCKS FOR THEIR BOWMEN!
THERE'S ONLY ONE WAY OUT!
YOU DON'T MEAN--
I HOPE YOU CAN SWIM!
AND IF I CAN'T...
SHOOT THEM!
4.

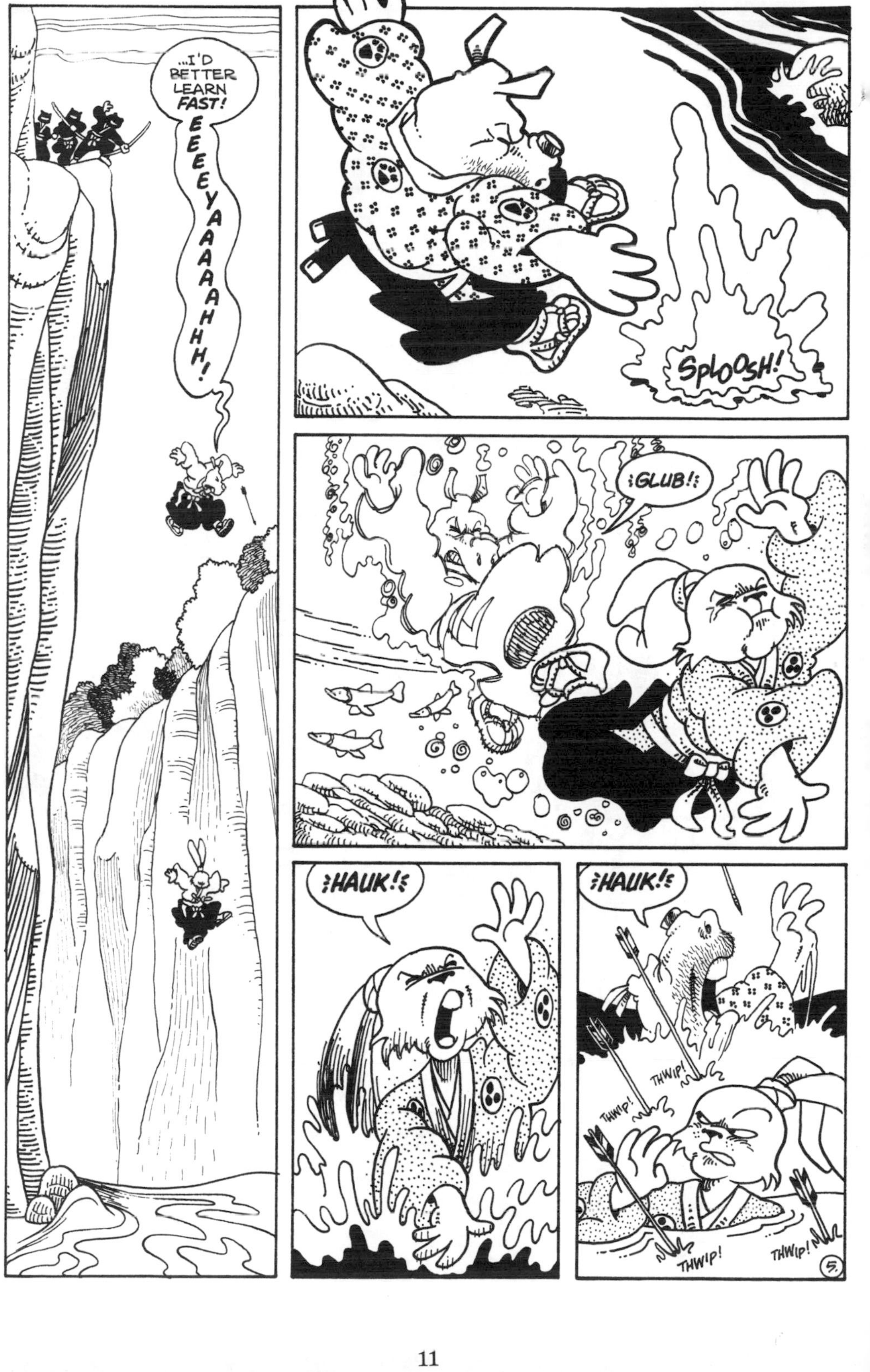
...I'D BETTER LEARN FAST!
EEEEYAAAAAAHHH!
SPLOOSH!
GLUB!
HAUK!
HAUK!
THWIP!
THWIP!
THWIP!
THWIP!
5.

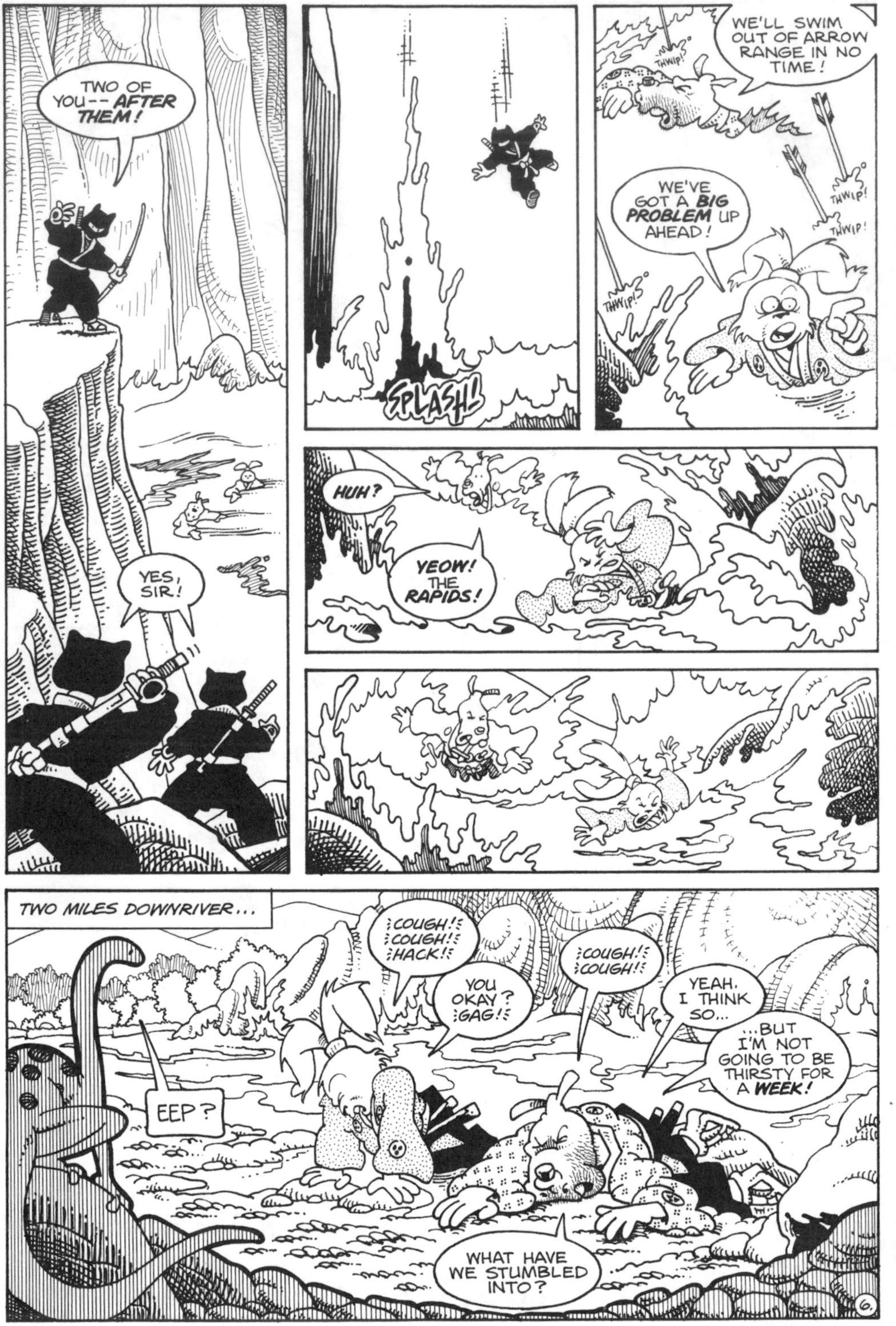
TWO OF YOU-- AFTER THEM!
YES, SIR!
SPLASH!
WE'LL SWIM OUT OF ARROW RANGE IN NO TIME!
THWIP!
WE'VE GOT A BIG PROBLEM UP AHEAD!
THWIP!
THWIP!
THWIP!
HUH?
YEOW! THE RAPIDS!
TWO MILES DOWNRIVER...
COUGH! COUGH! HACK!
YOU OKAY? GAG!
COUGH! COUGH!
YEAH. I THINK SO...
...BUT I'M NOT GOING TO BE THIRSTY FOR A WEEK!
EEP?
WHAT HAVE WE STUMBLED INTO?
6.

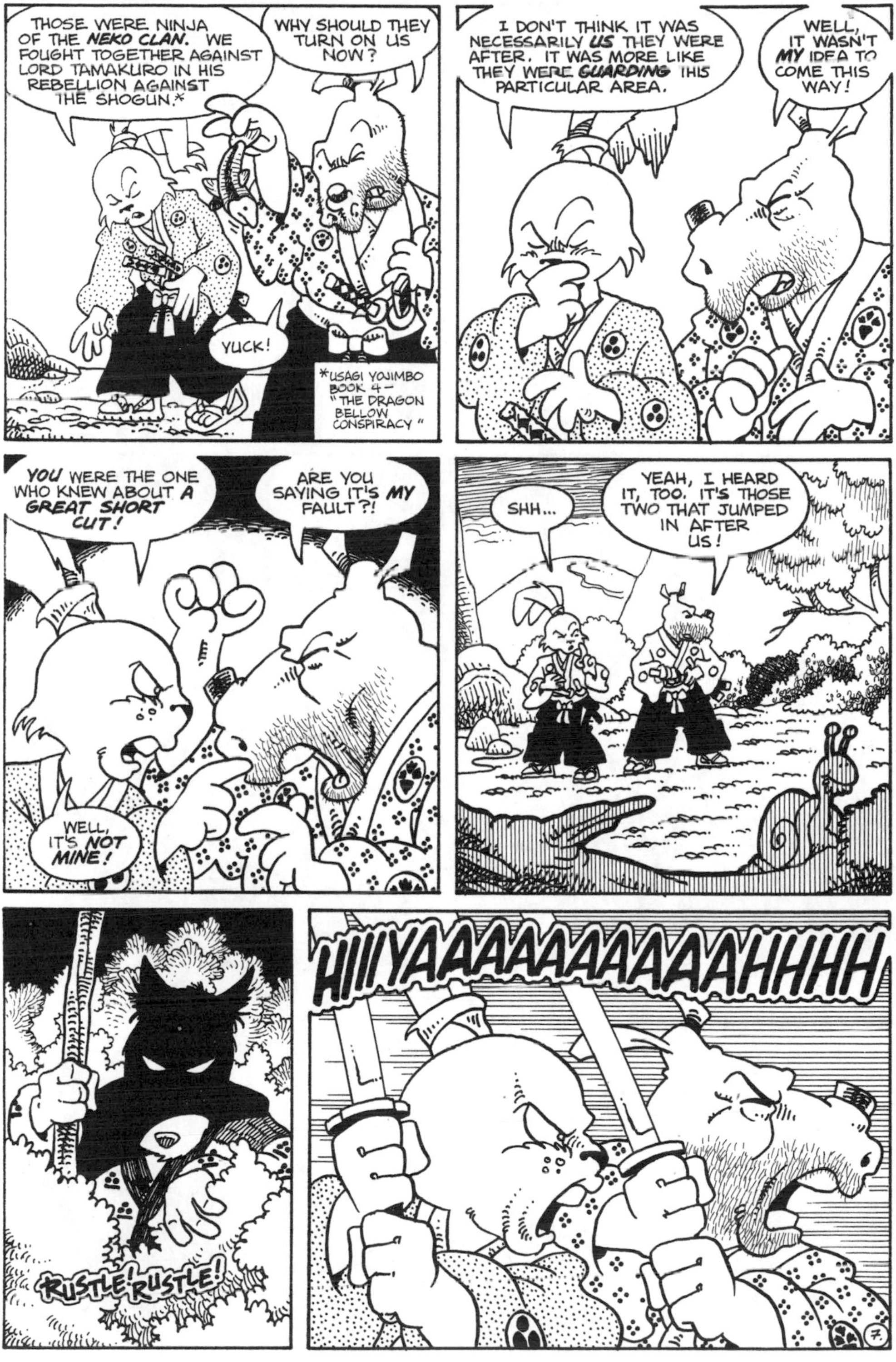
THOSE WERE NINJA OF THE NEKO CLAN. WE FOUGHT TOGETHER AGAINST LORD TAMAKURO IN HIS REBELLION AGAINST THE SHOGUN.*
WHY SHOULD THEY TURN ON US NOW?
YUCK!
*USAGI YOJIMBO BOOK 4— "THE DRAGON BELLOW CONSPIRACY"
I DON'T THINK IT WAS NECESSARILY US THEY WERE AFTER. IT WAS MORE LIKE THEY WERE GUARDING THIS PARTICULAR AREA.
WELL, IT WASN'T MY IDEA TO COME THIS WAY!
YOU WERE THE ONE WHO KNEW ABOUT A GREAT SHORT CUT!
ARE YOU SAYING IT'S MY FAULT?!
WELL, IT'S NOT MINE!
SHH...
YEAH, I HEARD IT, TOO. IT'S THOSE TWO THAT JUMPED IN AFTER US!
RUSTLE! RUSTLE!
HIIIYAAAAAAAAAAAHHHH

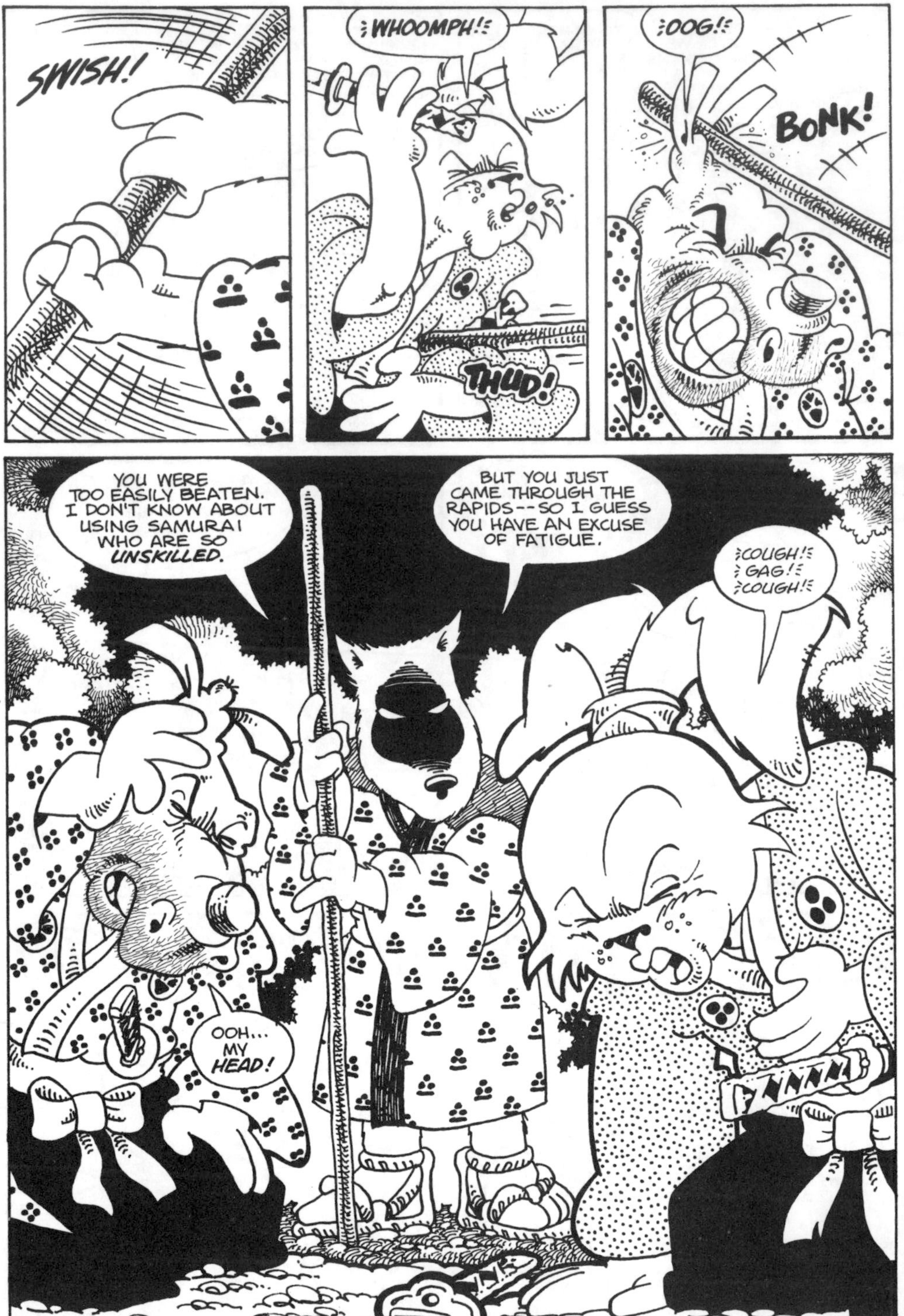
SWISH!
WHOOMPH!
THUD!
OOG!
BONK!
YOU WERE TOO EASILY BEATEN. I DON'T KNOW ABOUT USING SAMURAI WHO ARE SO UNSKILLED.
BUT YOU JUST CAME THROUGH THE RAPIDS--SO I GUESS YOU HAVE AN EXCUSE OF FATIGUE.
COUGH! GAG! COUGH!
OOH... MY HEAD!
8.

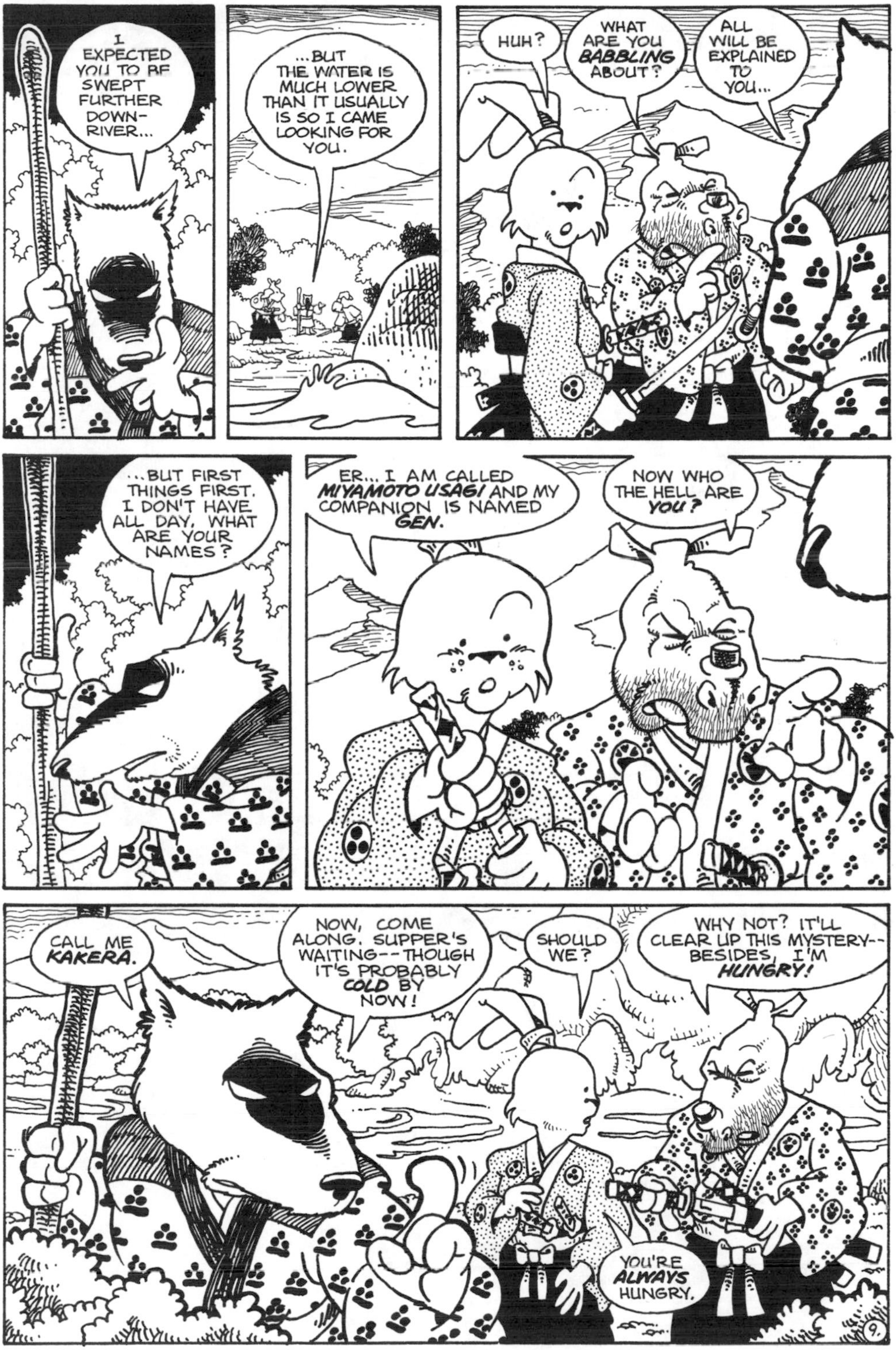
I EXPECTED YOU TO BE SWEPT FURTHER DOWN-RIVER...
...BUT THE WATER IS MUCH LOWER THAN IT USUALLY IS SO I CAME LOOKING FOR YOU.
HUH?
WHAT ARE YOU BABBLING ABOUT?
ALL WILL BE EXPLAINED TO YOU...
...BUT FIRST THINGS FIRST. I DON'T HAVE ALL DAY. WHAT ARE YOUR NAMES?
ER... I AM CALLED MIYAMOTO USAGI AND MY COMPANION IS NAMED GEN.
NOW WHO THE HELL ARE YOU?
CALL ME KAKERA.
NOW, COME ALONG. SUPPER'S WAITING--THOUGH IT'S PROBABLY COLD BY NOW!
SHOULD WE?
WHY NOT? IT'LL CLEAR UP THIS MYSTERY--BESIDES, I'M HUNGRY!
YOU'RE ALWAYS HUNGRY.
9.

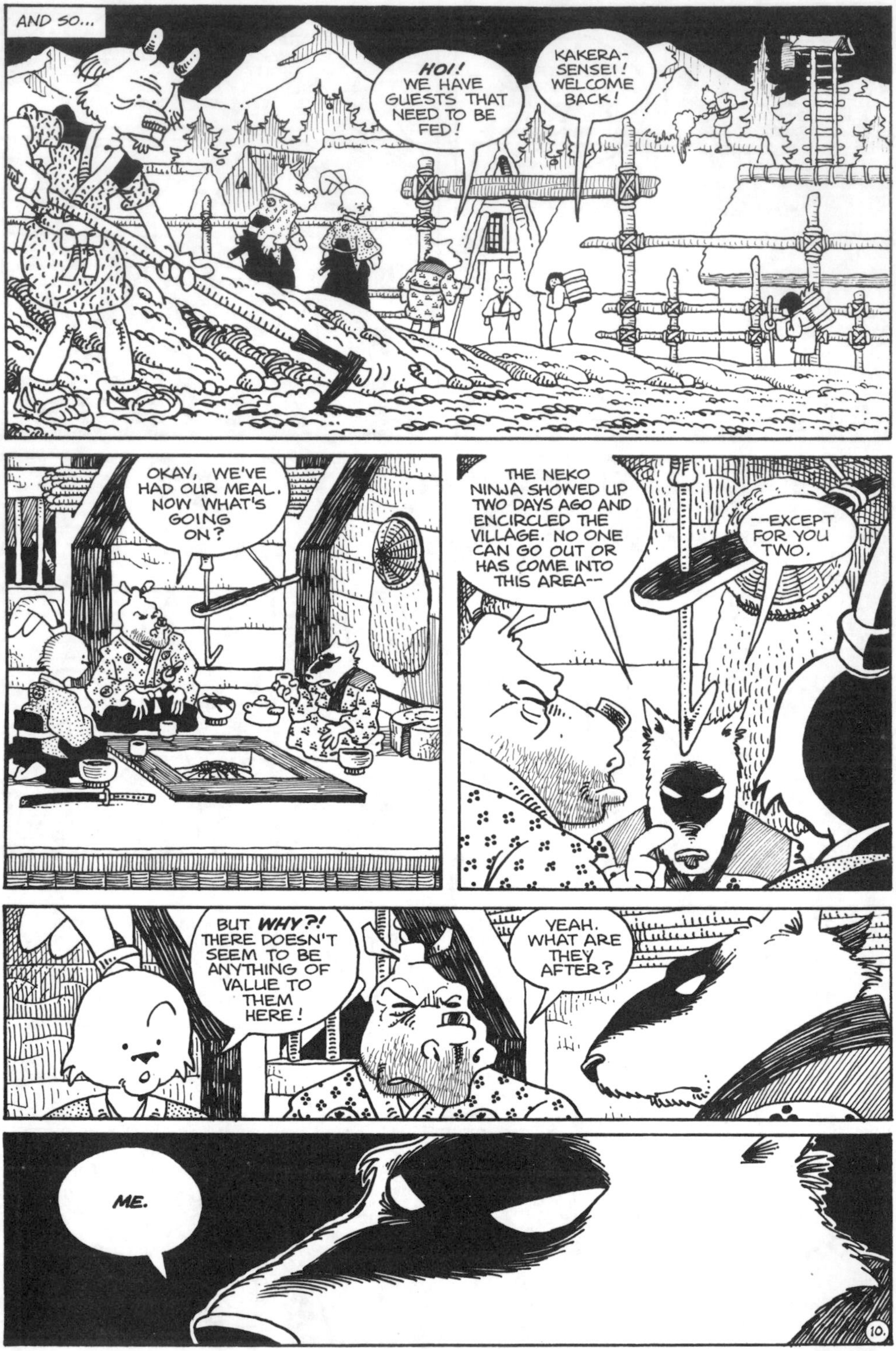
AND SO...
HOI! WE HAVE GUESTS THAT NEED TO BE FED!
KAKERA-SENSEI! WELCOME BACK!
OKAY, WE'VE HAD OUR MEAL. NOW WHAT'S GOING ON?
THE NEKO NINJA SHOWED UP TWO DAYS AGO AND ENCIRCLED THE VILLAGE. NO ONE CAN GO OUT OR HAS COME INTO THIS AREA--
--EXCEPT FOR YOU TWO.
BUT WHY?! THERE DOESN'T SEEM TO BE ANYTHING OF VALUE TO THEM HERE!
YEAH. WHAT ARE THEY AFTER?
ME.
10.

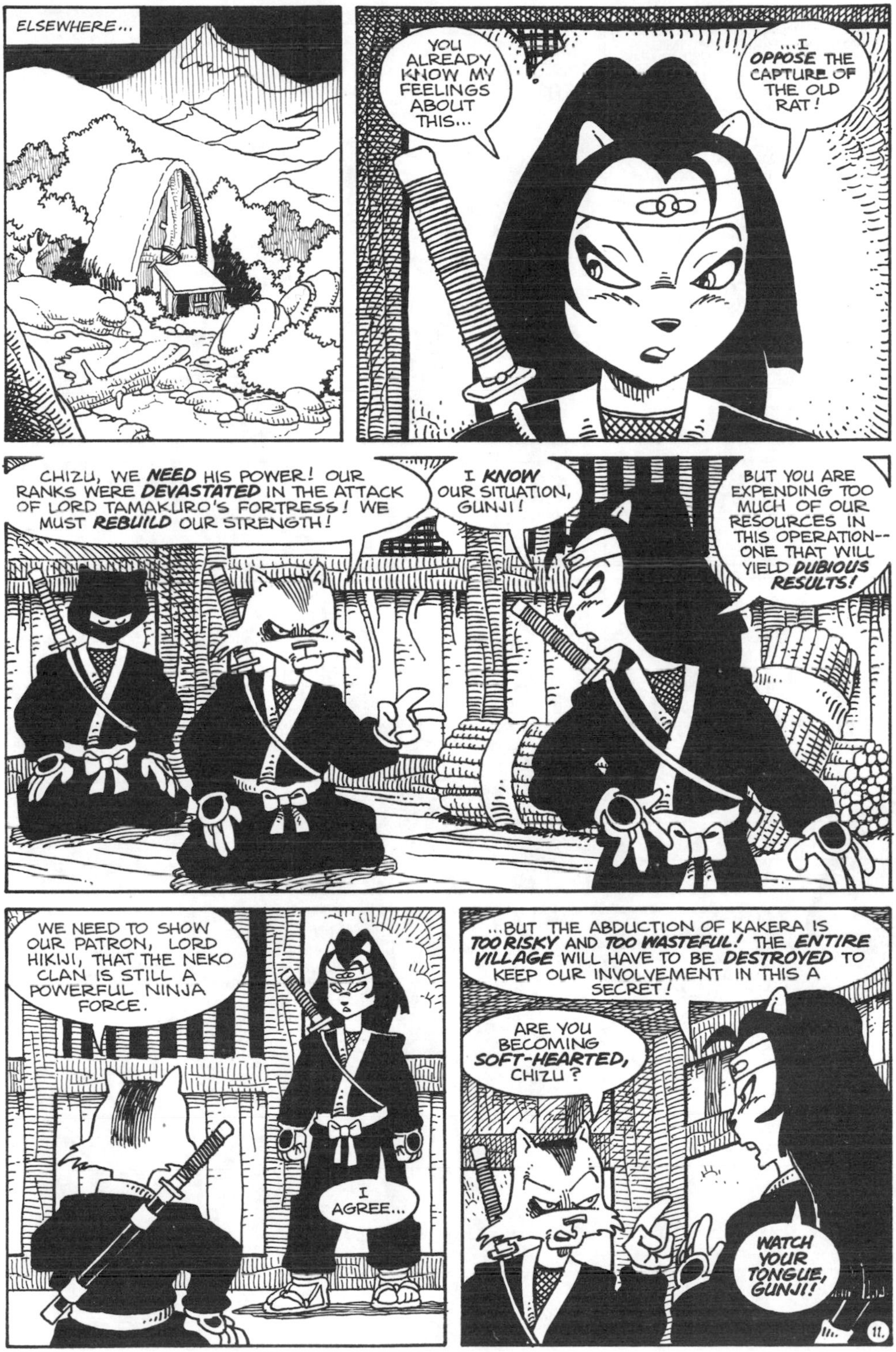

ELSEWHERE...
YOU ALREADY KNOW MY FEELINGS ABOUT THIS...
...I OPPOSE THE CAPTURE OF THE OLD RAT!
CHIZU, WE NEED HIS POWER! OUR RANKS WERE DEVASTATED IN THE ATTACK OF LORD TAMAKURO'S FORTRESS! WE MUST REBUILD OUR STRENGTH!
I KNOW OUR SITUATION, GUNJI!
BUT YOU ARE EXPENDING TOO MUCH OF OUR RESOURCES IN THIS OPERATION-- ONE THAT WILL YIELD DUBIOUS RESULTS!
WE NEED TO SHOW OUR PATRON, LORD HIKIJI, THAT THE NEKO CLAN IS STILL A POWERFUL NINJA FORCE.
I AGREE...
...BUT THE ABDUCTION OF KAKERA IS TOO RISKY AND TOO WASTEFUL! THE ENTIRE VILLAGE WILL HAVE TO BE DESTROYED TO KEEP OUR INVOLVEMENT IN THIS A SECRET!
ARE YOU BECOMING SOFT-HEARTED, CHIZU?
WATCH YOUR TONGUE, GUNJI!
11.

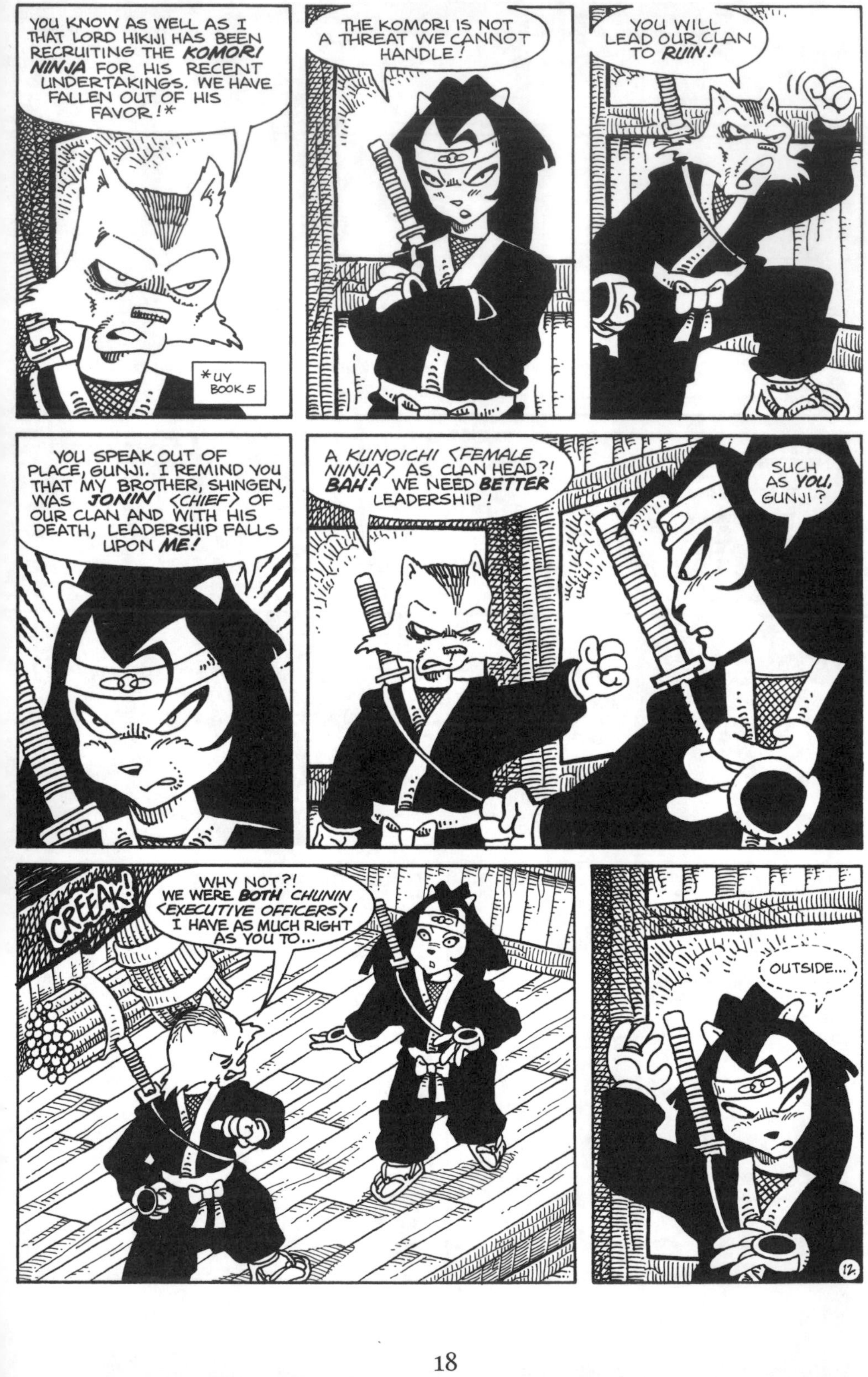

YOU KNOW AS WELL AS I THAT LORD HIKIJI HAS BEEN RECRUITING THE KOMORI NINJA FOR HIS RECENT UNDERTAKINGS. WE HAVE FALLEN OUT OF HIS FAVOR!*
*UY BOOK 5
THE KOMORI IS NOT A THREAT WE CANNOT HANDLE!
YOU WILL LEAD OUR CLAN TO RUIN!
YOU SPEAK OUT OF PLACE, GUNJI. I REMIND YOU THAT MY BROTHER, SHINGEN, WAS JONIN <CHIEF> OF OUR CLAN AND WITH HIS DEATH, LEADERSHIP FALLS UPON ME!
A KUNOICHI <FEMALE NINJA> AS CLAN HEAD?! BAH! WE NEED BETTER LEADERSHIP!
SUCH AS YOU, GUNJI?
CREEAK!
WHY NOT?! WE WERE BOTH CHUNIN <EXECUTIVE OFFICERS>! I HAVE AS MUCH RIGHT AS YOU TO...
OUTSIDE...
12.

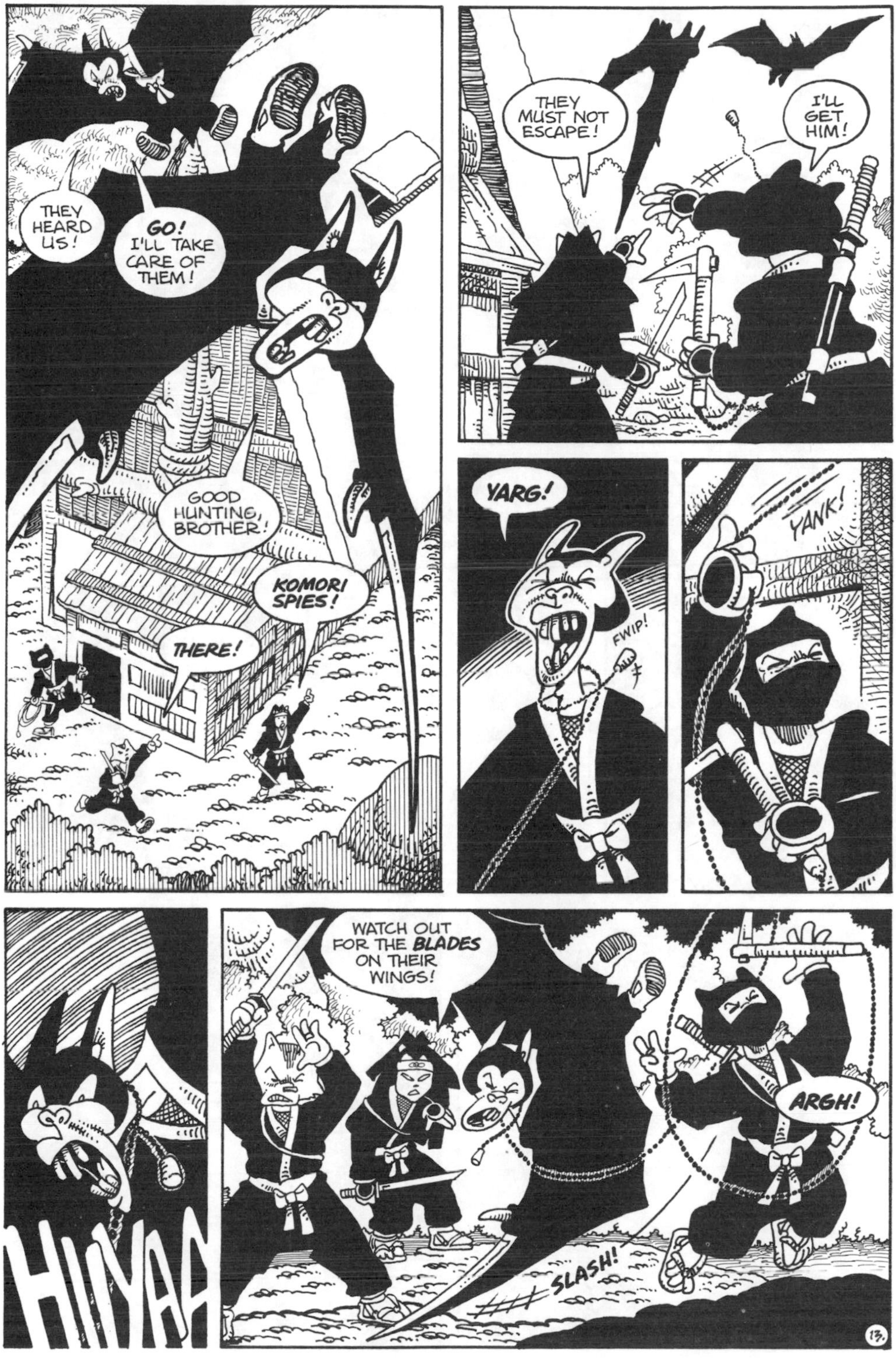
THEY HEARD US!
GO! I'LL TAKE CARE OF THEM!
GOOD HUNTING, BROTHER!
KOMORI SPIES!
THERE!
THEY MUST NOT ESCAPE!
I'LL GET HIM!
YARG!
FWIP!
YANK!
HIIYAA
WATCH OUT FOR THE BLADES ON THEIR WINGS!
SLASH!
ARGH!
13.

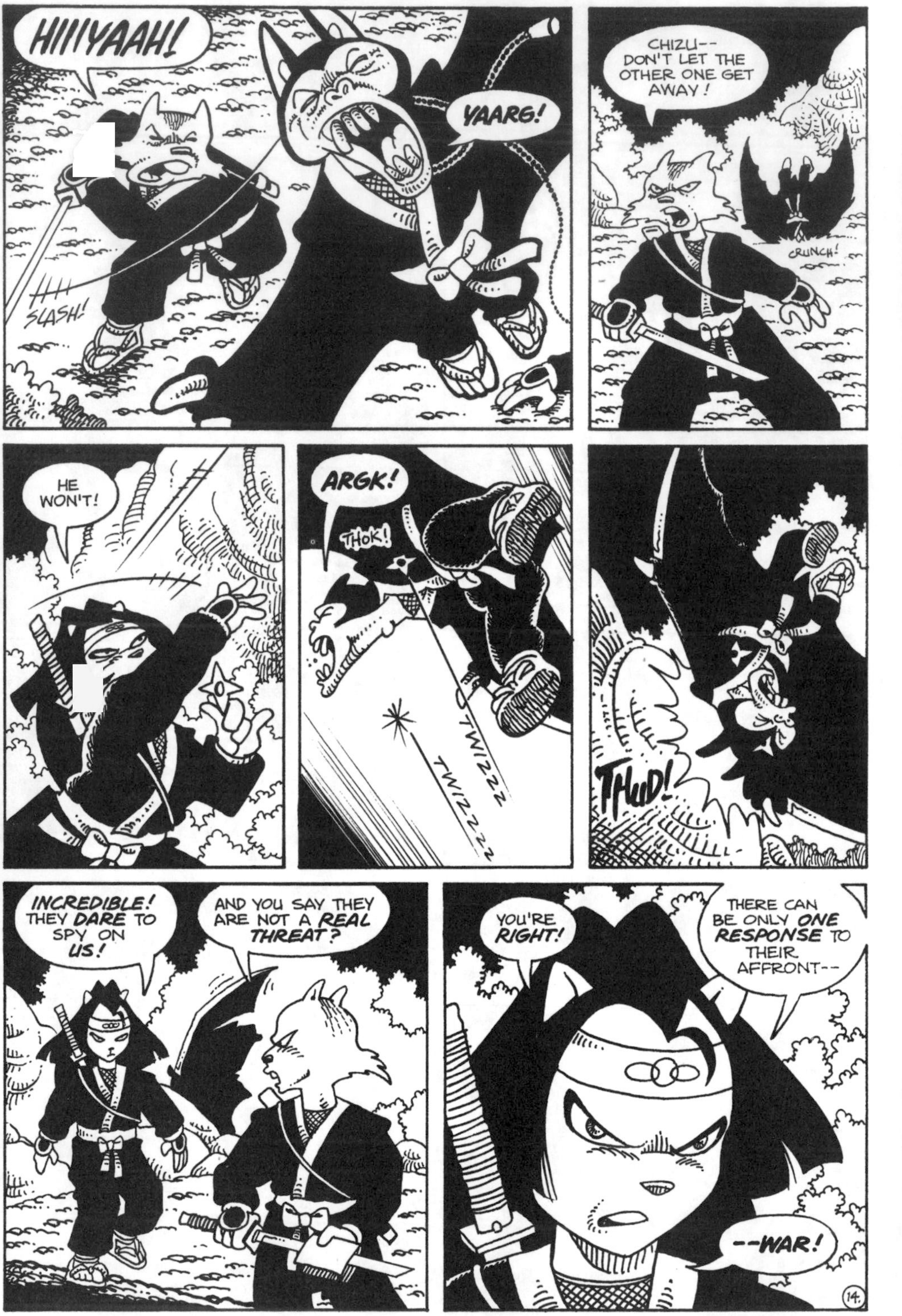
HIIIYAAH!
YAARG!
SLASH!
CHIZU-- DON'T LET THE OTHER ONE GET AWAY!
CRUNCH!
HE WON'T!
ARGK!
THOK!
TWIZZZ
TWIZZZZ
THUD!
INCREDIBLE! THEY DARE TO SPY ON US!
AND YOU SAY THEY ARE NOT A REAL THREAT?
YOU'RE RIGHT!
THERE CAN BE ONLY ONE RESPONSE TO THEIR AFFRONT--
--WAR!
14.

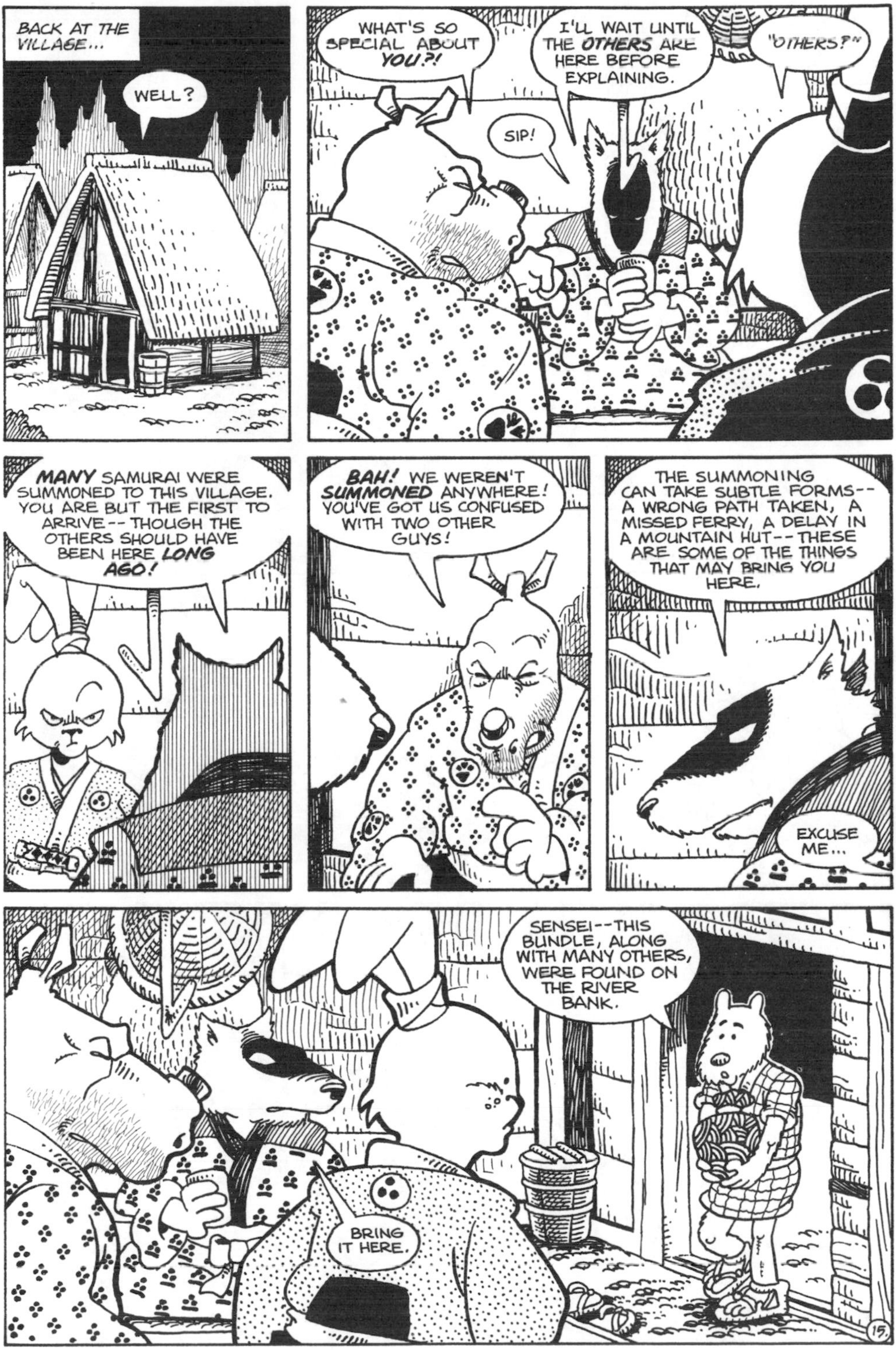
BACK AT THE VILLAGE...
WELL?
WHAT'S SO SPECIAL ABOUT YOU?!
SIP!
I'LL WAIT UNTIL THE OTHERS ARE HERE BEFORE EXPLAINING.
"OTHERS?"
MANY SAMURAI WERE SUMMONED TO THIS VILLAGE. YOU ARE BUT THE FIRST TO ARRIVE--THOUGH THE OTHERS SHOULD HAVE BEEN HERE LONG AGO!
BAH! WE WEREN'T SUMMONED ANYWHERE! YOU'VE GOT US CONFUSED WITH TWO OTHER GUYS!
THE SUMMONING CAN TAKE SUBTLE FORMS--A WRONG PATH TAKEN, A MISSED FERRY, A DELAY IN A MOUNTAIN HUT--THESE ARE SOME OF THE THINGS THAT MAY BRING YOU HERE.
EXCUSE ME...
SENSEI--THIS BUNDLE, ALONG WITH MANY OTHERS, WERE FOUND ON THE RIVER BANK.
BRING IT HERE.
15.

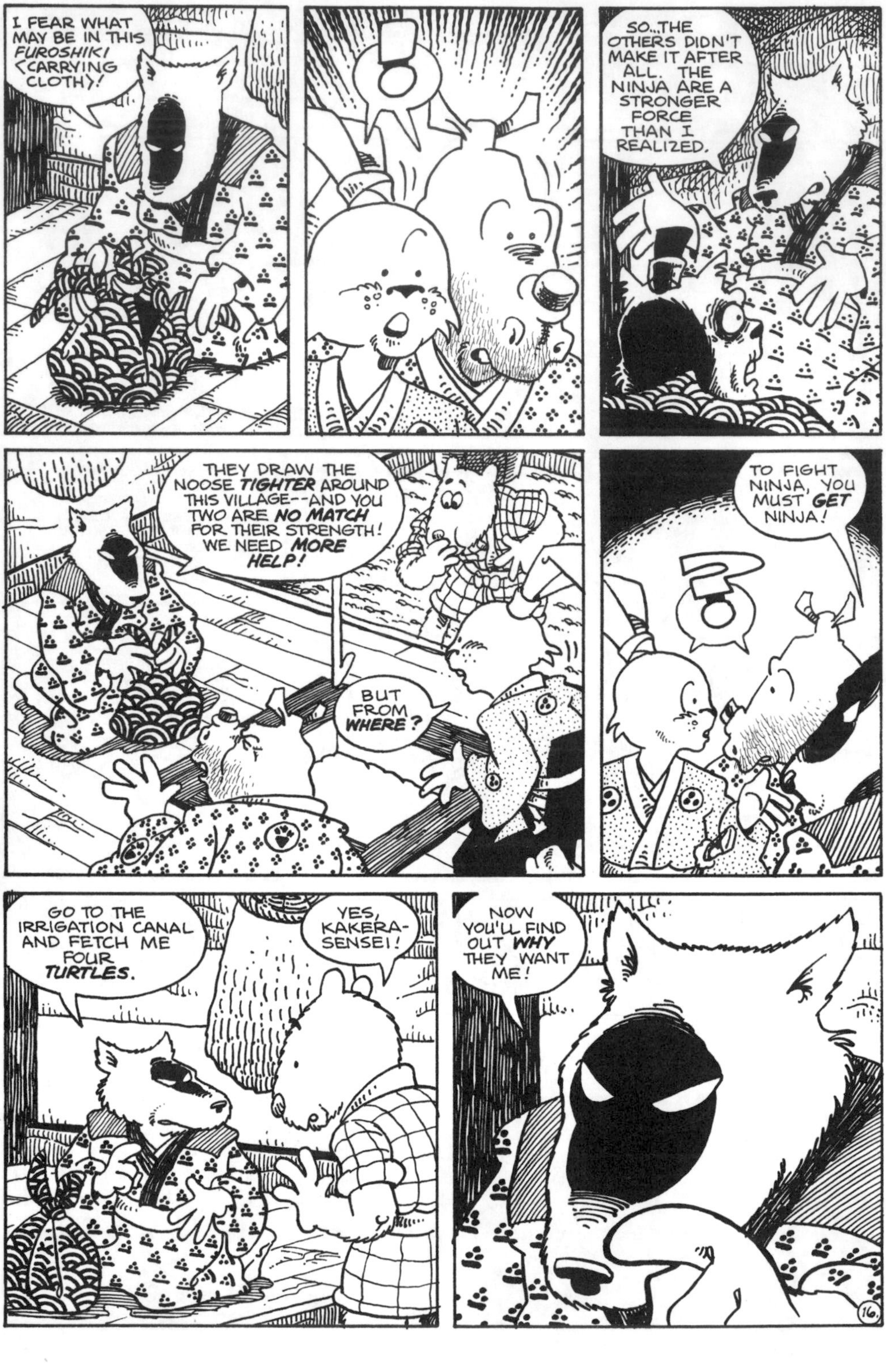
I FEAR WHAT MAY BE IN THIS *FUROSHIKI* <CARRYING CLOTH>!
!
SO...THE OTHERS DIDN'T MAKE IT AFTER ALL. THE NINJA ARE A STRONGER FORCE THAN I REALIZED.
THEY DRAW THE NOOSE *TIGHTER* AROUND THIS VILLAGE--AND YOU TWO ARE *NO MATCH* FOR THEIR STRENGTH! WE NEED *MORE HELP!*
BUT FROM *WHERE*?
TO FIGHT NINJA, YOU MUST *GET* NINJA!
?
GO TO THE IRRIGATION CANAL AND FETCH ME FOUR *TURTLES*.
YES, KAKERA-SENSEI!
NOW YOU'LL FIND OUT *WHY* THEY WANT ME!
16.

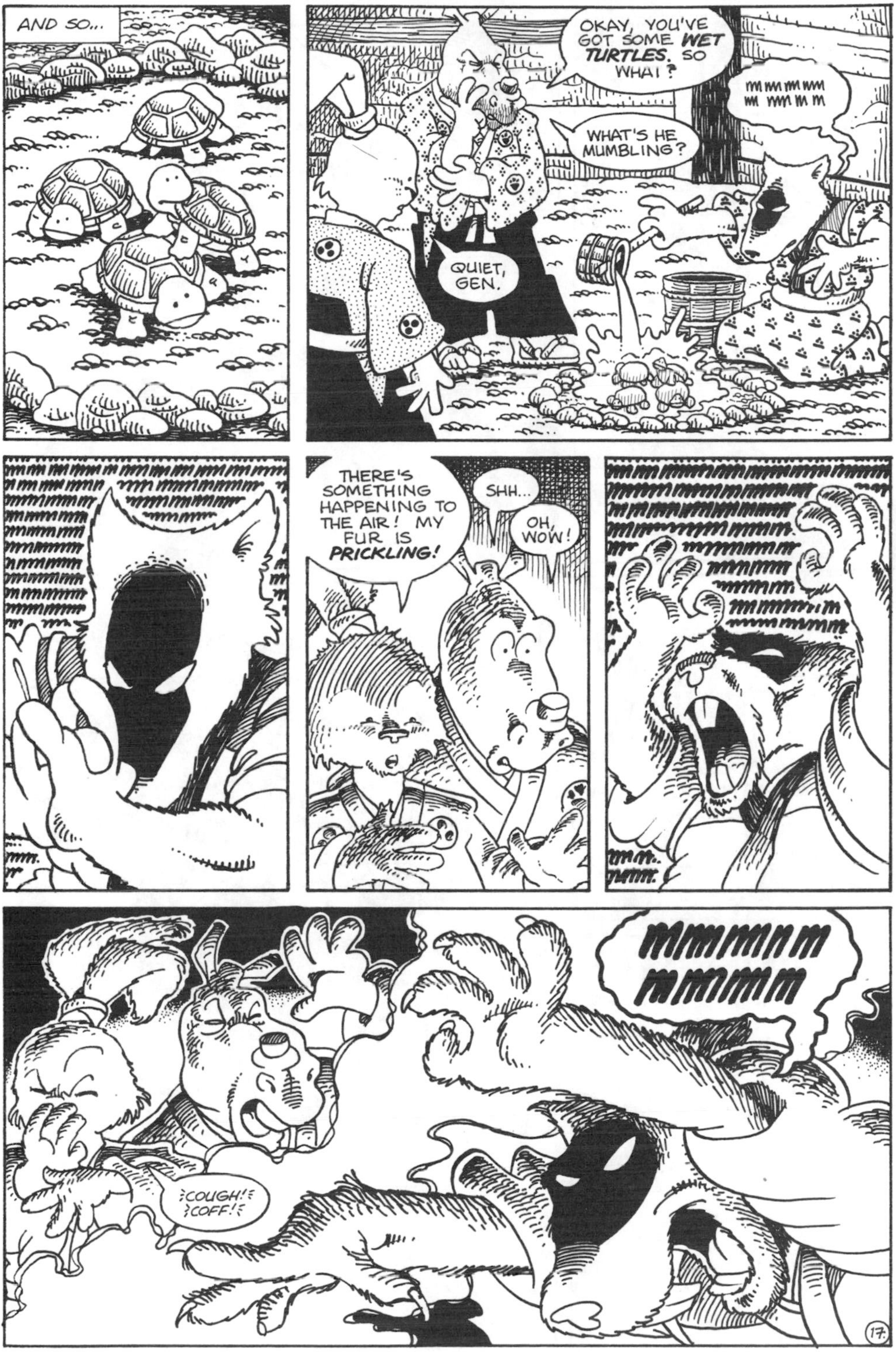
AND SO...
OKAY, YOU'VE GOT SOME WET TURTLES. SO WHAT?
WHAT'S HE MUMBLING?
QUIET, GEN.
THERE'S SOMETHING HAPPENING TO THE AIR! MY FUR IS PRICKLING!
SHH...
OH, WOW!
MMMMNM MMMMM
COUGH! COFF!
17.

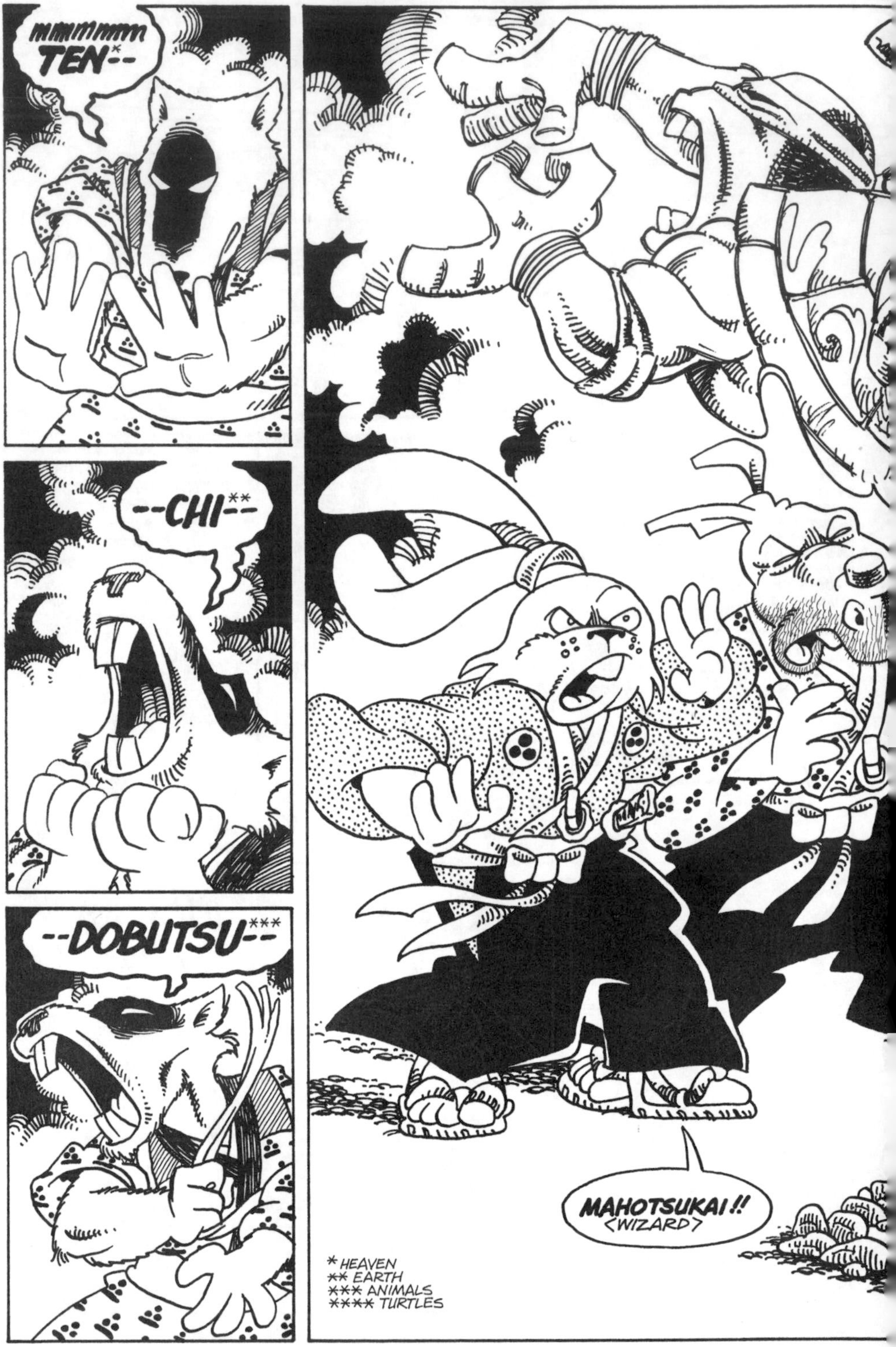
mmmmmm TEN*--
--CHI**--
--DOBUTSU***--
MAHOTSUKAI!! <WIZARD>
* HEAVEN
** EARTH
*** ANIMALS
**** TURTLES

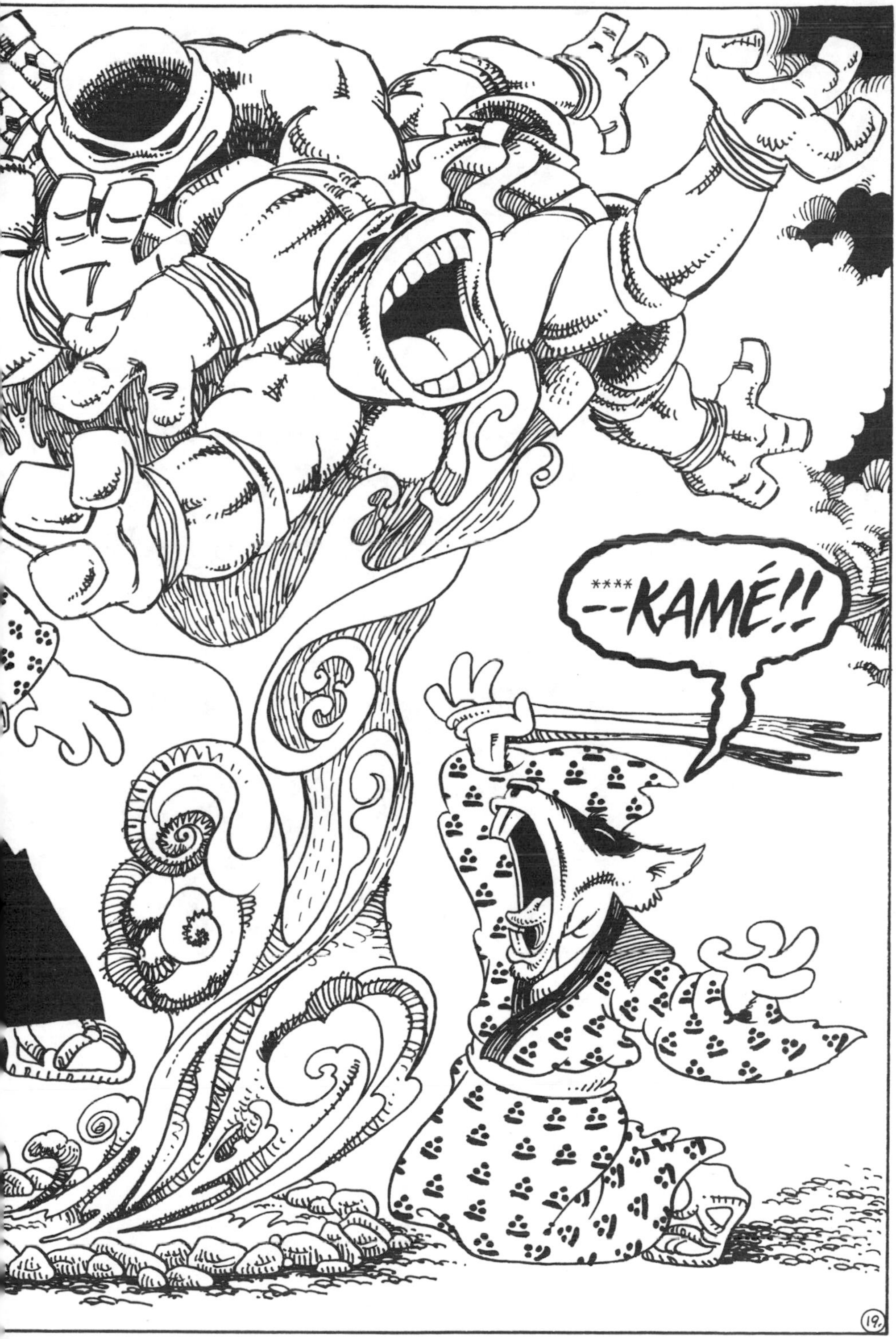
****--KAMÉ!!
19.

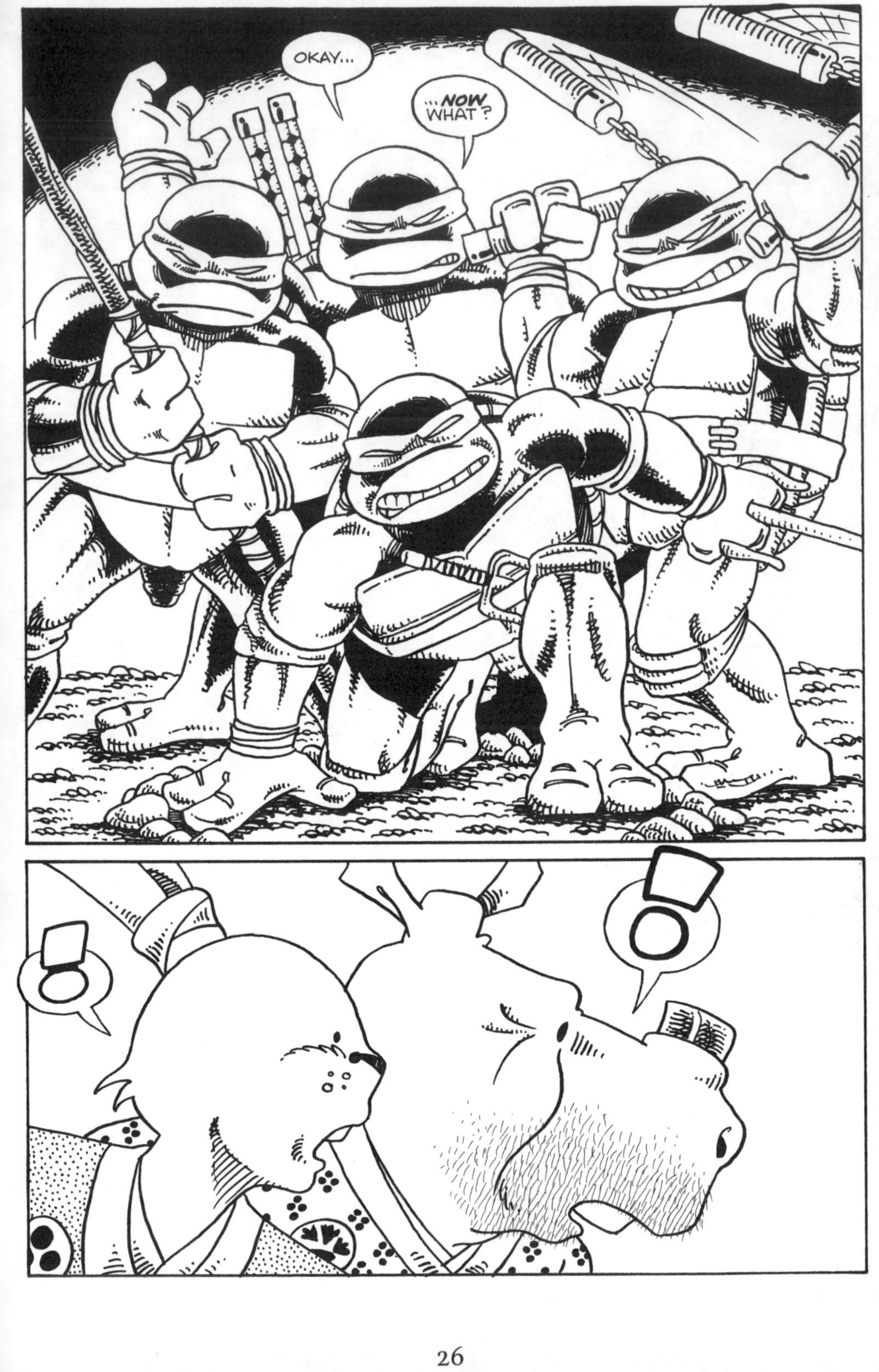
OKAY...
...NOW WHAT?
!
!

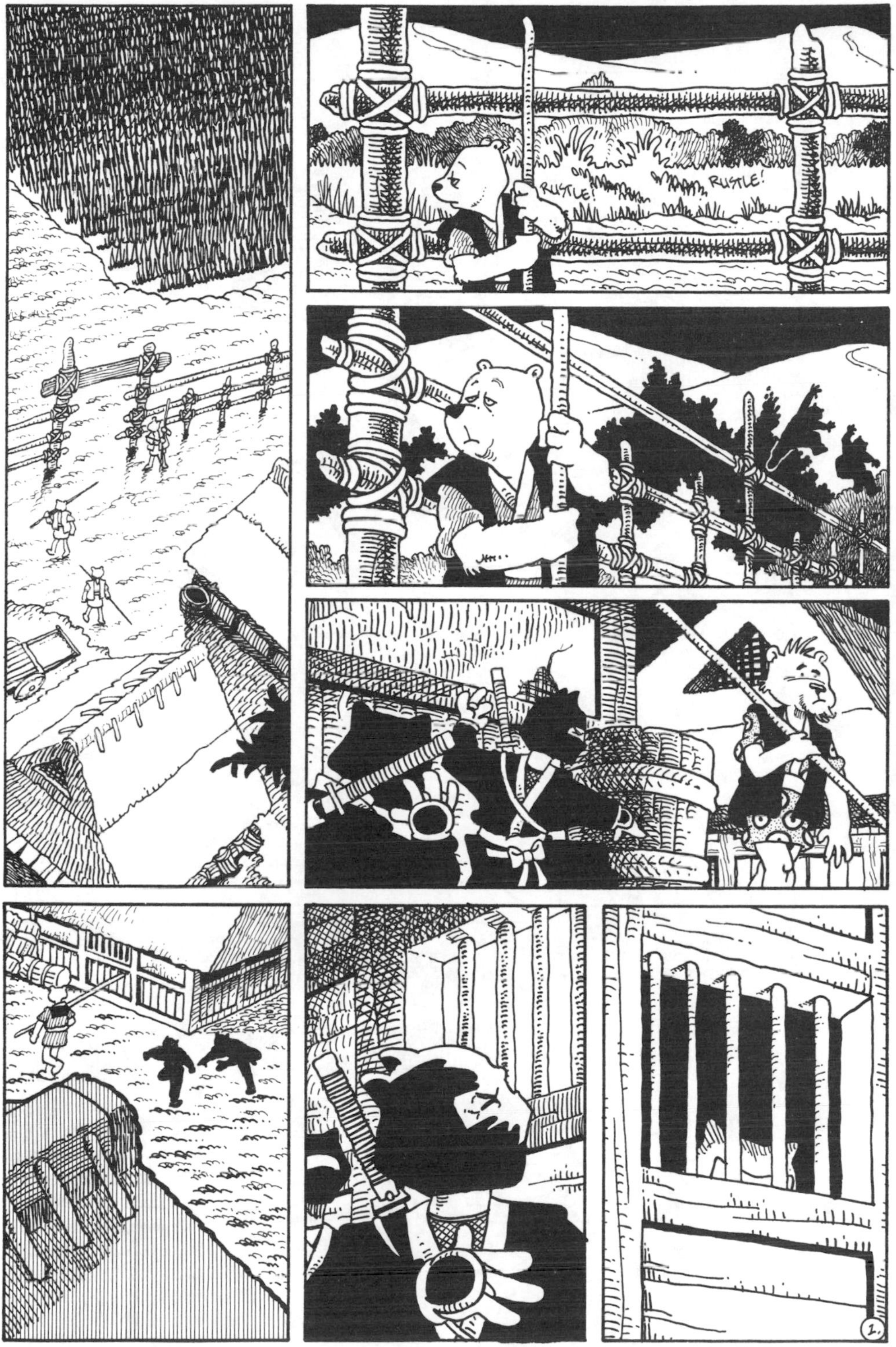
RUSTLE!
RUSTLE!

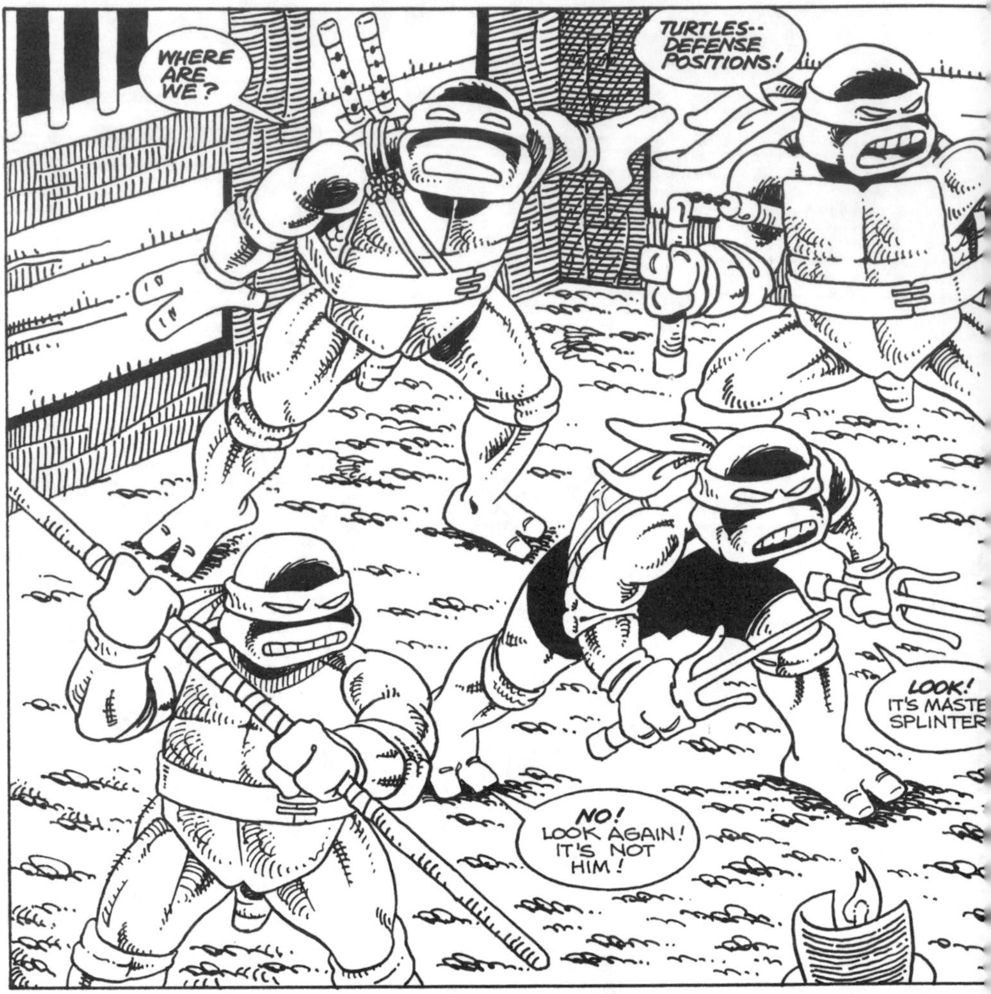
WHERE ARE WE?
TURTLES-- DEFENSE POSITIONS!
LOOK! IT'S MASTE SPLINTER
NO! LOOK AGAIN! IT'S NOT HIM!

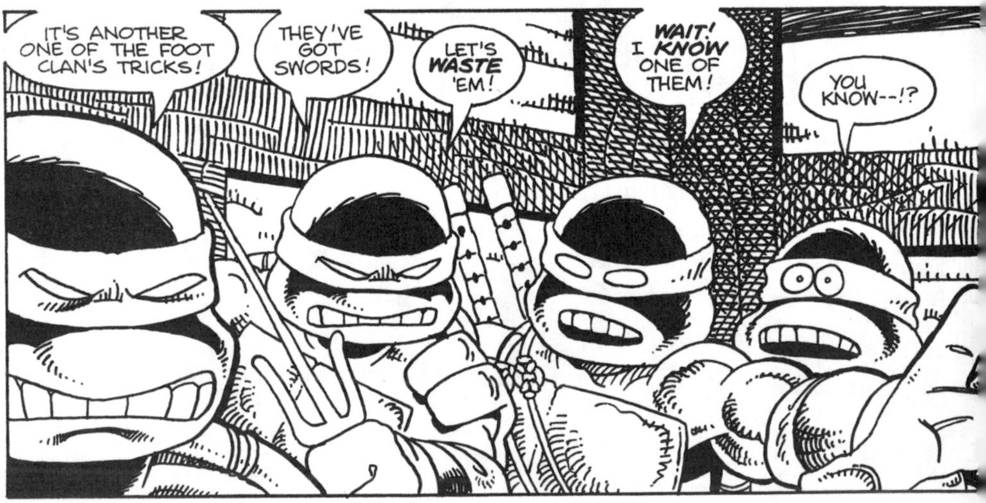
IT'S ANOTHER ONE OF THE FOOT CLAN'S TRICKS!
THEY'VE GOT SWORDS!
LET'S WASTE 'EM!
WAIT! I KNOW ONE OF THEM!
YOU KNOW--!?

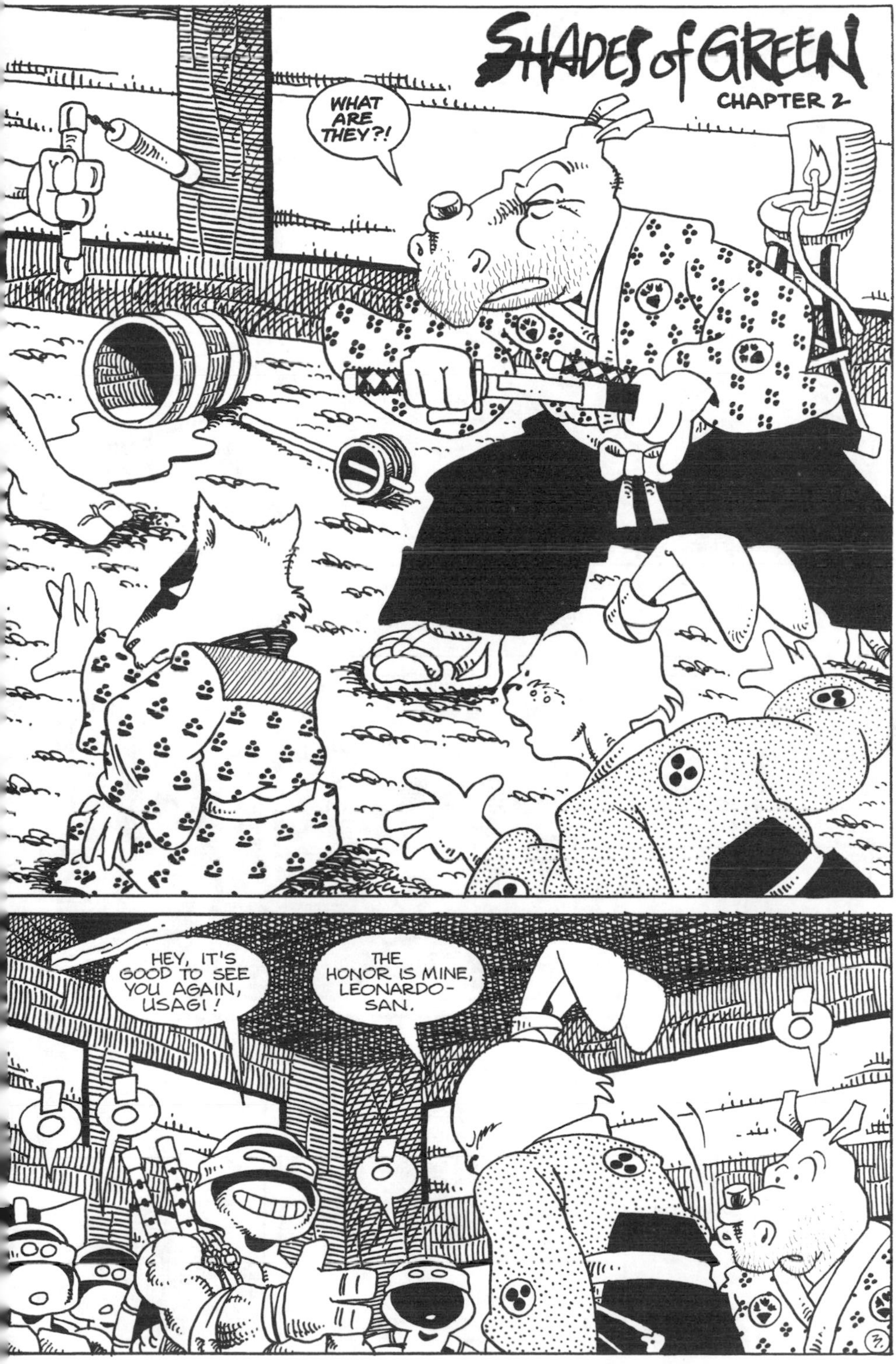
SHADES of GREEN
CHAPTER 2
WHAT ARE THEY?!
HEY, IT'S GOOD TO SEE YOU AGAIN, USAGI!
THE HONOR IS MINE, LEONARDO-SAN.

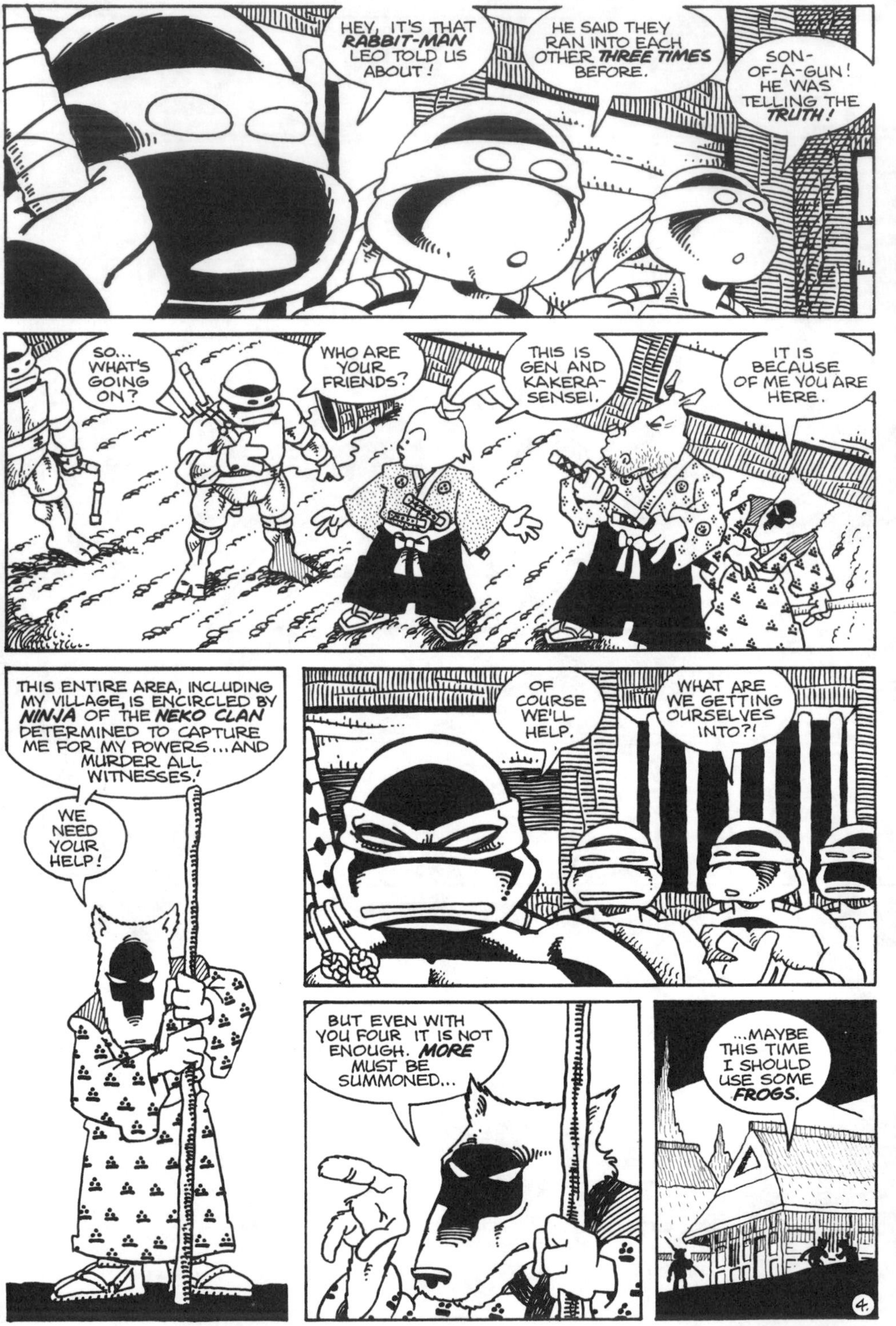

HEY, IT'S THAT RABBIT-MAN LEO TOLD US ABOUT!
HE SAID THEY RAN INTO EACH OTHER THREE TIMES BEFORE.
SON-OF-A-GUN! HE WAS TELLING THE TRUTH!
SO... WHAT'S GOING ON?
WHO ARE YOUR FRIENDS?
THIS IS GEN AND KAKERA-SENSEI.
IT IS BECAUSE OF ME YOU ARE HERE.
THIS ENTIRE AREA, INCLUDING MY VILLAGE, IS ENCIRCLED BY NINJA OF THE NEKO CLAN DETERMINED TO CAPTURE ME FOR MY POWERS... AND MURDER ALL WITNESSES!
WE NEED YOUR HELP!
OF COURSE WE'LL HELP.
WHAT ARE WE GETTING OURSELVES INTO?!
BUT EVEN WITH YOU FOUR IT IS NOT ENOUGH. MORE MUST BE SUMMONED...
...MAYBE THIS TIME I SHOULD USE SOME FROGS.
4.

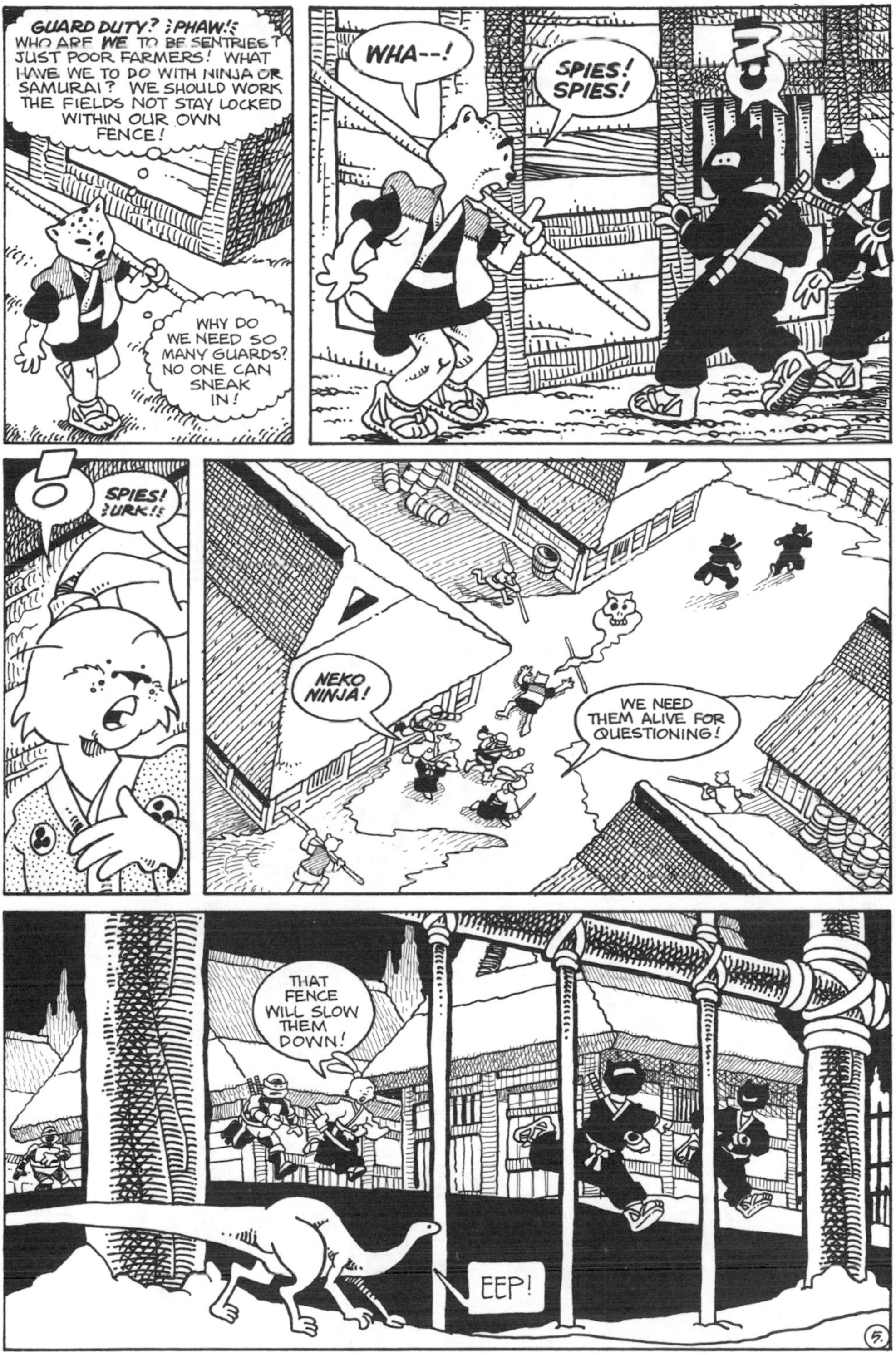
GUARD DUTY? ¡PHAW!¡ WHO ARE WE TO BE SENTRIES? JUST POOR FARMERS! WHAT HAVE WE TO DO WITH NINJA OR SAMURAI? WE SHOULD WORK THE FIELDS NOT STAY LOCKED WITHIN OUR OWN FENCE!
WHY DO WE NEED SO MANY GUARDS? NO ONE CAN SNEAK IN!
WHA--!
SPIES! SPIES!
!
SPIES! ¡URK!¡
NEKO NINJA!
WE NEED THEM ALIVE FOR QUESTIONING!
THAT FENCE WILL SLOW THEM DOWN!
EEP!
5.

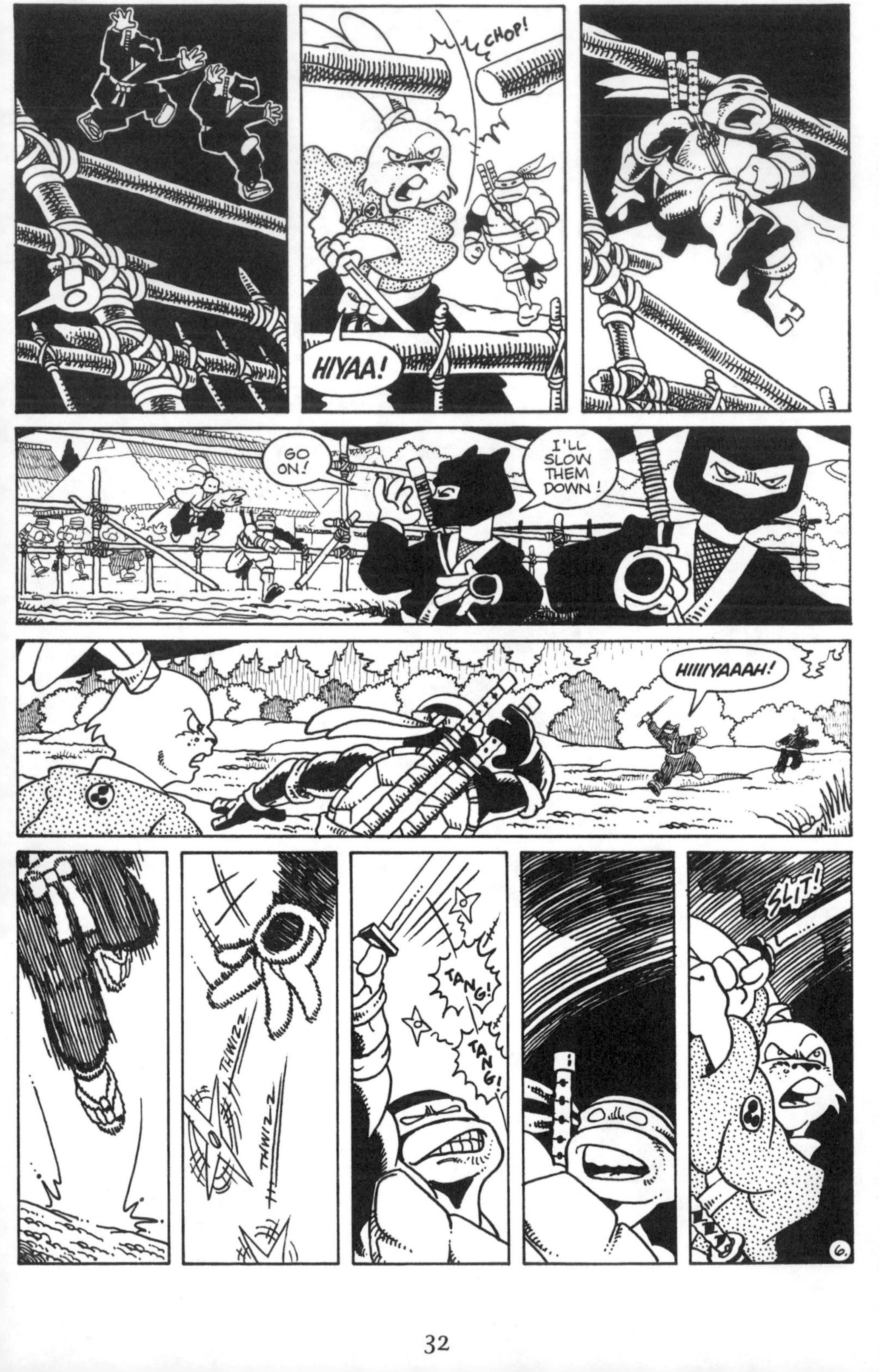
CHOP!
HIYAA!
GO ON!
I'LL SLOW THEM DOWN!
HIIIIYAAAH!
THWIZZ
THWIZZ
TANG!
TANG!
6.

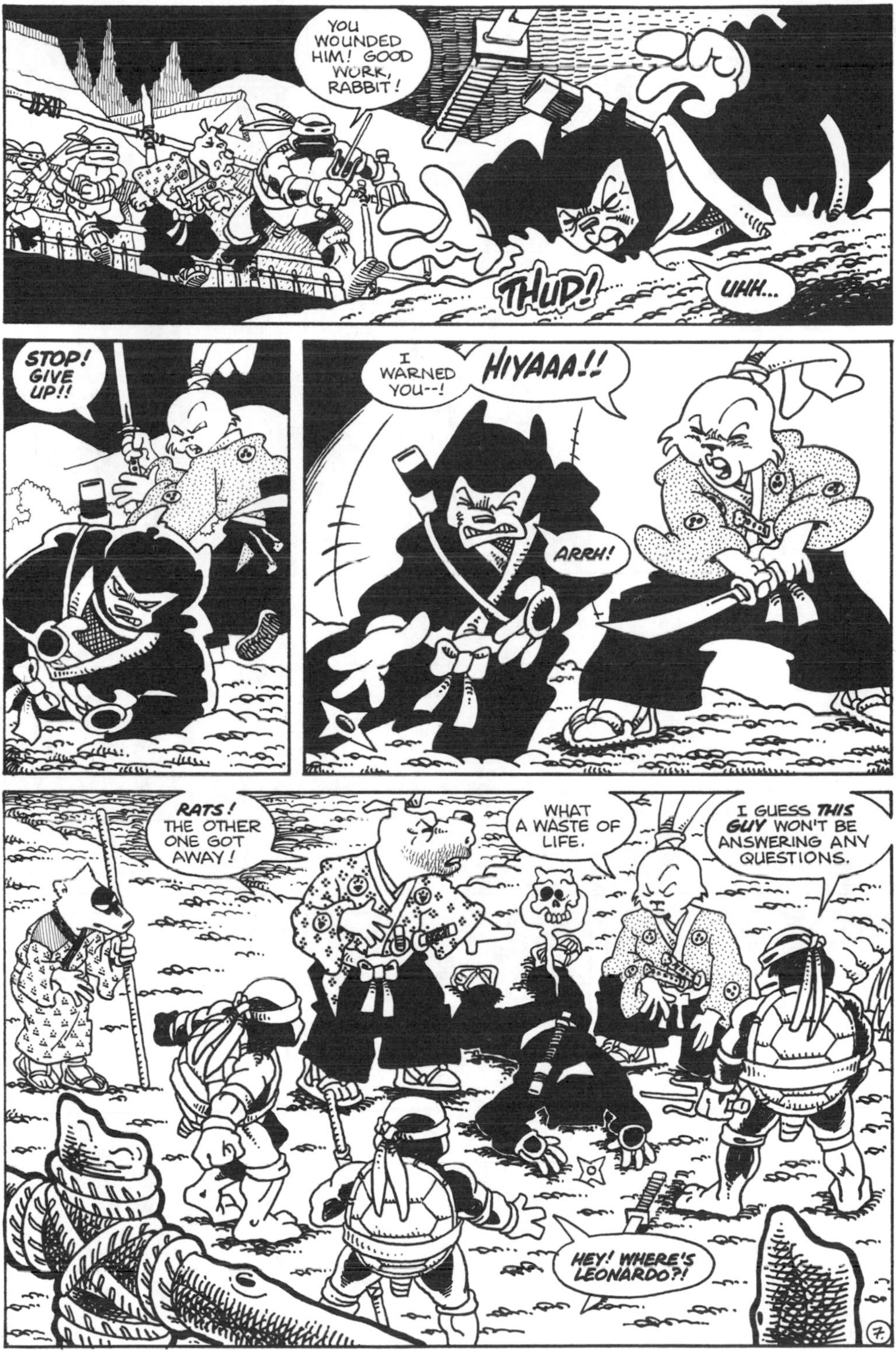
YOU WOUNDED HIM! GOOD WORK, RABBIT!
THUD!
UHH...
STOP! GIVE UP!!
I WARNED YOU--!
HIYAAA!!
ARRH!
RATS! THE OTHER ONE GOT AWAY!
WHAT A WASTE OF LIFE.
I GUESS THIS GUY WON'T BE ANSWERING ANY QUESTIONS.
HEY! WHERE'S LEONARDO?!
7.

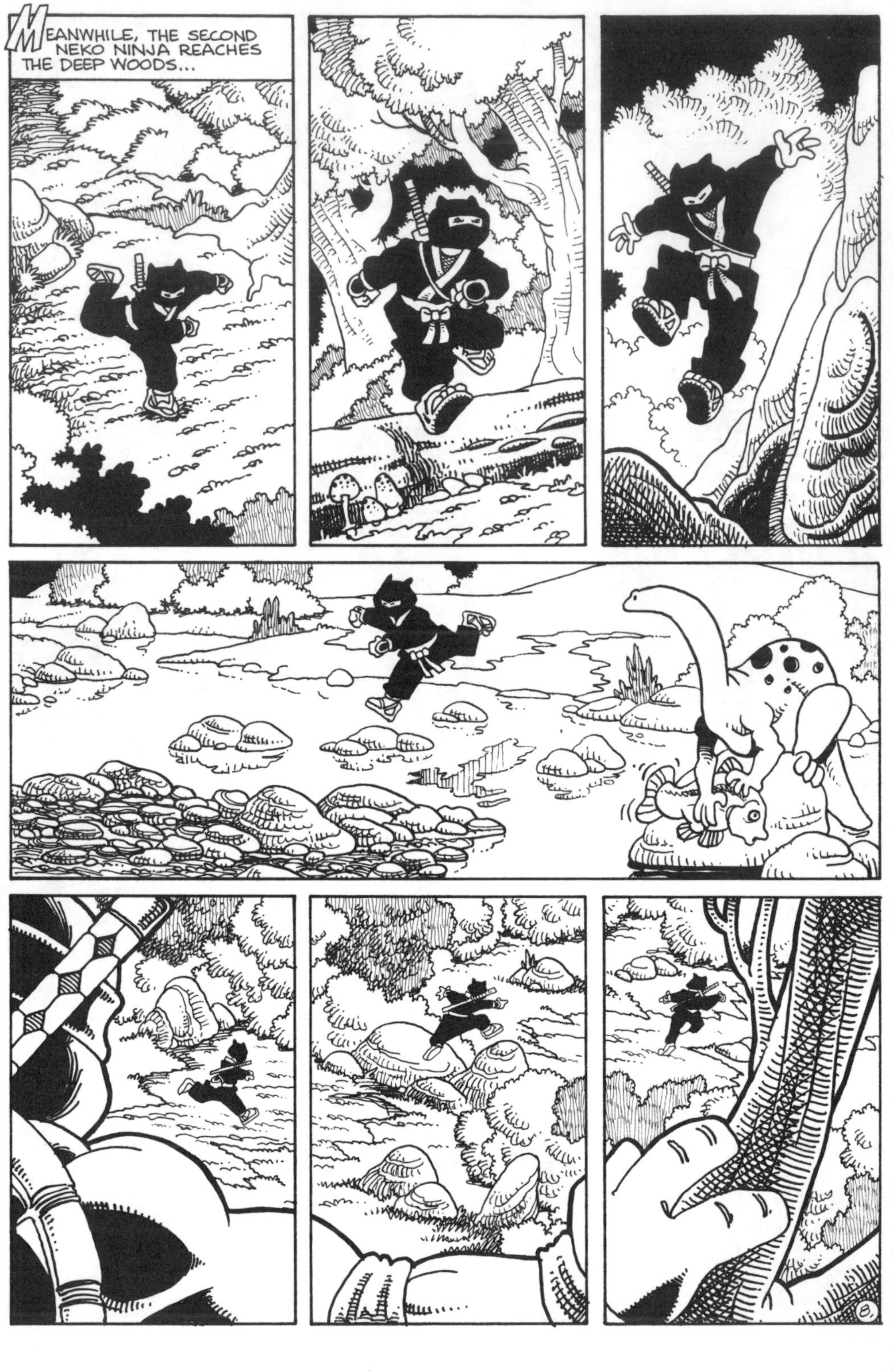
MEANWHILE, THE SECOND NEKO NINJA REACHES THE DEEP WOODS...

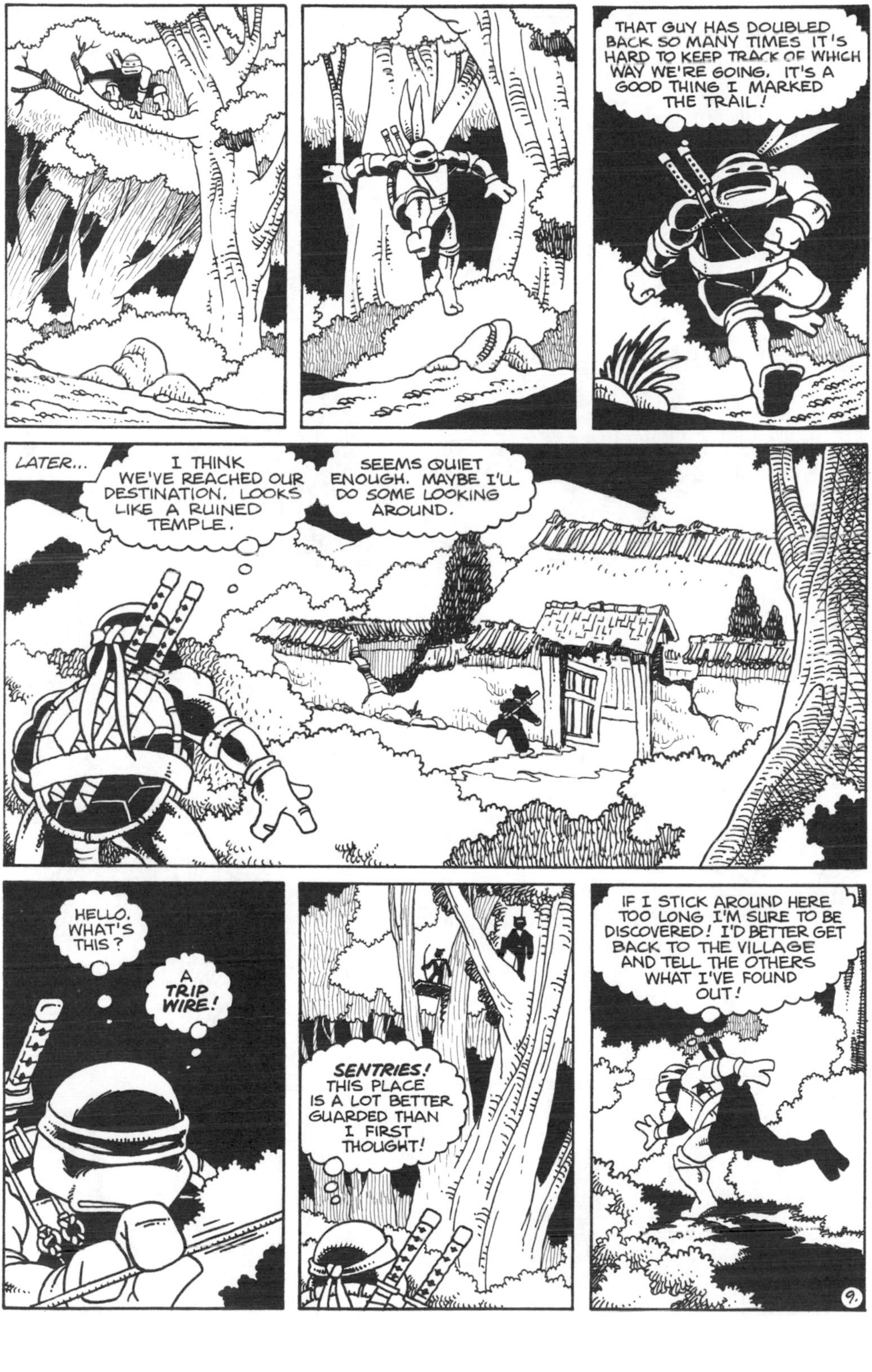

THAT GUY HAS DOUBLED BACK SO MANY TIMES IT'S HARD TO KEEP TRACK OF WHICH WAY WE'RE GOING. IT'S A GOOD THING I MARKED THE TRAIL!
LATER...
I THINK WE'VE REACHED OUR DESTINATION. LOOKS LIKE A RUINED TEMPLE.
SEEMS QUIET ENOUGH. MAYBE I'LL DO SOME LOOKING AROUND.
HELLO. WHAT'S THIS?
A TRIP WIRE!
SENTRIES! THIS PLACE IS A LOT BETTER GUARDED THAN I FIRST THOUGHT!
IF I STICK AROUND HERE TOO LONG I'M SURE TO BE DISCOVERED! I'D BETTER GET BACK TO THE VILLAGE AND TELL THE OTHERS WHAT I'VE FOUND OUT!
9.

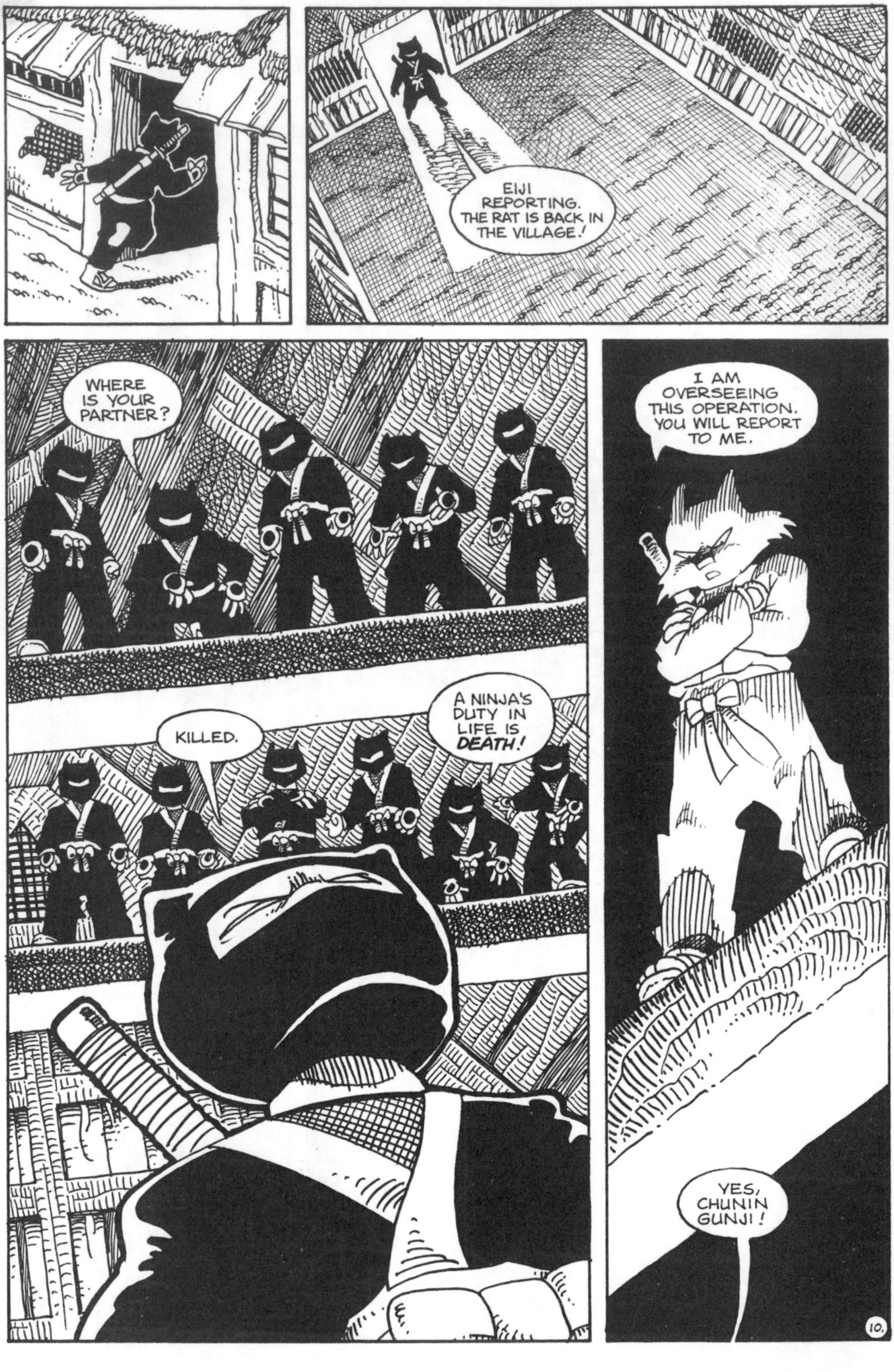
EIJI REPORTING. THE RAT IS BACK IN THE VILLAGE!
WHERE IS YOUR PARTNER?
KILLED.
A NINJA'S DUTY IN LIFE IS DEATH!
I AM OVERSEEING THIS OPERATION. YOU WILL REPORT TO ME.
YES, CHUNIN GUNJI!
10.

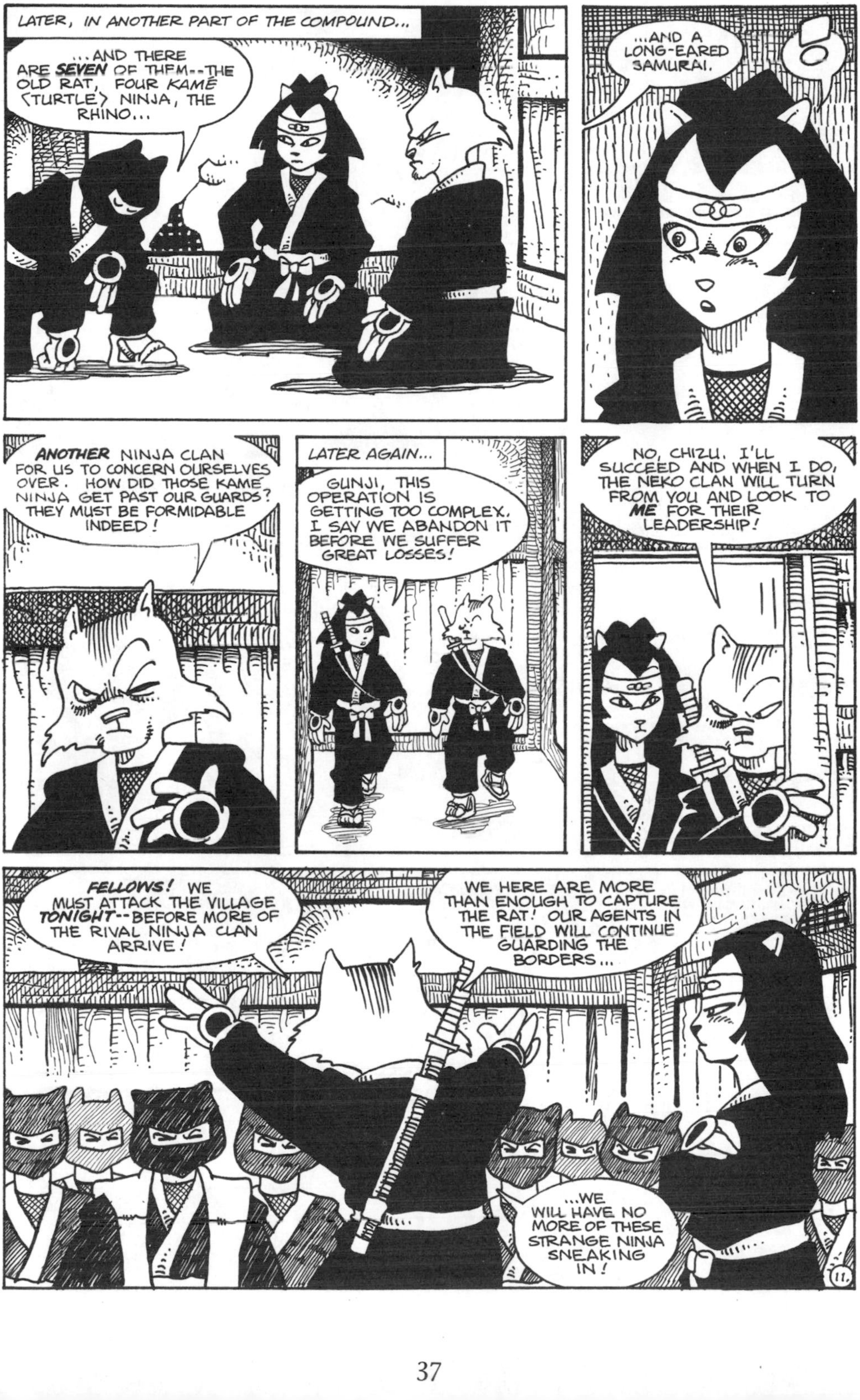
LATER, IN ANOTHER PART OF THE COMPOUND...
...AND THERE ARE SEVEN OF THEM--THE OLD RAT, FOUR KAME (TURTLE) NINJA, THE RHINO...
...AND A LONG-EARED SAMURAI.
ANOTHER NINJA CLAN FOR US TO CONCERN OURSELVES OVER. HOW DID THOSE KAME NINJA GET PAST OUR GUARDS? THEY MUST BE FORMIDABLE INDEED!
LATER AGAIN...
GUNJI, THIS OPERATION IS GETTING TOO COMPLEX. I SAY WE ABANDON IT BEFORE WE SUFFER GREAT LOSSES!
NO, CHIZU. I'LL SUCCEED AND WHEN I DO, THE NEKO CLAN WILL TURN FROM YOU AND LOOK TO ME FOR THEIR LEADERSHIP!
FELLOWS! WE MUST ATTACK THE VILLAGE TONIGHT--BEFORE MORE OF THE RIVAL NINJA CLAN ARRIVE!
WE HERE ARE MORE THAN ENOUGH TO CAPTURE THE RAT! OUR AGENTS IN THE FIELD WILL CONTINUE GUARDING THE BORDERS...
...WE WILL HAVE NO MORE OF THESE STRANGE NINJA SNEAKING IN!
11.

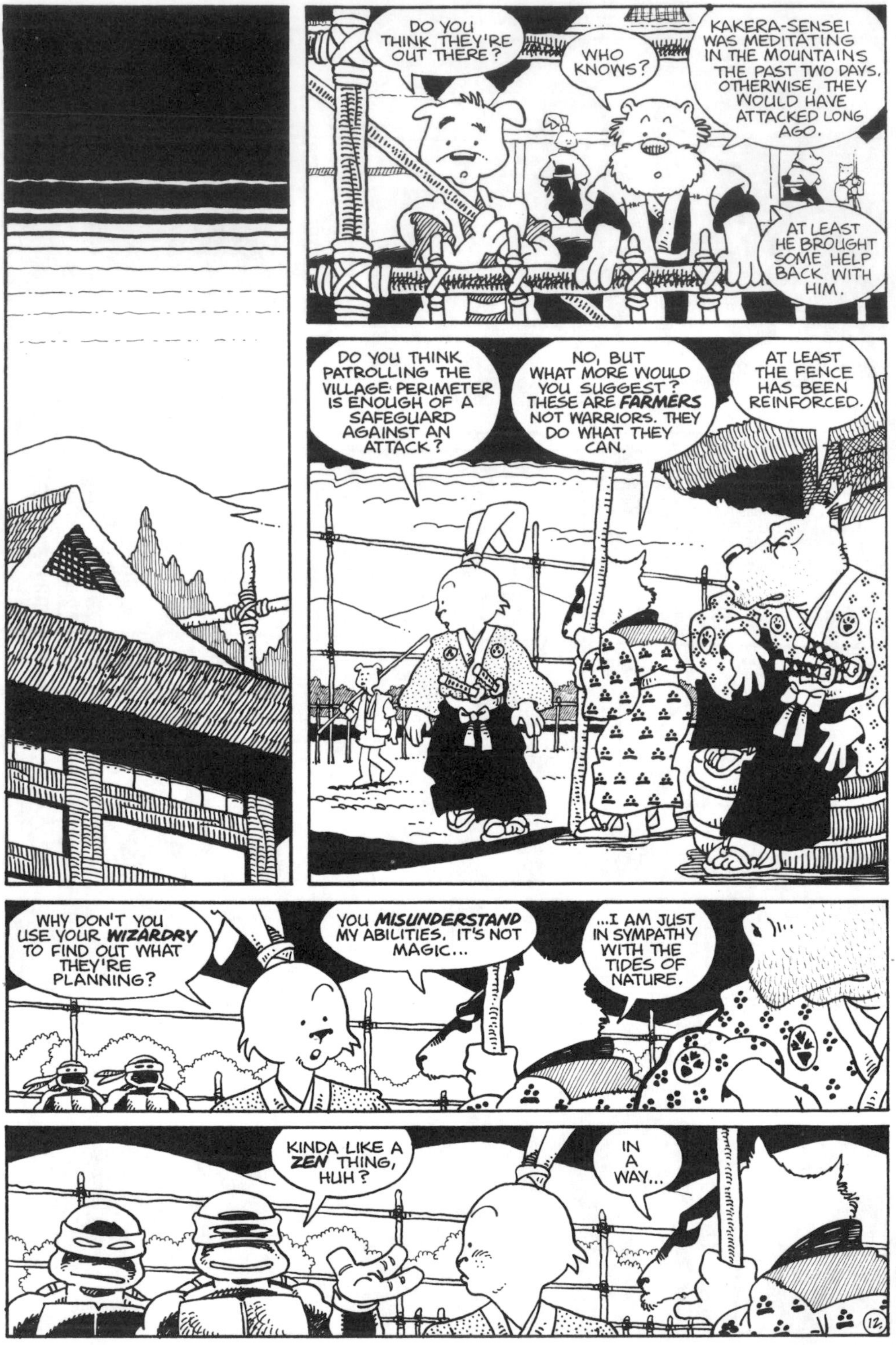
DO YOU THINK THEY'RE OUT THERE?
WHO KNOWS?
KAKERA-SENSEI WAS MEDITATING IN THE MOUNTAINS THE PAST TWO DAYS. OTHERWISE, THEY WOULD HAVE ATTACKED LONG AGO.
AT LEAST HE BROUGHT SOME HELP BACK WITH HIM.
DO YOU THINK PATROLLING THE VILLAGE PERIMETER IS ENOUGH OF A SAFEGUARD AGAINST AN ATTACK?
NO, BUT WHAT MORE WOULD YOU SUGGEST? THESE ARE FARMERS NOT WARRIORS. THEY DO WHAT THEY CAN.
AT LEAST THE FENCE HAS BEEN REINFORCED.
WHY DON'T YOU USE YOUR WIZARDRY TO FIND OUT WHAT THEY'RE PLANNING?
YOU MISUNDERSTAND MY ABILITIES. IT'S NOT MAGIC...
...I AM JUST IN SYMPATHY WITH THE TIDES OF NATURE.
KINDA LIKE A ZEN THING, HUH?
IN A WAY...
12

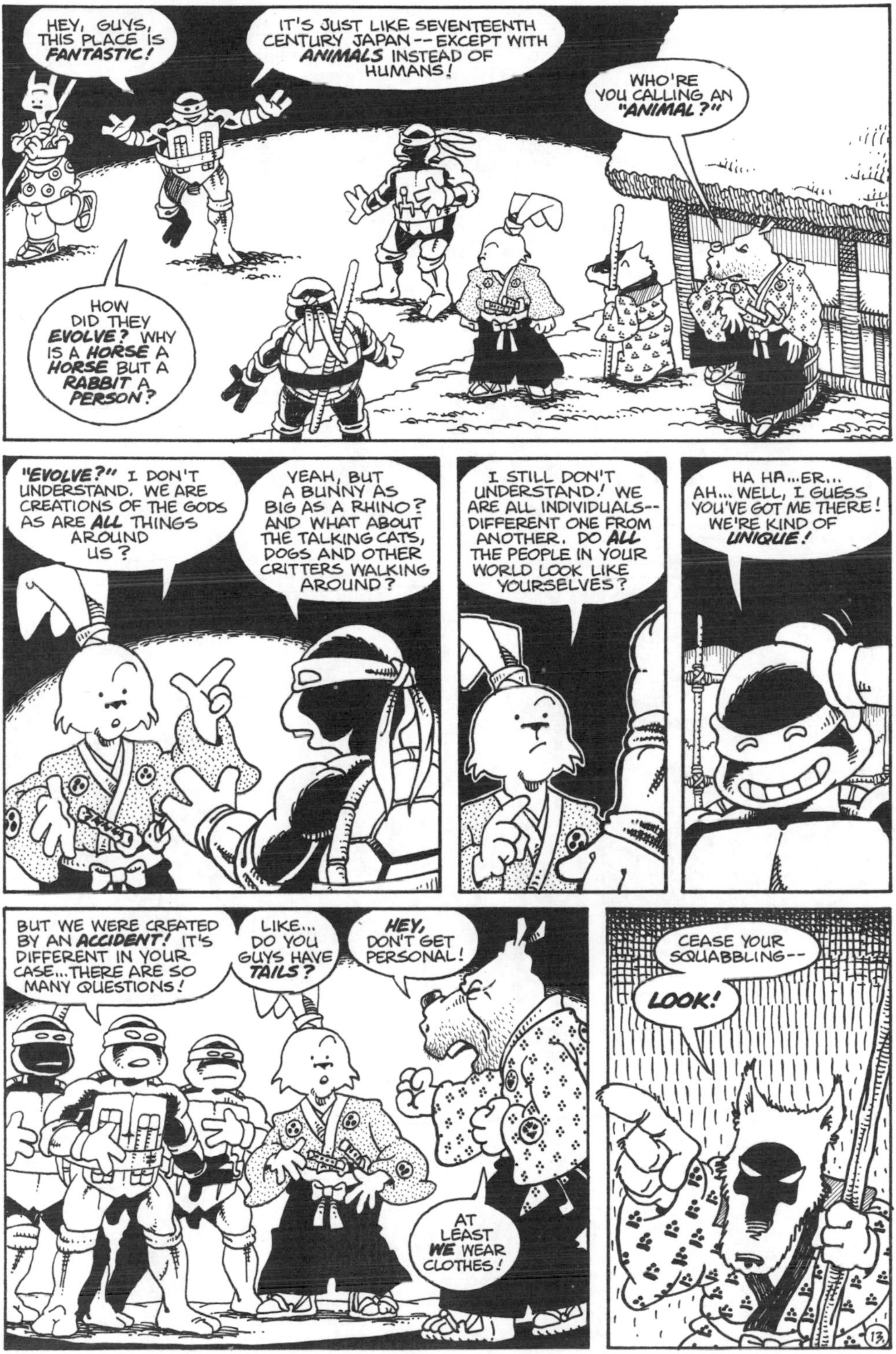
HEY, GUYS, THIS PLACE IS FANTASTIC!
IT'S JUST LIKE SEVENTEENTH CENTURY JAPAN--EXCEPT WITH ANIMALS INSTEAD OF HUMANS!
WHO'RE YOU CALLING AN "ANIMAL?"
HOW DID THEY EVOLVE? WHY IS A HORSE A HORSE BUT A RABBIT A PERSON?
"EVOLVE?" I DON'T UNDERSTAND. WE ARE CREATIONS OF THE GODS AS ARE ALL THINGS AROUND US?
YEAH, BUT A BUNNY AS BIG AS A RHINO? AND WHAT ABOUT THE TALKING CATS, DOGS AND OTHER CRITTERS WALKING AROUND?
I STILL DON'T UNDERSTAND! WE ARE ALL INDIVIDUALS--DIFFERENT ONE FROM ANOTHER. DO ALL THE PEOPLE IN YOUR WORLD LOOK LIKE YOURSELVES?
HA HA...ER... AH... WELL, I GUESS YOU'VE GOT ME THERE! WE'RE KIND OF UNIQUE!
BUT WE WERE CREATED BY AN ACCIDENT! IT'S DIFFERENT IN YOUR CASE...THERE ARE SO MANY QUESTIONS!
LIKE... DO YOU GUYS HAVE TAILS?
HEY, DON'T GET PERSONAL!
AT LEAST WE WEAR CLOTHES!
CEASE YOUR SQUABBLING--
LOOK!
13

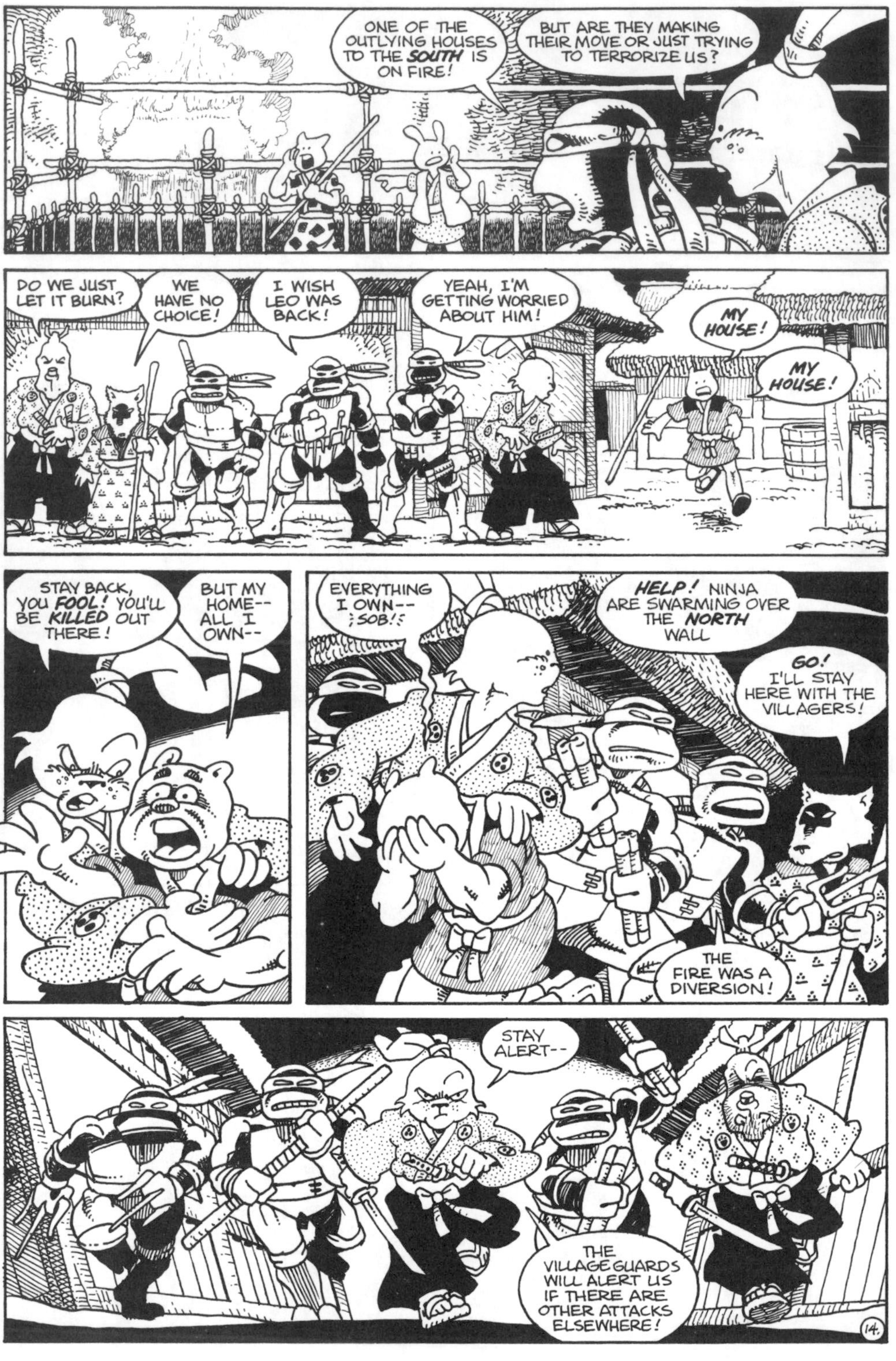
ONE OF THE OUTLYING HOUSES TO THE SOUTH IS ON FIRE!
BUT ARE THEY MAKING THEIR MOVE OR JUST TRYING TO TERRORIZE US?
DO WE JUST LET IT BURN?
WE HAVE NO CHOICE!
I WISH LEO WAS BACK!
YEAH, I'M GETTING WORRIED ABOUT HIM!
MY HOUSE!
MY HOUSE!
STAY BACK, YOU FOOL! YOU'LL BE KILLED OUT THERE!
BUT MY HOME-- ALL I OWN--
EVERYTHING I OWN-- ;SOB!;
HELP! NINJA ARE SWARMING OVER THE NORTH WALL
GO! I'LL STAY HERE WITH THE VILLAGERS!
THE FIRE WAS A DIVERSION!
STAY ALERT--
THE VILLAGE GUARDS WILL ALERT US IF THERE ARE OTHER ATTACKS ELSEWHERE!
14.

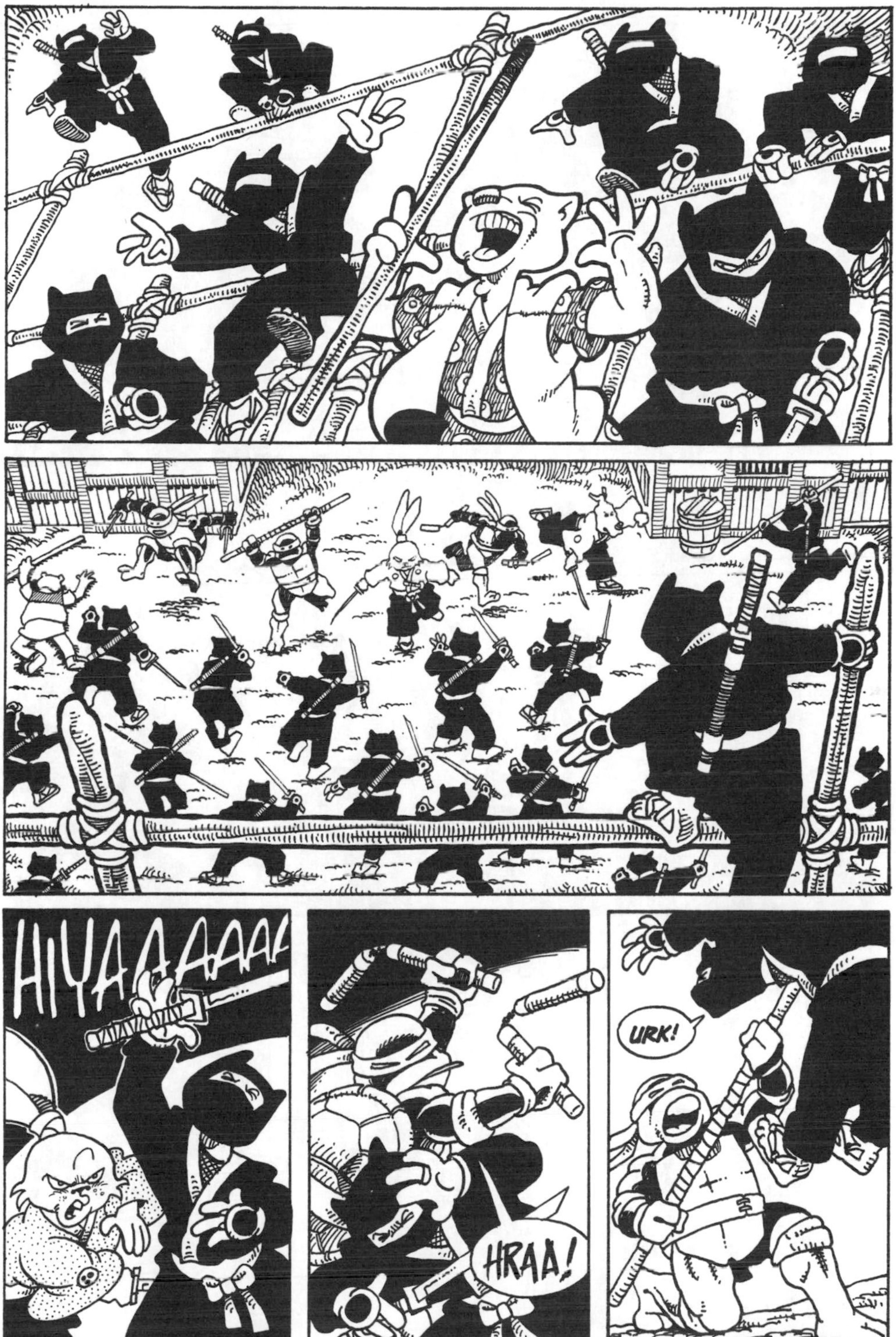
HIYAAAAA!
HRAA!
URK!

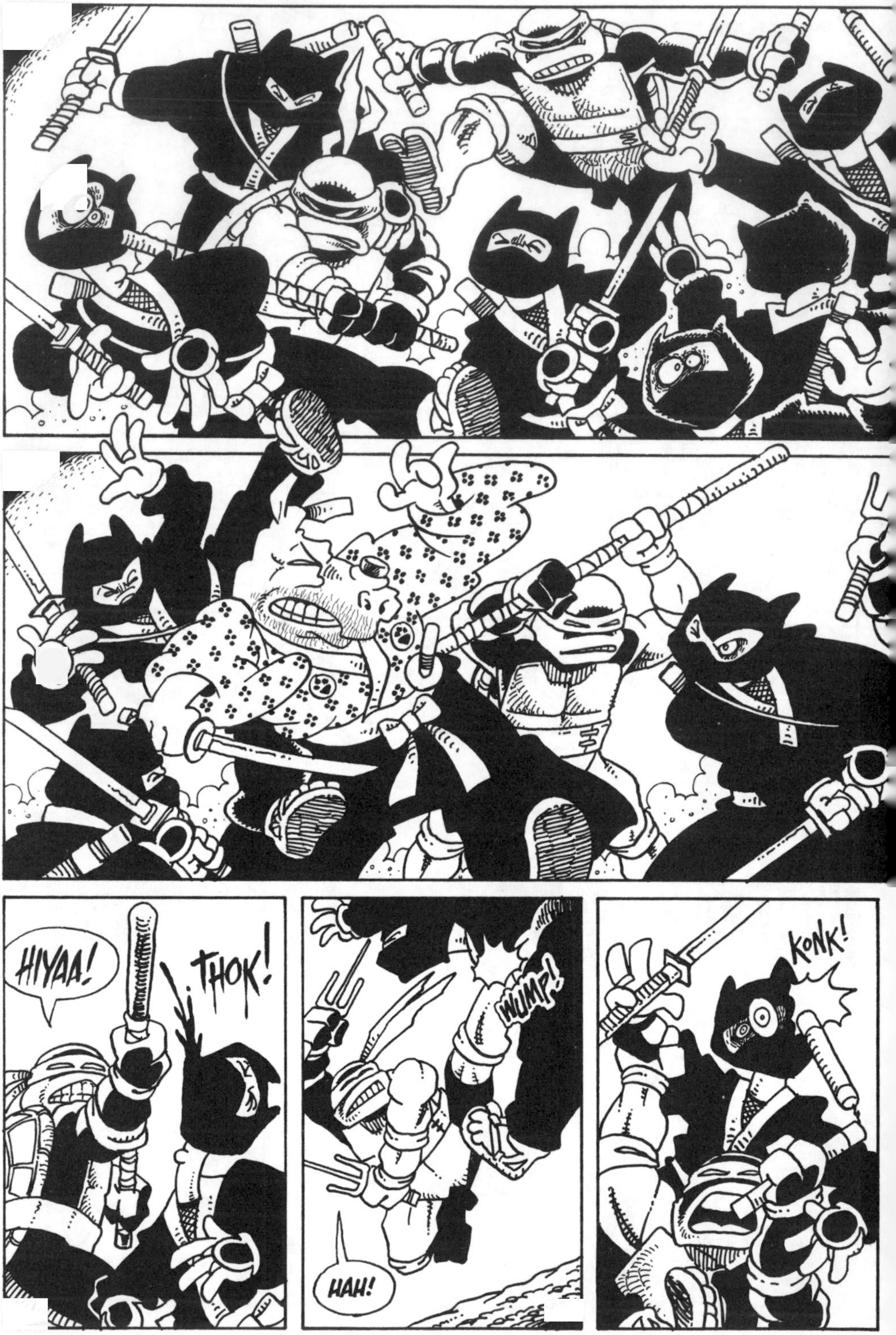
HIYAA!
THOK!
WUMP!
HAH!
KONK!

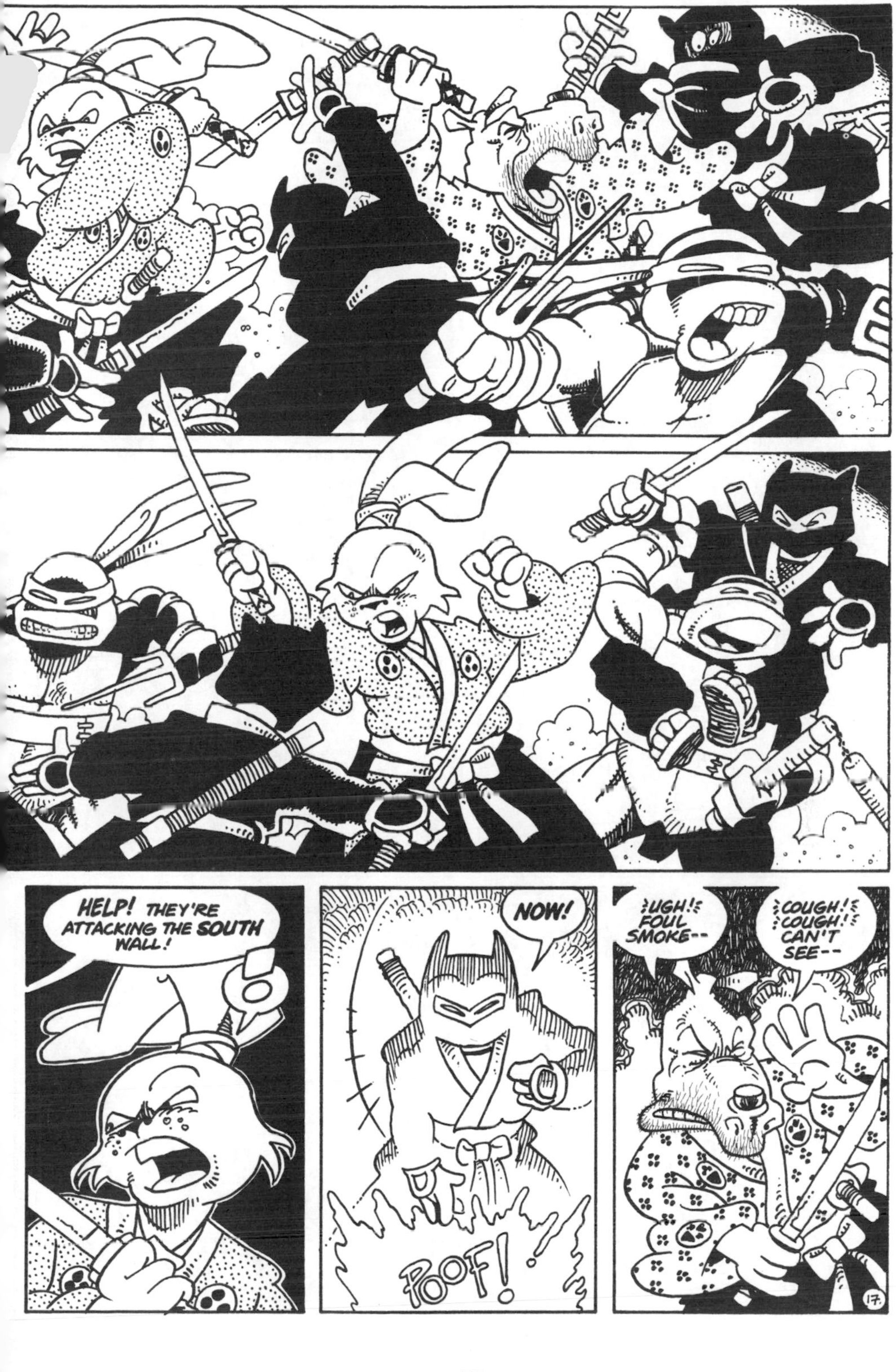
HELP! THEY'RE ATTACKING THE SOUTH WALL!
NOW!
POOF!
UGH! FOUL SMOKE--
COUGH! COUGH! CAN'T SEE--
17.

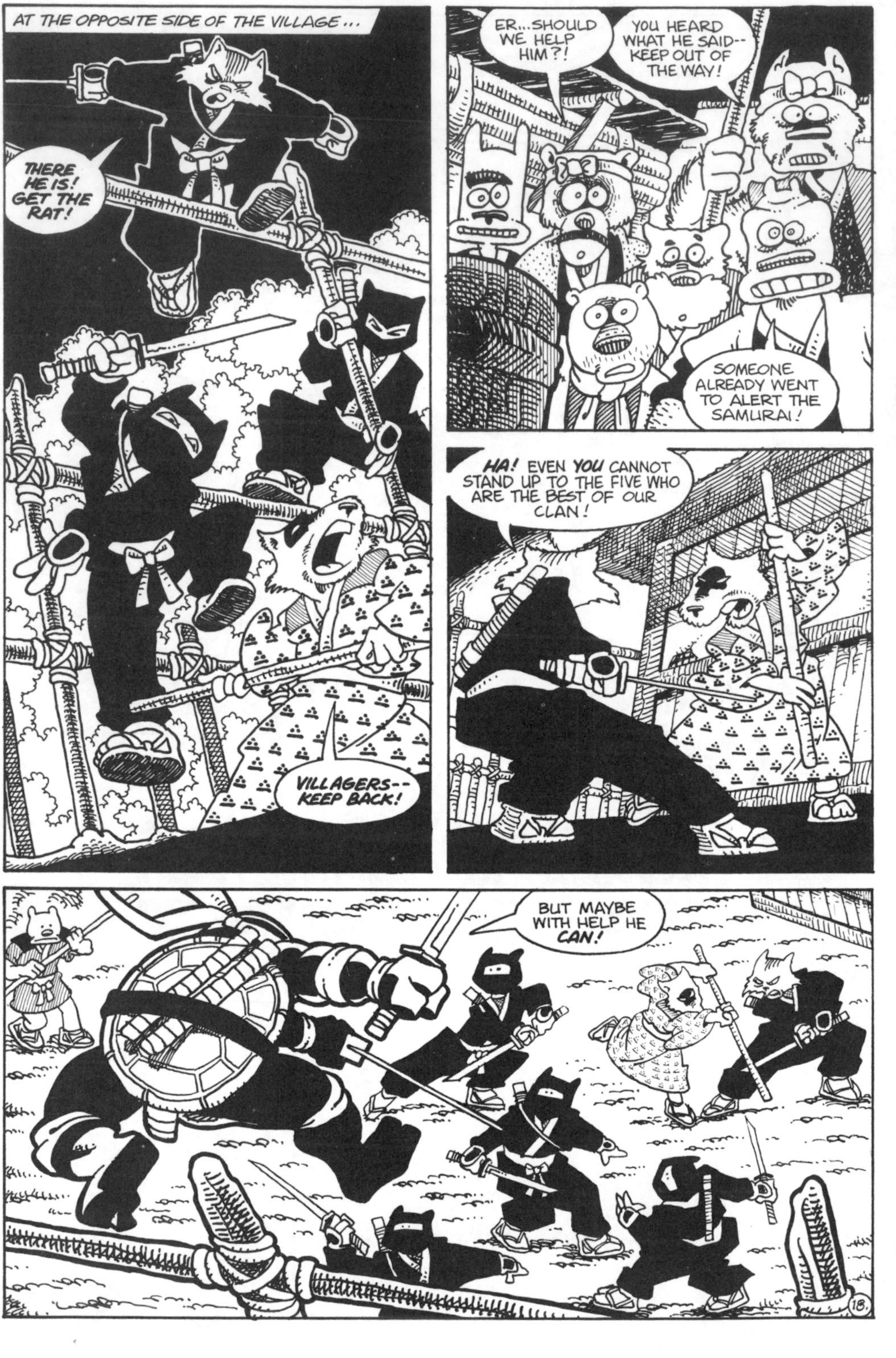
AT THE OPPOSITE SIDE OF THE VILLAGE...
THERE HE IS! GET THE RAT!
VILLAGERS-- KEEP BACK!
ER...SHOULD WE HELP HIM?!
YOU HEARD WHAT HE SAID-- KEEP OUT OF THE WAY!
SOMEONE ALREADY WENT TO ALERT THE SAMURAI!
HA! EVEN YOU CANNOT STAND UP TO THE FIVE WHO ARE THE BEST OF OUR CLAN!
BUT MAYBE WITH HELP HE CAN!
18.

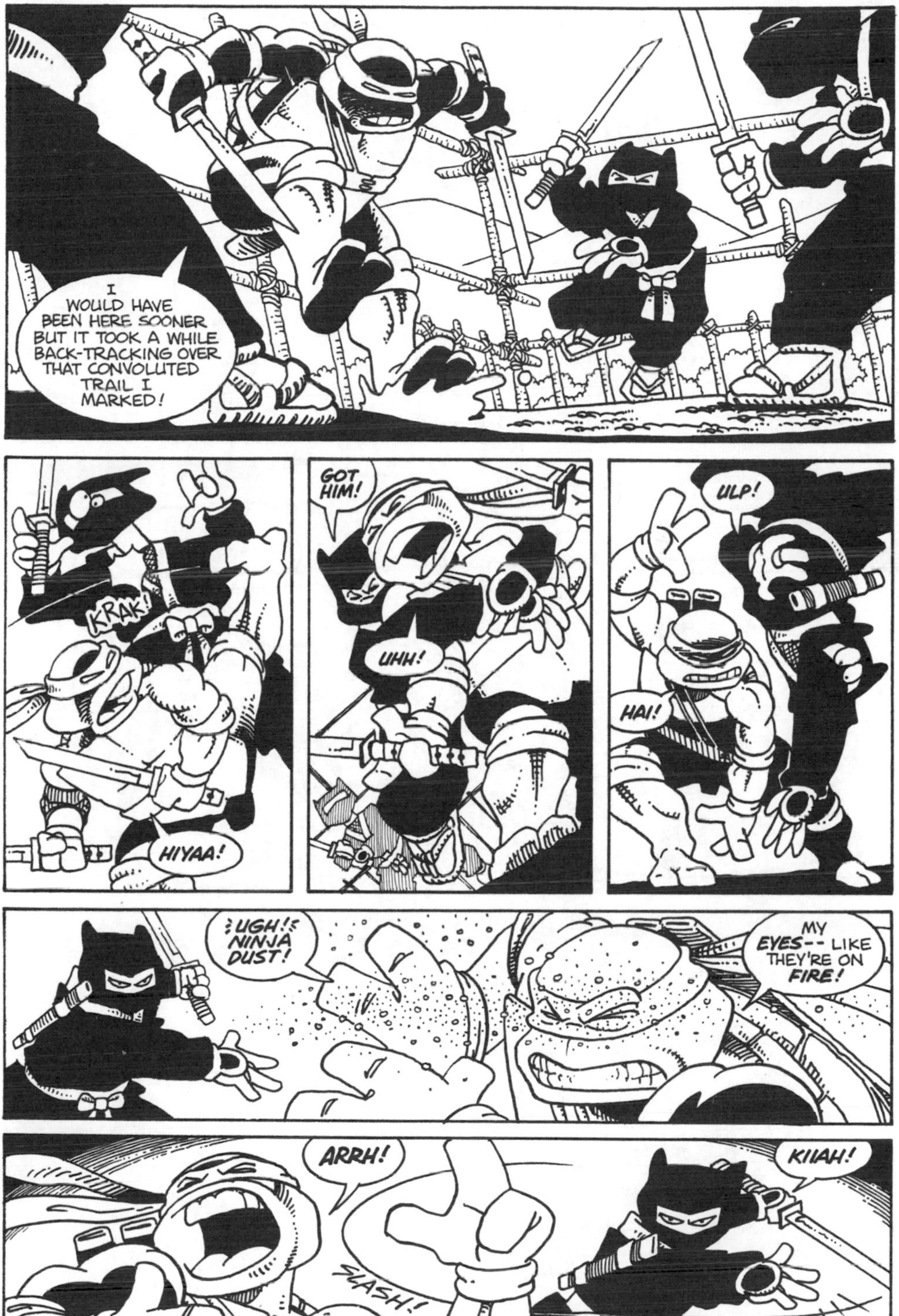
I WOULD HAVE BEEN HERE SOONER BUT IT TOOK A WHILE BACK-TRACKING OVER THAT CONVOLUTED TRAIL I MARKED!
KRAK!
HIYAA!
GOT HIM!
UHH!
ULP!
HAI!
UGH! NINJA DUST!
MY EYES-- LIKE THEY'RE ON FIRE!
ARRH!
KIIAH!
SLASH!
19.

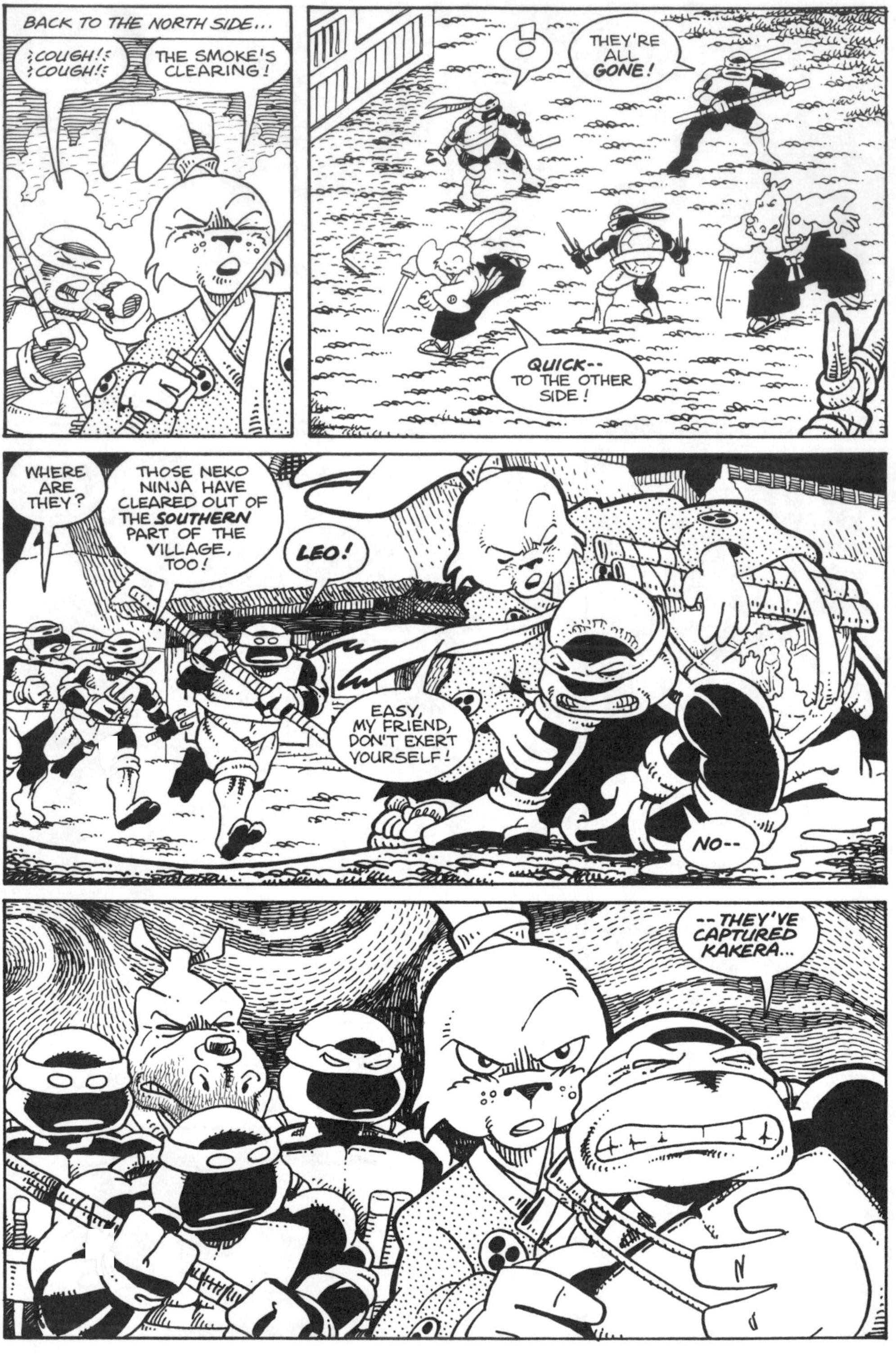
BACK TO THE NORTH SIDE...
;COUGH!; ;COUGH!;
THE SMOKE'S CLEARING!
!
O
THEY'RE ALL GONE!
QUICK-- TO THE OTHER SIDE!
WHERE ARE THEY?
THOSE NEKO NINJA HAVE CLEARED OUT OF THE SOUTHERN PART OF THE VILLAGE, TOO!
LEO!
EASY, MY FRIEND, DON'T EXERT YOURSELF!
NO--
--THEY'VE CAPTURED KAKERA...

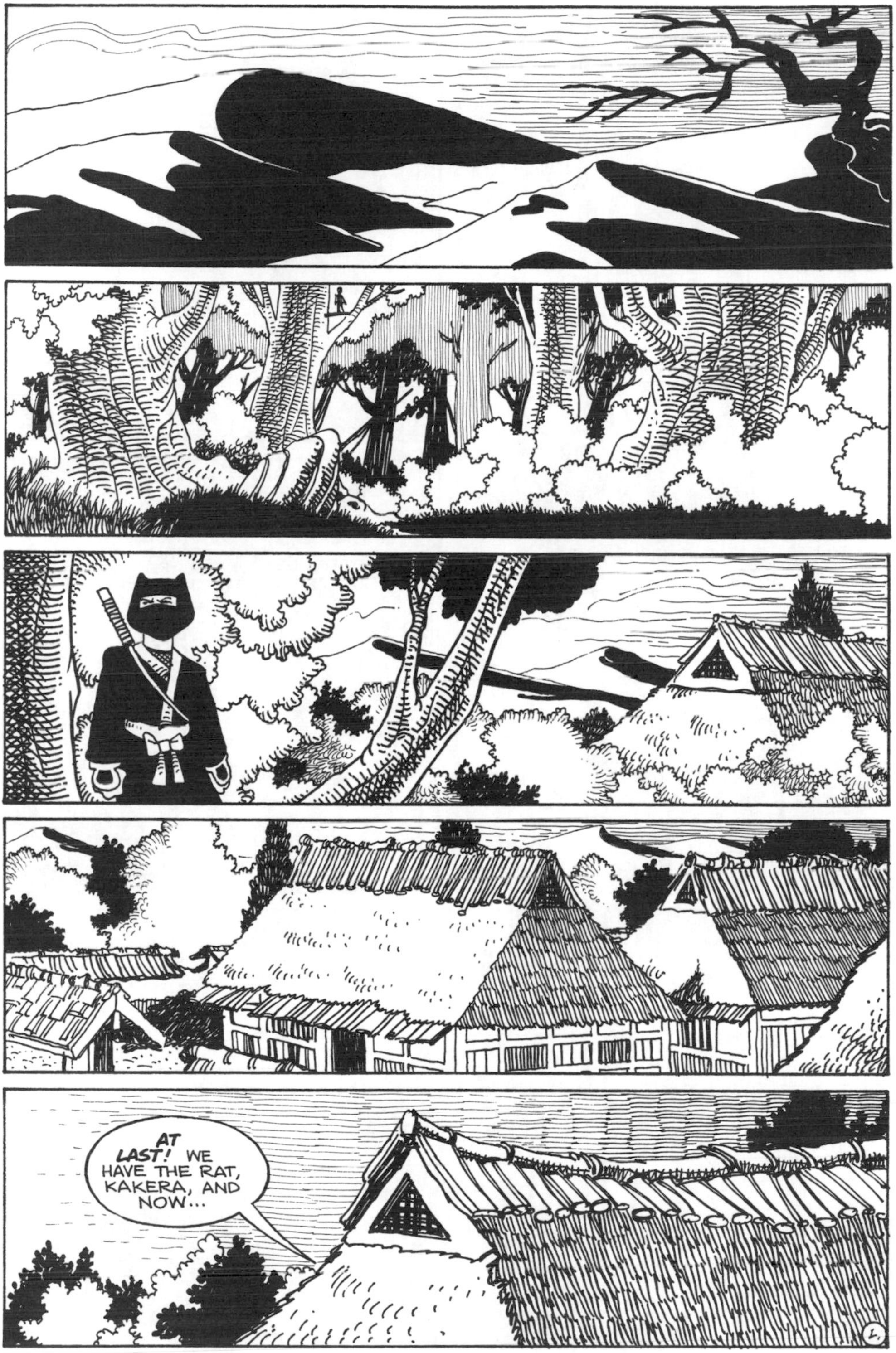
AT LAST! WE HAVE THE RAT, KAKERA, AND NOW...

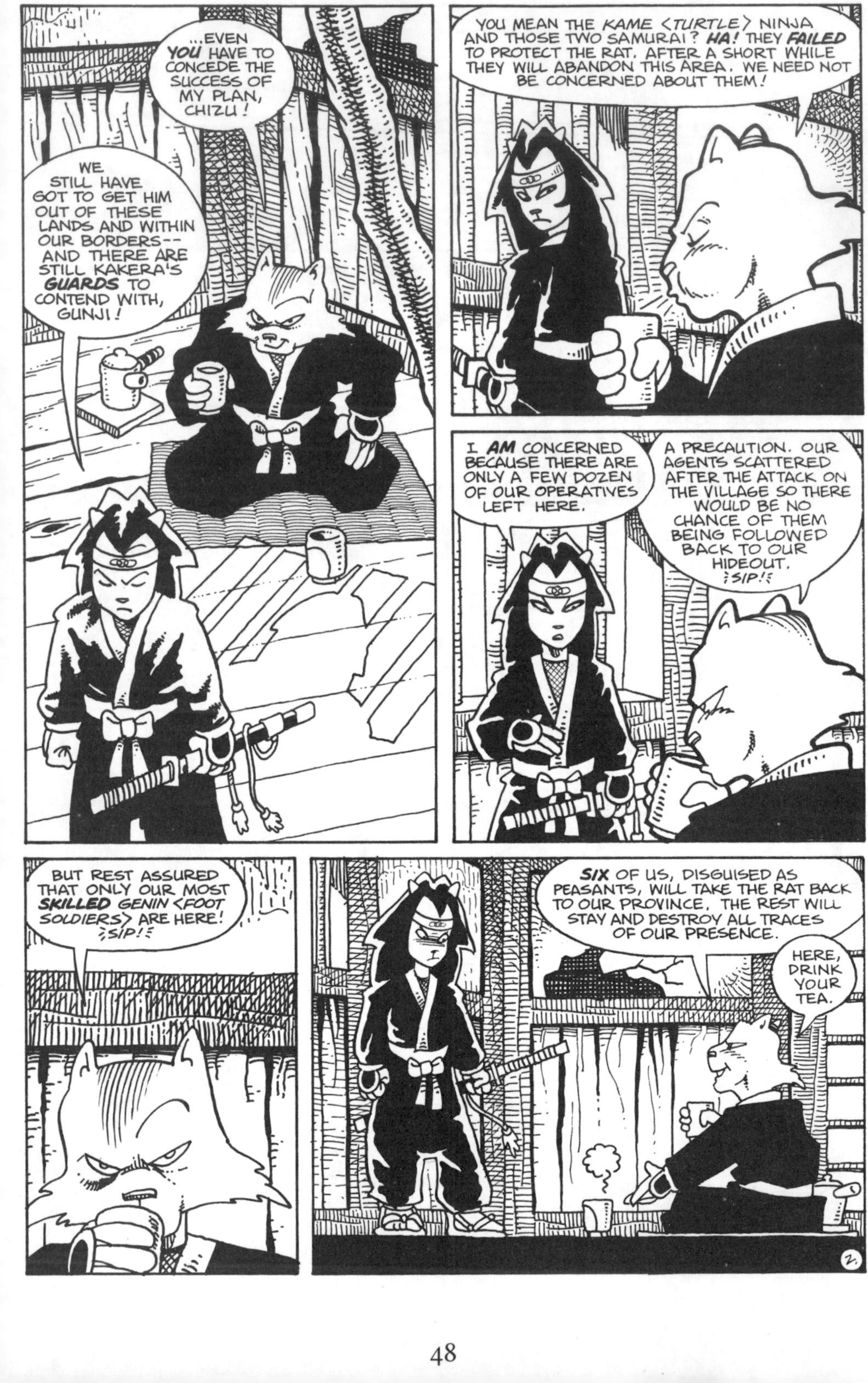
...EVEN YOU HAVE TO CONCEDE THE SUCCESS OF MY PLAN, CHIZU!
WE STILL HAVE GOT TO GET HIM OUT OF THESE LANDS AND WITHIN OUR BORDERS-- AND THERE ARE STILL KAKERA'S GUARDS TO CONTEND WITH, GUNJI!
YOU MEAN THE KAME <TURTLE> NINJA AND THOSE TWO SAMURAI? HA! THEY FAILED TO PROTECT THE RAT. AFTER A SHORT WHILE THEY WILL ABANDON THIS AREA. WE NEED NOT BE CONCERNED ABOUT THEM!
I AM CONCERNED BECAUSE THERE ARE ONLY A FEW DOZEN OF OUR OPERATIVES LEFT HERE.
A PRECAUTION. OUR AGENTS SCATTERED AFTER THE ATTACK ON THE VILLAGE SO THERE WOULD BE NO CHANCE OF THEM BEING FOLLOWED BACK TO OUR HIDEOUT.
SIP!
BUT REST ASSURED THAT ONLY OUR MOST SKILLED GENIN <FOOT SOLDIERS> ARE HERE!
SIP!
SIX OF US, DISGUISED AS PEASANTS, WILL TAKE THE RAT BACK TO OUR PROVINCE. THE REST WILL STAY AND DESTROY ALL TRACES OF OUR PRESENCE.
HERE, DRINK YOUR TEA.
2.

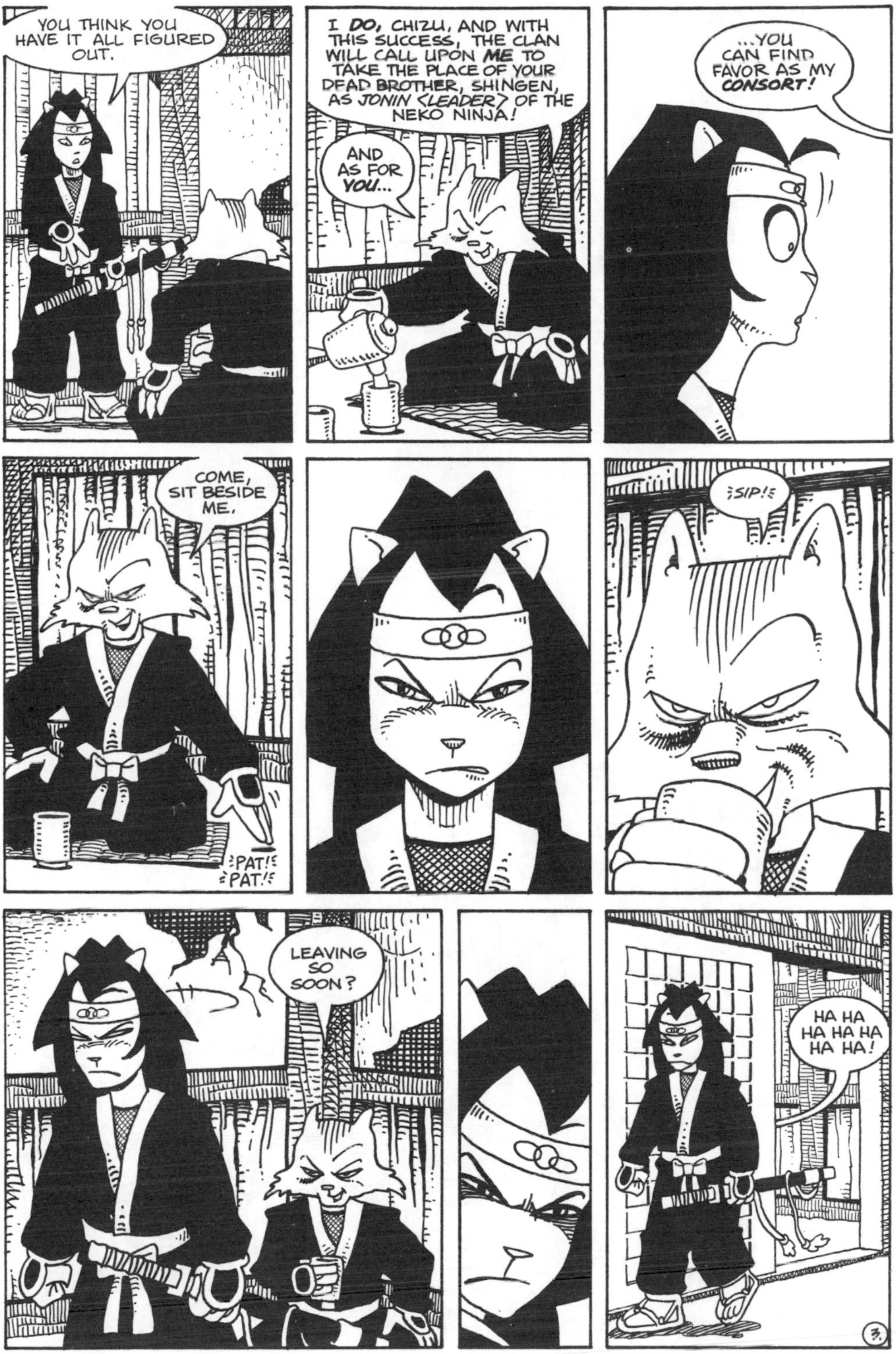
YOU THINK YOU HAVE IT ALL FIGURED OUT.
I DO, CHIZU, AND WITH THIS SUCCESS, THE CLAN WILL CALL UPON ME TO TAKE THE PLACE OF YOUR DEAD BROTHER, SHINGEN, AS JONIN <LEADER> OF THE NEKO NINJA!
AND AS FOR YOU...
...YOU CAN FIND FAVOR AS MY CONSORT!
COME, SIT BESIDE ME.
PAT! PAT!
SIP!
LEAVING SO SOON?
HA HA HA HA HA HA HA!
3.

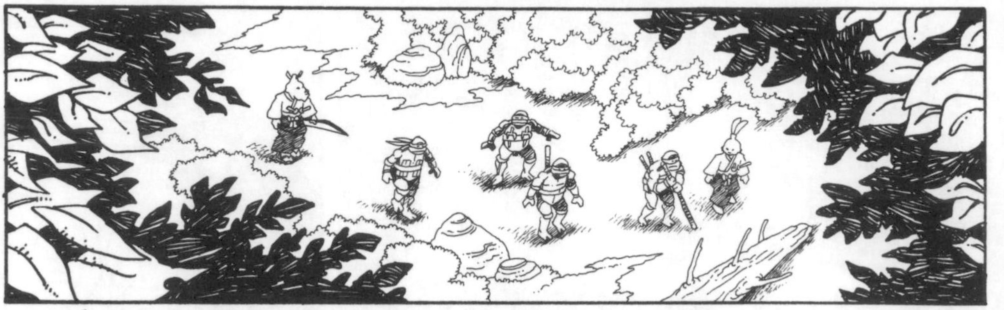

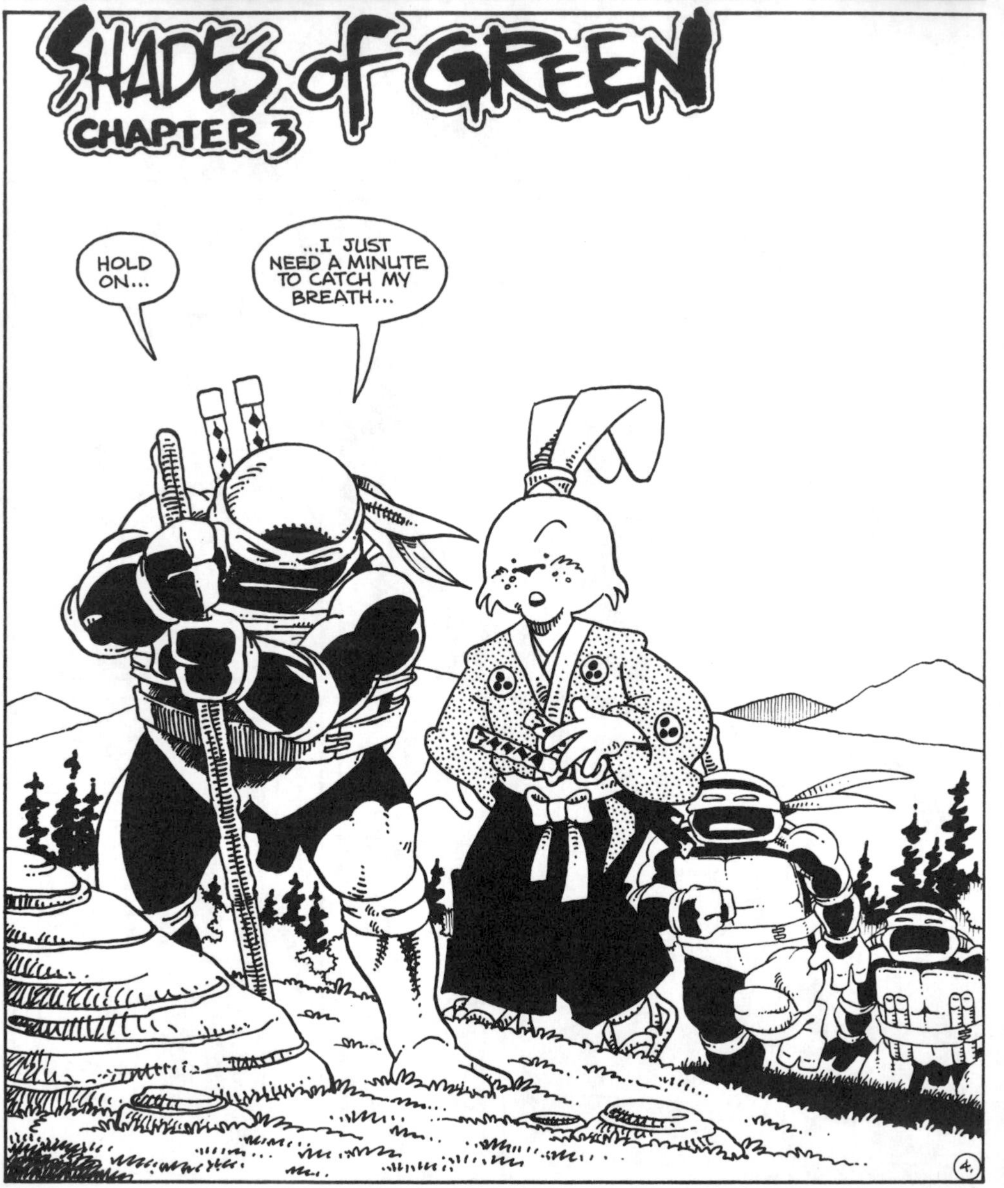
SHADES OF GREEN
CHAPTER 3
HOLD ON...
...I JUST NEED A MINUTE TO CATCH MY BREATH...
4.

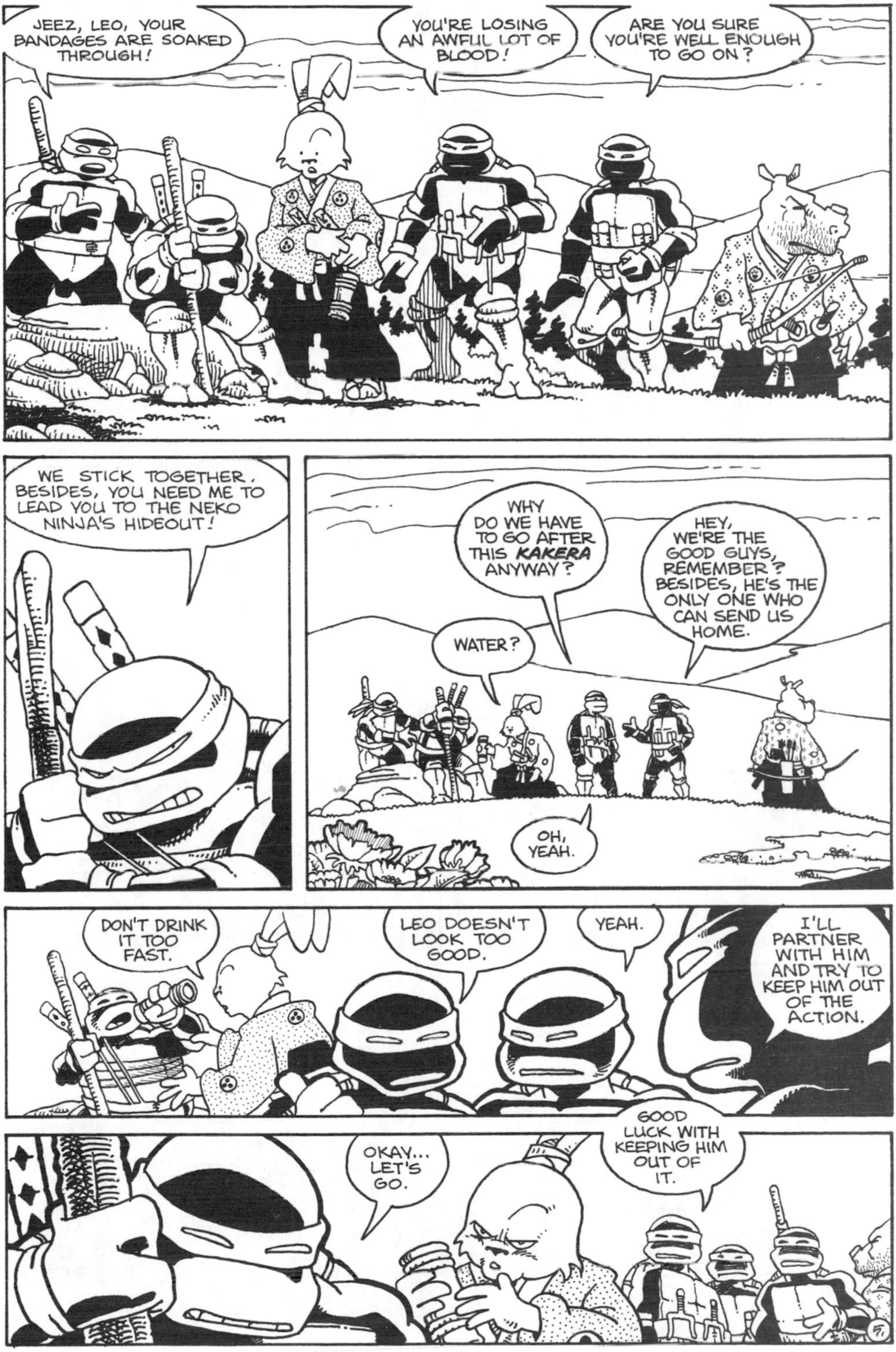
JEEZ, LEO, YOUR BANDAGES ARE SOAKED THROUGH!
YOU'RE LOSING AN AWFUL LOT OF BLOOD!
ARE YOU SURE YOU'RE WELL ENOUGH TO GO ON?
WE STICK TOGETHER. BESIDES, YOU NEED ME TO LEAD YOU TO THE NEKO NINJA'S HIDEOUT!
WATER?
WHY DO WE HAVE TO GO AFTER THIS KAKERA ANYWAY?
HEY, WE'RE THE GOOD GUYS, REMEMBER? BESIDES, HE'S THE ONLY ONE WHO CAN SEND US HOME.
OH, YEAH.
DON'T DRINK IT TOO FAST.
LEO DOESN'T LOOK TOO GOOD.
YEAH.
I'LL PARTNER WITH HIM AND TRY TO KEEP HIM OUT OF THE ACTION.
OKAY... LET'S GO.
GOOD LUCK WITH KEEPING HIM OUT OF IT.

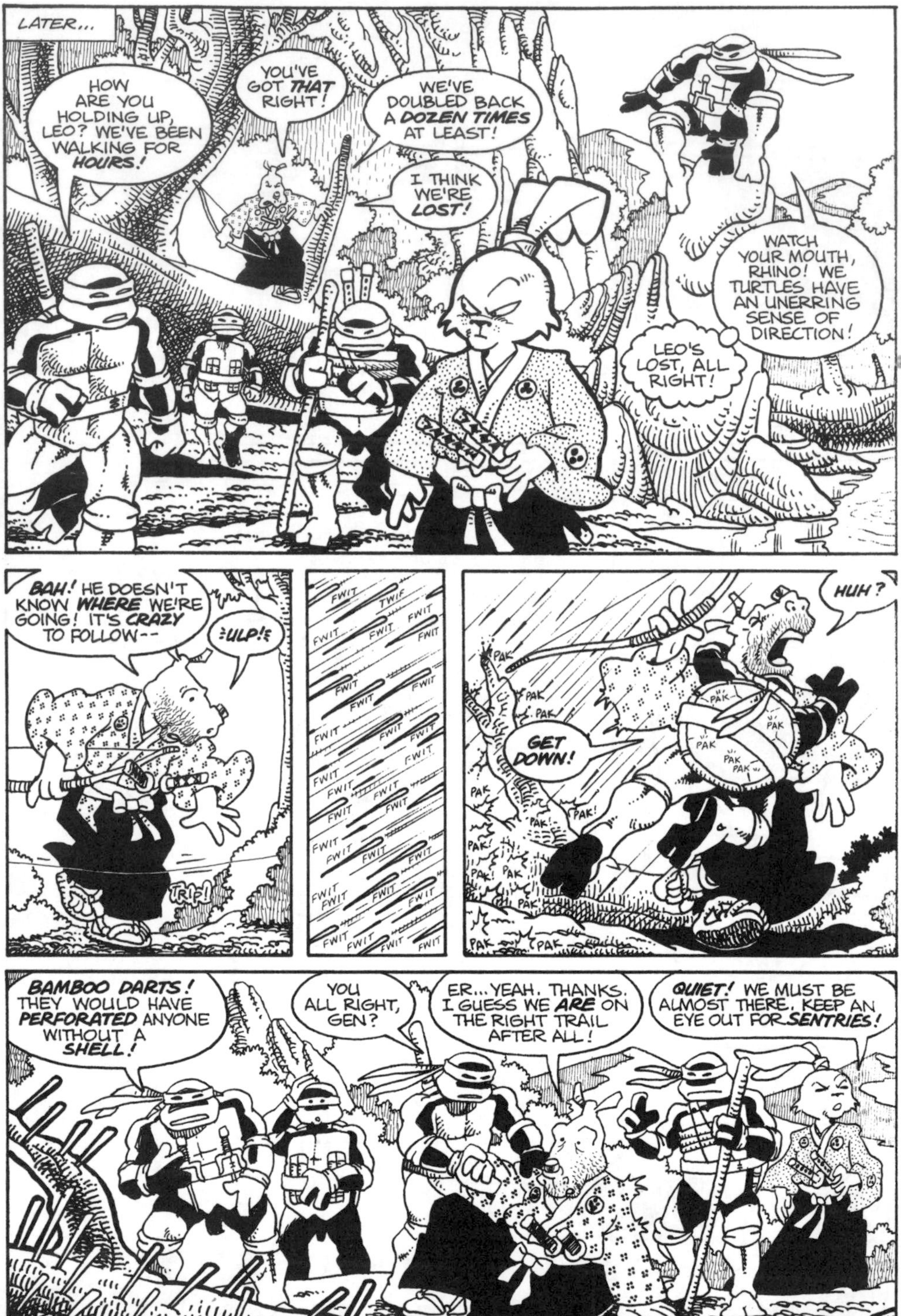
LATER...
HOW ARE YOU HOLDING UP, LEO? WE'VE BEEN WALKING FOR HOURS!
YOU'VE GOT THAT RIGHT!
WE'VE DOUBLED BACK A DOZEN TIMES AT LEAST!
I THINK WE'RE LOST!
WATCH YOUR MOUTH, RHINO! WE TURTLES HAVE AN UNERRING SENSE OF DIRECTION!
LEO'S LOST, ALL RIGHT!
BAH! HE DOESN'T KNOW WHERE WE'RE GOING! IT'S CRAZY TO FOLLOW--
ULP!
TRIP!
FWIT
TWIF
HUH?
GET DOWN!
PAK
BAMBOO DARTS! THEY WOULD HAVE PERFORATED ANYONE WITHOUT A SHELL!
YOU ALL RIGHT, GEN?
ER...YEAH. THANKS. I GUESS WE ARE ON THE RIGHT TRAIL AFTER ALL!
QUIET! WE MUST BE ALMOST THERE. KEEP AN EYE OUT FOR SENTRIES!
6.

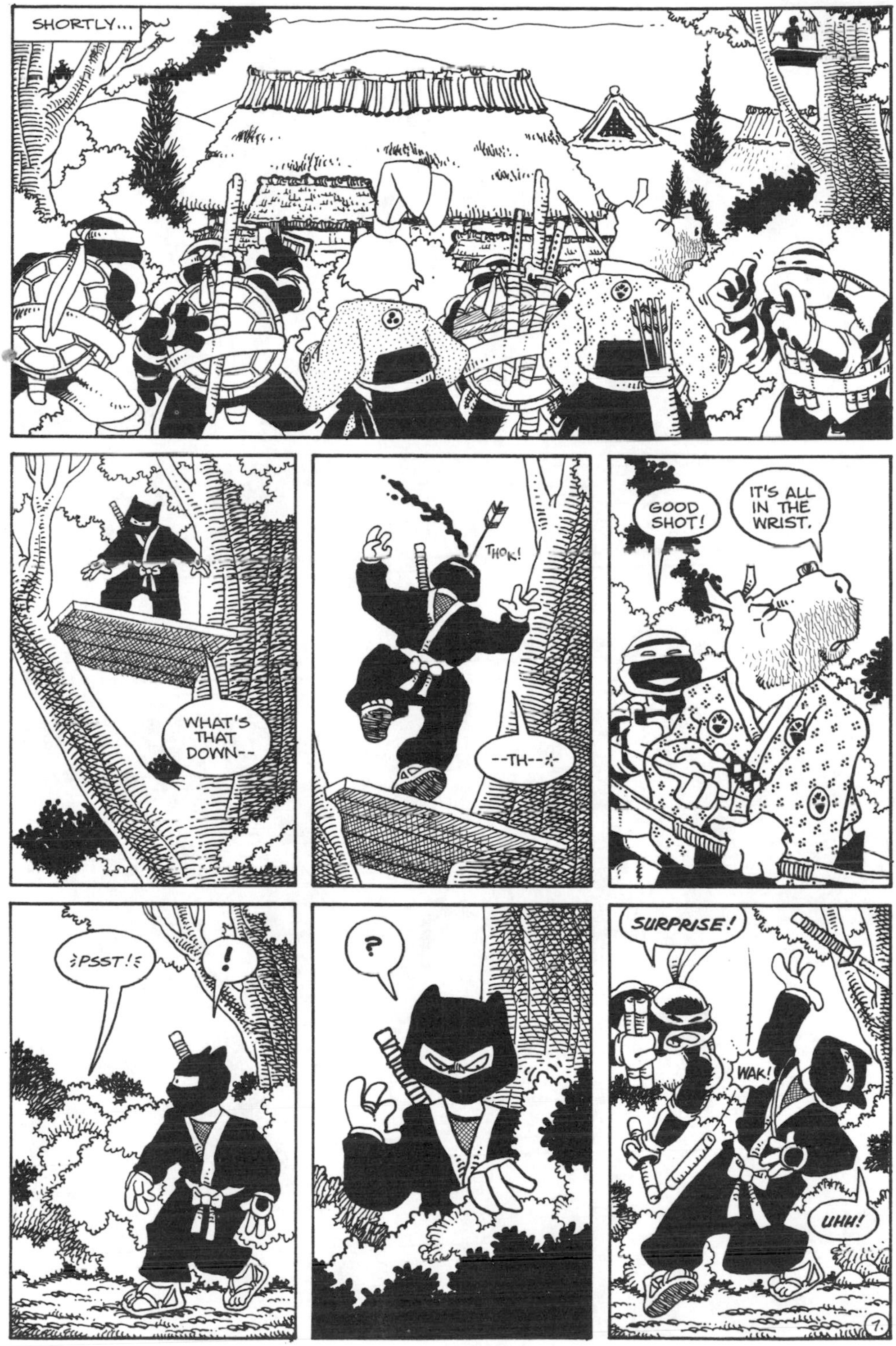
SHORTLY...
WHAT'S THAT DOWN--
THOK!
--TH--
GOOD SHOT!
IT'S ALL IN THE WRIST.
PSST!
!
?
SURPRISE!
WAK!
UHH!
7.

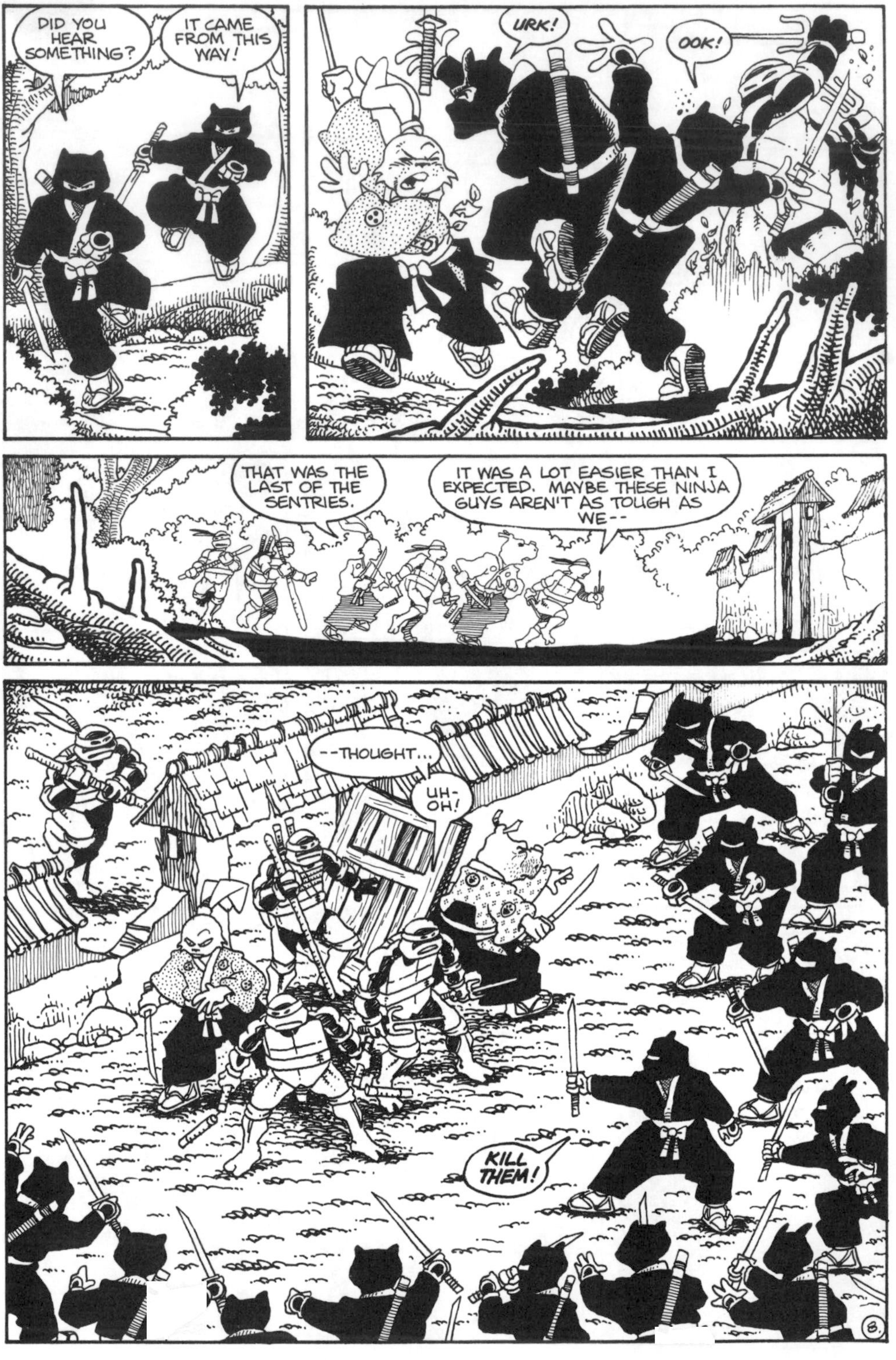
DID YOU HEAR SOMETHING?
IT CAME FROM THIS WAY!
URK!
OOK!
THAT WAS THE LAST OF THE SENTRIES.
IT WAS A LOT EASIER THAN I EXPECTED. MAYBE THESE NINJA GUYS AREN'T AS TOUGH AS WE--
--THOUGHT...
UH-OH!
KILL THEM!
8.

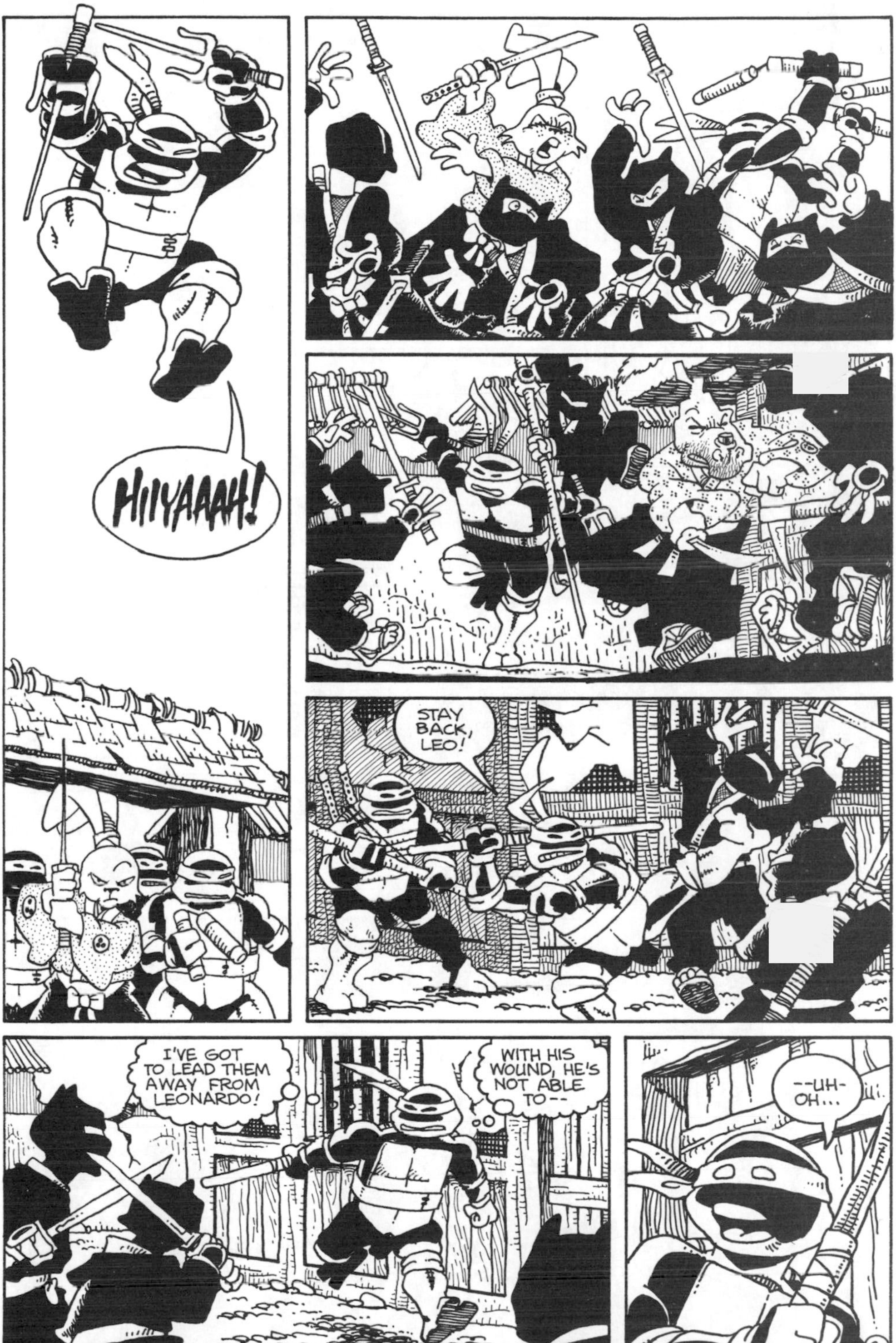
HIIYAAAH!
STAY BACK, LEO!
I'VE GOT TO LEAD THEM AWAY FROM LEONARDO!
WITH HIS WOUND, HE'S NOT ABLE TO--
--UH-OH...
9.

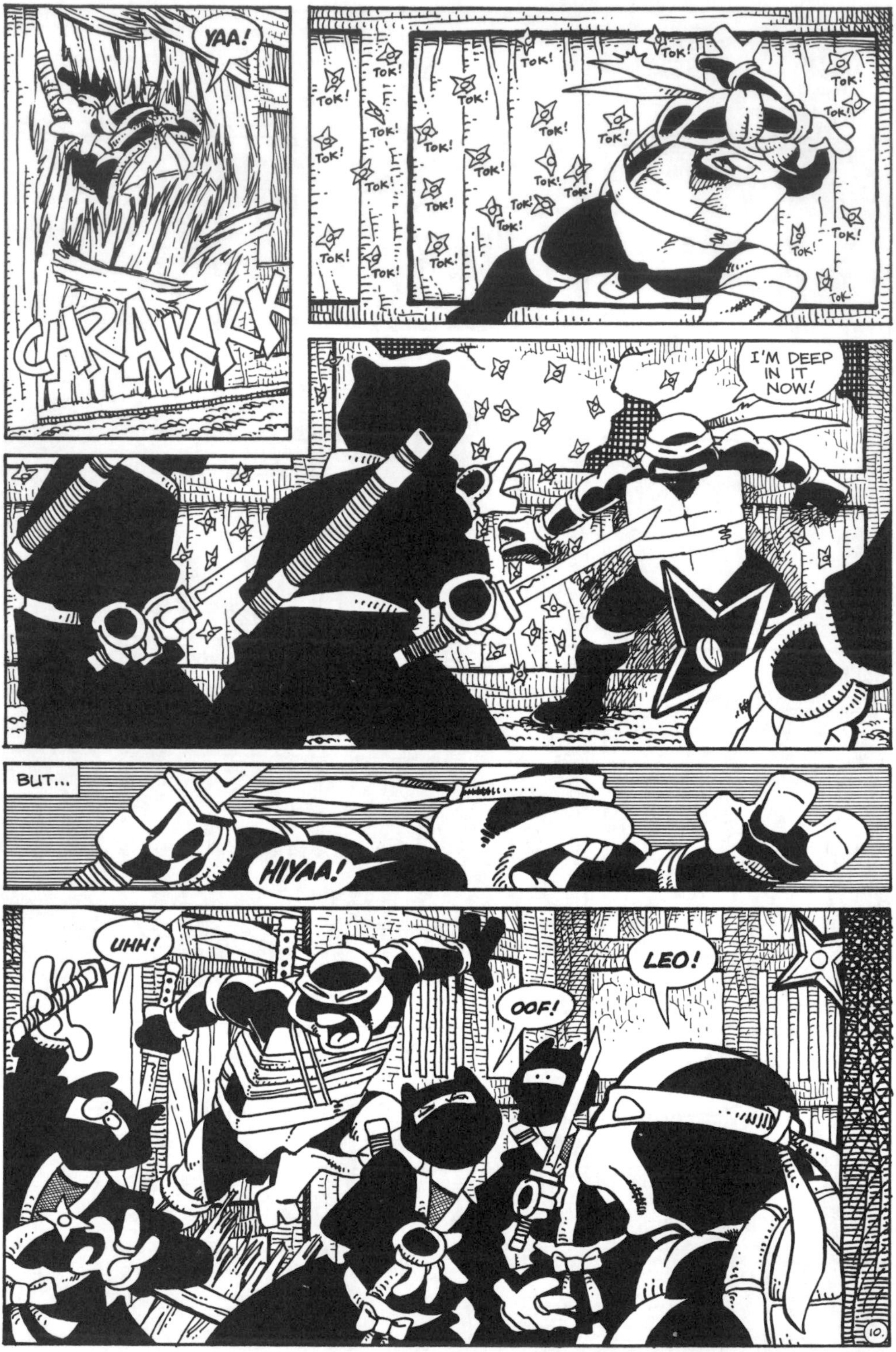
YAA!
CHRAKKK
TOK!
TOK!
TOK!
TOK!
I'M DEEP IN IT NOW!
BUT...
HIYAA!
UHH!
OOF!
LEO!
10.

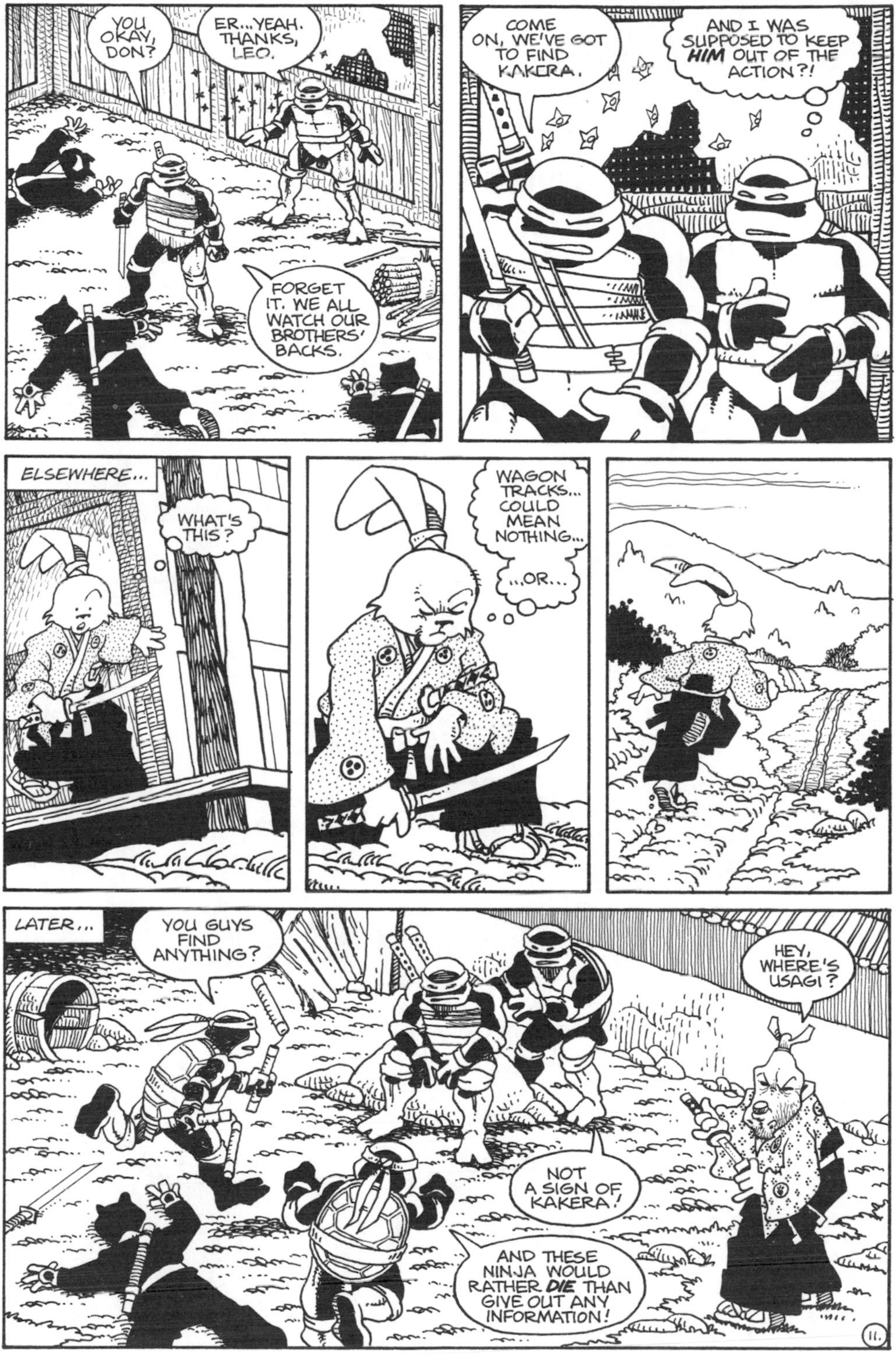
YOU OKAY, DON?
ER...YEAH. THANKS, LEO.
FORGET IT. WE ALL WATCH OUR BROTHERS' BACKS.
COME ON, WE'VE GOT TO FIND KAKERA.
AND I WAS SUPPOSED TO KEEP HIM OUT OF THE ACTION?!
ELSEWHERE...
WHAT'S THIS?
WAGON TRACKS... COULD MEAN NOTHING...
...OR...
LATER...
YOU GUYS FIND ANYTHING?
HEY, WHERE'S USAGI?
NOT A SIGN OF KAKERA!
AND THESE NINJA WOULD RATHER DIE THAN GIVE OUT ANY INFORMATION!
11.

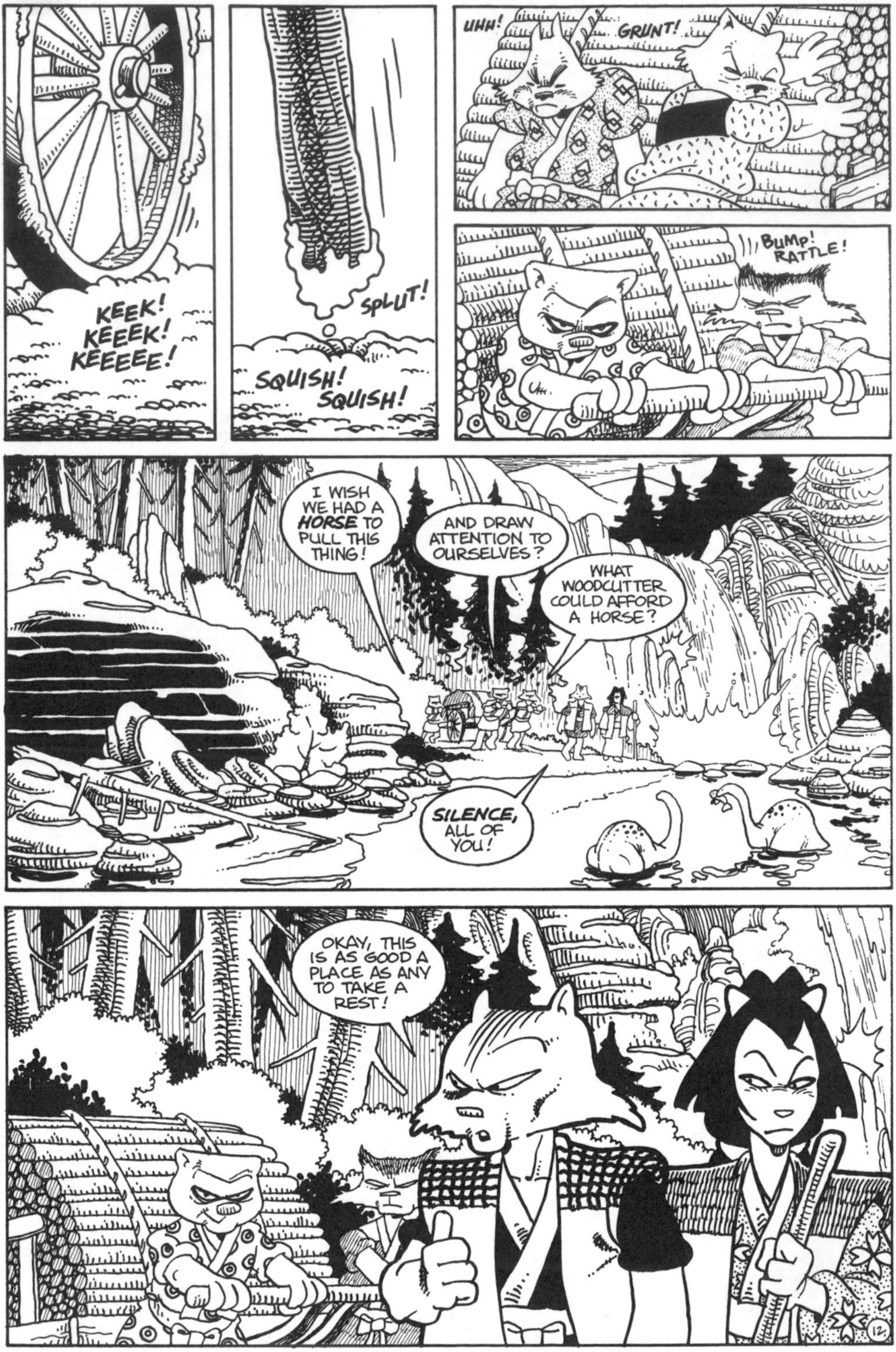
KEEK!
KEEEK!
KEEEEE!
SPLUT!
SQUISH!
SQUISH!
UHH!
GRUNT!
BUMP!
RATTLE!
I WISH WE HAD A HORSE TO PULL THIS THING!
AND DRAW ATTENTION TO OURSELVES?
WHAT WOODCUTTER COULD AFFORD A HORSE?
SILENCE, ALL OF YOU!
OKAY, THIS IS AS GOOD A PLACE AS ANY TO TAKE A REST!
12

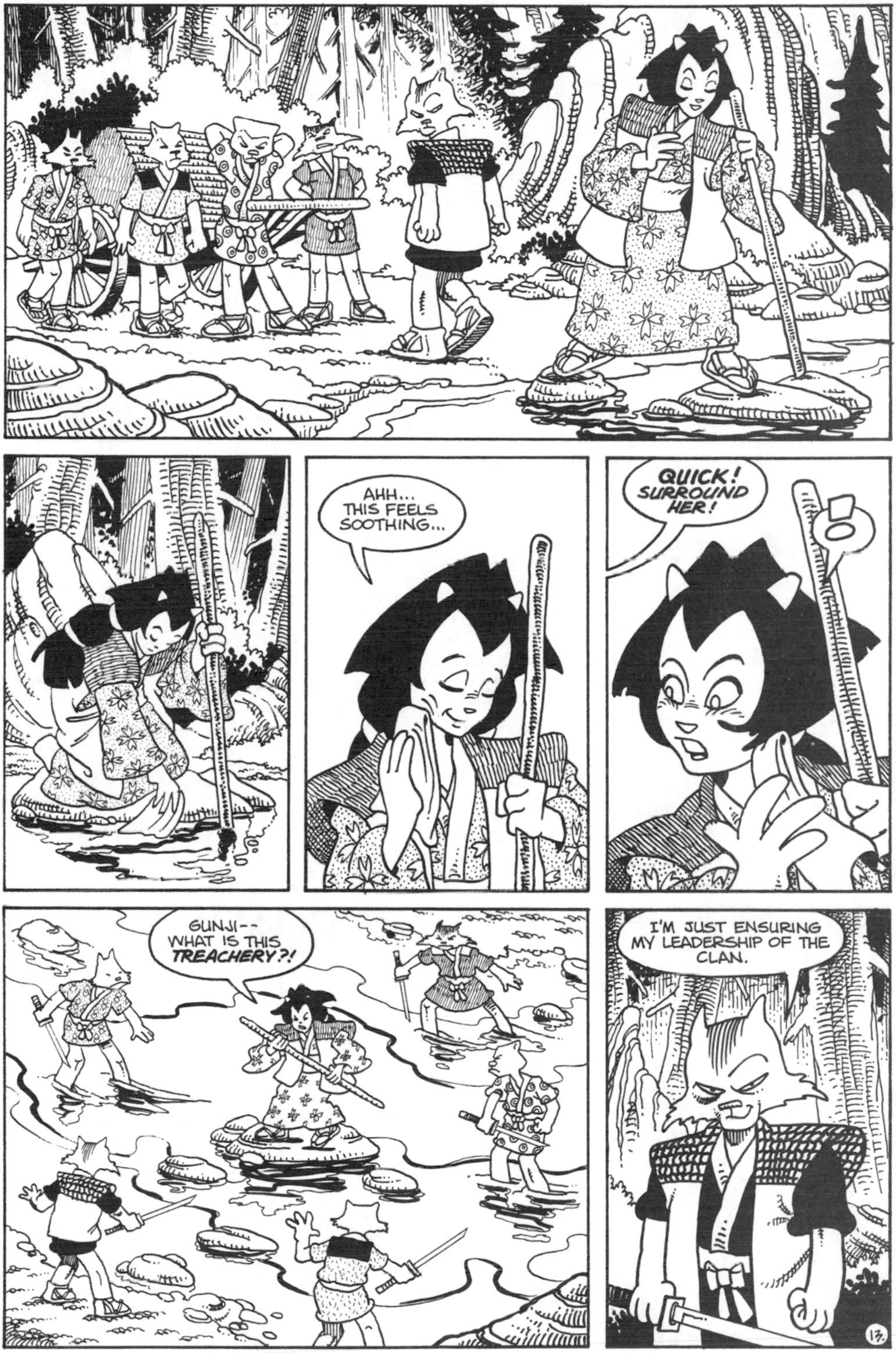
AHH... THIS FEELS SOOTHING...
QUICK! SURROUND HER!
!
GUNJI-- WHAT IS THIS TREACHERY?!
I'M JUST ENSURING MY LEADERSHIP OF THE CLAN.
13.

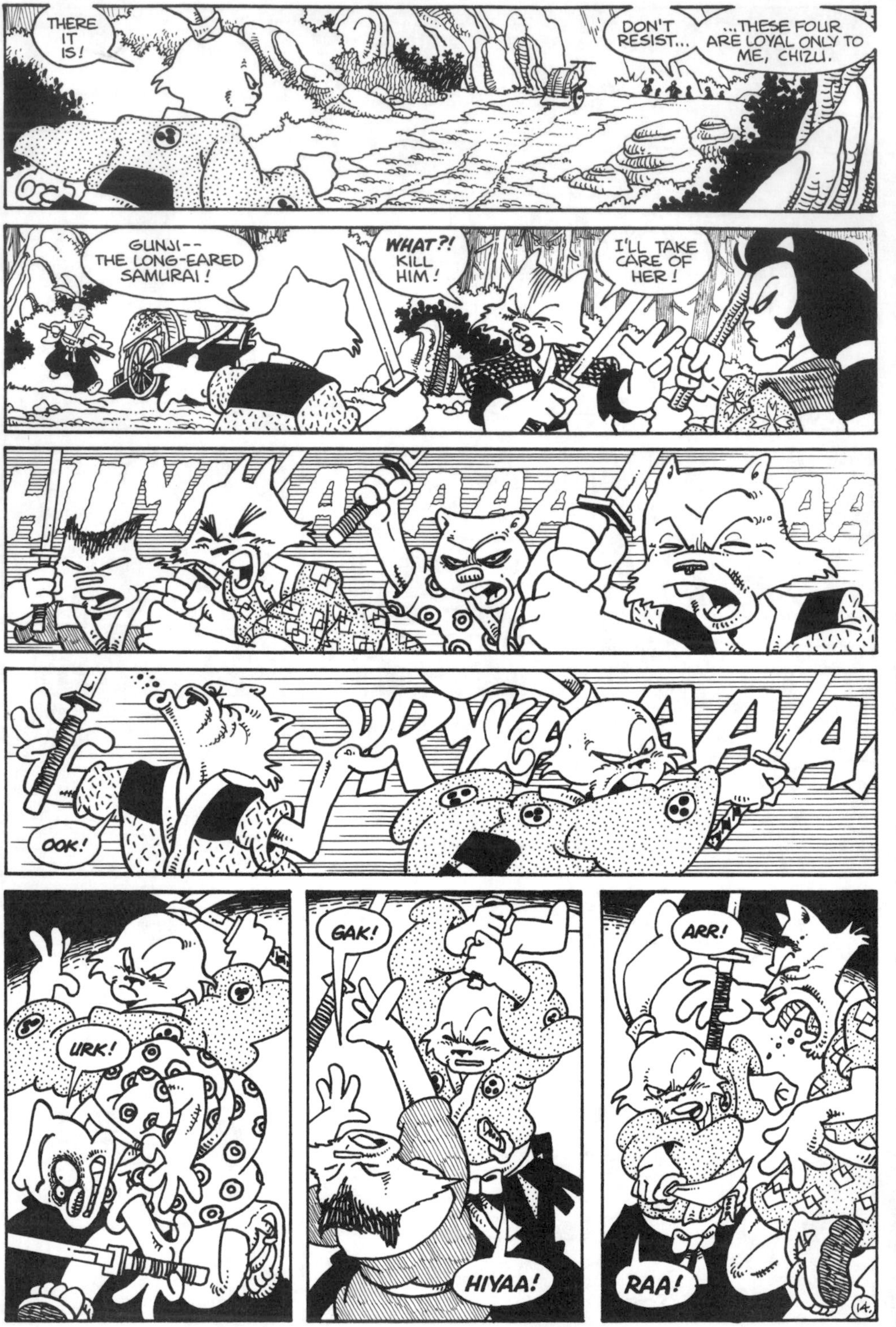
THERE IT IS!
DON'T RESIST...
...THESE FOUR ARE LOYAL ONLY TO ME, CHIZU.
GUNJI-- THE LONG-EARED SAMURAI!
WHAT?! KILL HIM!
I'LL TAKE CARE OF HER!
HIIYAAAAAA
YRYAAAAA
OOK!
URK!
GAK!
HIYAA!
ARR!
RAA!
14.

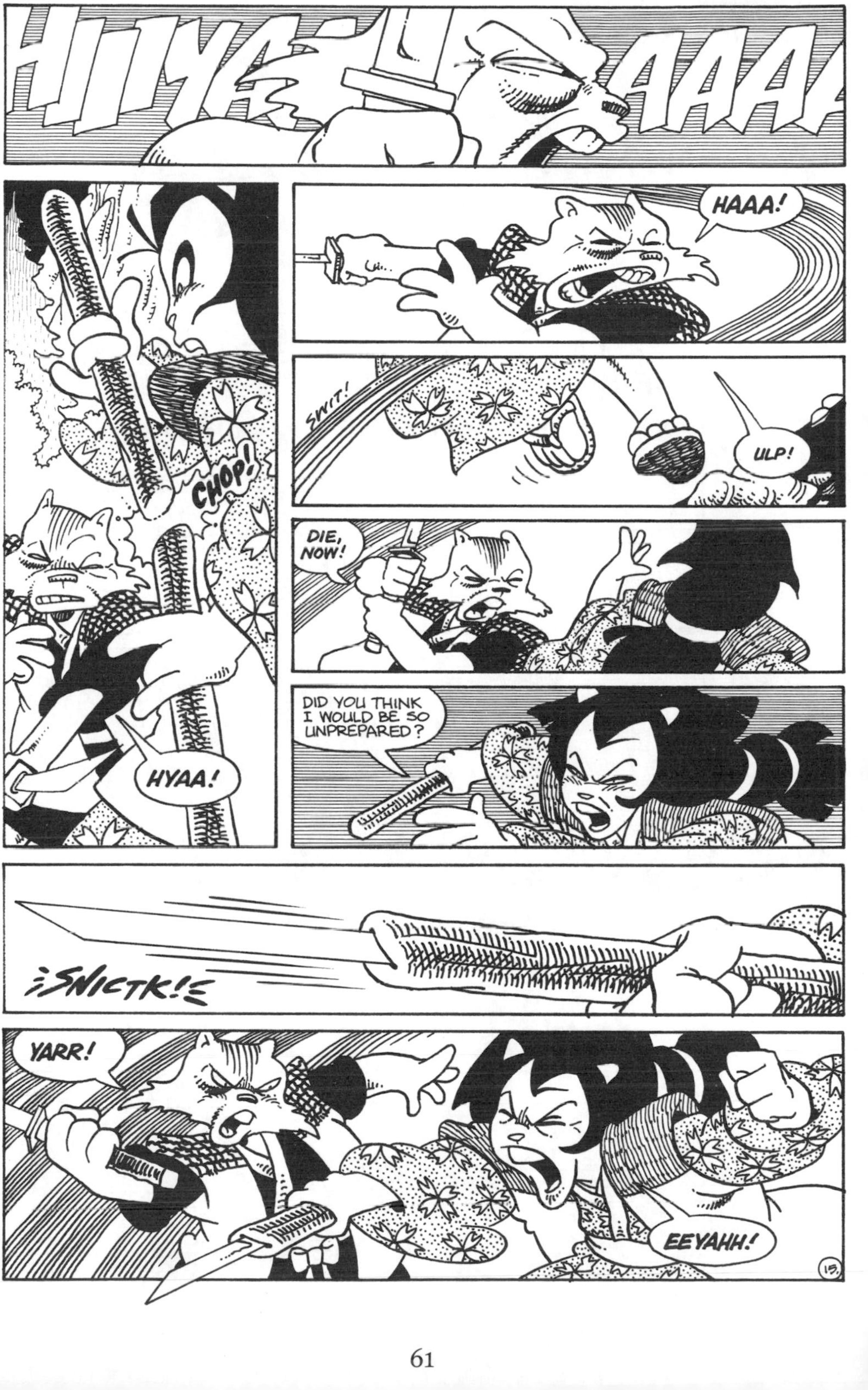
HIIYAAAAA
HAAA!
CHOP!
SWIT!
ULP!
HYAA!
DIE, NOW!
DID YOU THINK I WOULD BE SO UNPREPARED?
SNICTK!
YARR!
EEYAHH!
15

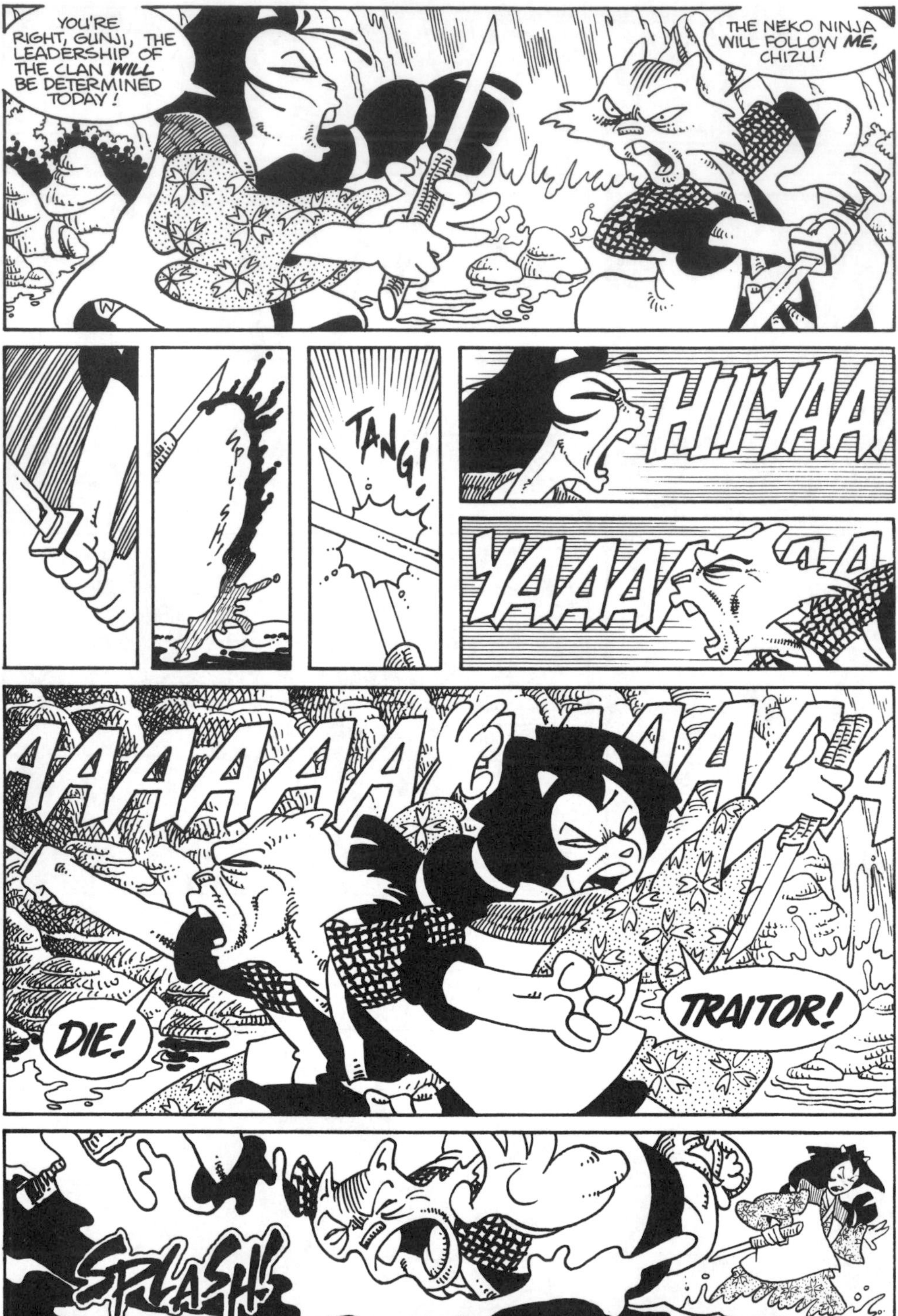

YOU'RE RIGHT, GUNJI, THE LEADERSHIP OF THE CLAN WILL BE DETERMINED TODAY!
THE NEKO NINJA WILL FOLLOW ME, CHIZU!
SPLISH!
TANG!
HIIYAA
YAAA
AAAAAA
DIE!
TRAITOR!
SPLASH!
16.

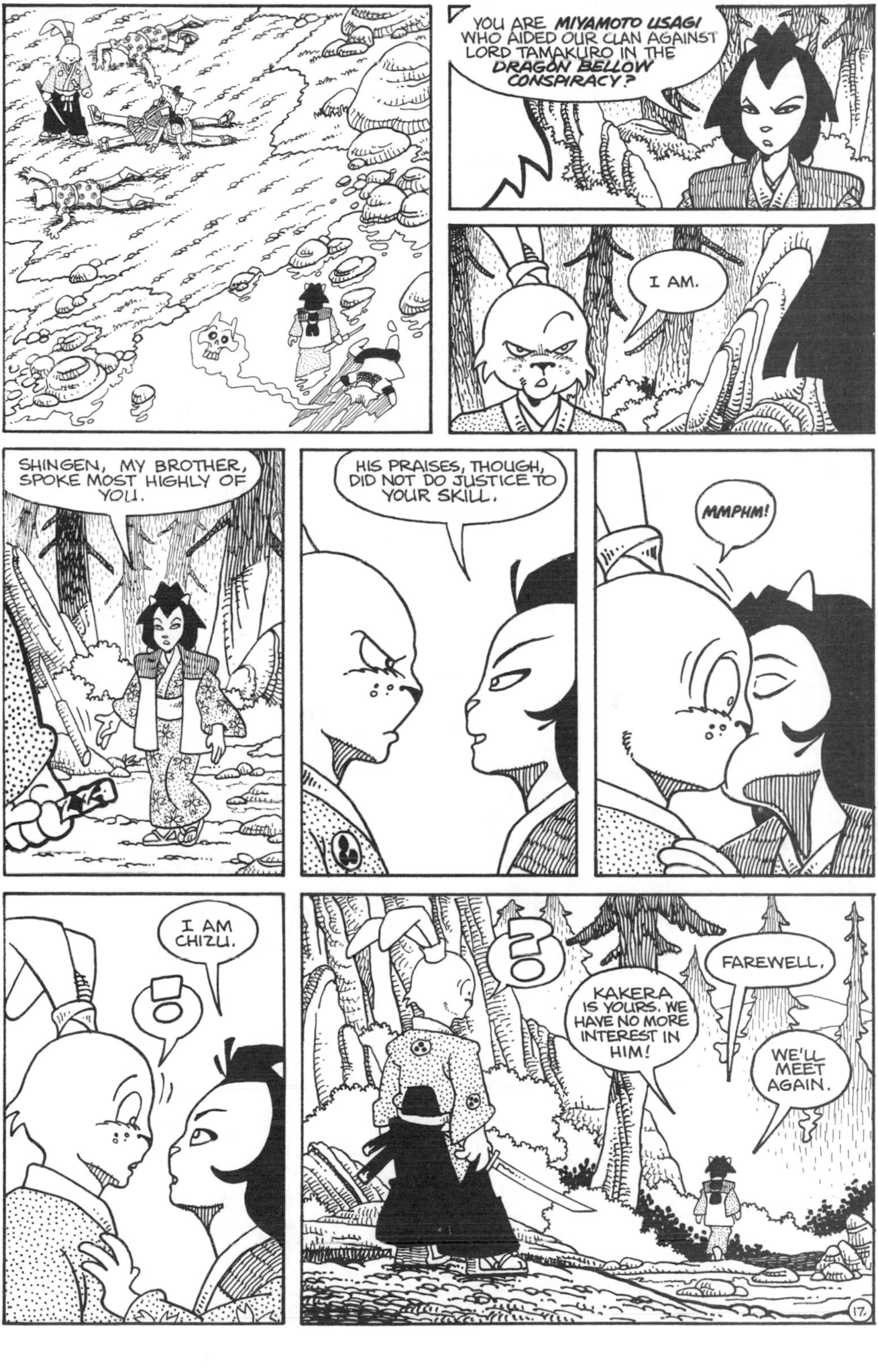
YOU ARE MIYAMOTO USAGI WHO AIDED OUR CLAN AGAINST LORD TAMAKURO IN THE DRAGON BELLOW CONSPIRACY?
I AM.
SHINGEN, MY BROTHER, SPOKE MOST HIGHLY OF YOU.
HIS PRAISES, THOUGH, DID NOT DO JUSTICE TO YOUR SKILL.
MMPHM!
I AM CHIZU.
KAKERA IS YOURS. WE HAVE NO MORE INTEREST IN HIM!
FAREWELL.
WE'LL MEET AGAIN.
17.

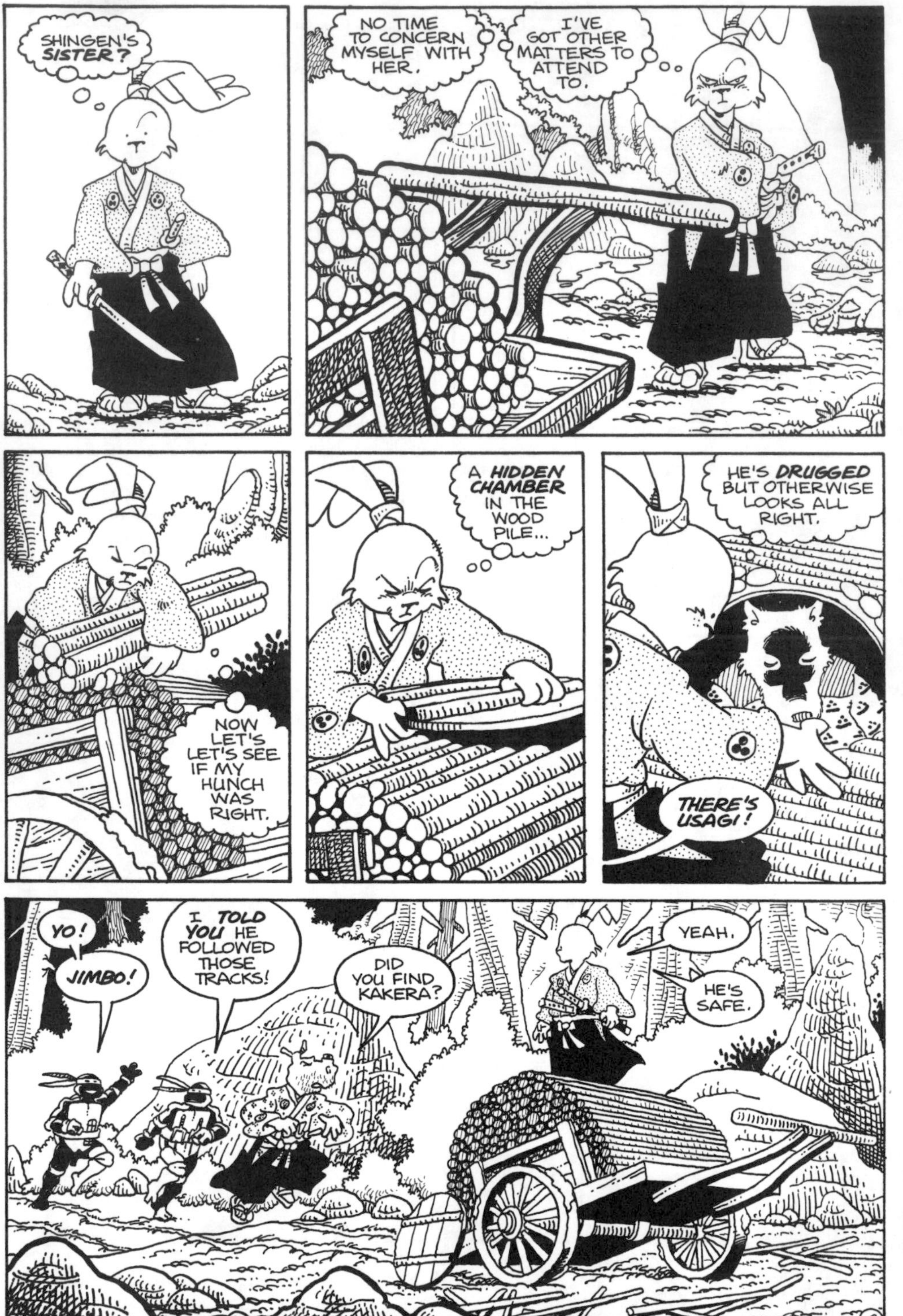
SHINGEN'S SISTER?
NO TIME TO CONCERN MYSELF WITH HER.
I'VE GOT OTHER MATTERS TO ATTEND TO.
NOW LET'S SEE IF MY HUNCH WAS RIGHT.
A HIDDEN CHAMBER IN THE WOOD PILE...
HE'S DRUGGED BUT OTHERWISE LOOKS ALL RIGHT.
THERE'S USAGI!
YO!
JIMBO!
I TOLD YOU HE FOLLOWED THOSE TRACKS!
DID YOU FIND KAKERA?
YEAH.
HE'S SAFE.
18.

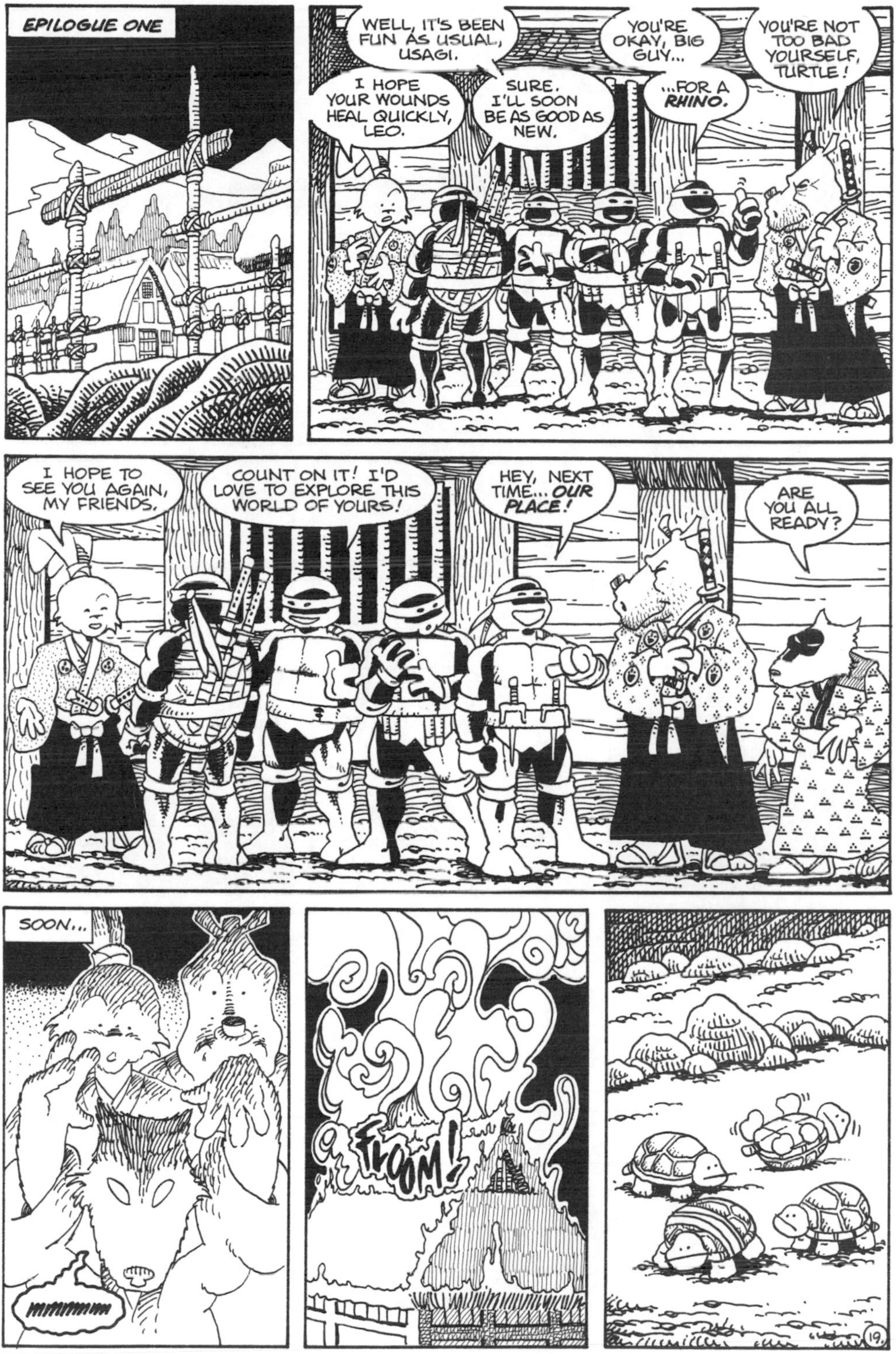
EPILOGUE ONE
WELL, IT'S BEEN FUN AS USUAL, USAGI.
I HOPE YOUR WOUNDS HEAL QUICKLY, LEO.
SURE. I'LL SOON BE AS GOOD AS NEW.
YOU'RE OKAY, BIG GUY...
...FOR A RHINO.
YOU'RE NOT TOO BAD YOURSELF, TURTLE!
I HOPE TO SEE YOU AGAIN, MY FRIENDS.
COUNT ON IT! I'D LOVE TO EXPLORE THIS WORLD OF YOURS!
HEY, NEXT TIME... OUR PLACE!
ARE YOU ALL READY?
SOON...
MMMMMM
FROOM!
19

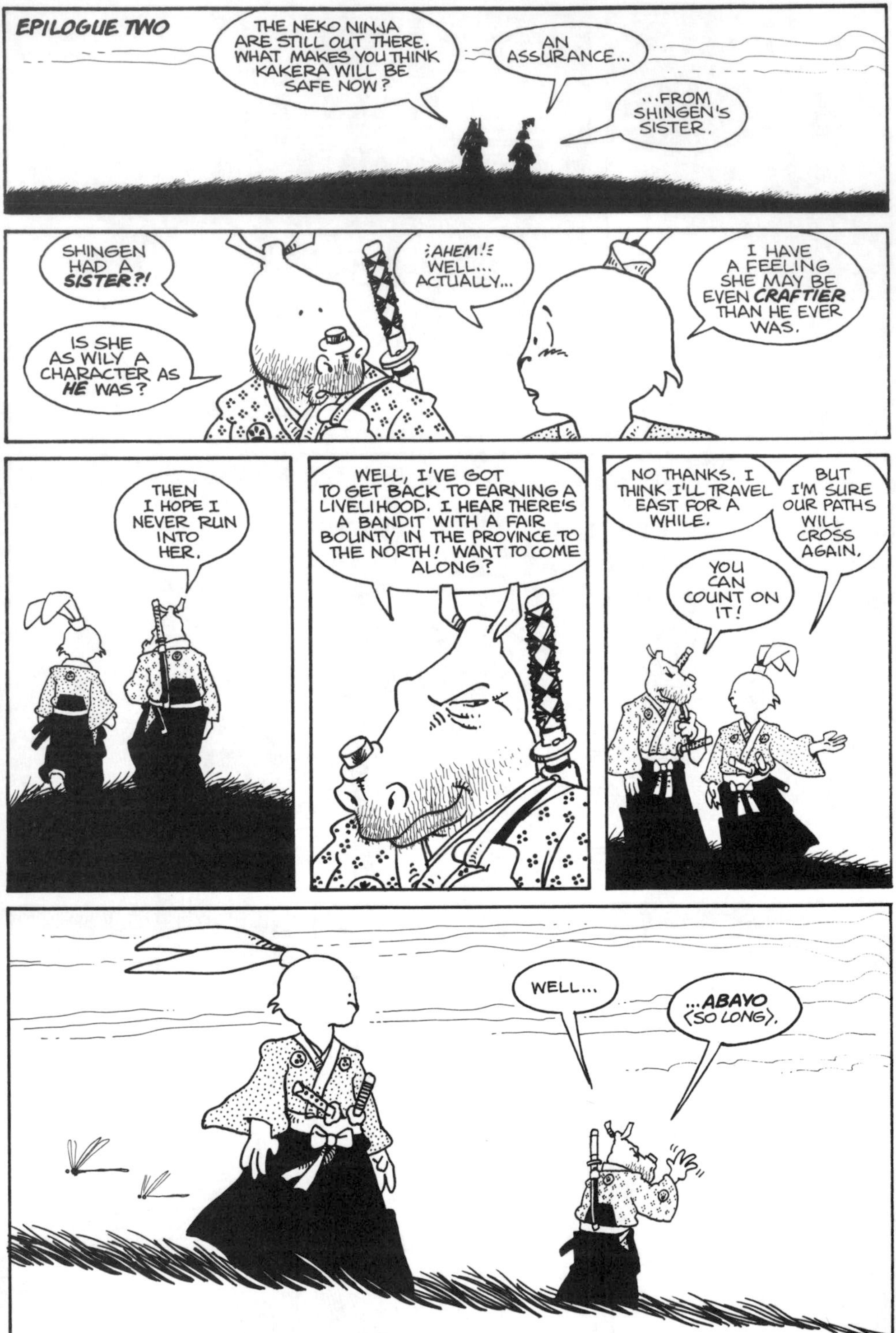
EPILOGUE TWO
THE NEKO NINJA ARE STILL OUT THERE. WHAT MAKES YOU THINK KAKERA WILL BE SAFE NOW?
AN ASSURANCE...
...FROM SHINGEN'S SISTER.
SHINGEN HAD A SISTER?!
IS SHE AS WILY A CHARACTER AS HE WAS?
AHEM! WELL... ACTUALLY...
I HAVE A FEELING SHE MAY BE EVEN CRAFTIER THAN HE EVER WAS.
THEN I HOPE I NEVER RUN INTO HER.
WELL, I'VE GOT TO GET BACK TO EARNING A LIVELIHOOD. I HEAR THERE'S A BANDIT WITH A FAIR BOUNTY IN THE PROVINCE TO THE NORTH! WANT TO COME ALONG?
NO THANKS. I THINK I'LL TRAVEL EAST FOR A WHILE.
BUT I'M SURE OUR PATHS WILL CROSS AGAIN.
YOU CAN COUNT ON IT!
WELL...
...ABAYO 〈SO LONG〉.

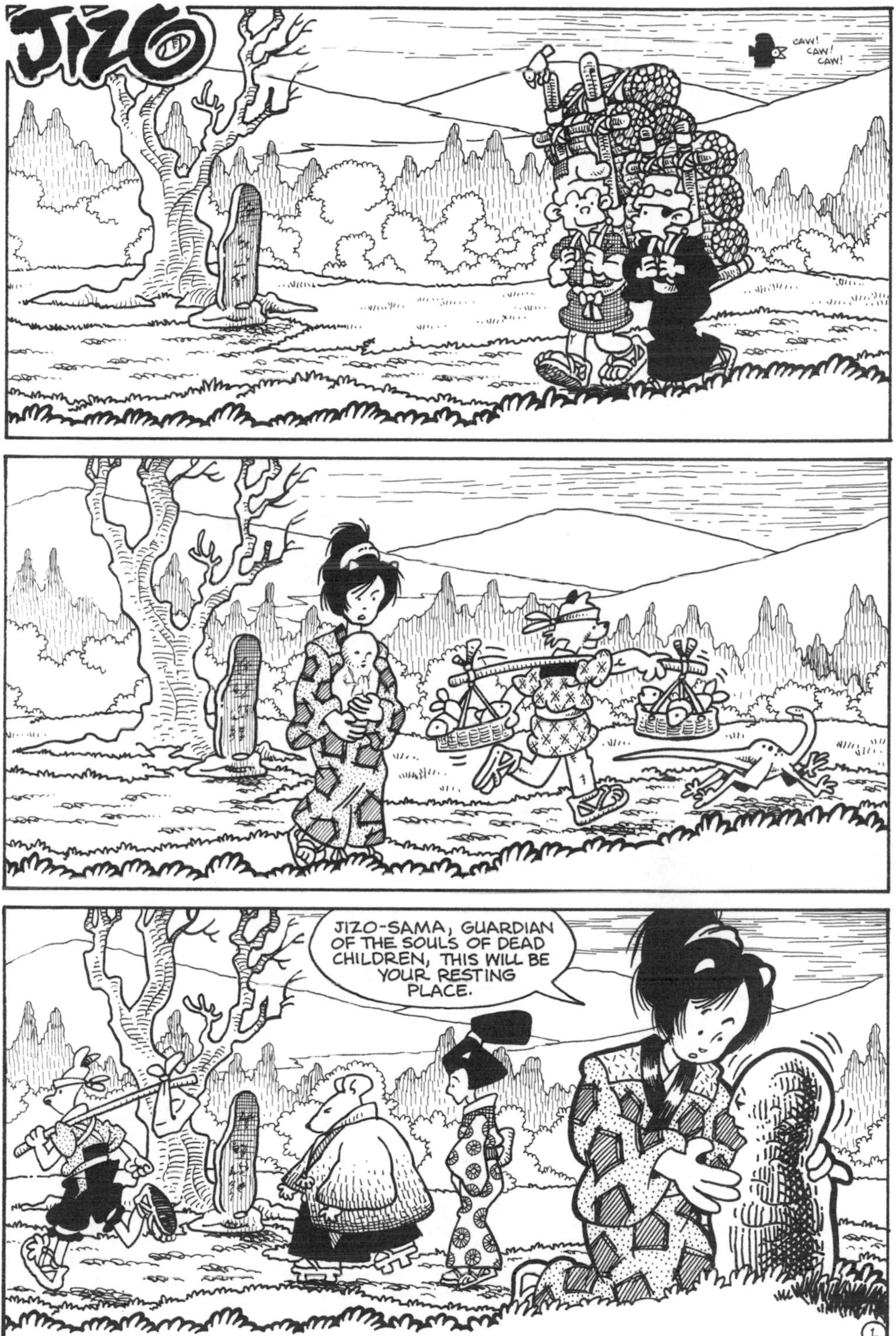
JIZO
CAW! CAW! CAW!
JIZO-SAMA, GUARDIAN OF THE SOULS OF DEAD CHILDREN, THIS WILL BE YOUR RESTING PLACE.
1

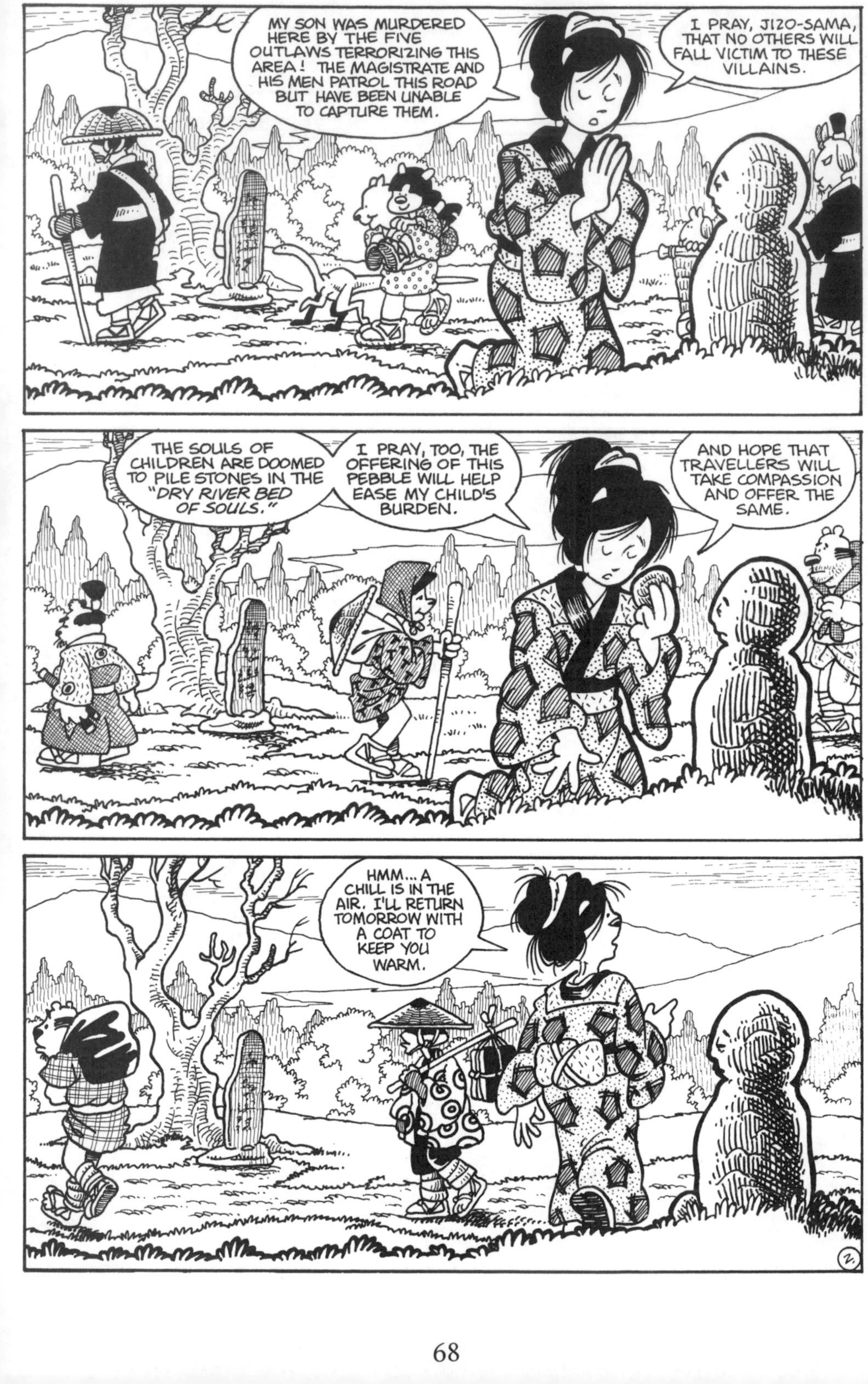
MY SON WAS MURDERED HERE BY THE FIVE OUTLAWS TERRORIZING THIS AREA! THE MAGISTRATE AND HIS MEN PATROL THIS ROAD BUT HAVE BEEN UNABLE TO CAPTURE THEM.
I PRAY, JIZO-SAMA, THAT NO OTHERS WILL FALL VICTIM TO THESE VILLAINS.
THE SOULS OF CHILDREN ARE DOOMED TO PILE STONES IN THE "DRY RIVER BED OF SOULS."
I PRAY, TOO, THE OFFERING OF THIS PEBBLE WILL HELP EASE MY CHILD'S BURDEN.
AND HOPE THAT TRAVELLERS WILL TAKE COMPASSION AND OFFER THE SAME.
HMM... A CHILL IS IN THE AIR. I'LL RETURN TOMORROW WITH A COAT TO KEEP YOU WARM.
2.

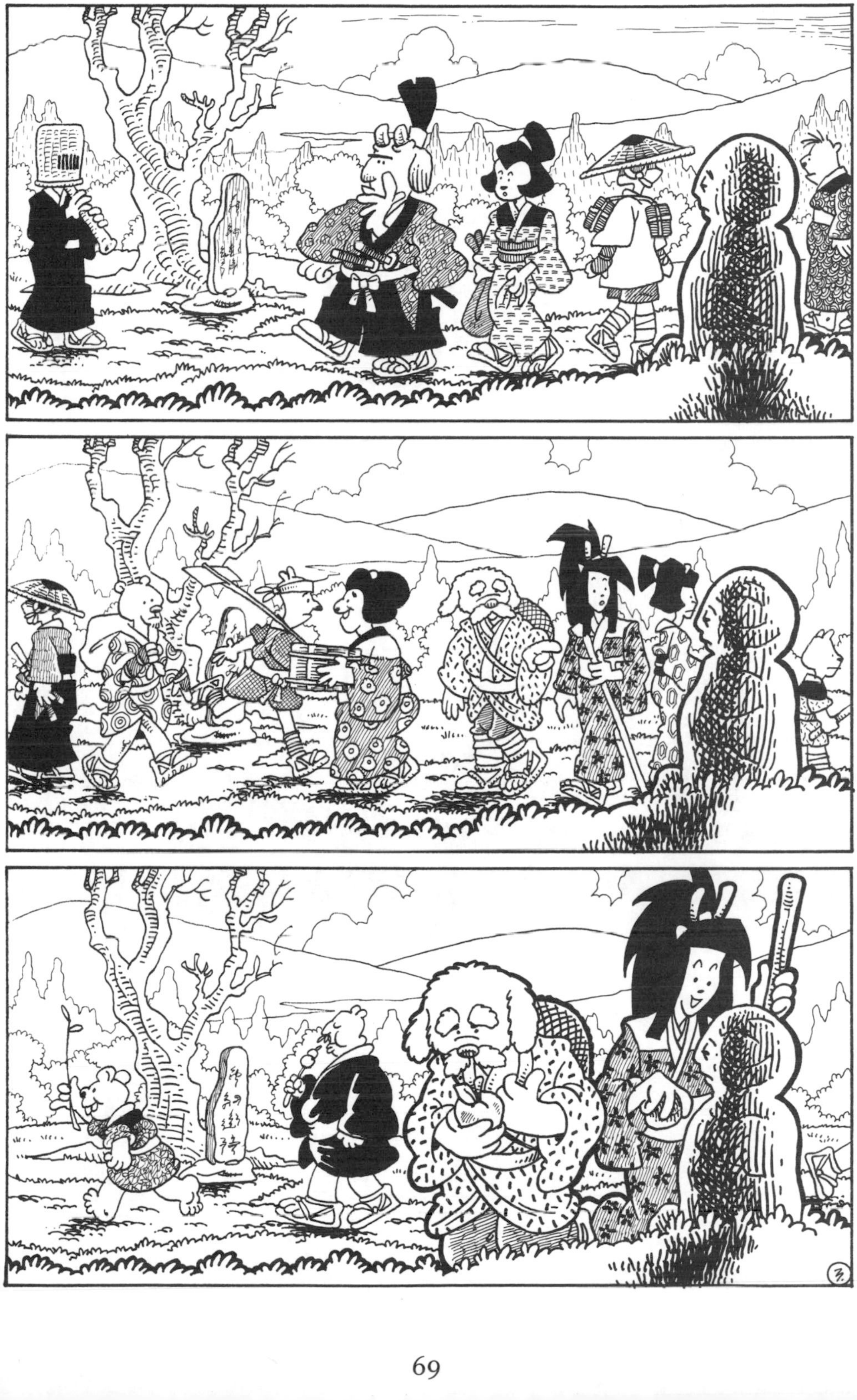

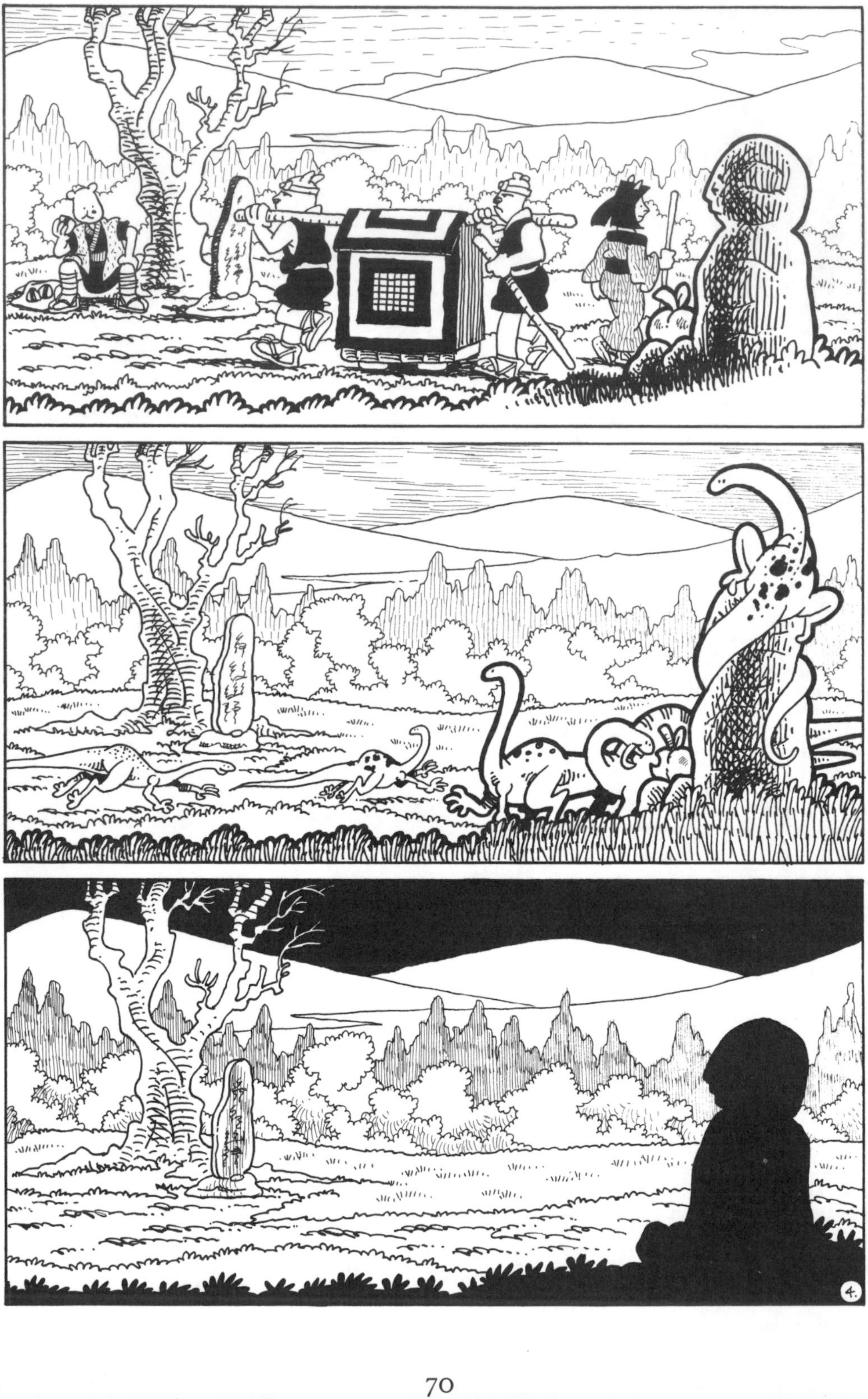
4.

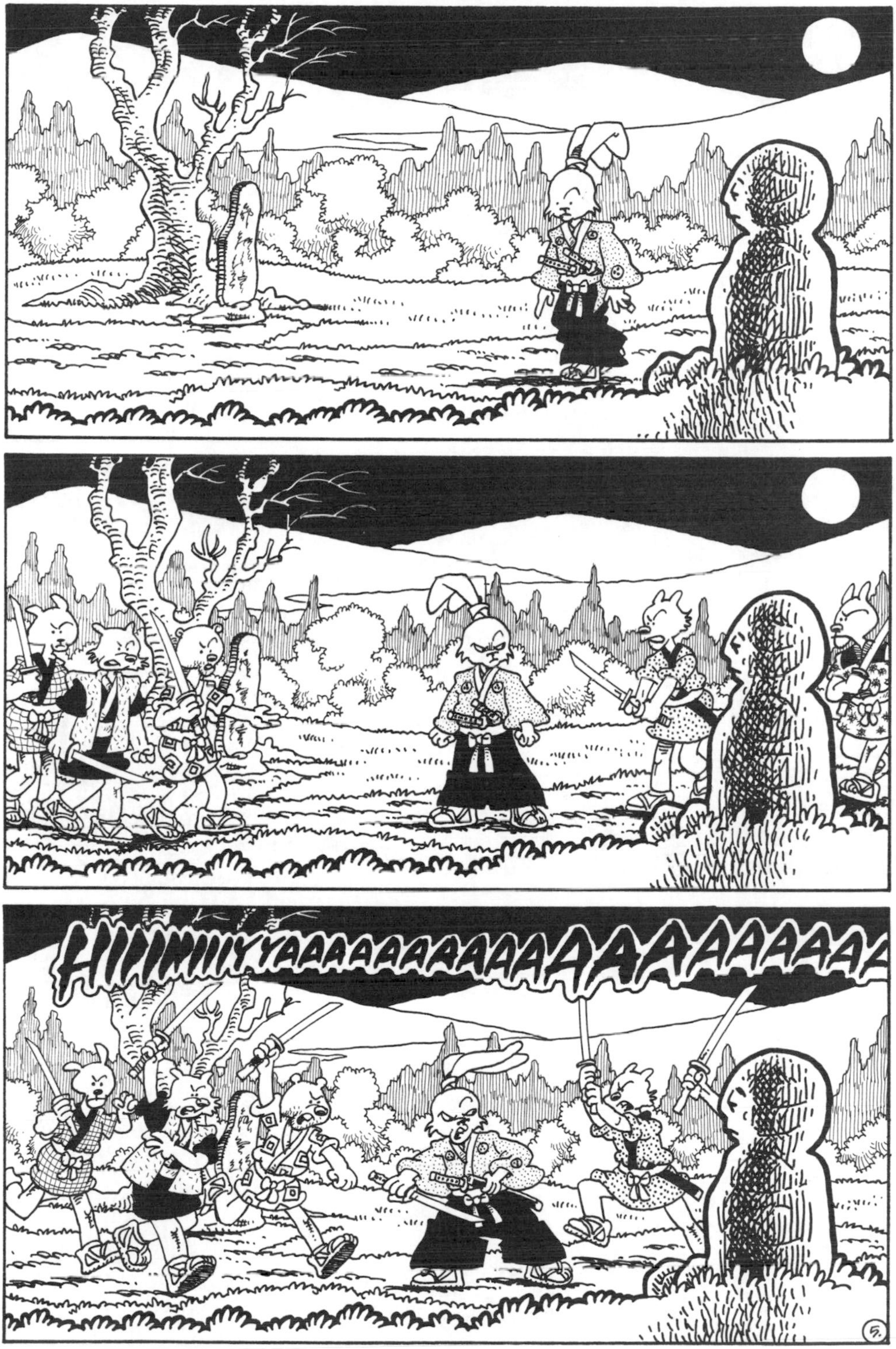
HIIIIIIIYAAAAAAAAAAAAAAAAAAAAA

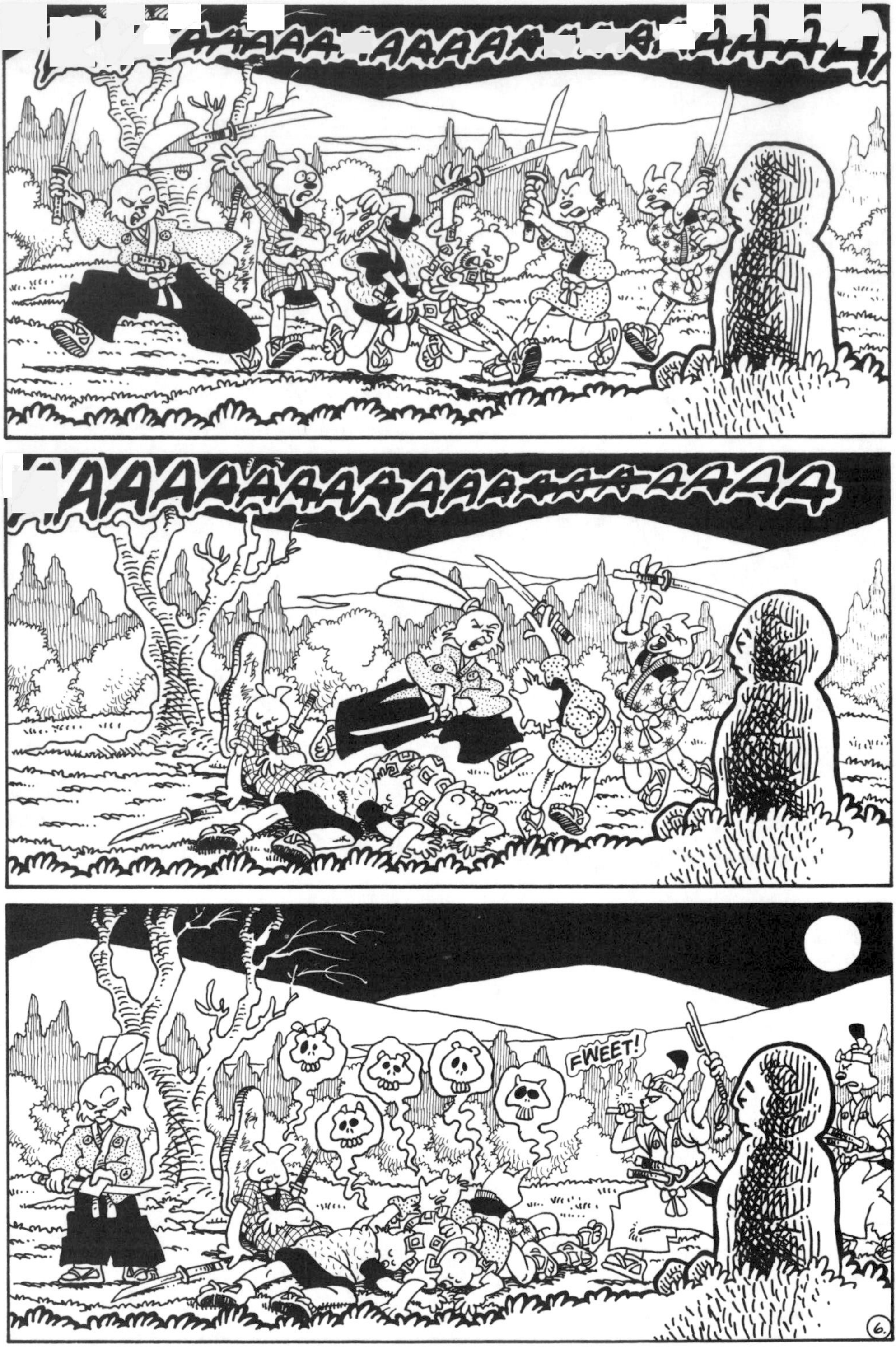
FWEET!
6.

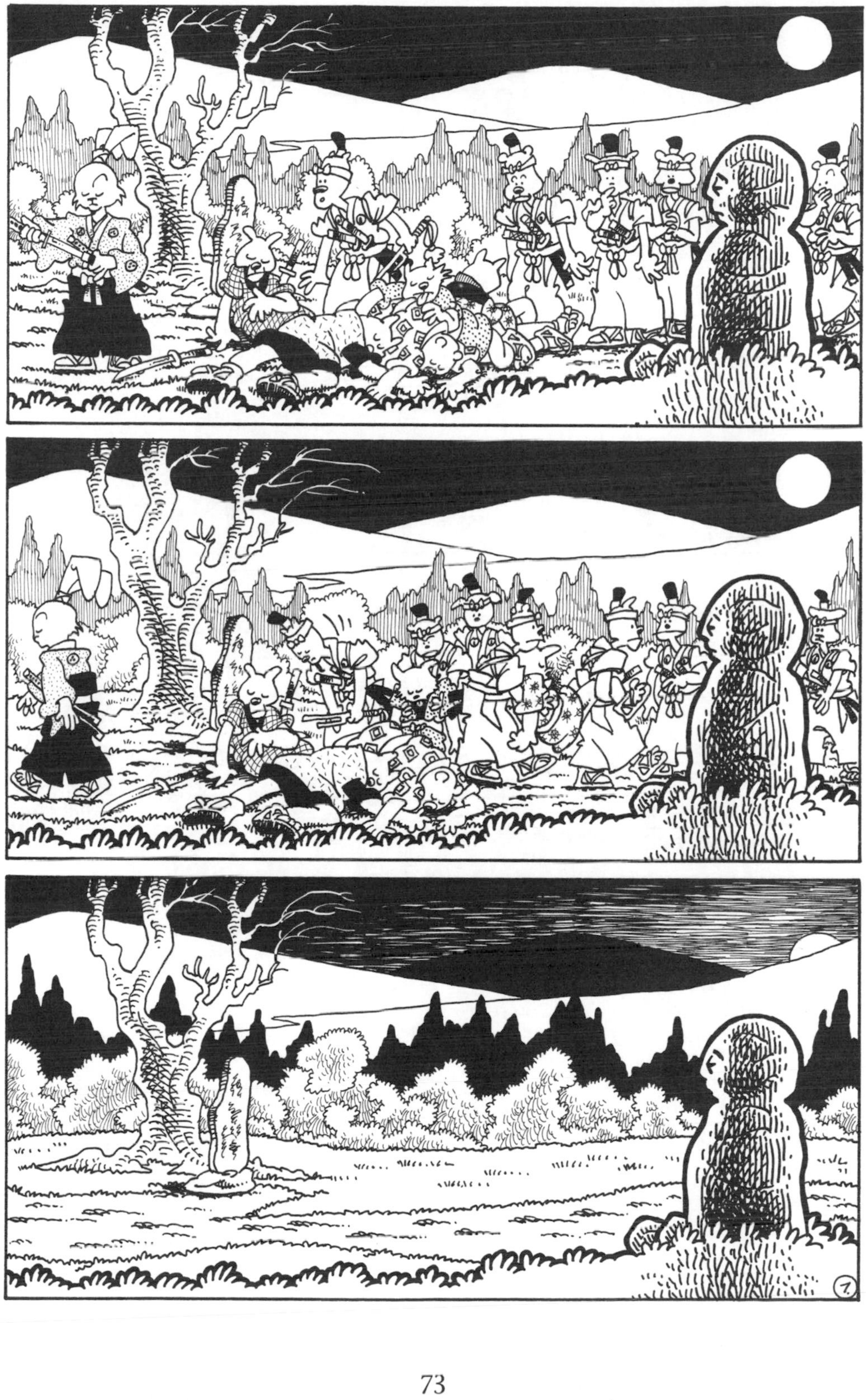

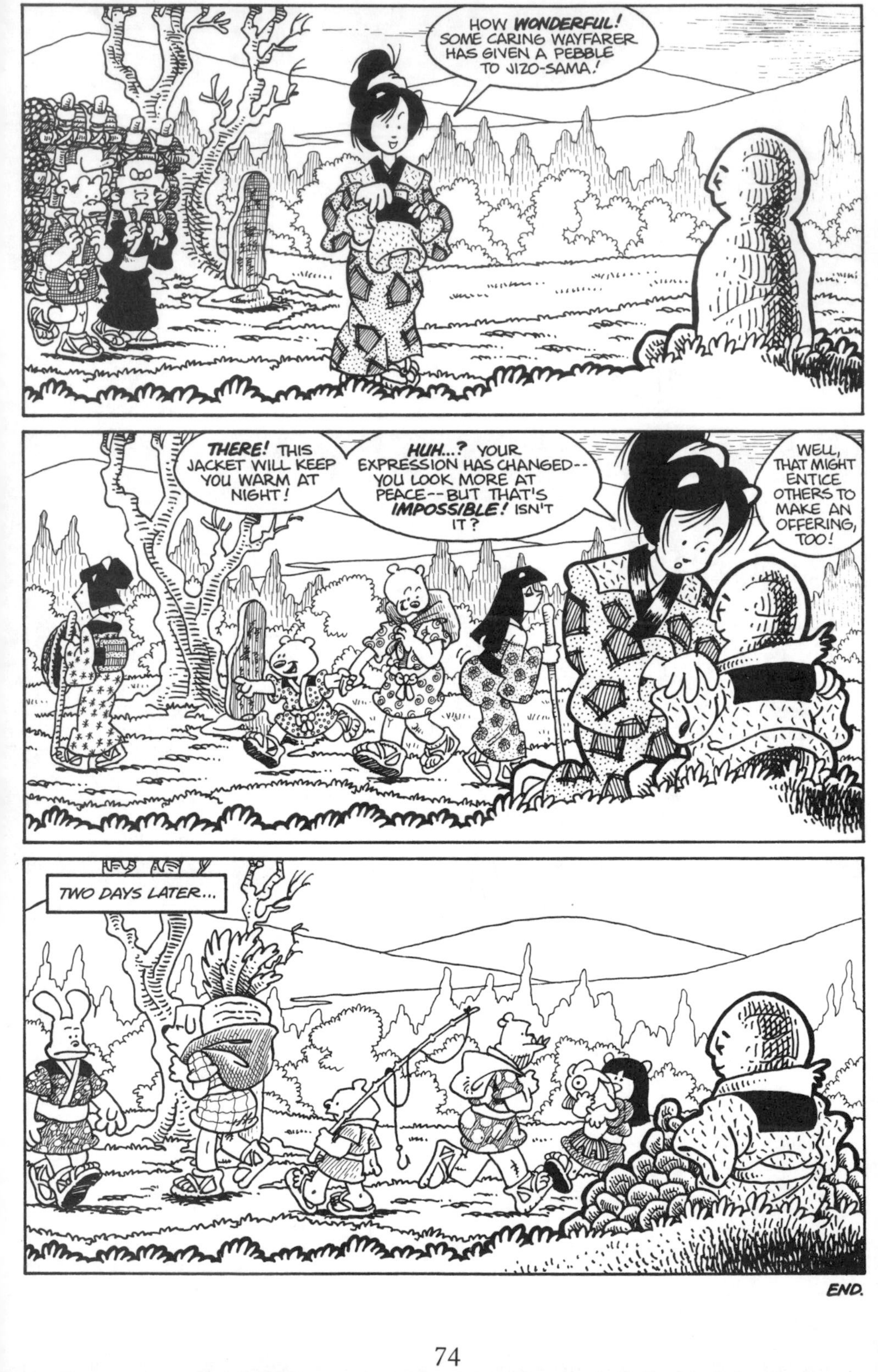
HOW WONDERFUL! SOME CARING WAYFARER HAS GIVEN A PEBBLE TO JIZO-SAMA!
THERE! THIS JACKET WILL KEEP YOU WARM AT NIGHT!
HUH...? YOUR EXPRESSION HAS CHANGED-- YOU LOOK MORE AT PEACE--BUT THAT'S IMPOSSIBLE! ISN'T IT?
WELL, THAT MIGHT ENTICE OTHERS TO MAKE AN OFFERING, TOO!
TWO DAYS LATER...
END.

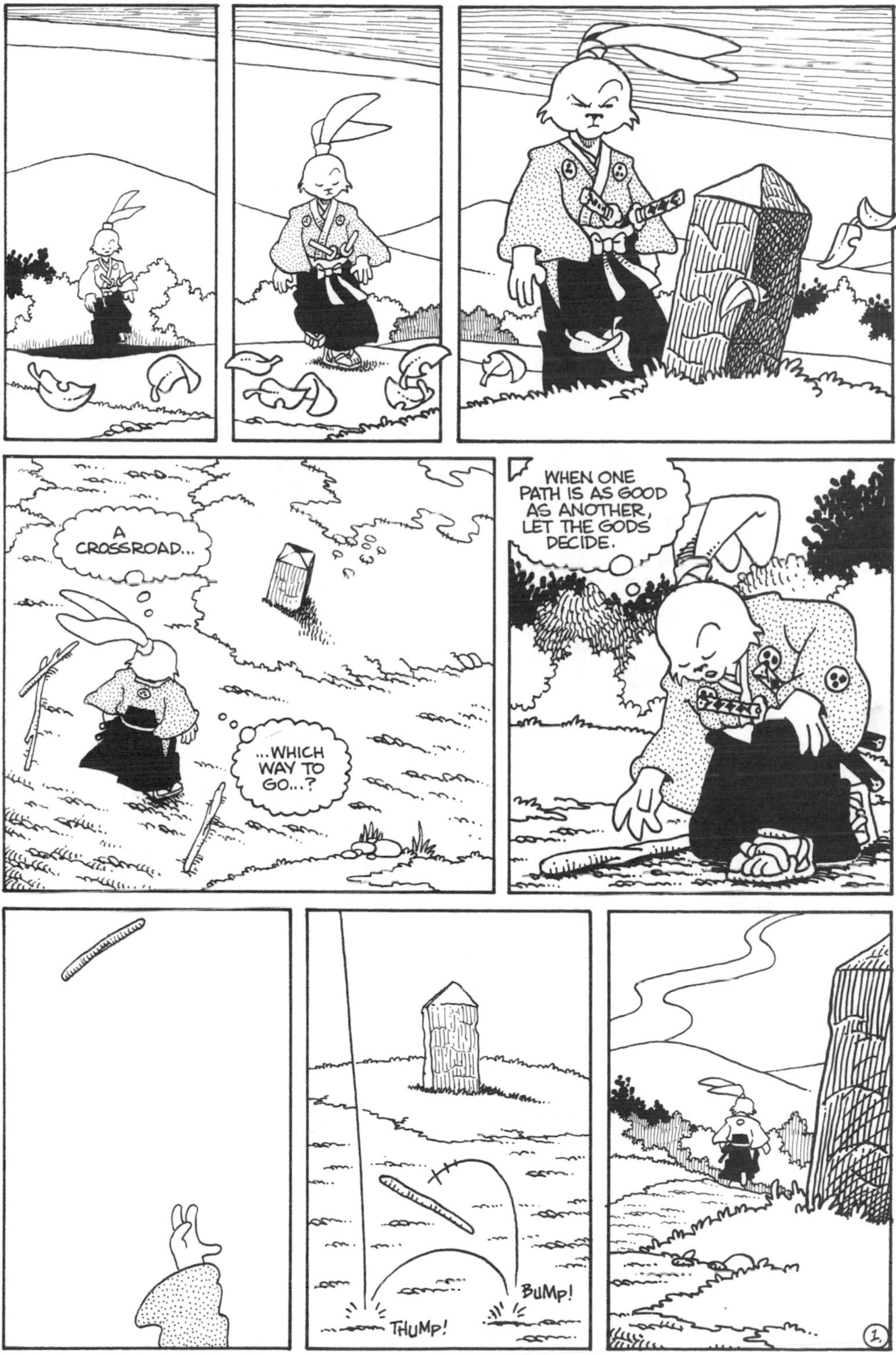
A CROSSROAD...
...WHICH WAY TO GO...?
WHEN ONE PATH IS AS GOOD AS ANOTHER, LET THE GODS DECIDE.
THUMP!
BUMP!
1

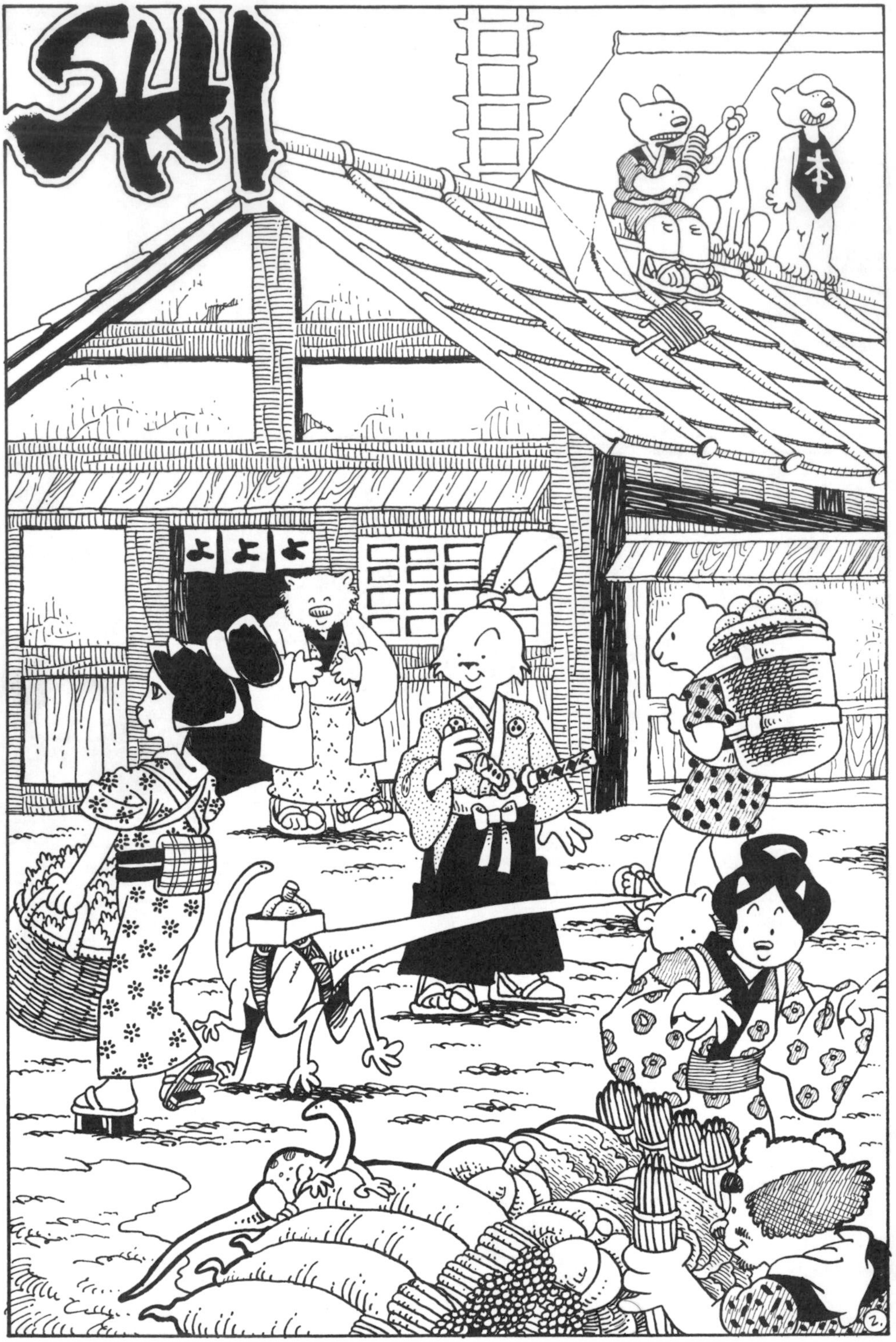
よよよ

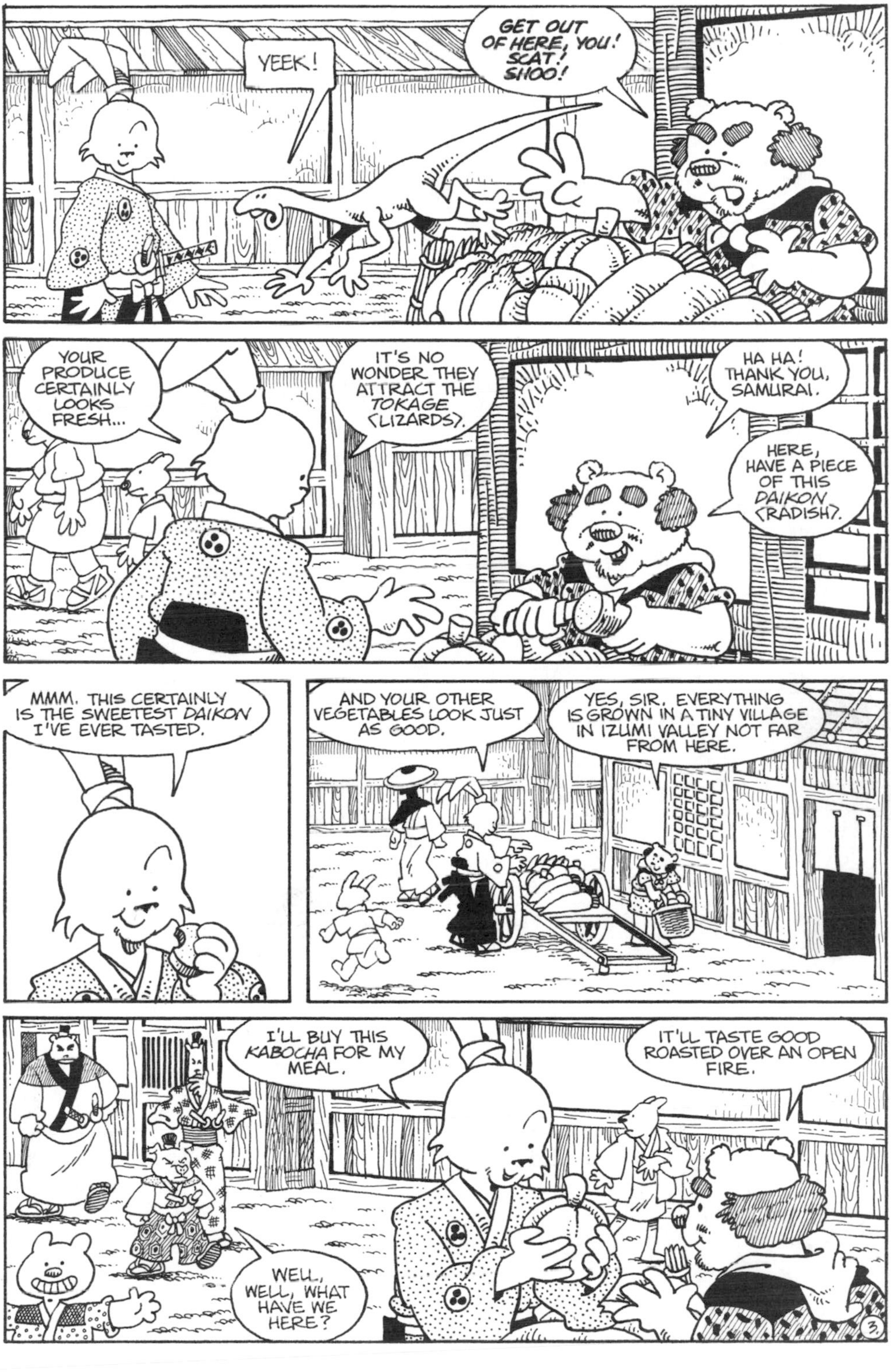
YEEK!
GET OUT OF HERE, YOU! SCAT! SHOO!
YOUR PRODUCE CERTAINLY LOOKS FRESH...
IT'S NO WONDER THEY ATTRACT THE TOKAGE (LIZARDS).
HA HA! THANK YOU, SAMURAI.
HERE, HAVE A PIECE OF THIS DAIKON (RADISH).
MMM. THIS CERTAINLY IS THE SWEETEST DAIKON I'VE EVER TASTED.
AND YOUR OTHER VEGETABLES LOOK JUST AS GOOD.
YES, SIR. EVERYTHING IS GROWN IN A TINY VILLAGE IN IZUMI VALLEY NOT FAR FROM HERE.
I'LL BUY THIS KABOCHA FOR MY MEAL.
IT'LL TASTE GOOD ROASTED OVER AN OPEN FIRE.
WELL, WELL, WHAT HAVE WE HERE?
3.

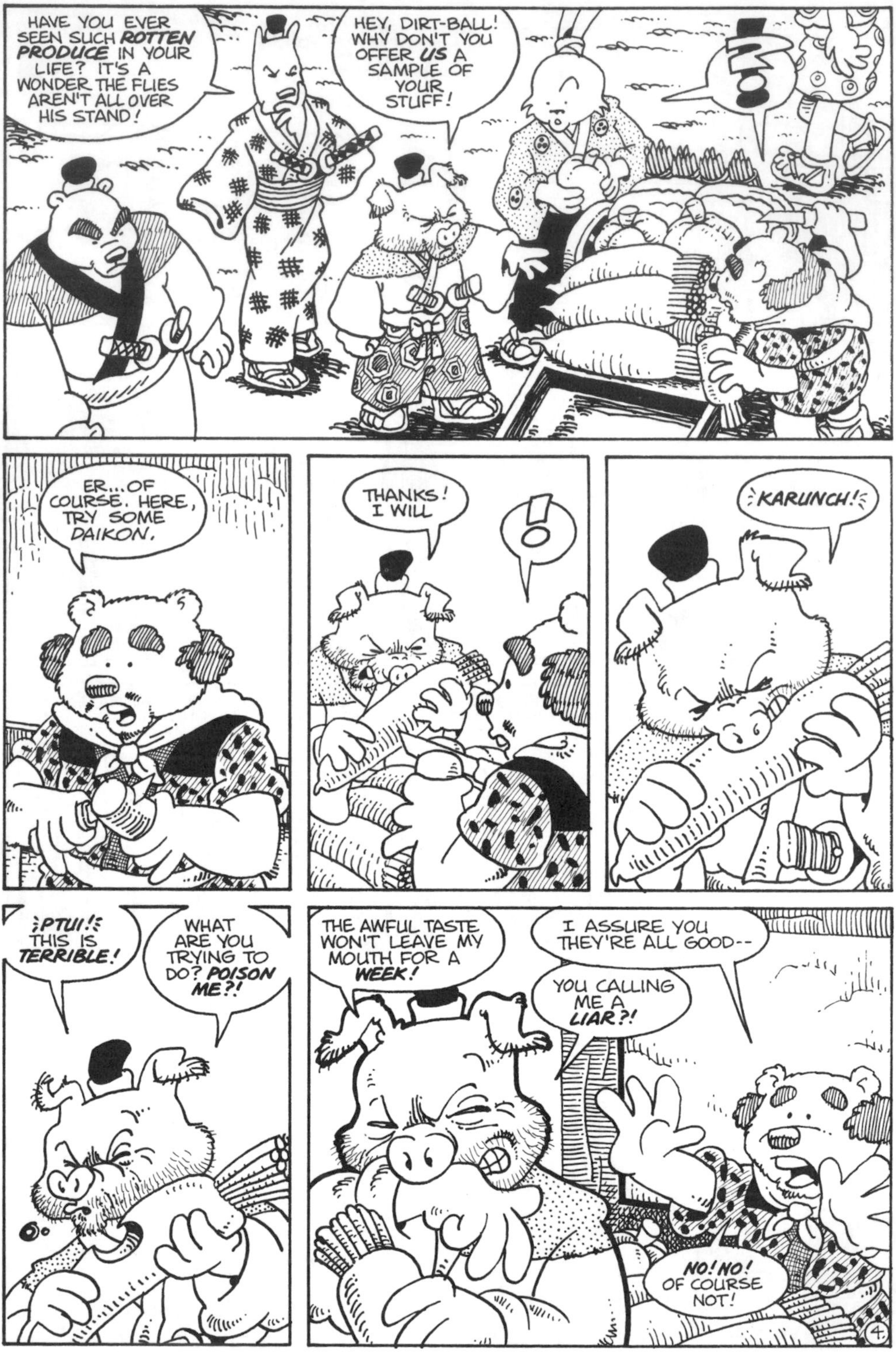

HAVE YOU EVER SEEN SUCH ROTTEN PRODUCE IN YOUR LIFE? IT'S A WONDER THE FLIES AREN'T ALL OVER HIS STAND!
HEY, DIRT-BALL! WHY DON'T YOU OFFER US A SAMPLE OF YOUR STUFF!
?
ER...OF COURSE. HERE, TRY SOME DAIKON.
THANKS! I WILL
!
KARUNCH!
PTUI! THIS IS TERRIBLE!
WHAT ARE YOU TRYING TO DO? POISON ME?!
THE AWFUL TASTE WON'T LEAVE MY MOUTH FOR A WEEK!
I ASSURE YOU THEY'RE ALL GOOD--
YOU CALLING ME A LIAR?!
NO! NO! OF COURSE NOT!
4

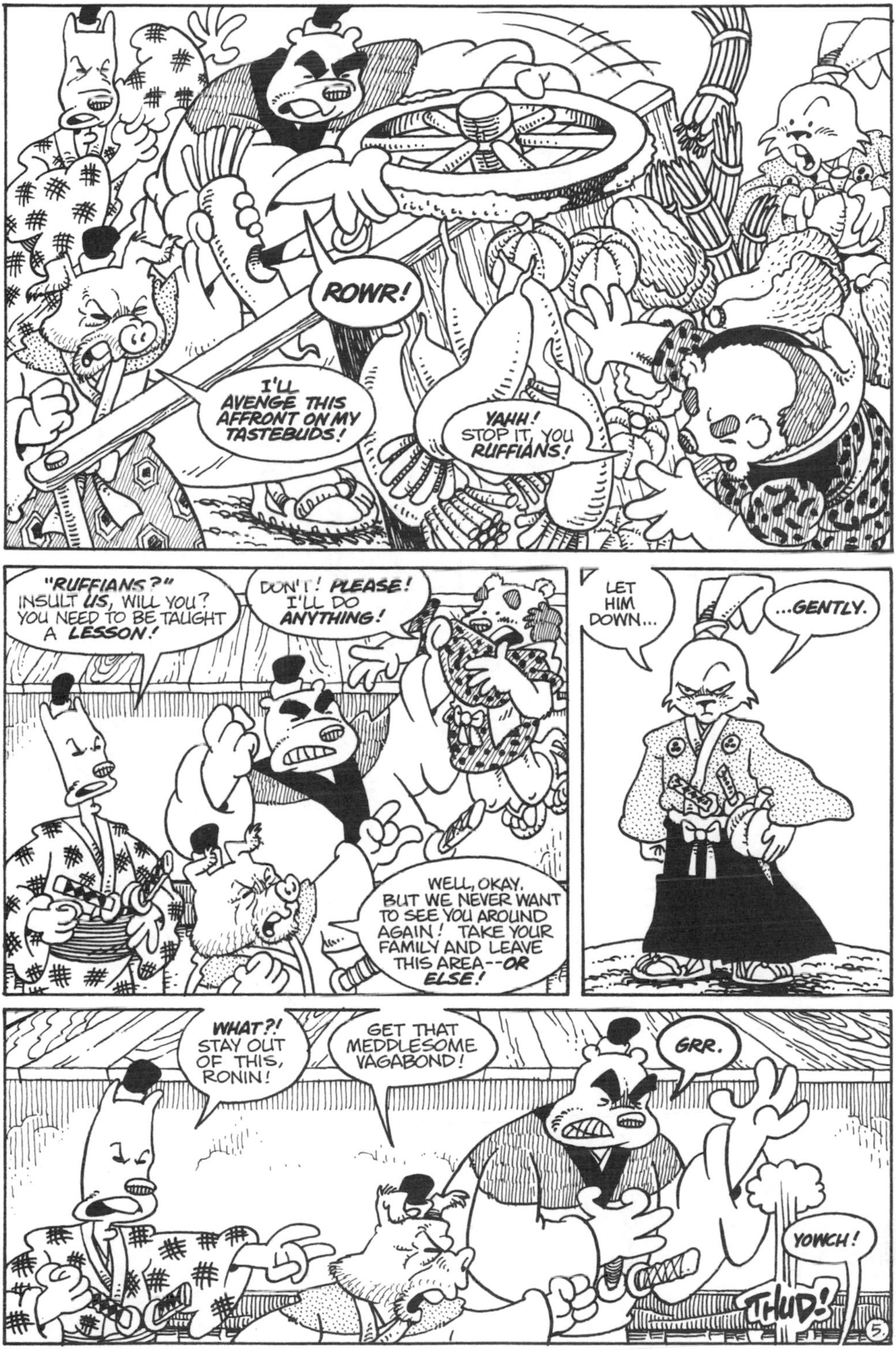
ROWR!
I'LL AVENGE THIS AFFRONT ON MY TASTEBUDS!
YAHH! STOP IT, YOU RUFFIANS!
"RUFFIANS?" INSULT US, WILL YOU? YOU NEED TO BE TAUGHT A LESSON!
DON'T! PLEASE! I'LL DO ANYTHING!
WELL, OKAY. BUT WE NEVER WANT TO SEE YOU AROUND AGAIN! TAKE YOUR FAMILY AND LEAVE THIS AREA--OR ELSE!
LET HIM DOWN...
...GENTLY.
WHAT?! STAY OUT OF THIS, RONIN!
GET THAT MEDDLESOME VAGABOND!
GRR.
YOWCH!
THUD!
5

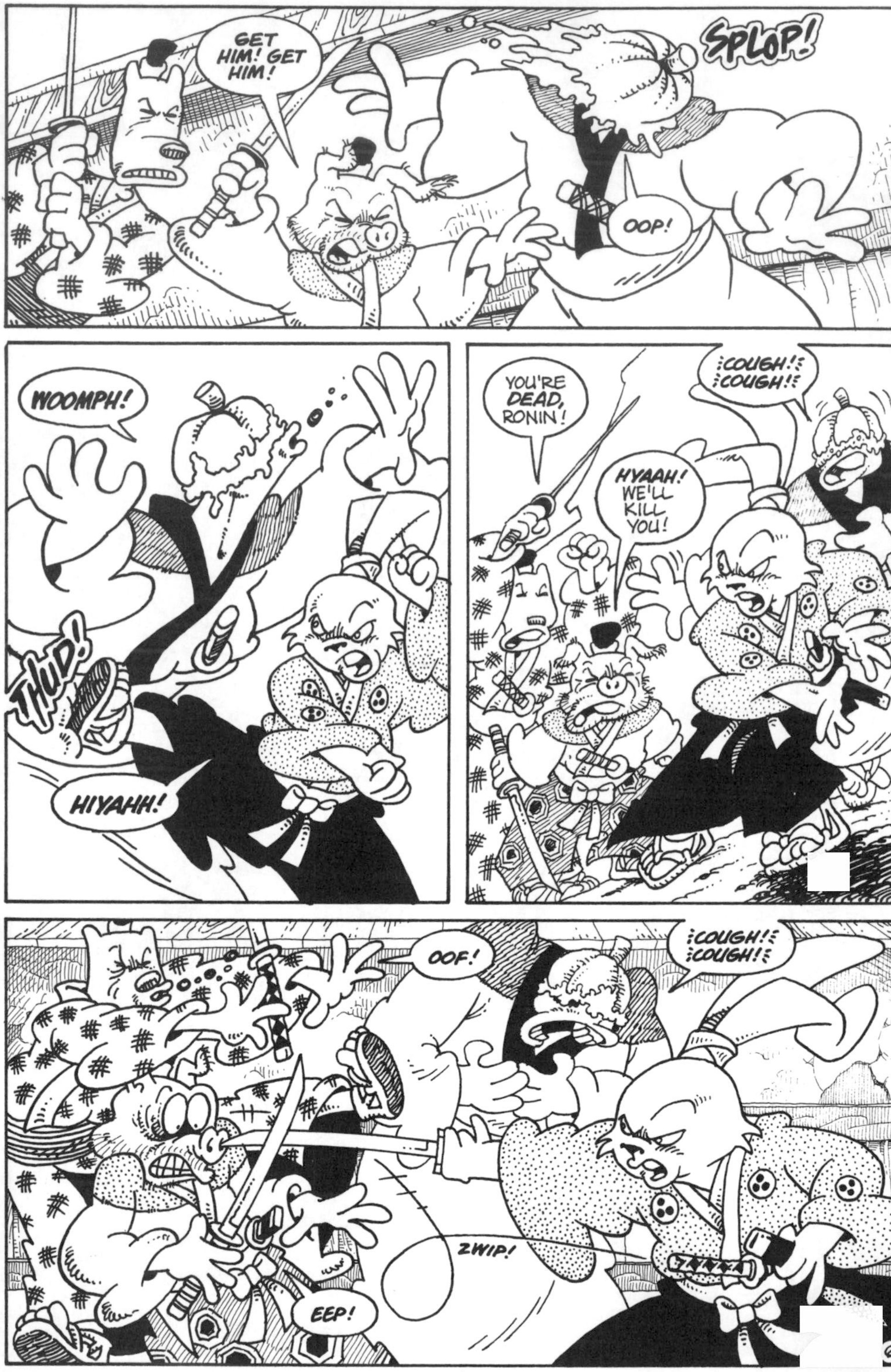
GET HIM! GET HIM!
SPLOP!
OOP!
WOOMPH!
THUD!
HIYAHH!
YOU'RE DEAD, RONIN!
COUGH! COUGH!
HYAAH! WE'LL KILL YOU!
OOF!
COUGH! COUGH!
ZWIP!
EEP!

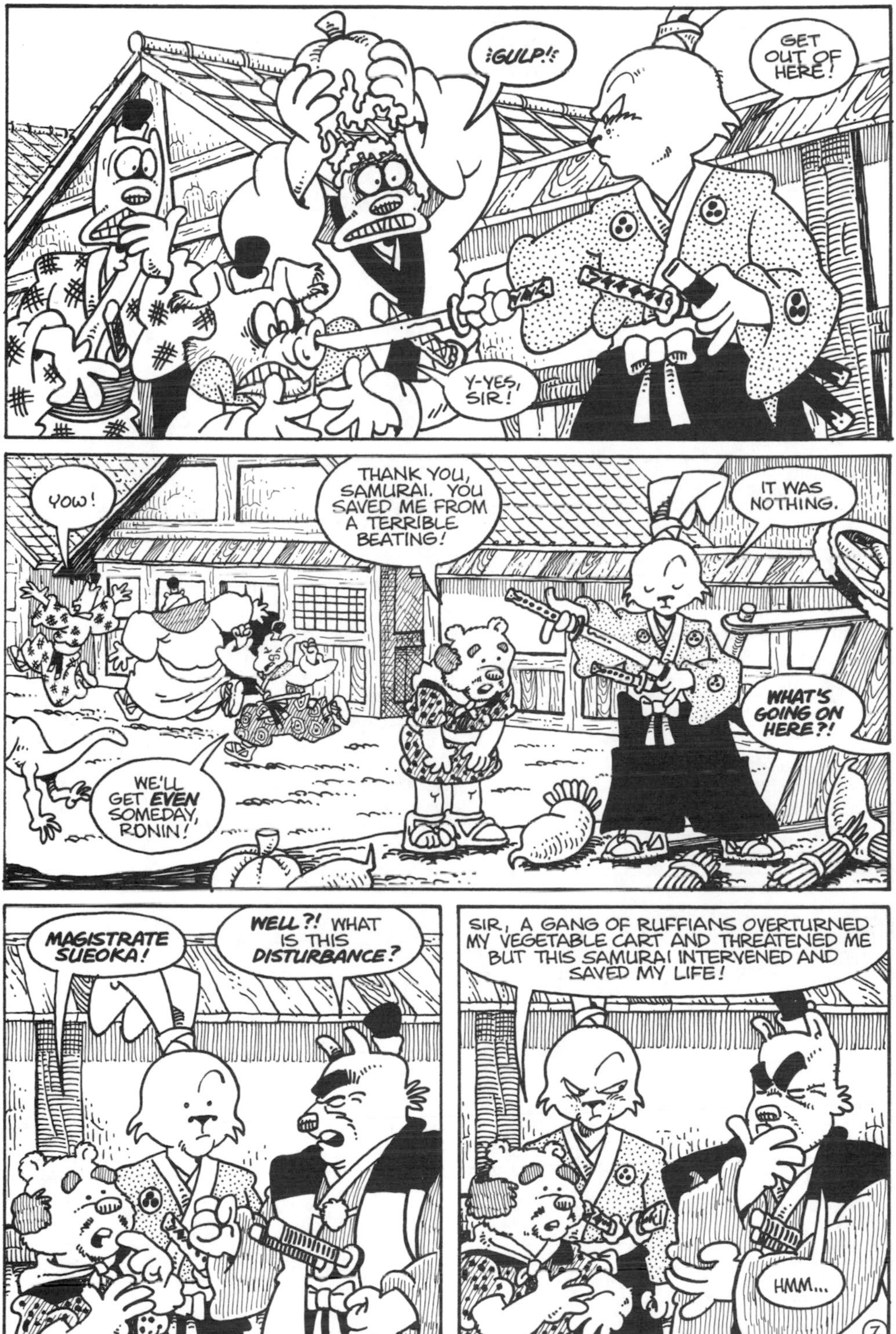
¡GULP!¡
GET OUT OF HERE!
Y-YES, SIR!
YOW!
THANK YOU, SAMURAI. YOU SAVED ME FROM A TERRIBLE BEATING!
IT WAS NOTHING.
WHAT'S GOING ON HERE?!
WE'LL GET EVEN SOMEDAY, RONIN!
MAGISTRATE SUEOKA!
WELL?! WHAT IS THIS DISTURBANCE?
SIR, A GANG OF RUFFIANS OVERTURNED MY VEGETABLE CART AND THREATENED ME BUT THIS SAMURAI INTERVENED AND SAVED MY LIFE!
HMM...
7.

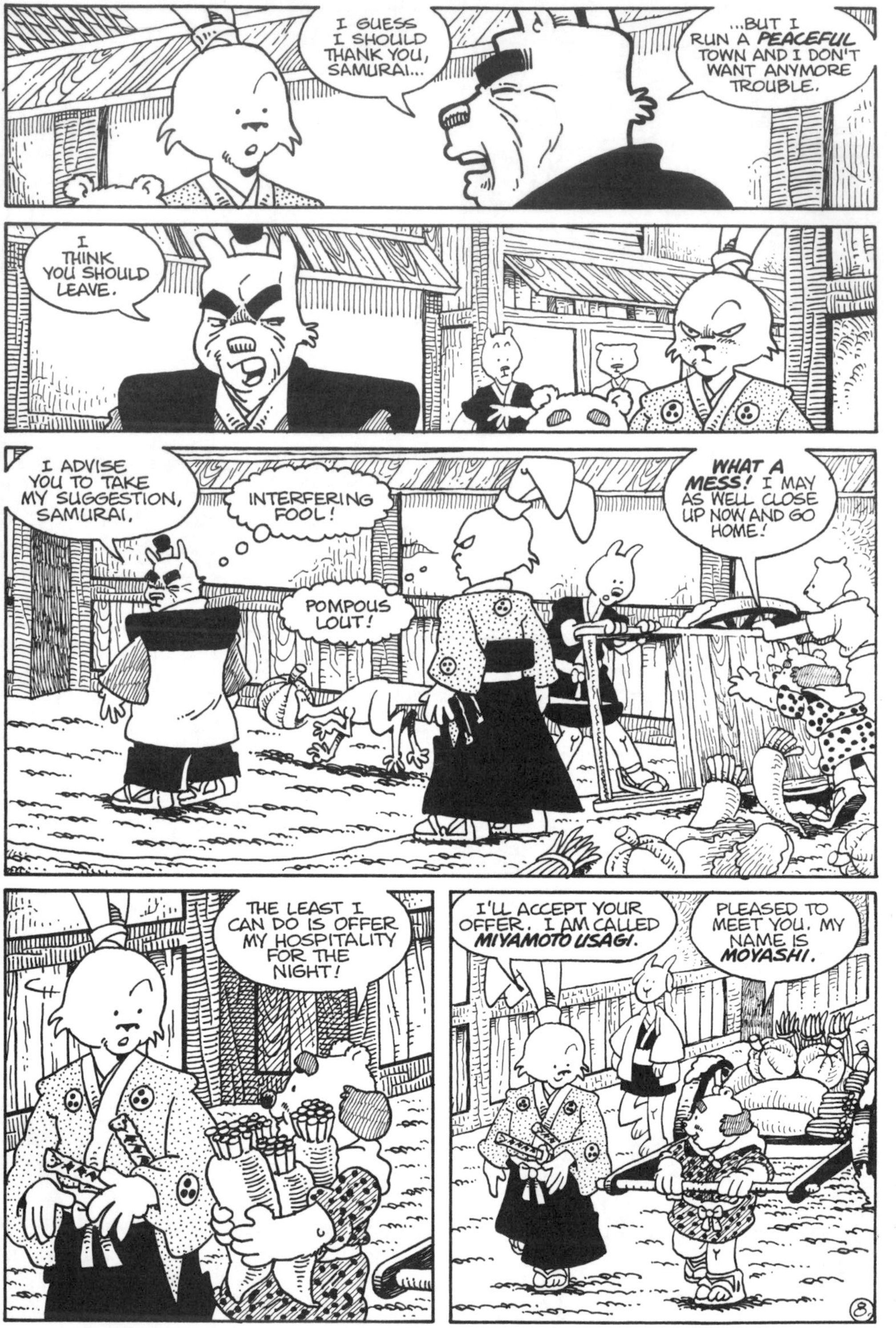
I GUESS I SHOULD THANK YOU, SAMURAI...
...BUT I RUN A PEACEFUL TOWN AND I DON'T WANT ANYMORE TROUBLE.
I THINK YOU SHOULD LEAVE.
I ADVISE YOU TO TAKE MY SUGGESTION, SAMURAI.
INTERFERING FOOL!
POMPOUS LOUT!
WHAT A MESS! I MAY AS WELL CLOSE UP NOW AND GO HOME!
THE LEAST I CAN DO IS OFFER MY HOSPITALITY FOR THE NIGHT!
I'LL ACCEPT YOUR OFFER. I AM CALLED MIYAMOTO USAGI.
PLEASED TO MEET YOU. MY NAME IS MOYASHI.
8

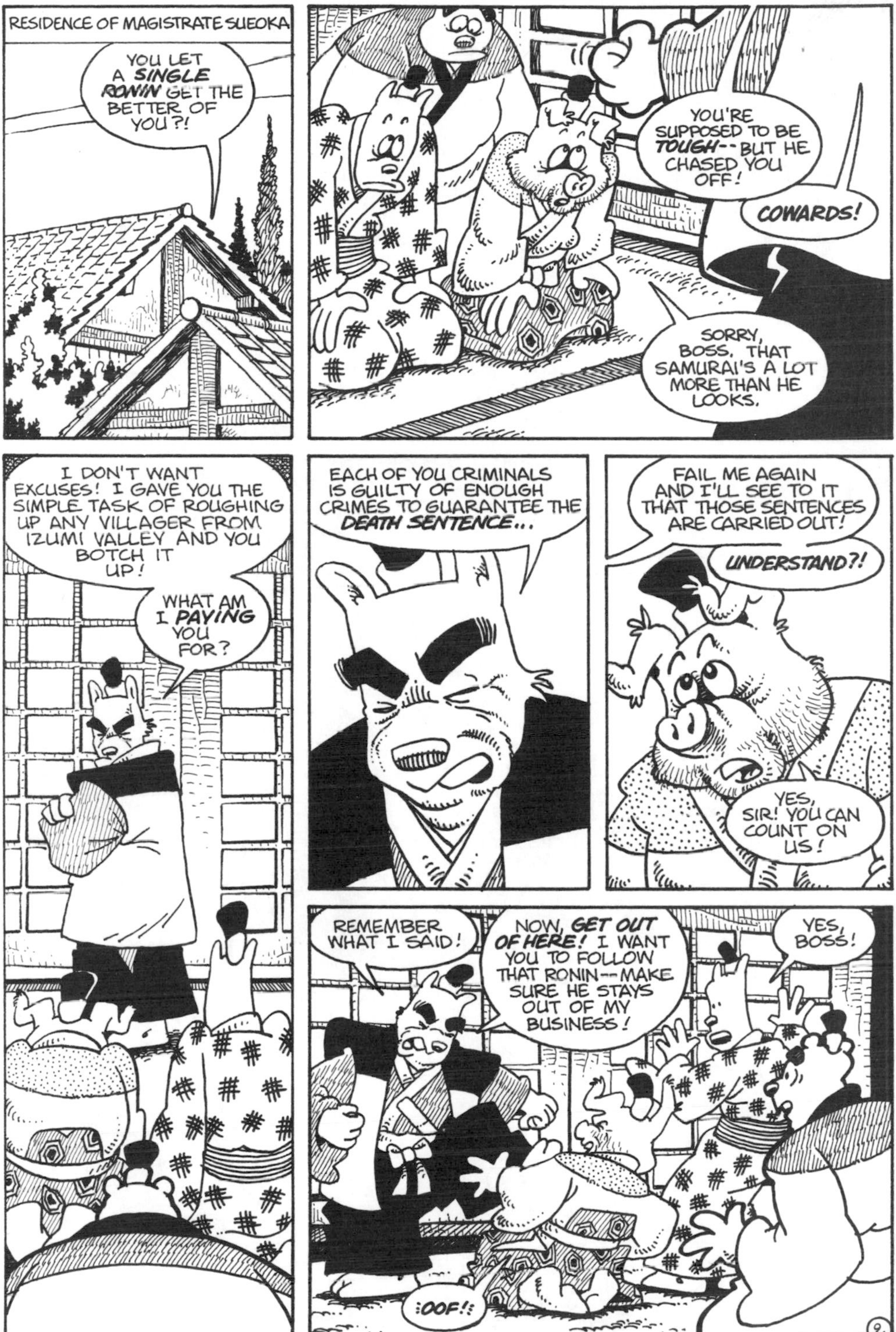
RESIDENCE OF MAGISTRATE SUEOKA
YOU LET A SINGLE RONIN GET THE BETTER OF YOU?!
YOU'RE SUPPOSED TO BE TOUGH-- BUT HE CHASED YOU OFF!
COWARDS!
SORRY, BOSS. THAT SAMURAI'S A LOT MORE THAN HE LOOKS.
I DON'T WANT EXCUSES! I GAVE YOU THE SIMPLE TASK OF ROUGHING UP ANY VILLAGER FROM IZUMI VALLEY AND YOU BOTCH IT UP!
WHAT AM I PAYING YOU FOR?
EACH OF YOU CRIMINALS IS GUILTY OF ENOUGH CRIMES TO GUARANTEE THE DEATH SENTENCE...
FAIL ME AGAIN AND I'LL SEE TO IT THAT THOSE SENTENCES ARE CARRIED OUT!
UNDERSTAND?!
YES, SIR! YOU CAN COUNT ON US!
REMEMBER WHAT I SAID!
NOW, GET OUT OF HERE! I WANT YOU TO FOLLOW THAT RONIN--MAKE SURE HE STAYS OUT OF MY BUSINESS!
YES, BOSS!
OOF!
9.

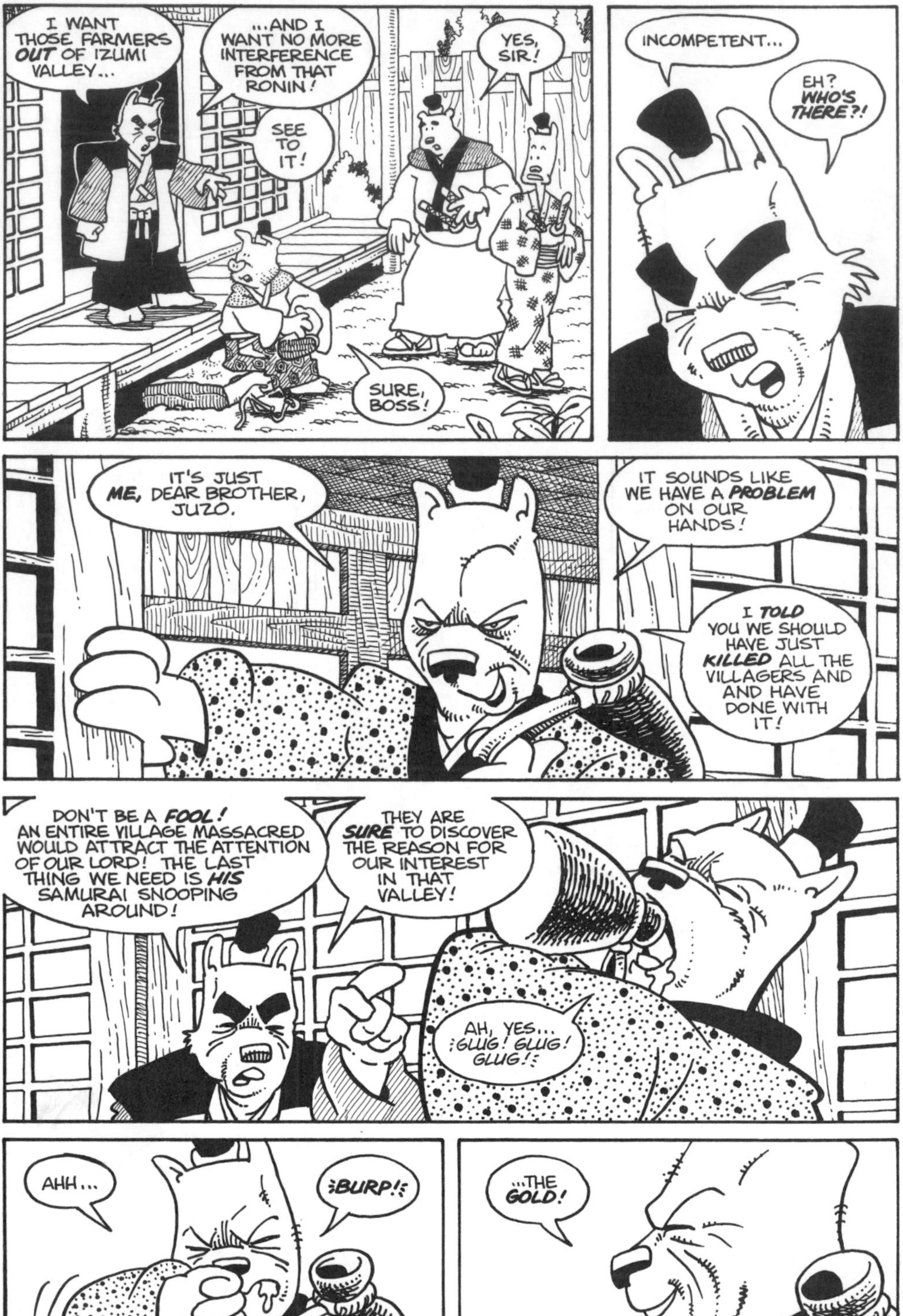
I WANT THOSE FARMERS OUT OF IZUMI VALLEY...
...AND I WANT NO MORE INTERFERENCE FROM THAT RONIN!
SEE TO IT!
YES, SIR!
SURE, BOSS!
INCOMPETENT...
EH? WHO'S THERE?!
IT'S JUST ME, DEAR BROTHER, JUZO.
IT SOUNDS LIKE WE HAVE A PROBLEM ON OUR HANDS!
I TOLD YOU WE SHOULD HAVE JUST KILLED ALL THE VILLAGERS AND AND HAVE DONE WITH IT!
DON'T BE A FOOL! AN ENTIRE VILLAGE MASSACRED WOULD ATTRACT THE ATTENTION OF OUR LORD! THE LAST THING WE NEED IS HIS SAMURAI SNOOPING AROUND!
THEY ARE SURE TO DISCOVER THE REASON FOR OUR INTEREST IN THAT VALLEY!
AH, YES... GLUG! GLUG! GLUG!
AHH...
BURP!
...THE GOLD!
10.

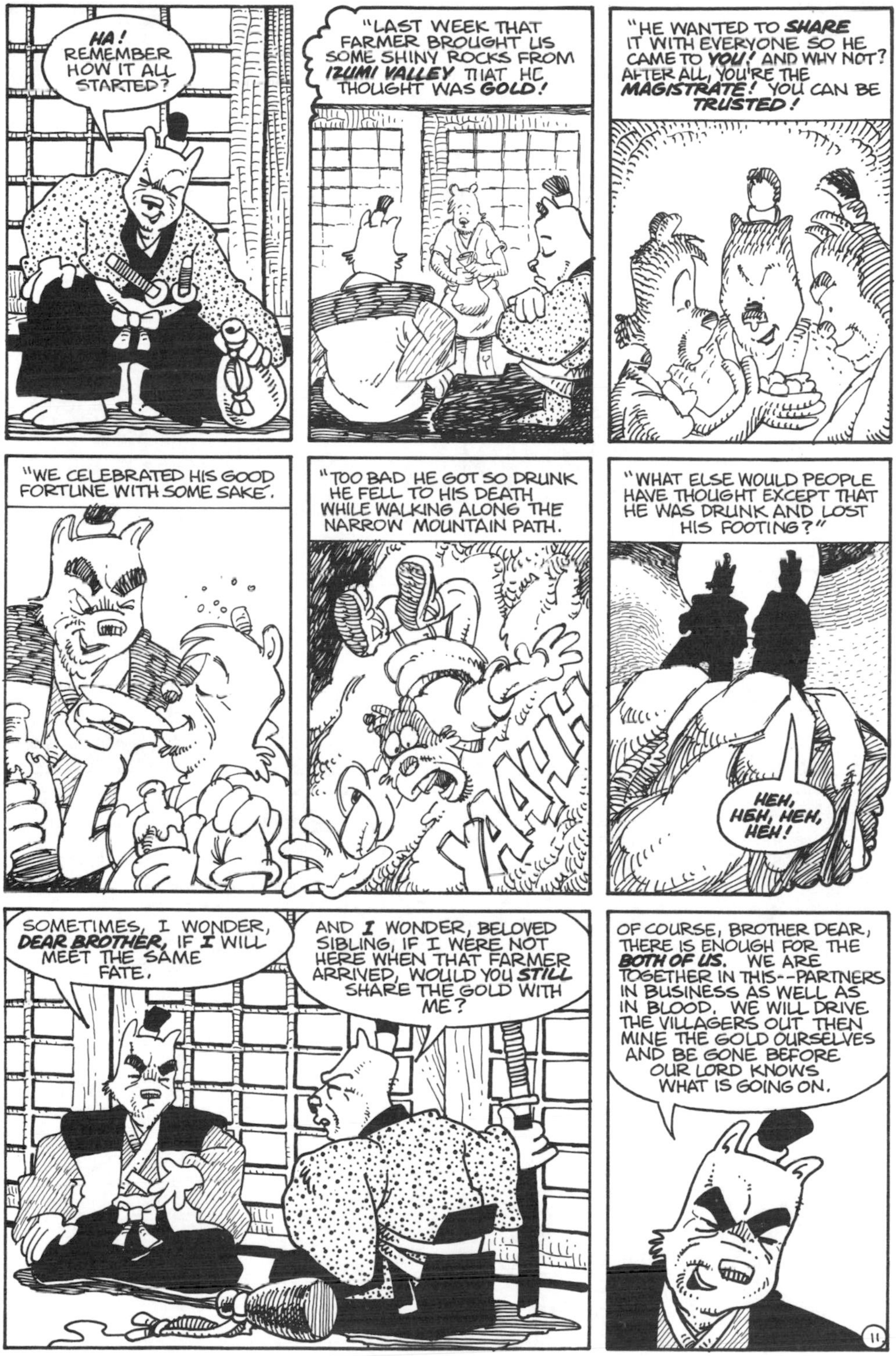
HA! REMEMBER HOW IT ALL STARTED?
"LAST WEEK THAT FARMER BROUGHT US SOME SHINY ROCKS FROM IZUMI VALLEY THAT HE THOUGHT WAS GOLD!
"HE WANTED TO SHARE IT WITH EVERYONE SO HE CAME TO YOU! AND WHY NOT? AFTER ALL, YOU'RE THE MAGISTRATE! YOU CAN BE TRUSTED!
"WE CELEBRATED HIS GOOD FORTUNE WITH SOME SAKE.
"TOO BAD HE GOT SO DRUNK HE FELL TO HIS DEATH WHILE WALKING ALONG THE NARROW MOUNTAIN PATH.
YAAHH
"WHAT ELSE WOULD PEOPLE HAVE THOUGHT EXCEPT THAT HE WAS DRUNK AND LOST HIS FOOTING?"
HEH, HEH, HEH, HEH!
SOMETIMES, I WONDER, DEAR BROTHER, IF I WILL MEET THE SAME FATE.
AND I WONDER, BELOVED SIBLING, IF I WERE NOT HERE WHEN THAT FARMER ARRIVED, WOULD YOU STILL SHARE THE GOLD WITH ME?
OF COURSE, BROTHER DEAR, THERE IS ENOUGH FOR THE BOTH OF US. WE ARE TOGETHER IN THIS--PARTNERS IN BUSINESS AS WELL AS IN BLOOD. WE WILL DRIVE THE VILLAGERS OUT THEN MINE THE GOLD OURSELVES AND BE GONE BEFORE OUR LORD KNOWS WHAT IS GOING ON.
11

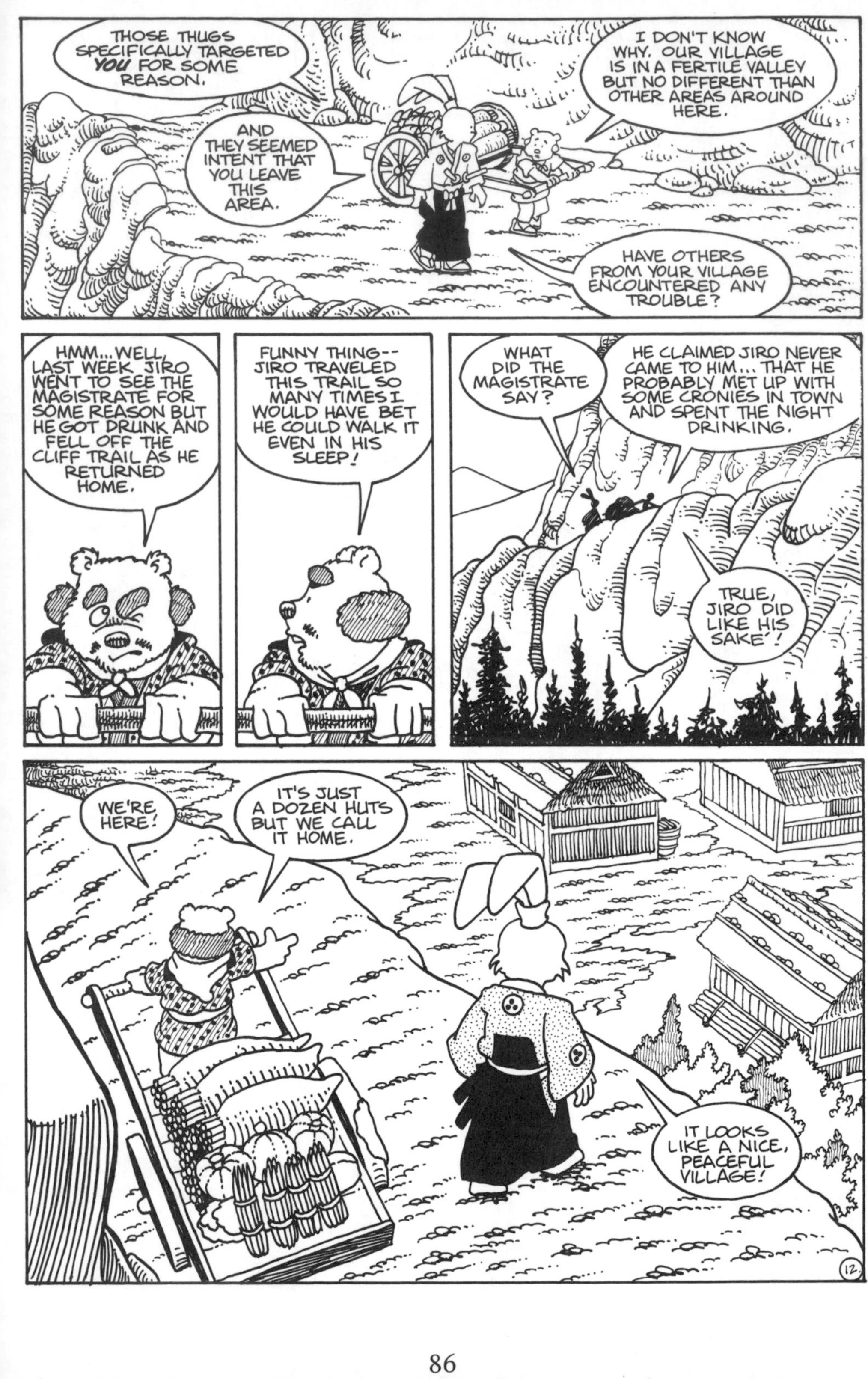
THOSE THUGS SPECIFICALLY TARGETED *YOU* FOR SOME REASON.
AND THEY SEEMED INTENT THAT YOU LEAVE THIS AREA.
I DON'T KNOW WHY. OUR VILLAGE IS IN A FERTILE VALLEY BUT NO DIFFERENT THAN OTHER AREAS AROUND HERE.
HAVE OTHERS FROM YOUR VILLAGE ENCOUNTERED ANY TROUBLE?
HMM... WELL, LAST WEEK JIRO WENT TO SEE THE MAGISTRATE FOR SOME REASON BUT HE GOT DRUNK AND FELL OFF THE CLIFF TRAIL AS HE RETURNED HOME.
FUNNY THING-- JIRO TRAVELED THIS TRAIL SO MANY TIMES I WOULD HAVE BET HE COULD WALK IT EVEN IN HIS SLEEP!
WHAT DID THE MAGISTRATE SAY?
HE CLAIMED JIRO NEVER CAME TO HIM... THAT HE PROBABLY MET UP WITH SOME CRONIES IN TOWN AND SPENT THE NIGHT DRINKING.
TRUE, JIRO DID LIKE HIS SAKE'!
WE'RE HERE!
IT'S JUST A DOZEN HUTS BUT WE CALL IT HOME.
IT LOOKS LIKE A NICE, PEACEFUL VILLAGE!
12.

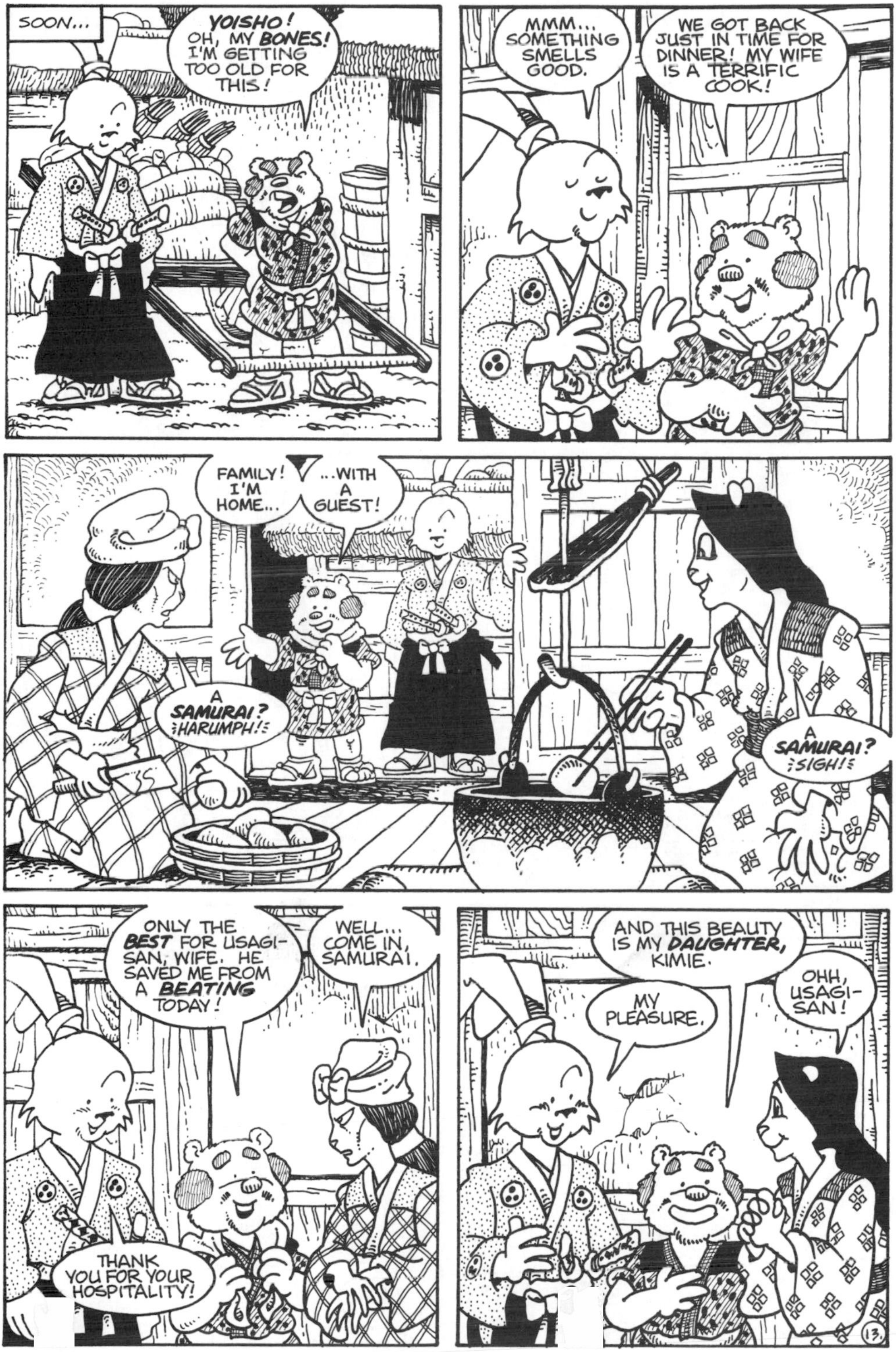
SOON...
YOISHO! OH, MY BONES! I'M GETTING TOO OLD FOR THIS!
MMM... SOMETHING SMELLS GOOD.
WE GOT BACK JUST IN TIME FOR DINNER! MY WIFE IS A TERRIFIC COOK!
FAMILY! I'M HOME...
...WITH A GUEST!
A SAMURAI? HARUMPH!
A SAMURAI? SIGH!
ONLY THE BEST FOR USAGI-SAN, WIFE. HE SAVED ME FROM A BEATING TODAY!
WELL... COME IN, SAMURAI.
THANK YOU FOR YOUR HOSPITALITY!
AND THIS BEAUTY IS MY DAUGHTER, KIMIE.
MY PLEASURE.
OHH, USAGI-SAN!
13.

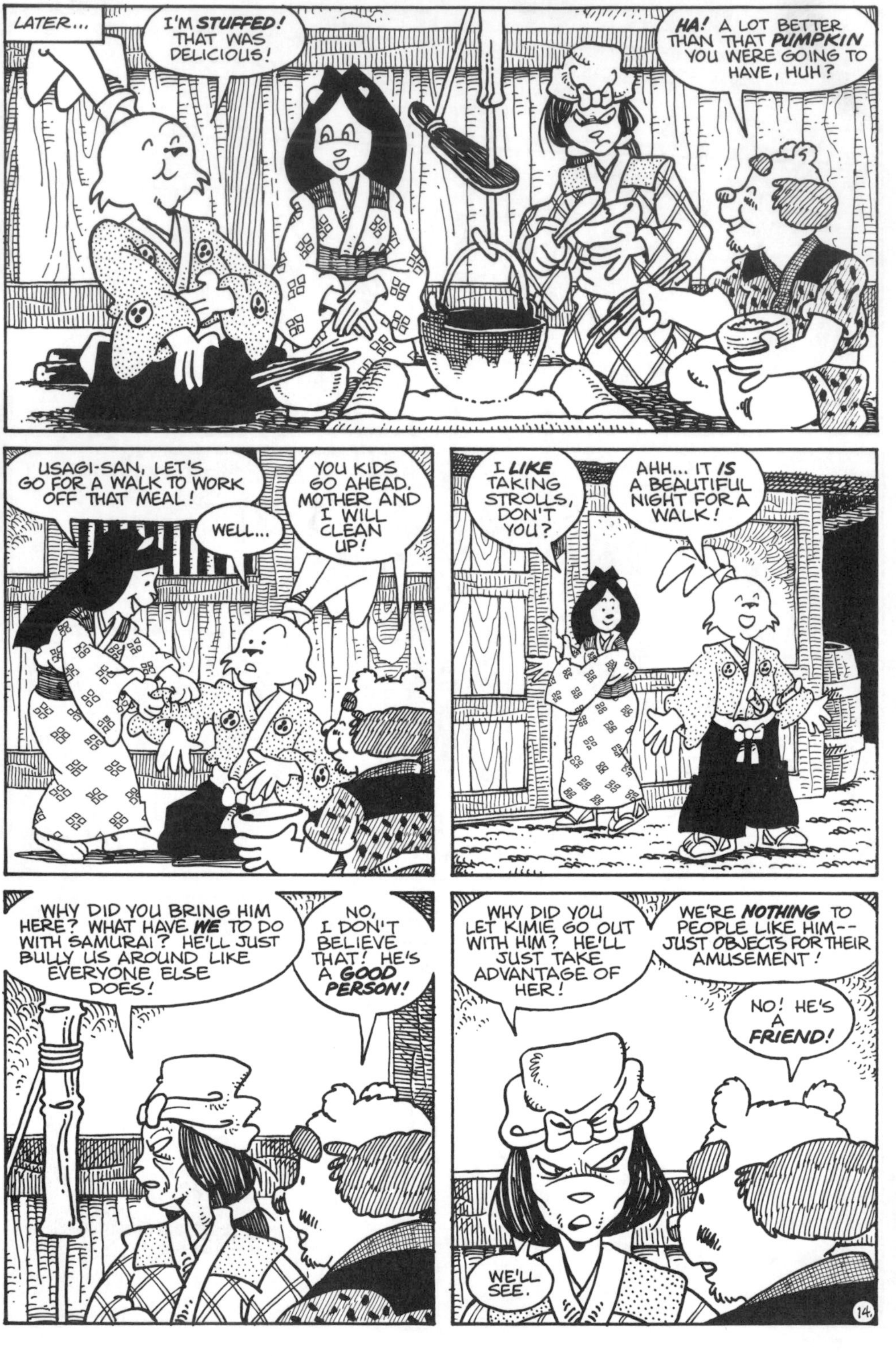
LATER...
I'M STUFFED! THAT WAS DELICIOUS!
HA! A LOT BETTER THAN THAT PUMPKIN YOU WERE GOING TO HAVE, HUH?
USAGI-SAN, LET'S GO FOR A WALK TO WORK OFF THAT MEAL!
WELL...
YOU KIDS GO AHEAD. MOTHER AND I WILL CLEAN UP!
I LIKE TAKING STROLLS, DON'T YOU?
AHH... IT IS A BEAUTIFUL NIGHT FOR A WALK!
WHY DID YOU BRING HIM HERE? WHAT HAVE WE TO DO WITH SAMURAI? HE'LL JUST BULLY US AROUND LIKE EVERYONE ELSE DOES!
NO, I DON'T BELIEVE THAT! HE'S A GOOD PERSON!
WHY DID YOU LET KIMIE GO OUT WITH HIM? HE'LL JUST TAKE ADVANTAGE OF HER!
WE'RE NOTHING TO PEOPLE LIKE HIM-- JUST OBJECTS FOR THEIR AMUSEMENT!
NO! HE'S A FRIEND!
WE'LL SEE.
14.

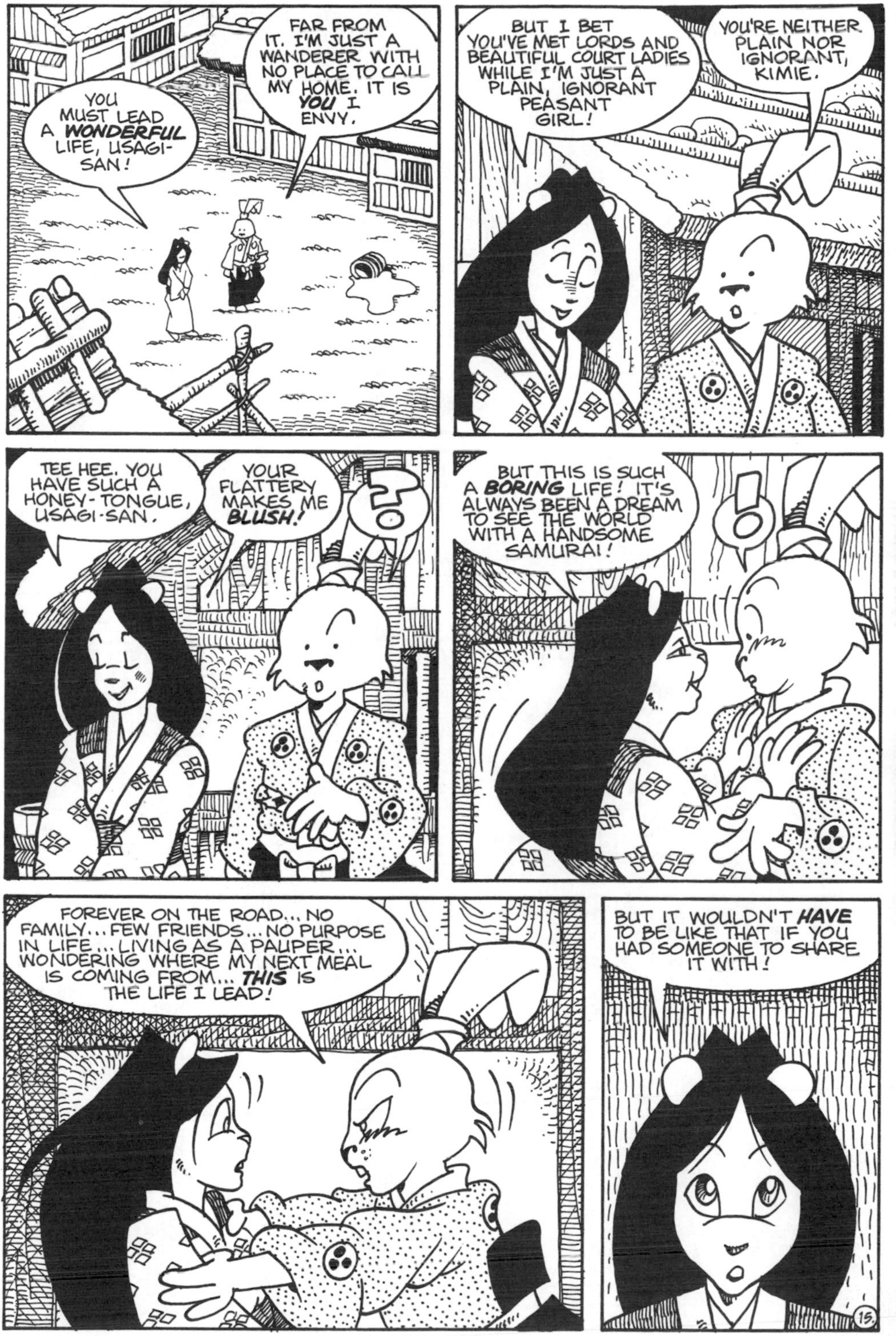

YOU MUST LEAD A WONDERFUL LIFE, USAGI-SAN!
FAR FROM IT. I'M JUST A WANDERER WITH NO PLACE TO CALL MY HOME. IT IS YOU I ENVY.
BUT I BET YOU'VE MET LORDS AND BEAUTIFUL COURT LADIES WHILE I'M JUST A PLAIN, IGNORANT PEASANT GIRL!
YOU'RE NEITHER PLAIN NOR IGNORANT, KIMIE.
TEE HEE. YOU HAVE SUCH A HONEY-TONGUE, USAGI-SAN.
YOUR FLATTERY MAKES ME BLUSH!
?
BUT THIS IS SUCH A BORING LIFE! IT'S ALWAYS BEEN A DREAM TO SEE THE WORLD WITH A HANDSOME SAMURAI!
!
FOREVER ON THE ROAD... NO FAMILY... FEW FRIENDS... NO PURPOSE IN LIFE... LIVING AS A PAUPER... WONDERING WHERE MY NEXT MEAL IS COMING FROM... THIS IS THE LIFE I LEAD!
BUT IT WOULDN'T HAVE TO BE LIKE THAT IF YOU HAD SOMEONE TO SHARE IT WITH!
15

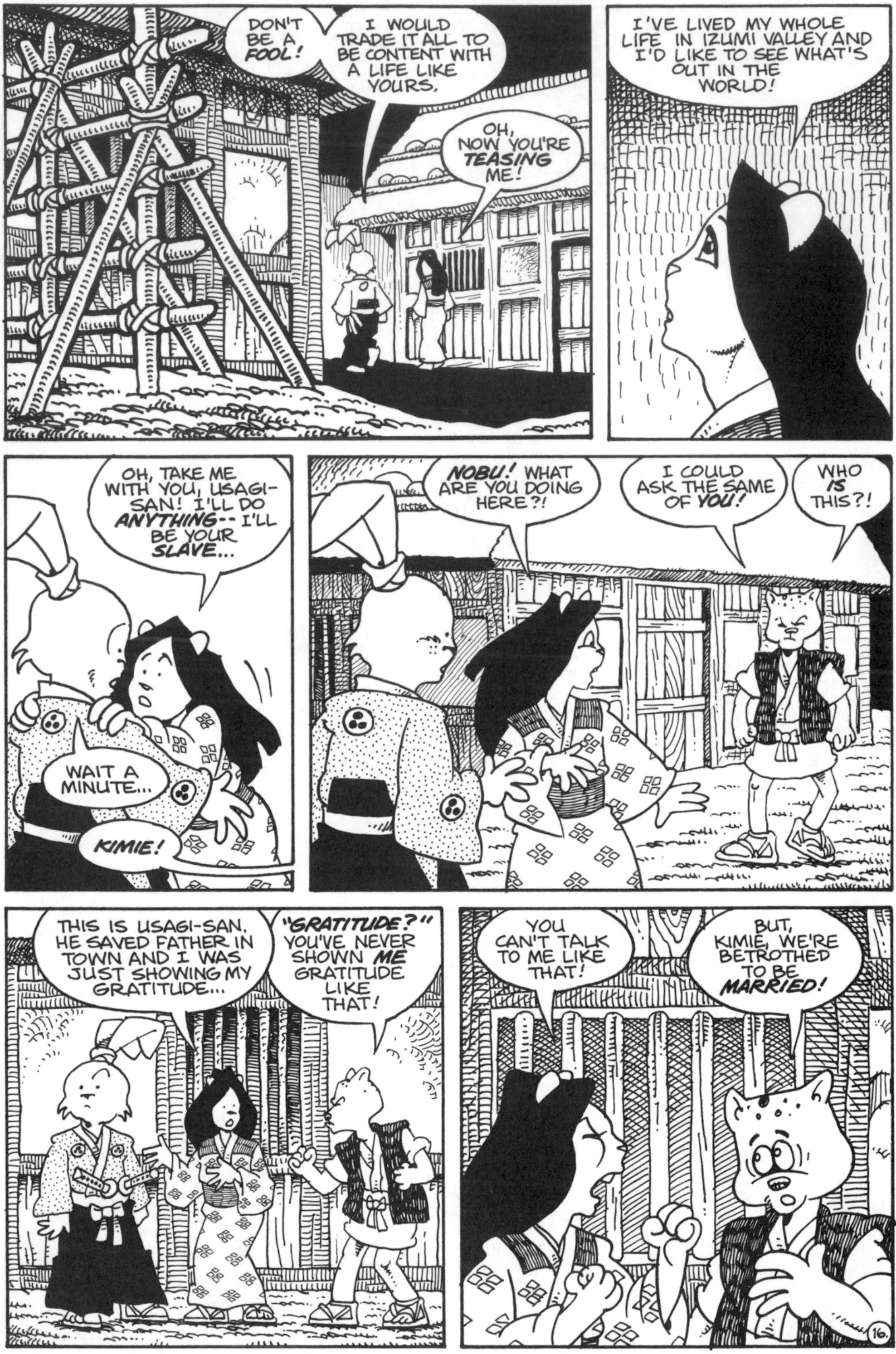
DON'T BE A FOOL!
I WOULD TRADE IT ALL TO BE CONTENT WITH A LIFE LIKE YOURS.
OH, NOW YOU'RE TEASING ME!
I'VE LIVED MY WHOLE LIFE IN IZUMI VALLEY AND I'D LIKE TO SEE WHAT'S OUT IN THE WORLD!
OH, TAKE ME WITH YOU, USAGI-SAN! I'LL DO ANYTHING-- I'LL BE YOUR SLAVE...
WAIT A MINUTE...
KIMIE!
NOBU! WHAT ARE YOU DOING HERE?!
I COULD ASK THE SAME OF YOU!
WHO IS THIS?!
THIS IS USAGI-SAN. HE SAVED FATHER IN TOWN AND I WAS JUST SHOWING MY GRATITUDE...
"GRATITUDE?" YOU'VE NEVER SHOWN ME GRATITUDE LIKE THAT!
YOU CAN'T TALK TO ME LIKE THAT!
BUT, KIMIE, WE'RE BETROTHED TO BE MARRIED!
16.

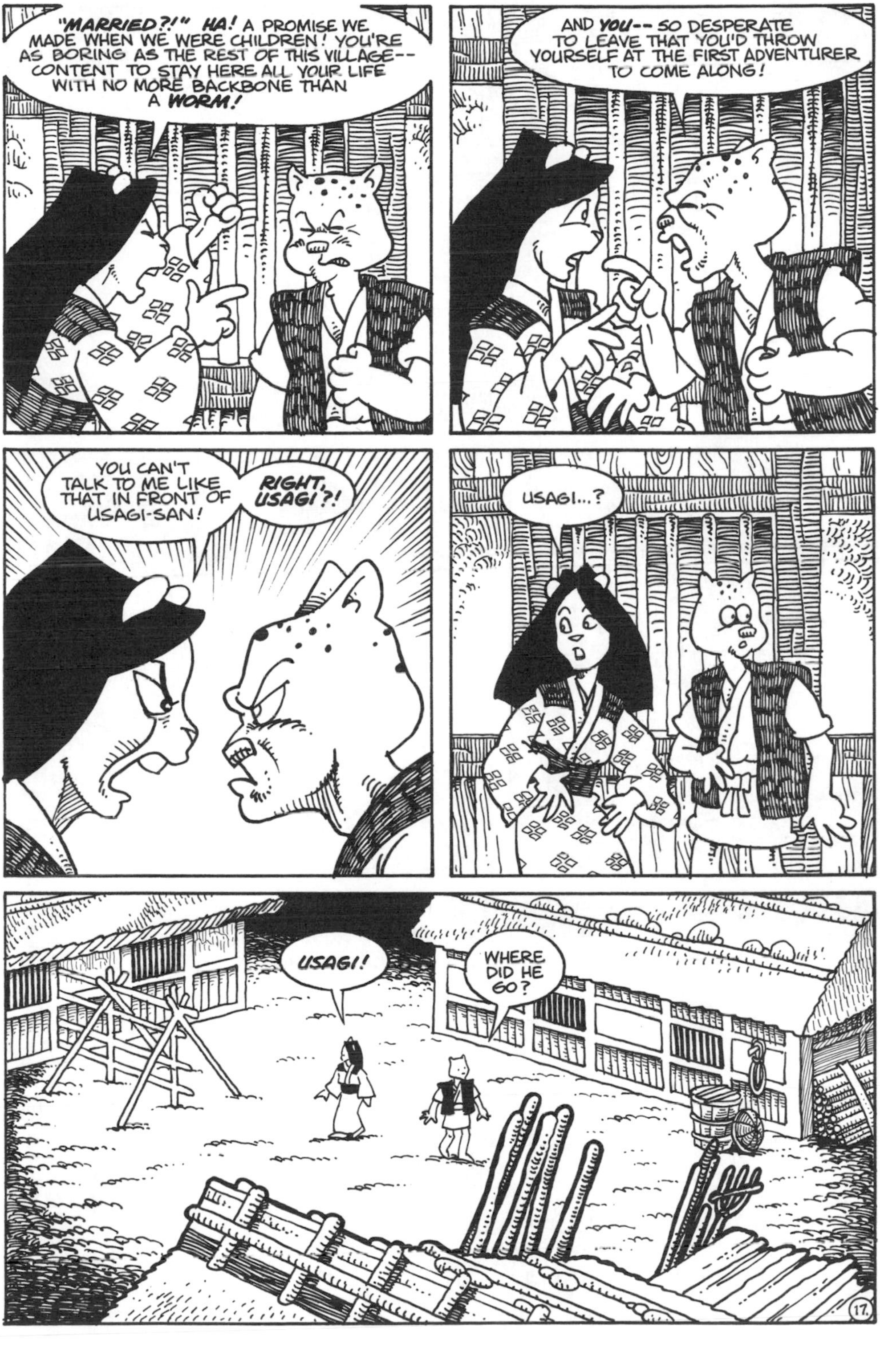
"MARRIED?!" HA! A PROMISE WE MADE WHEN WE WERE CHILDREN! YOU'RE AS BORING AS THE REST OF THIS VILLAGE-- CONTENT TO STAY HERE ALL YOUR LIFE WITH NO MORE BACKBONE THAN A WORM!
AND YOU-- SO DESPERATE TO LEAVE THAT YOU'D THROW YOURSELF AT THE FIRST ADVENTURER TO COME ALONG!
YOU CAN'T TALK TO ME LIKE THAT IN FRONT OF USAGI-SAN!
RIGHT, USAGI?!
USAGI...?
USAGI!
WHERE DID HE GO?
17.

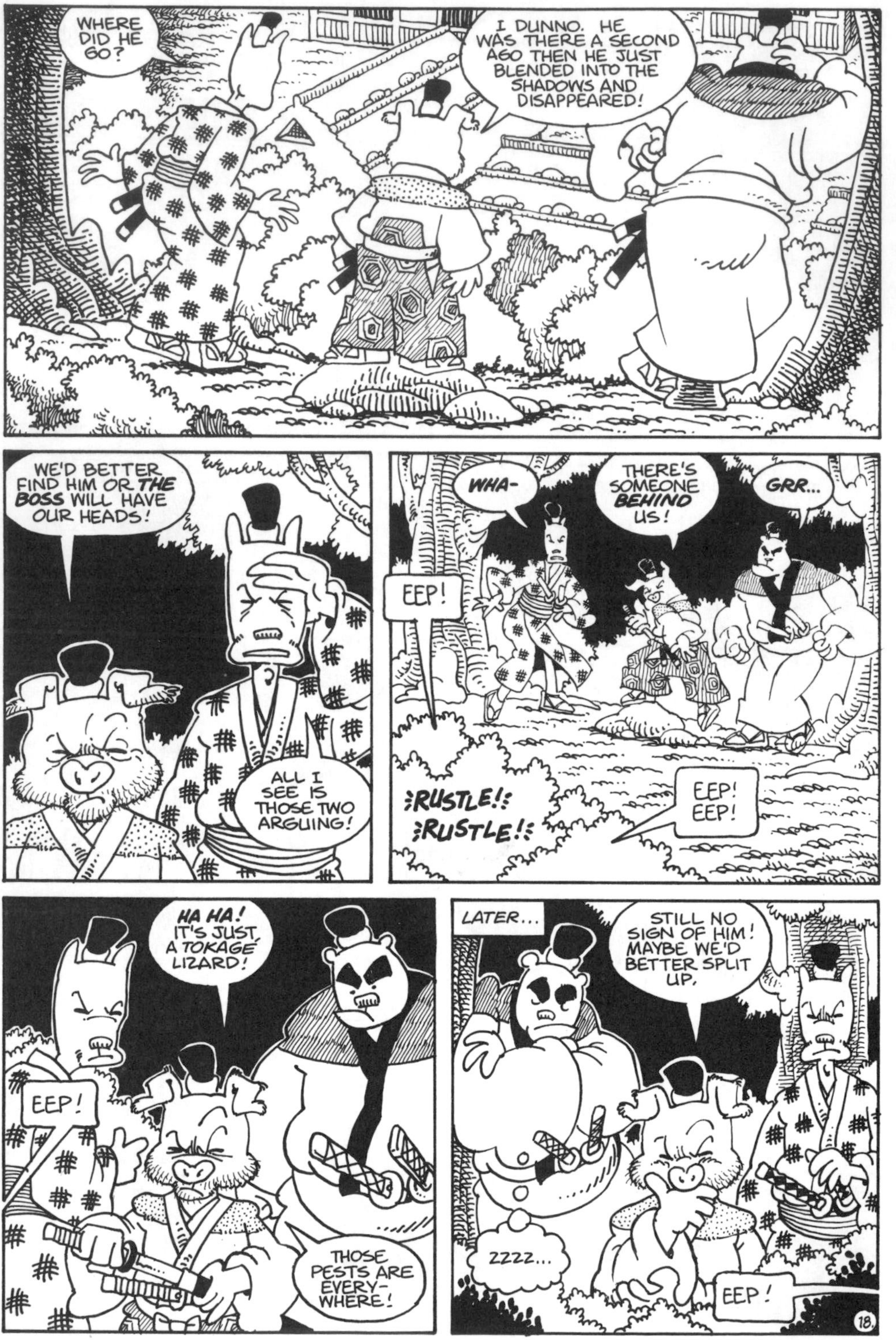
WHERE DID HE GO?
I DUNNO. HE WAS THERE A SECOND AGO THEN HE JUST BLENDED INTO THE SHADOWS AND DISAPPEARED!
WE'D BETTER FIND HIM OR THE BOSS WILL HAVE OUR HEADS!
ALL I SEE IS THOSE TWO ARGUING!
WHA-
THERE'S SOMEONE BEHIND US!
GRR...
EEP!
RUSTLE! RUSTLE!
EEP! EEP!
HA HA! IT'S JUST A TOKAGE LIZARD!
EEP!
THOSE PESTS ARE EVERY-WHERE!
LATER...
STILL NO SIGN OF HIM! MAYBE WE'D BETTER SPLIT UP.
ZZZZ...
EEP!
18.

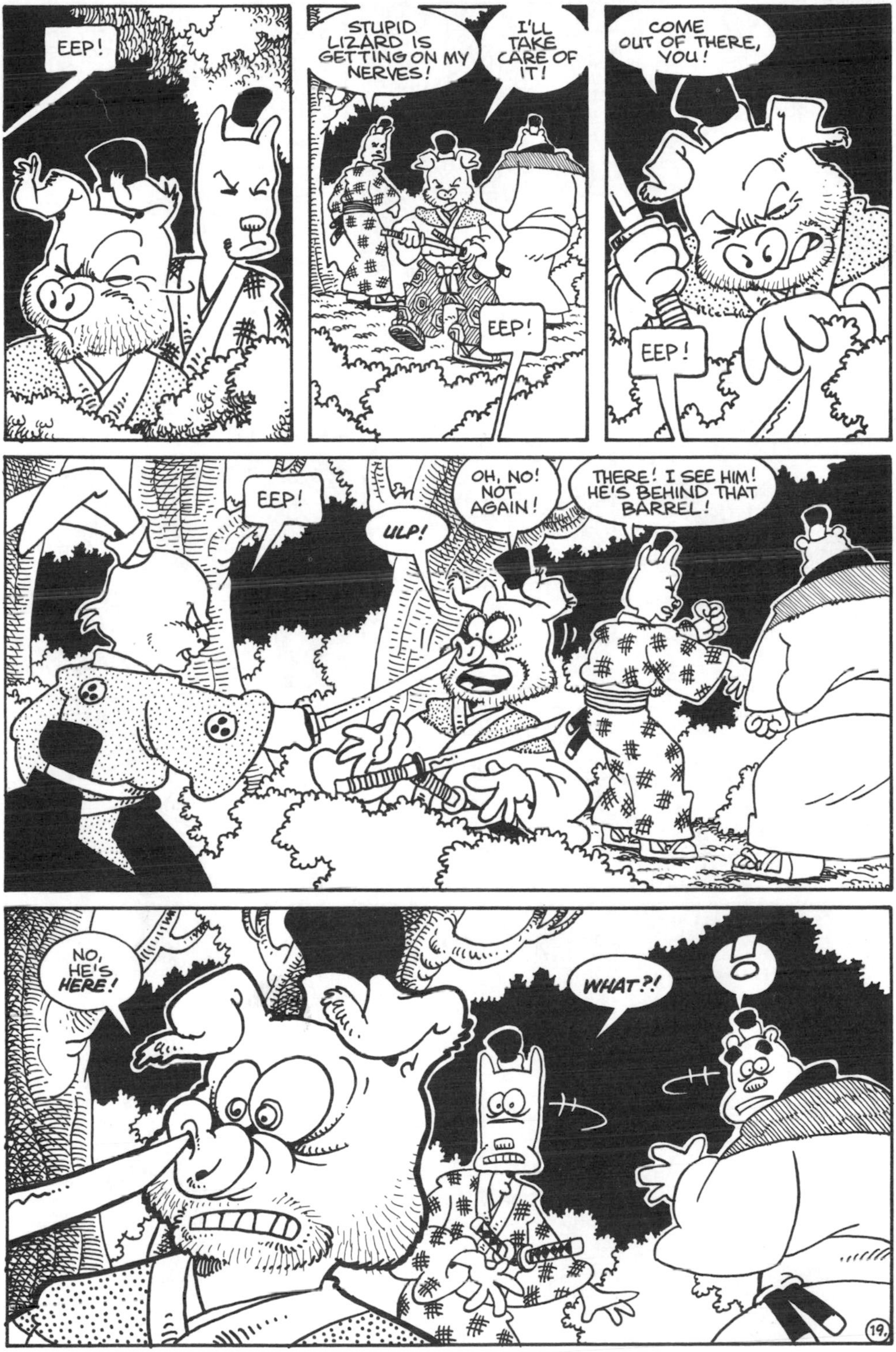
EEP!
STUPID LIZARD IS GETTING ON MY NERVES!
I'LL TAKE CARE OF IT!
EEP!
COME OUT OF THERE, YOU!
EEP!
EEP!
ULP!
OH, NO! NOT AGAIN!
THERE! I SEE HIM! HE'S BEHIND THAT BARREL!
NO, HE'S HERE!
WHAT?!
!
19.

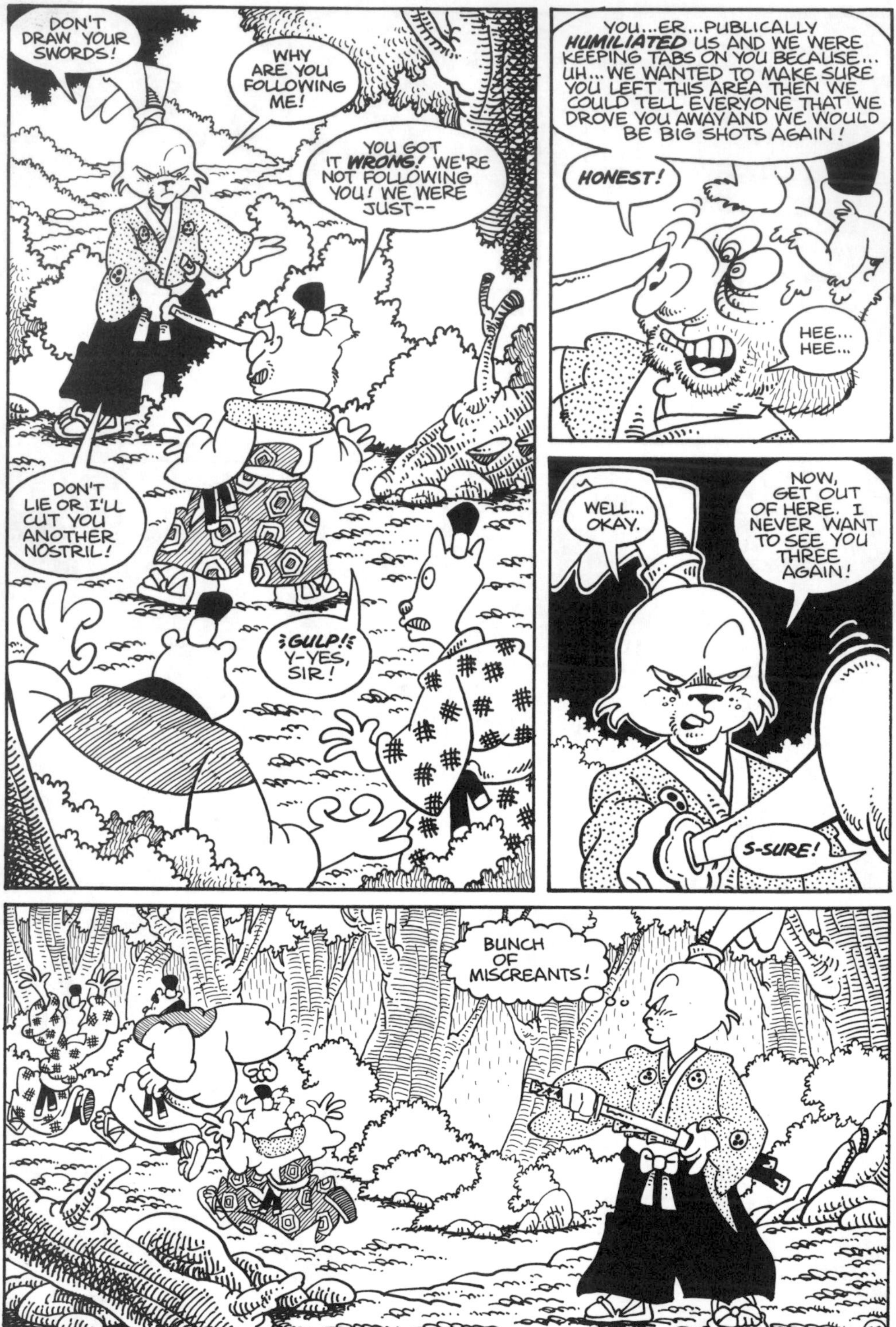
DON'T DRAW YOUR SWORDS!
WHY ARE YOU FOLLOWING ME!
YOU GOT IT WRONG! WE'RE NOT FOLLOWING YOU! WE WERE JUST--
DON'T LIE OR I'LL CUT YOU ANOTHER NOSTRIL!
GULP! Y-YES, SIR!
YOU...ER...PUBLICALLY HUMILIATED US AND WE WERE KEEPING TABS ON YOU BECAUSE... UH... WE WANTED TO MAKE SURE YOU LEFT THIS AREA THEN WE COULD TELL EVERYONE THAT WE DROVE YOU AWAY AND WE WOULD BE BIG SHOTS AGAIN!
HONEST!
HEE... HEE...
WELL... OKAY.
NOW, GET OUT OF HERE. I NEVER WANT TO SEE YOU THREE AGAIN!
S-SURE!
BUNCH OF MISCREANTS!
20

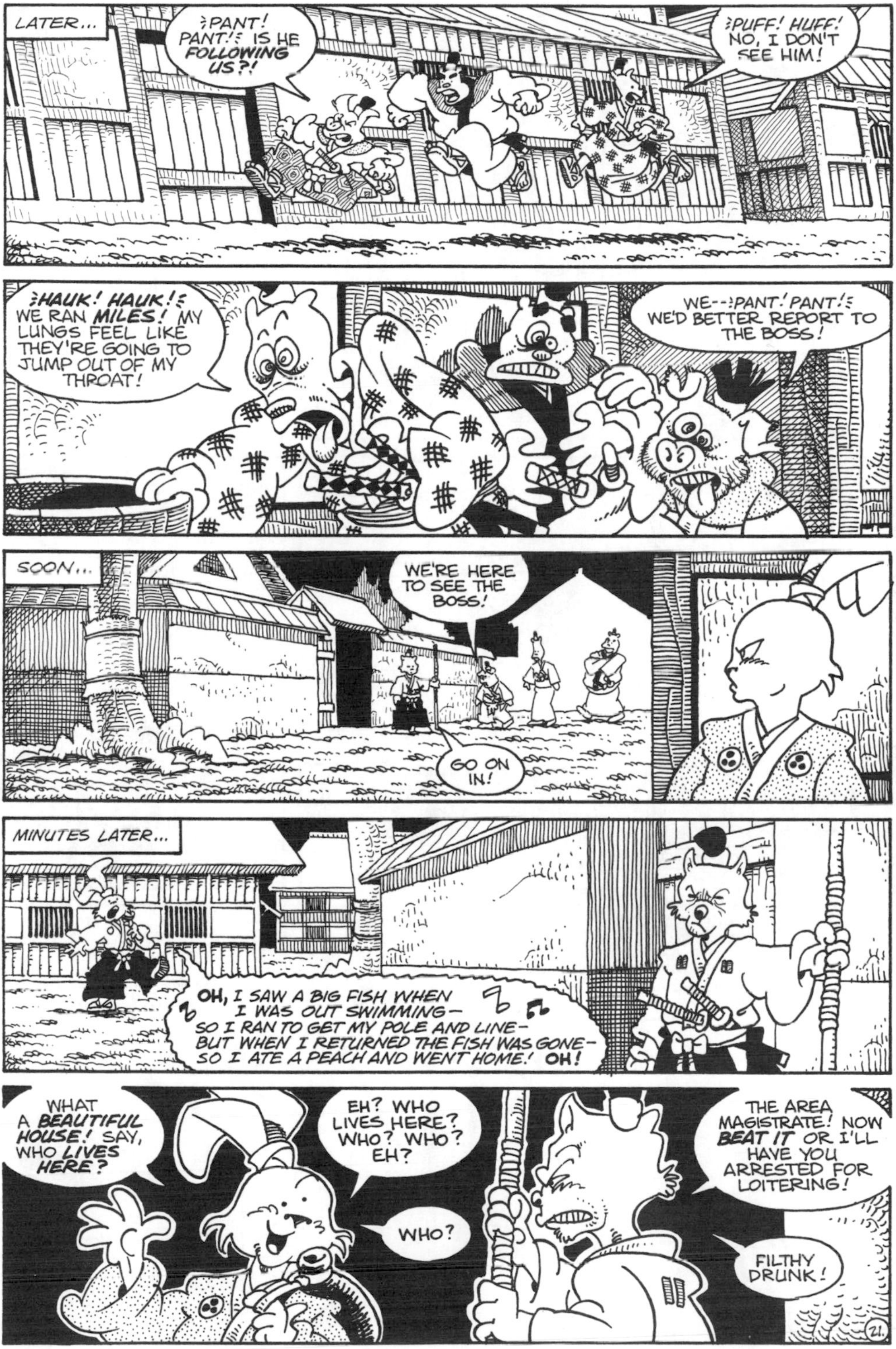
LATER...
¡PANT! PANT! IS HE FOLLOWING US?!
¡PUFF! HUFF! NO, I DON'T SEE HIM!
¡HAUK! HAUK! WE RAN MILES! MY LUNGS FEEL LIKE THEY'RE GOING TO JUMP OUT OF MY THROAT!
WE--¡PANT! PANT! WE'D BETTER REPORT TO THE BOSS!
SOON...
WE'RE HERE TO SEE THE BOSS!
GO ON IN!
MINUTES LATER...
OH, I SAW A BIG FISH WHEN I WAS OUT SWIMMING- SO I RAN TO GET MY POLE AND LINE- BUT WHEN I RETURNED THE FISH WAS GONE- SO I ATE A PEACH AND WENT HOME! OH!
WHAT A BEAUTIFUL HOUSE! SAY, WHO LIVES HERE?
EH? WHO LIVES HERE? WHO? WHO? EH?
WHO?
THE AREA MAGISTRATE! NOW BEAT IT OR I'LL HAVE YOU ARRESTED FOR LOITERING!
FILTHY DRUNK!
21.

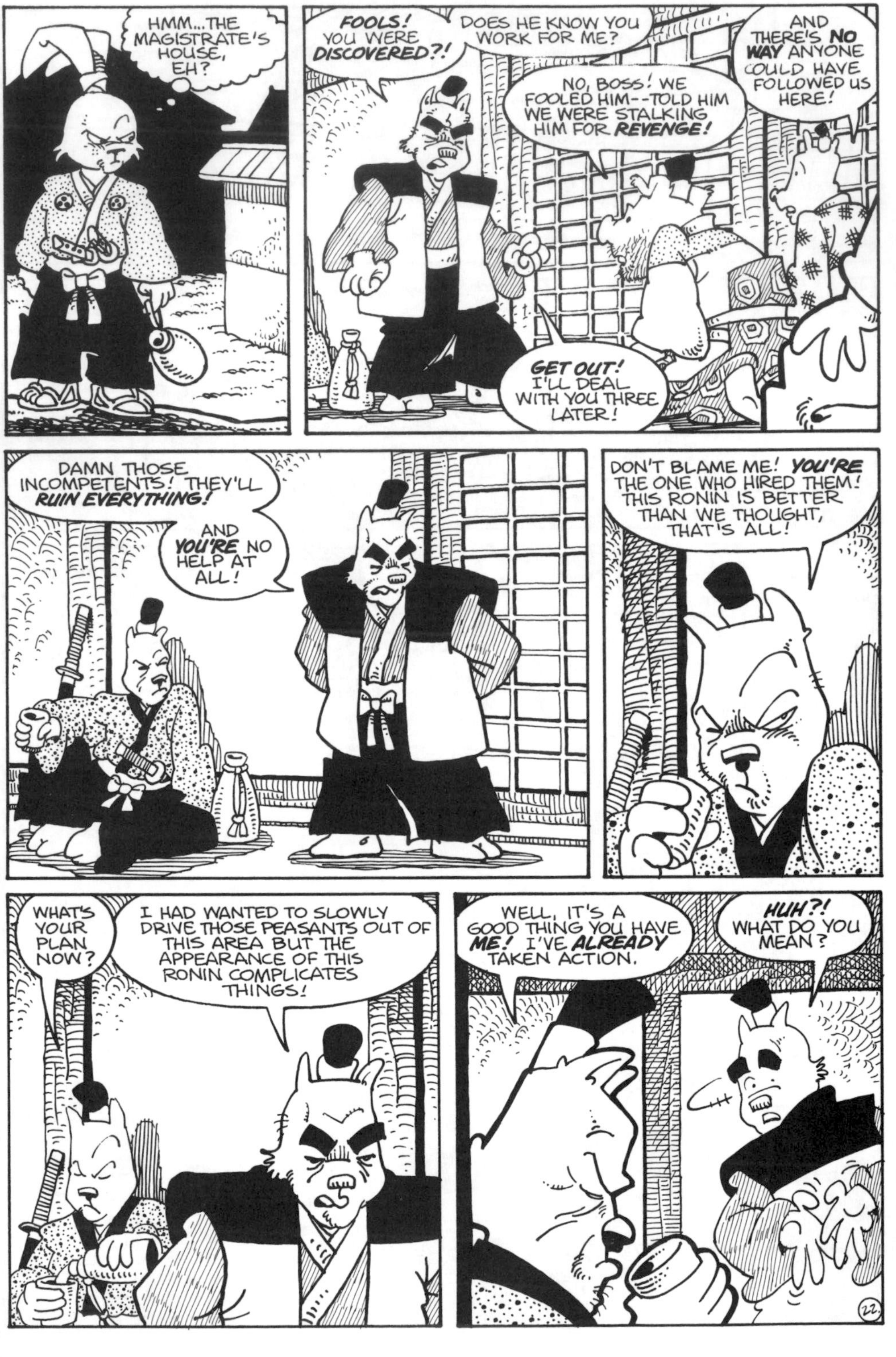
HMM... THE MAGISTRATE'S HOUSE, EH?
FOOLS! YOU WERE DISCOVERED?!
DOES HE KNOW YOU WORK FOR ME?
NO, BOSS! WE FOOLED HIM--TOLD HIM WE WERE STALKING HIM FOR REVENGE!
AND THERE'S NO WAY ANYONE COULD HAVE FOLLOWED US HERE!
GET OUT! I'LL DEAL WITH YOU THREE LATER!
DAMN THOSE INCOMPETENTS! THEY'LL RUIN EVERYTHING!
AND YOU'RE NO HELP AT ALL!
DON'T BLAME ME! YOU'RE THE ONE WHO HIRED THEM! THIS RONIN IS BETTER THAN WE THOUGHT, THAT'S ALL!
WHAT'S YOUR PLAN NOW?
I HAD WANTED TO SLOWLY DRIVE THOSE PEASANTS OUT OF THIS AREA BUT THE APPEARANCE OF THIS RONIN COMPLICATES THINGS!
WELL, IT'S A GOOD THING YOU HAVE ME! I'VE ALREADY TAKEN ACTION.
HUH?! WHAT DO YOU MEAN?
22.

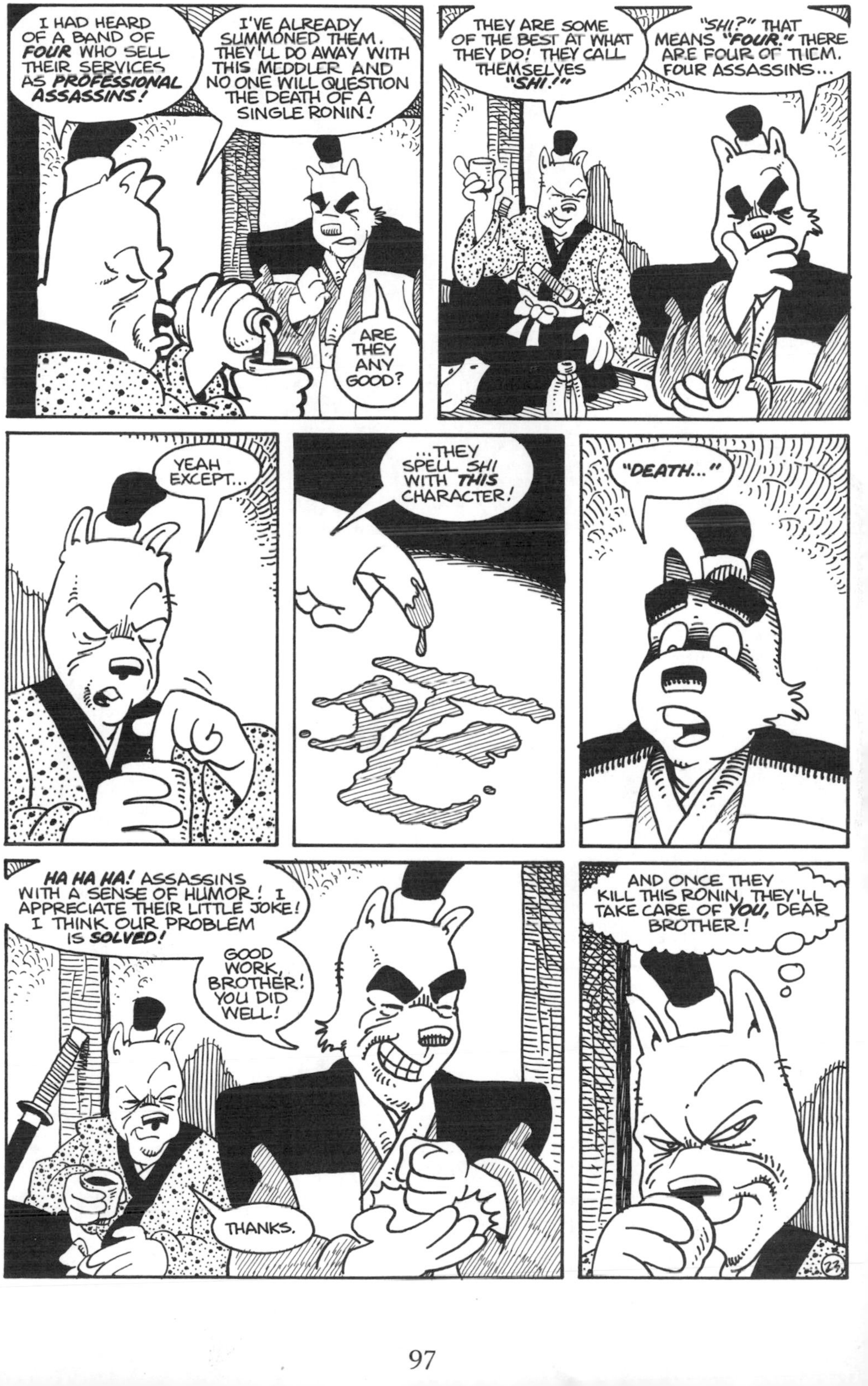
I HAD HEARD OF A BAND OF FOUR WHO SELL THEIR SERVICES AS PROFESSIONAL ASSASSINS!
I'VE ALREADY SUMMONED THEM. THEY'LL DO AWAY WITH THIS MEDDLER AND NO ONE WILL QUESTION THE DEATH OF A SINGLE RONIN!
ARE THEY ANY GOOD?
THEY ARE SOME OF THE BEST AT WHAT THEY DO! THEY CALL THEMSELVES "SHI!"
"SHI?" THAT MEANS "FOUR." THERE ARE FOUR OF THEM. FOUR ASSASSINS...
YEAH EXCEPT...
...THEY SPELL SHI WITH THIS CHARACTER!
"DEATH..."
HA HA HA! ASSASSINS WITH A SENSE OF HUMOR! I APPRECIATE THEIR LITTLE JOKE! I THINK OUR PROBLEM IS SOLVED!
GOOD WORK, BROTHER! YOU DID WELL!
THANKS.
AND ONCE THEY KILL THIS RONIN, THEY'LL TAKE CARE OF YOU, DEAR BROTHER!
23

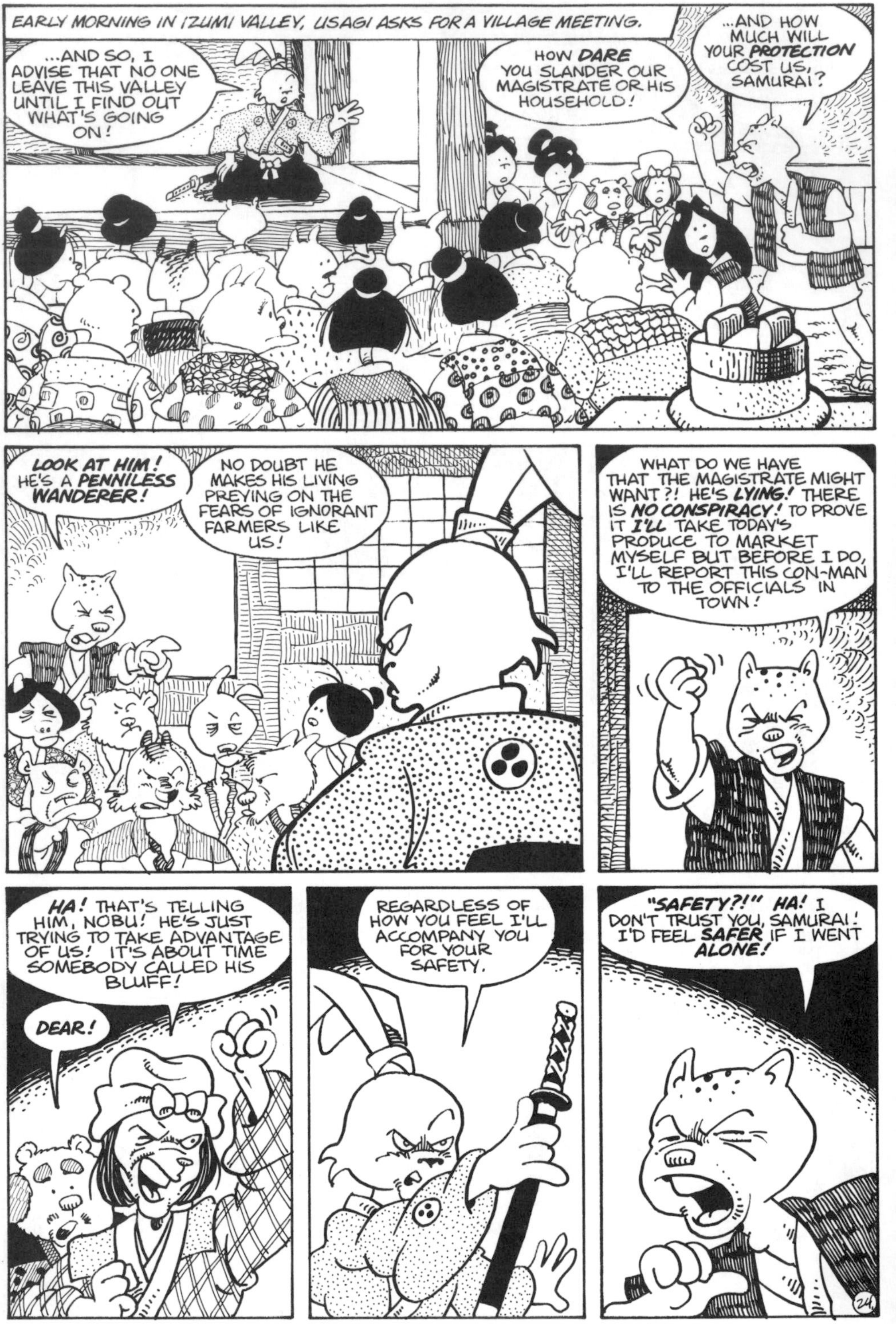
EARLY MORNING IN IZUMI VALLEY, USAGI ASKS FOR A VILLAGE MEETING.
...AND SO, I ADVISE THAT NO ONE LEAVE THIS VALLEY UNTIL I FIND OUT WHAT'S GOING ON!
HOW DARE YOU SLANDER OUR MAGISTRATE OR HIS HOUSEHOLD!
...AND HOW MUCH WILL YOUR PROTECTION COST US, SAMURAI?
LOOK AT HIM! HE'S A PENNILESS WANDERER!
NO DOUBT HE MAKES HIS LIVING PREYING ON THE FEARS OF IGNORANT FARMERS LIKE US!
WHAT DO WE HAVE THAT THE MAGISTRATE MIGHT WANT?! HE'S LYING! THERE IS NO CONSPIRACY! TO PROVE IT I'LL TAKE TODAY'S PRODUCE TO MARKET MYSELF BUT BEFORE I DO, I'LL REPORT THIS CON-MAN TO THE OFFICIALS IN TOWN!
HA! THAT'S TELLING HIM, NOBU! HE'S JUST TRYING TO TAKE ADVANTAGE OF US! IT'S ABOUT TIME SOMEBODY CALLED HIS BLUFF!
DEAR!
REGARDLESS OF HOW YOU FEEL I'LL ACCOMPANY YOU FOR YOUR SAFETY.
"SAFETY?!" HA! I DON'T TRUST YOU, SAMURAI! I'D FEEL SAFER IF I WENT ALONE!
24

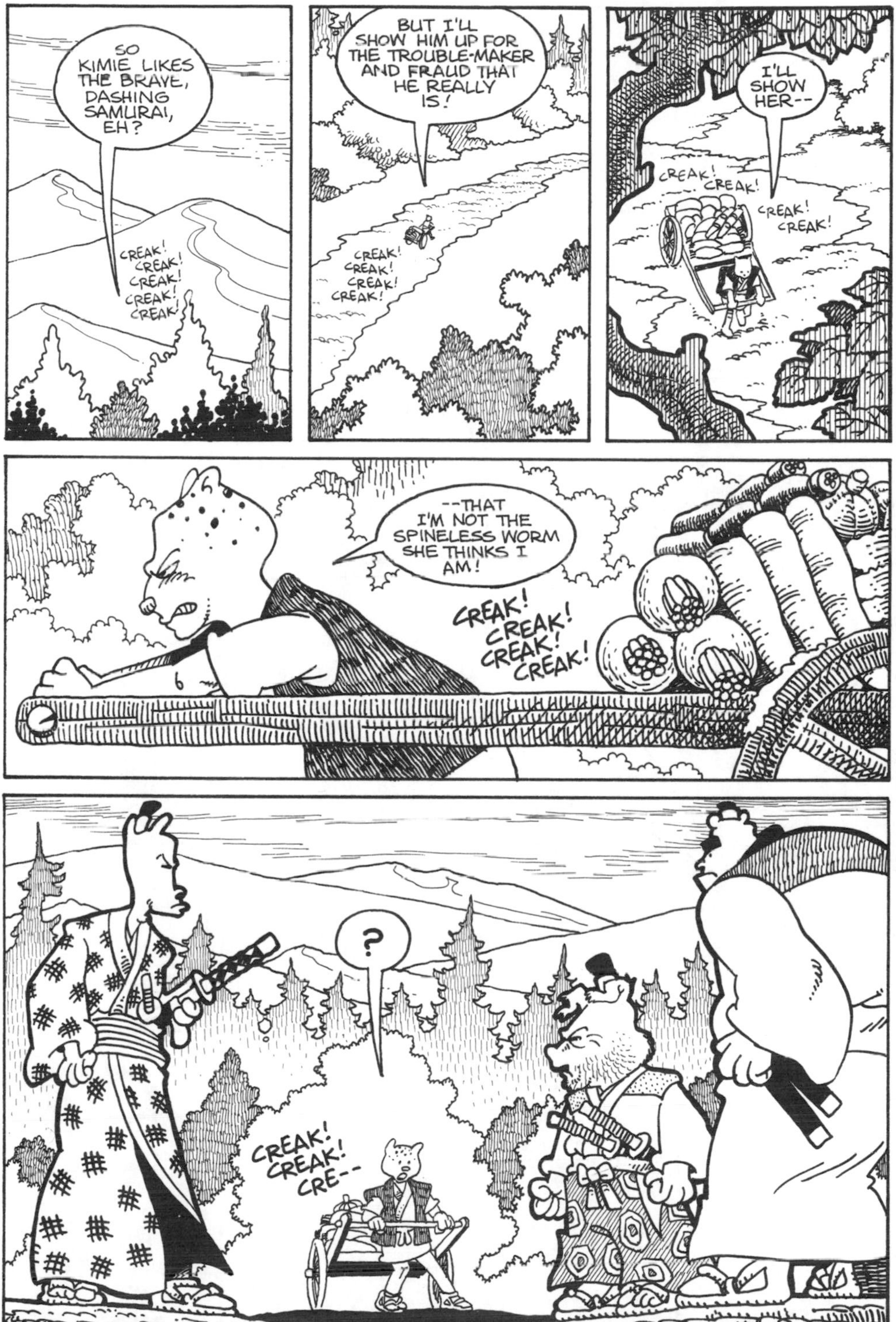
SO KIMIE LIKES THE BRAVE, DASHING SAMURAI, EH?
CREAK! CREAK! CREAK! CREAK! CREAK!
BUT I'LL SHOW HIM UP FOR THE TROUBLE-MAKER AND FRAUD THAT HE REALLY IS!
CREAK! CREAK! CREAK! CREAK!
I'LL SHOW HER--
CREAK! CREAK!
CREAK! CREAK!
--THAT I'M NOT THE SPINELESS WORM SHE THINKS I AM!
CREAK! CREAK! CREAK! CREAK!
?
CREAK! CREAK! CRE--
25.

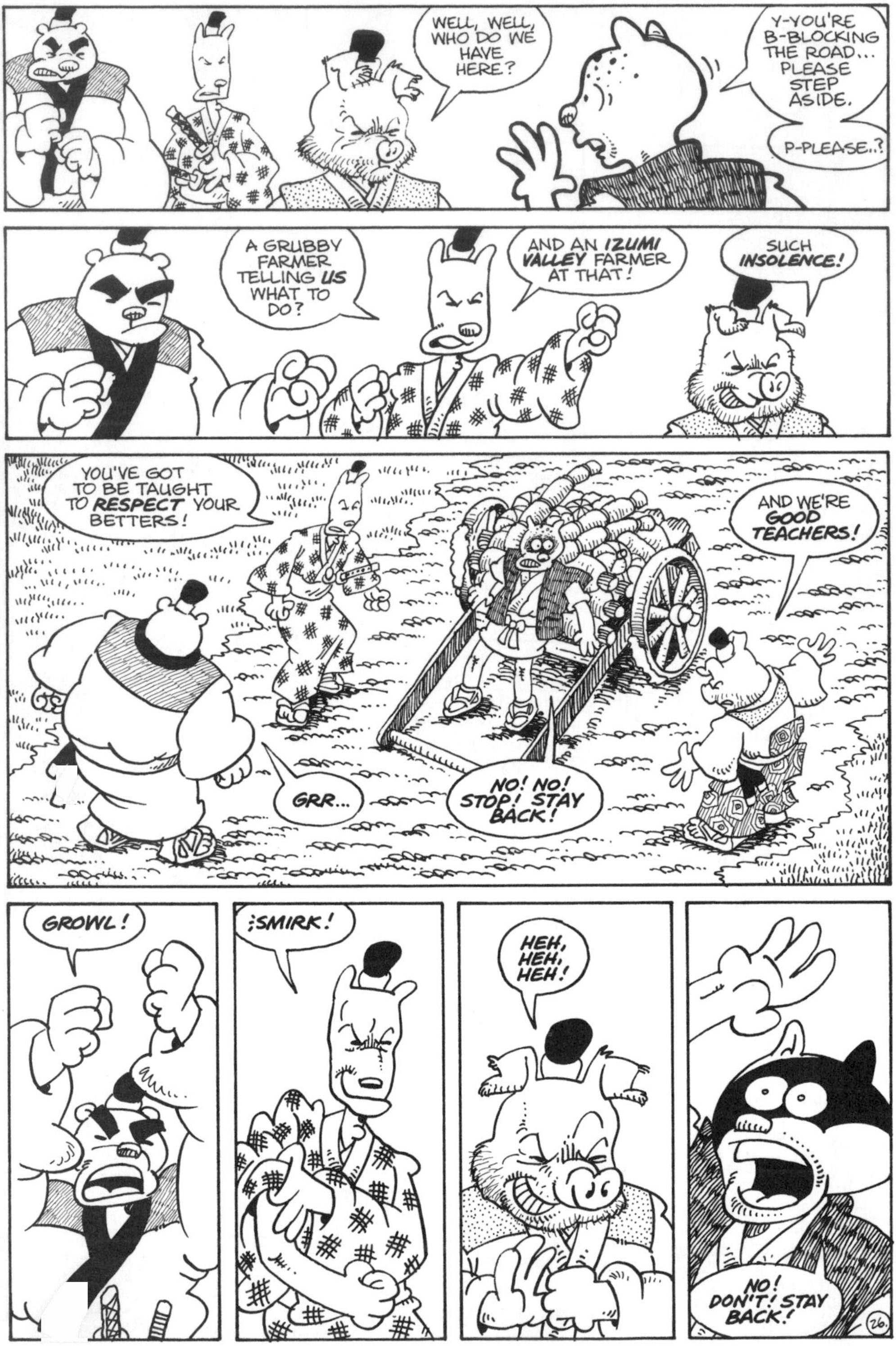

WELL, WELL, WHO DO WE HAVE HERE?
Y-YOU'RE B-BLOCKING THE ROAD... PLEASE STEP ASIDE.
P-PLEASE..?
A GRUBBY FARMER TELLING US WHAT TO DO?
AND AN IZUMI VALLEY FARMER AT THAT!
SUCH INSOLENCE!
YOU'VE GOT TO BE TAUGHT TO RESPECT YOUR BETTERS!
AND WE'RE GOOD TEACHERS!
GRR...
NO! NO! STOP! STAY BACK!
GROWL!
¡SMIRK!
HEH, HEH, HEH!
NO! DON'T! STAY BACK!
26.

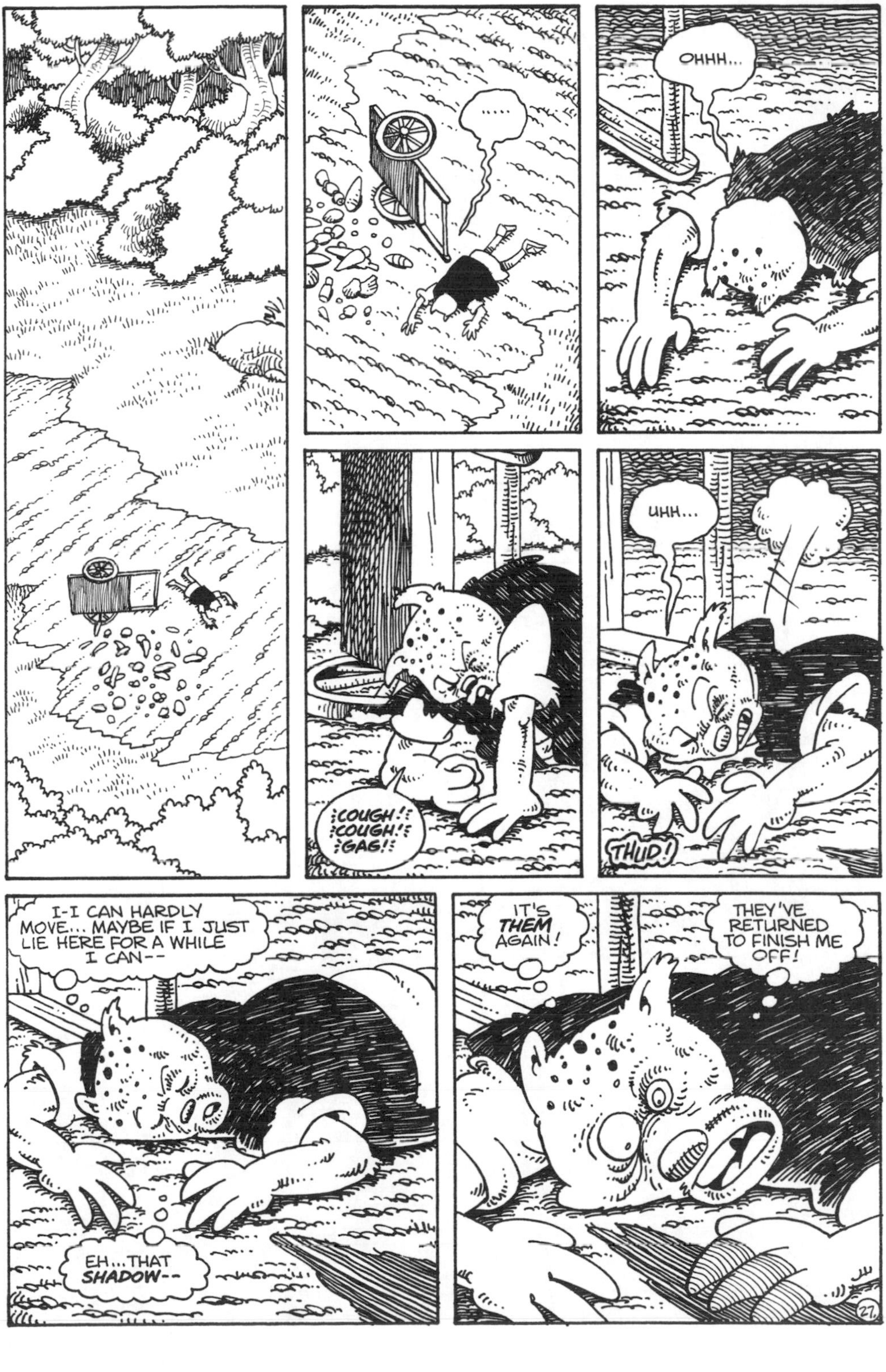
.....
OHHH...
:COUGH! :COUGH! :GAG!
UHH...
THUD!
I-I CAN HARDLY MOVE... MAYBE IF I JUST LIE HERE FOR A WHILE I CAN--
EH...THAT SHADOW--
IT'S THEM AGAIN!
THEY'VE RETURNED TO FINISH ME OFF!
27.

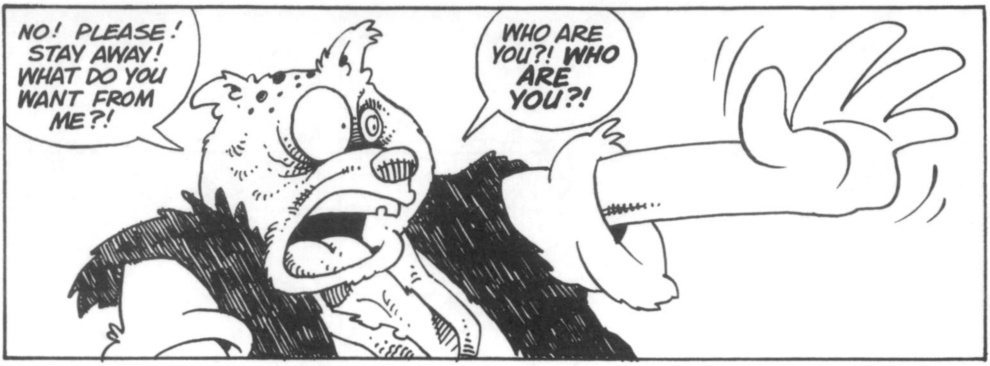
NO! PLEASE! STAY AWAY! WHAT DO YOU WANT FROM ME?!
WHO ARE YOU?! WHO ARE YOU?!

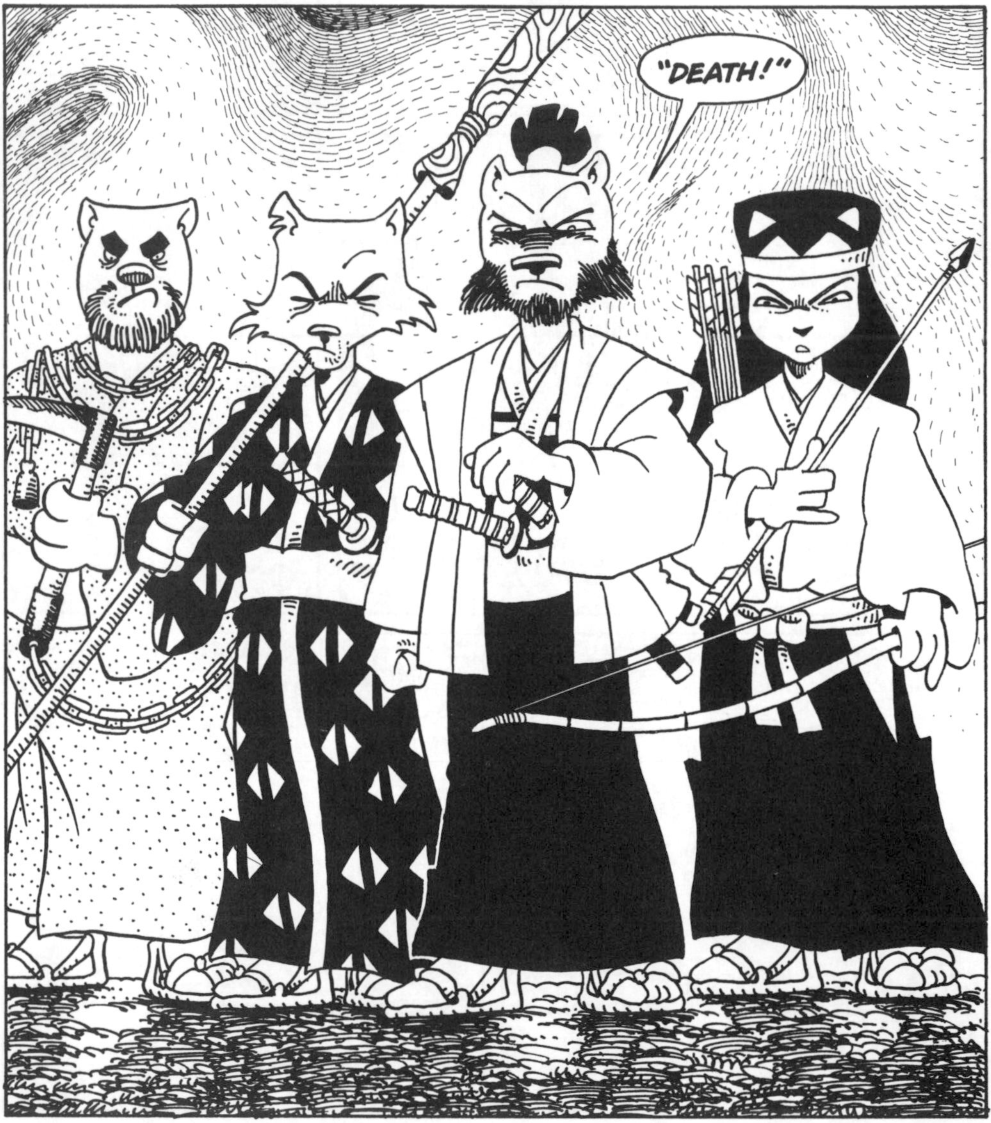
"DEATH!"

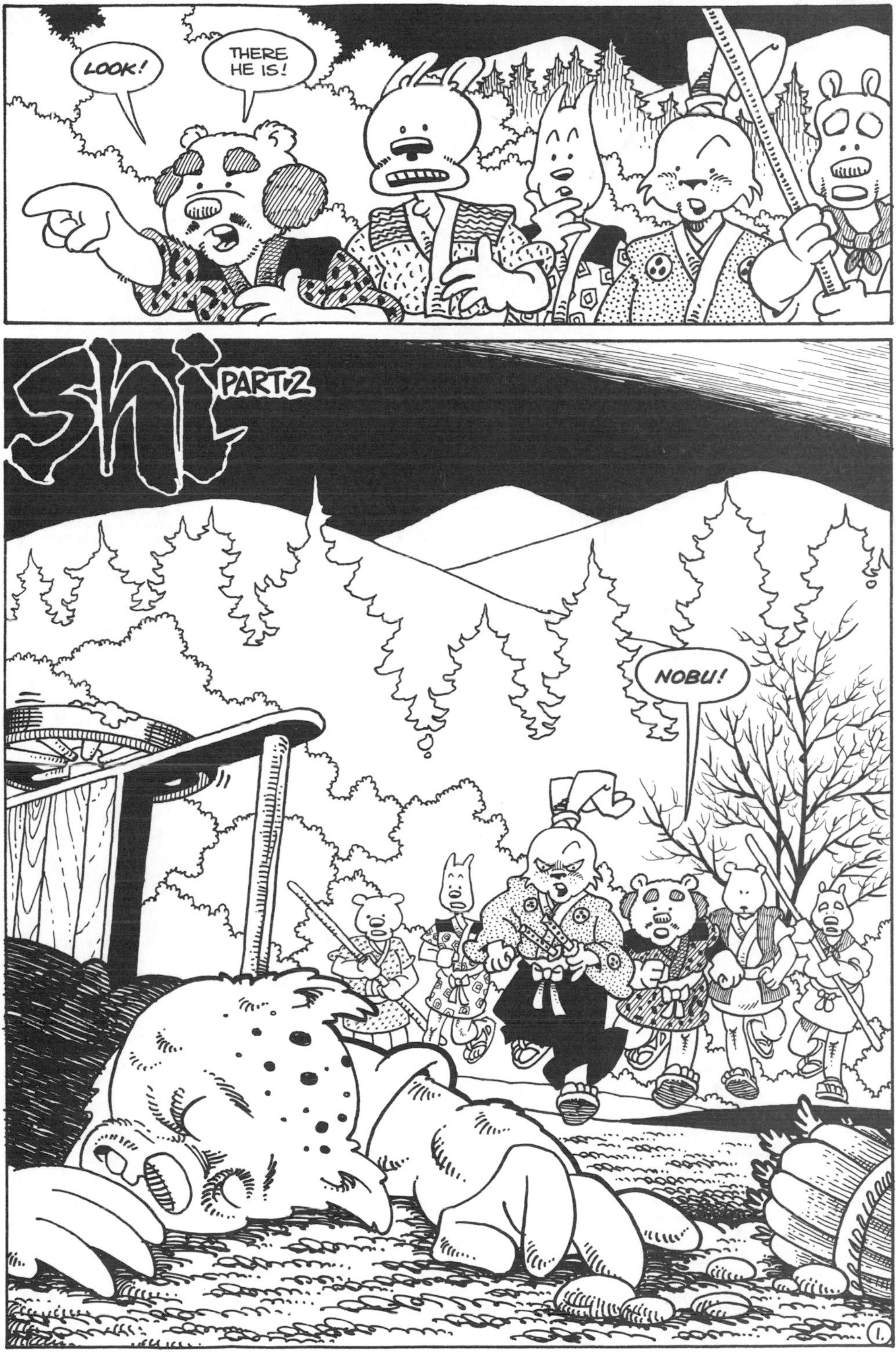
LOOK!
THERE HE IS!
Shi PART 2
NOBU!
1.

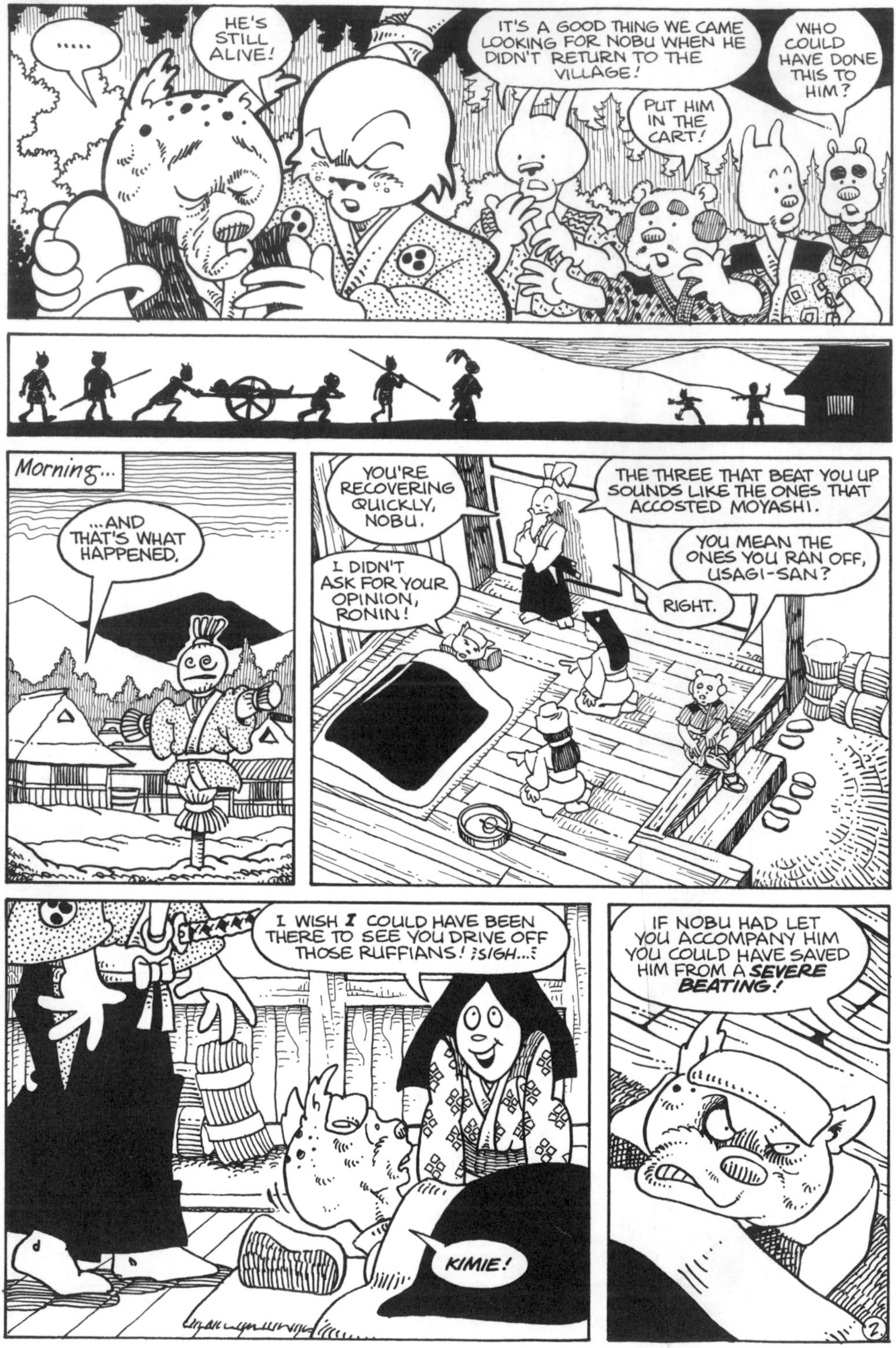
.....
HE'S STILL ALIVE!
IT'S A GOOD THING WE CAME LOOKING FOR NOBU WHEN HE DIDN'T RETURN TO THE VILLAGE!
WHO COULD HAVE DONE THIS TO HIM?
PUT HIM IN THE CART!
Morning...
...AND THAT'S WHAT HAPPENED.
YOU'RE RECOVERING QUICKLY, NOBU.
THE THREE THAT BEAT YOU UP SOUNDS LIKE THE ONES THAT ACCOSTED MOYASHI.
I DIDN'T ASK FOR YOUR OPINION, RONIN!
YOU MEAN THE ONES YOU RAN OFF, USAGI-SAN?
RIGHT.
I WISH I COULD HAVE BEEN THERE TO SEE YOU DRIVE OFF THOSE RUFFIANS! SIGH...
KIMIE!
IF NOBU HAD LET YOU ACCOMPANY HIM YOU COULD HAVE SAVED HIM FROM A SEVERE BEATING!
2.

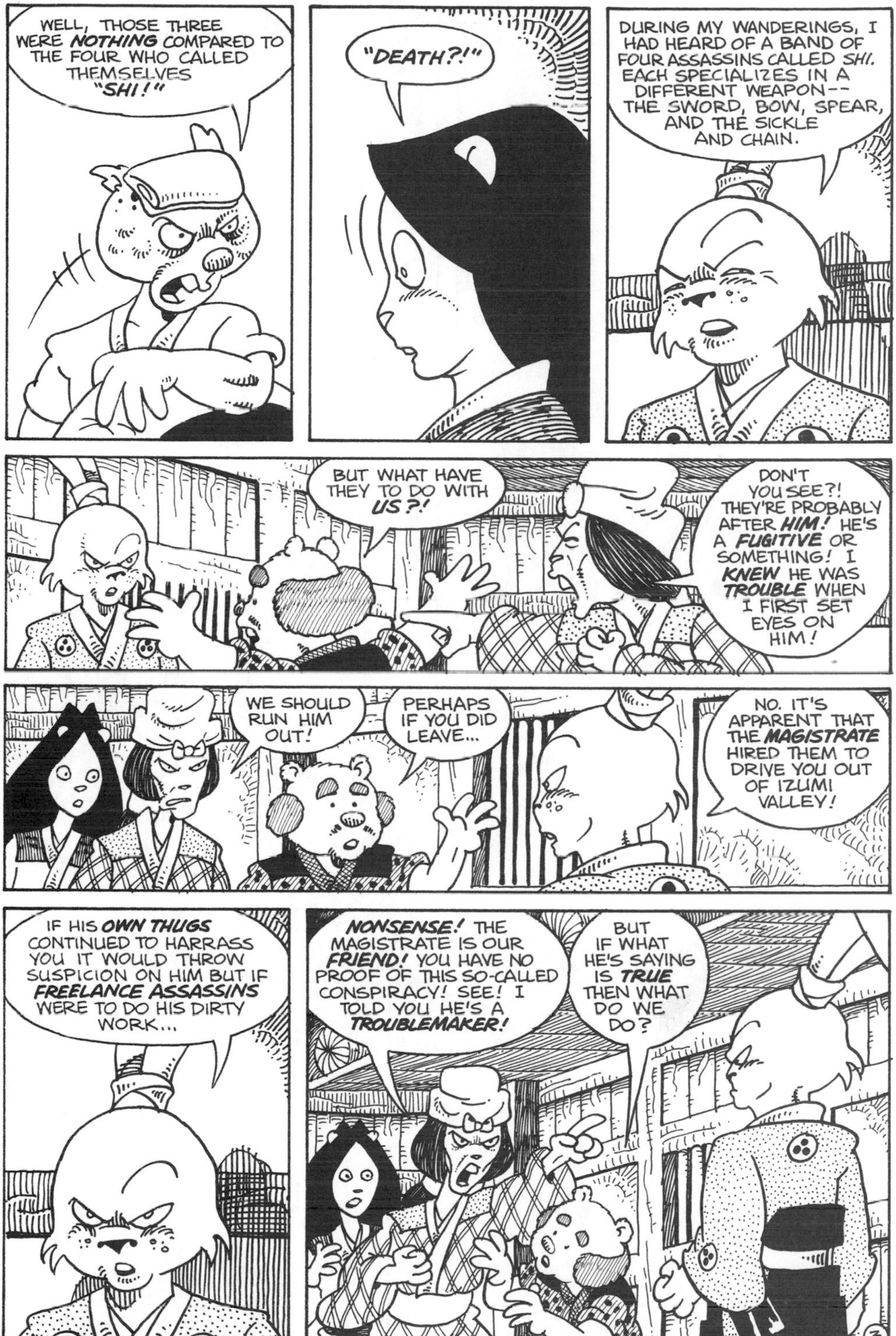
WELL, THOSE THREE WERE NOTHING COMPARED TO THE FOUR WHO CALLED THEMSELVES "SHI!"
"DEATH?!"
DURING MY WANDERINGS, I HAD HEARD OF A BAND OF FOUR ASSASSINS CALLED SHI. EACH SPECIALIZES IN A DIFFERENT WEAPON-- THE SWORD, BOW, SPEAR, AND THE SICKLE AND CHAIN.
BUT WHAT HAVE THEY TO DO WITH US?!
DON'T YOU SEE?! THEY'RE PROBABLY AFTER HIM! HE'S A FUGITIVE OR SOMETHING! I KNEW HE WAS TROUBLE WHEN I FIRST SET EYES ON HIM!
WE SHOULD RUN HIM OUT!
PERHAPS IF YOU DID LEAVE...
NO. IT'S APPARENT THAT THE MAGISTRATE HIRED THEM TO DRIVE YOU OUT OF IZUMI VALLEY!
IF HIS OWN THUGS CONTINUED TO HARRASS YOU IT WOULD THROW SUSPICION ON HIM BUT IF FREELANCE ASSASSINS WERE TO DO HIS DIRTY WORK...
NONSENSE! THE MAGISTRATE IS OUR FRIEND! YOU HAVE NO PROOF OF THIS SO-CALLED CONSPIRACY! SEE! I TOLD YOU HE'S A TROUBLEMAKER!
BUT IF WHAT HE'S SAYING IS TRUE THEN WHAT DO WE DO?
3

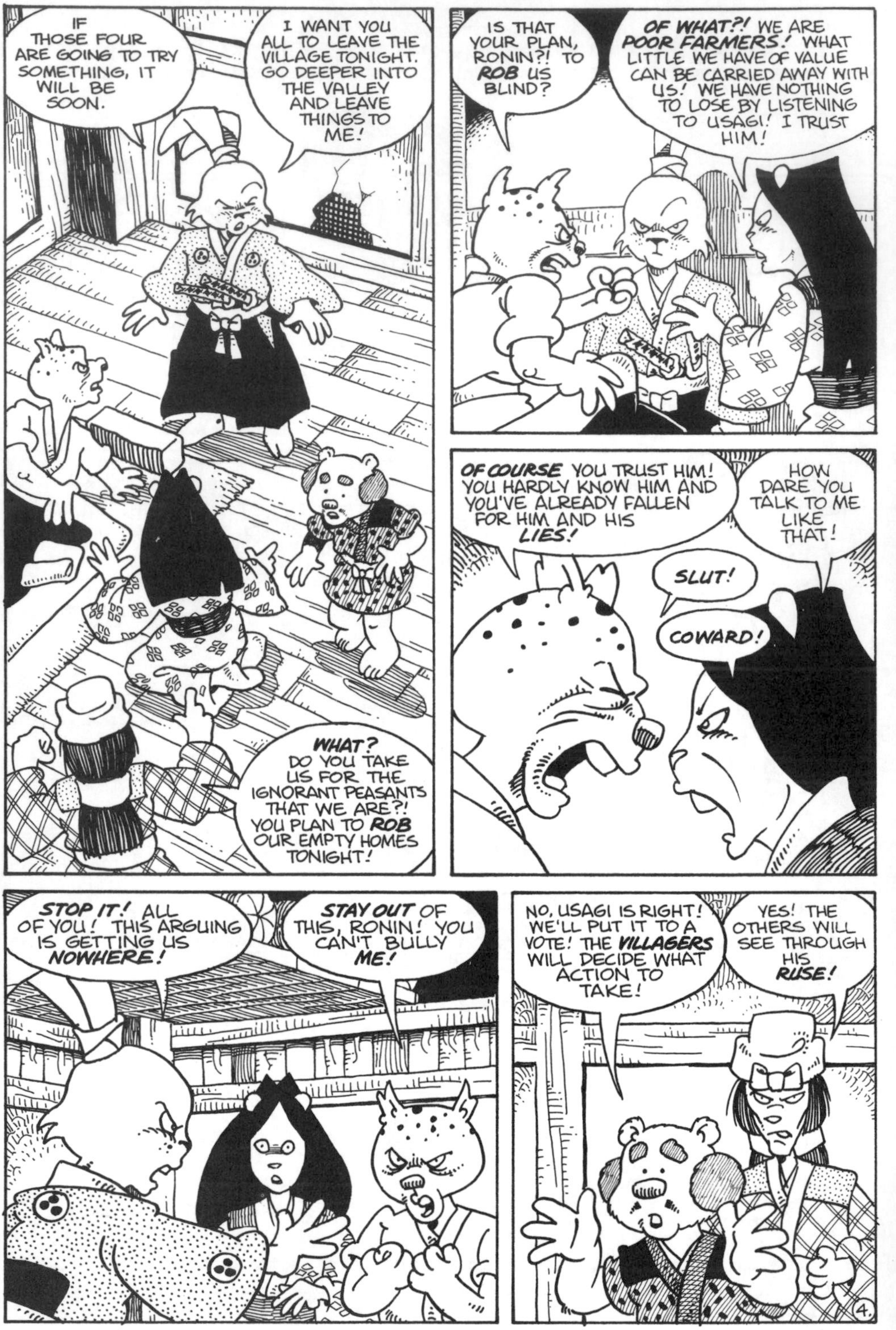
IF THOSE FOUR ARE GOING TO TRY SOMETHING, IT WILL BE SOON.
I WANT YOU ALL TO LEAVE THE VILLAGE TONIGHT. GO DEEPER INTO THE VALLEY AND LEAVE THINGS TO ME!
WHAT? DO YOU TAKE US FOR THE IGNORANT PEASANTS THAT WE ARE?! YOU PLAN TO ROB OUR EMPTY HOMES TONIGHT!
IS THAT YOUR PLAN, RONIN?! TO ROB US BLIND?
OF WHAT?! WE ARE POOR FARMERS! WHAT LITTLE WE HAVE OF VALUE CAN BE CARRIED AWAY WITH US! WE HAVE NOTHING TO LOSE BY LISTENING TO USAGI! I TRUST HIM!
OF COURSE YOU TRUST HIM! YOU HARDLY KNOW HIM AND YOU'VE ALREADY FALLEN FOR HIM AND HIS LIES!
HOW DARE YOU TALK TO ME LIKE THAT!
SLUT!
COWARD!
STOP IT! ALL OF YOU! THIS ARGUING IS GETTING US NOWHERE!
STAY OUT OF THIS, RONIN! YOU CAN'T BULLY ME!
NO, USAGI IS RIGHT! WE'LL PUT IT TO A VOTE! THE VILLAGERS WILL DECIDE WHAT ACTION TO TAKE!
YES! THE OTHERS WILL SEE THROUGH HIS RUSE!
4.

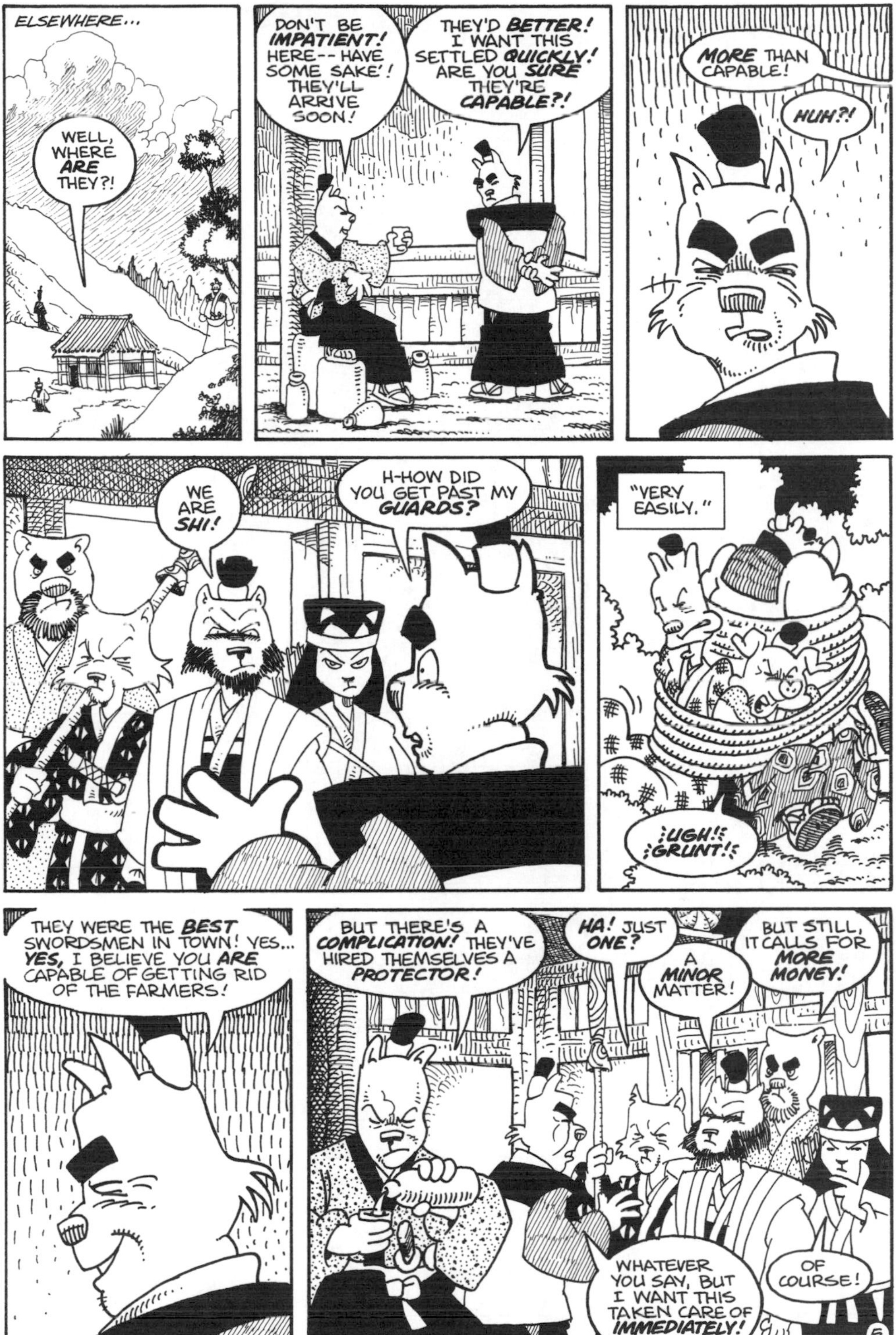
ELSEWHERE...
WELL, WHERE ARE THEY?!
DON'T BE IMPATIENT! HERE-- HAVE SOME SAKE'! THEY'LL ARRIVE SOON!
THEY'D BETTER! I WANT THIS SETTLED QUICKLY! ARE YOU SURE THEY'RE CAPABLE?!
MORE THAN CAPABLE!
HUH?!
WE ARE SHI!
H-HOW DID YOU GET PAST MY GUARDS?
"VERY EASILY."
UGH! GRUNT!
THEY WERE THE BEST SWORDSMEN IN TOWN! YES... YES, I BELIEVE YOU ARE CAPABLE OF GETTING RID OF THE FARMERS!
BUT THERE'S A COMPLICATION! THEY'VE HIRED THEMSELVES A PROTECTOR!
HA! JUST ONE?
A MINOR MATTER!
BUT STILL, IT CALLS FOR MORE MONEY!
WHATEVER YOU SAY, BUT I WANT THIS TAKEN CARE OF IMMEDIATELY!
OF COURSE!
5.

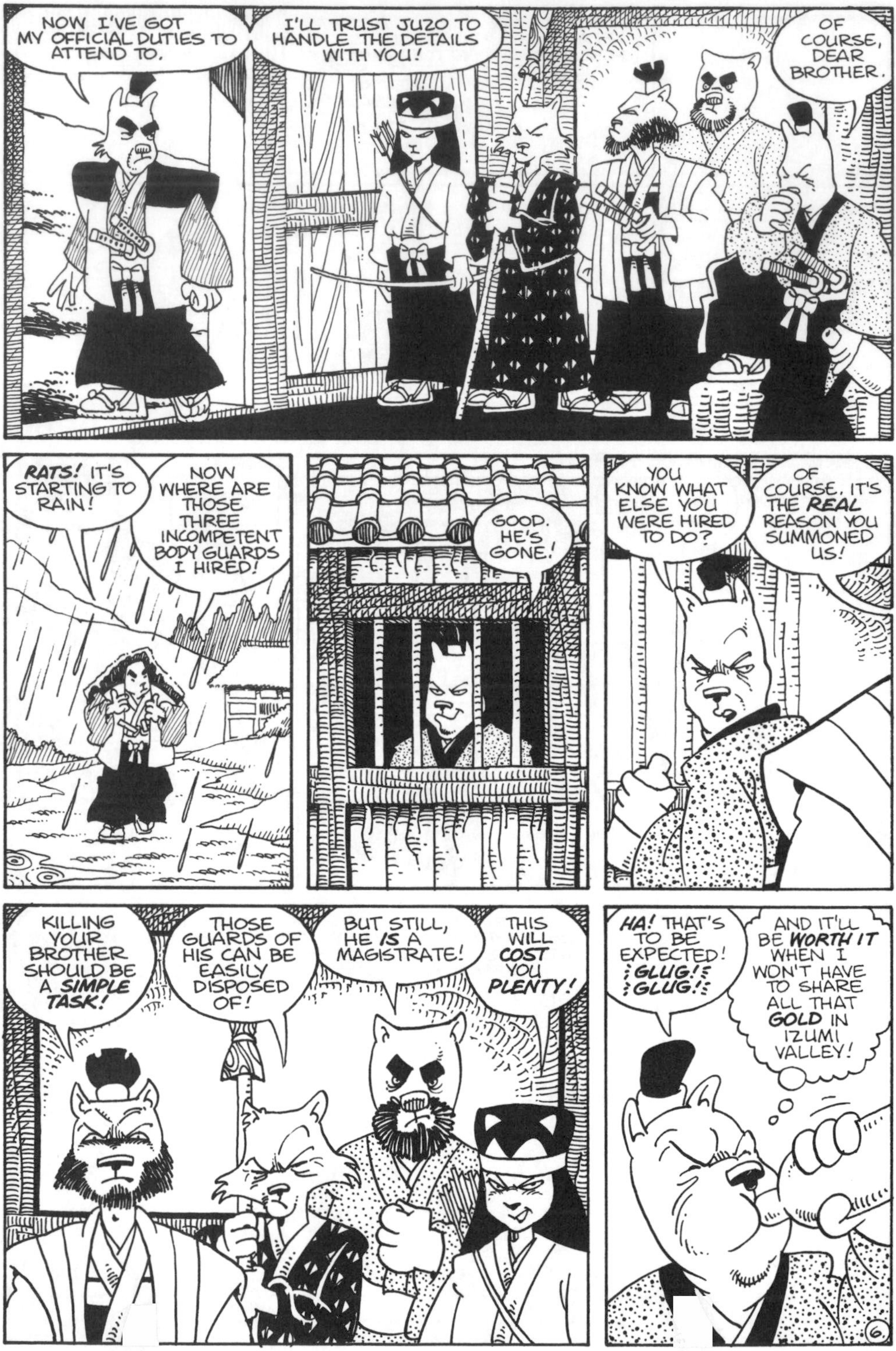
NOW I'VE GOT MY OFFICIAL DUTIES TO ATTEND TO.
I'LL TRUST JUZO TO HANDLE THE DETAILS WITH YOU!
OF COURSE, DEAR BROTHER.
RATS! IT'S STARTING TO RAIN!
NOW WHERE ARE THOSE THREE INCOMPETENT BODY GUARDS I HIRED!
GOOD. HE'S GONE!
YOU KNOW WHAT ELSE YOU WERE HIRED TO DO?
OF COURSE. IT'S THE REAL REASON YOU SUMMONED US!
KILLING YOUR BROTHER SHOULD BE A SIMPLE TASK!
THOSE GUARDS OF HIS CAN BE EASILY DISPOSED OF!
BUT STILL, HE IS A MAGISTRATE!
THIS WILL COST YOU PLENTY!
HA! THAT'S TO BE EXPECTED! GLUG! GLUG!
AND IT'LL BE WORTH IT WHEN I WON'T HAVE TO SHARE ALL THAT GOLD IN IZUMI VALLEY!
6.

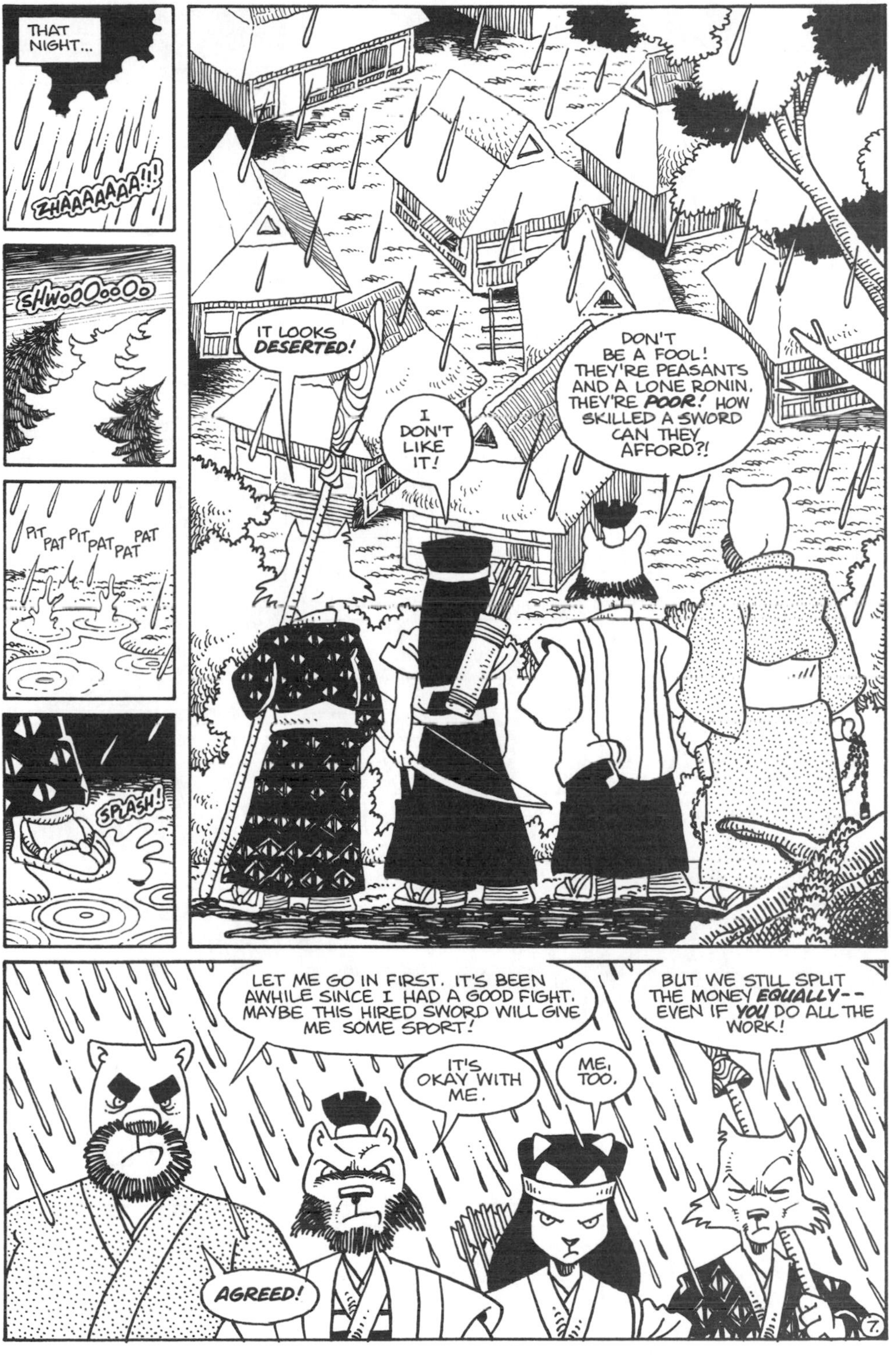
THAT NIGHT...
ZHAAAAAAA!!!
SHWoOOoOo
PIT PAT PIT PAT PAT PAT
SPLASH!
IT LOOKS DESERTED!
I DON'T LIKE IT!
DON'T BE A FOOL! THEY'RE PEASANTS AND A LONE RONIN. THEY'RE POOR! HOW SKILLED A SWORD CAN THEY AFFORD?!
LET ME GO IN FIRST. IT'S BEEN AWHILE SINCE I HAD A GOOD FIGHT. MAYBE THIS HIRED SWORD WILL GIVE ME SOME SPORT!
IT'S OKAY WITH ME.
ME, TOO.
BUT WE STILL SPLIT THE MONEY EQUALLY-- EVEN IF YOU DO ALL THE WORK!
AGREED!
7

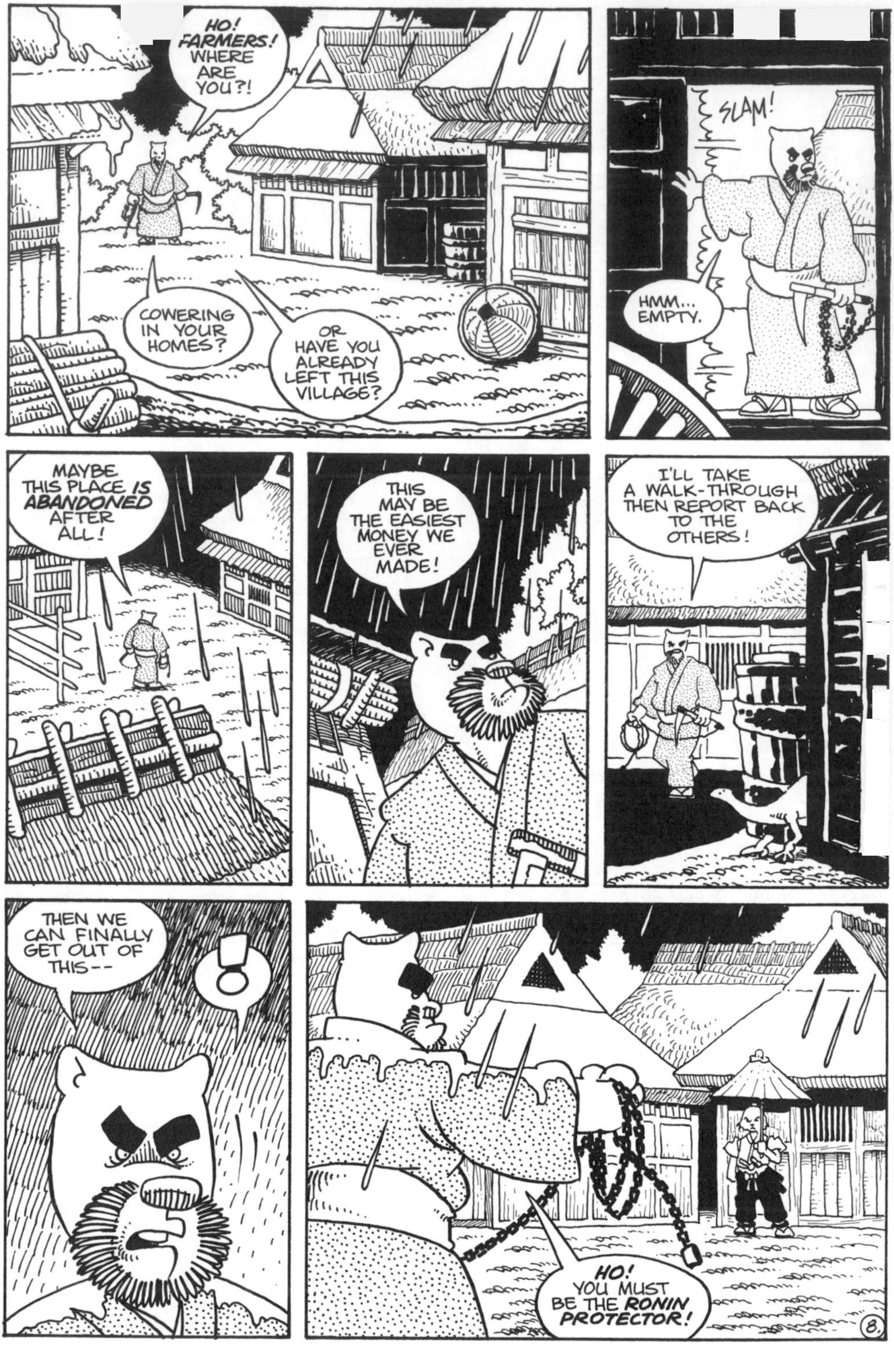
HO! FARMERS! WHERE ARE YOU?!
COWERING IN YOUR HOMES?
OR HAVE YOU ALREADY LEFT THIS VILLAGE?
SLAM!
HMM... EMPTY.
MAYBE THIS PLACE IS ABANDONED AFTER ALL!
THIS MAY BE THE EASIEST MONEY WE EVER MADE!
I'LL TAKE A WALK-THROUGH THEN REPORT BACK TO THE OTHERS!
THEN WE CAN FINALLY GET OUT OF THIS--
!
HO! YOU MUST BE THE RONIN PROTECTOR!
8.

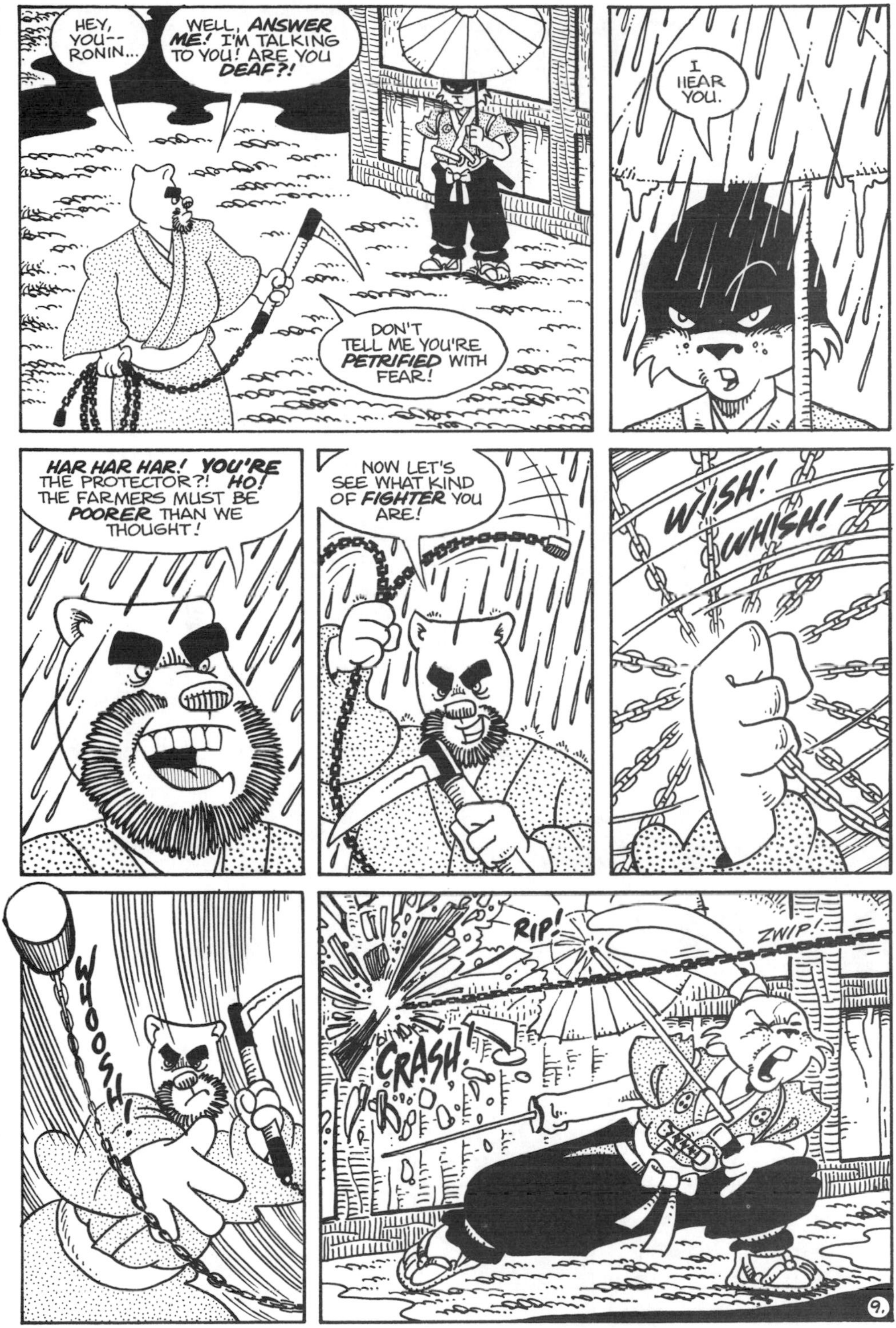
HEY, YOU-- RONIN...
WELL, ANSWER ME! I'M TALKING TO YOU! ARE YOU DEAF?!
DON'T TELL ME YOU'RE PETRIFIED WITH FEAR!
I HEAR YOU.
HAR HAR HAR! YOU'RE THE PROTECTOR?! HO! THE FARMERS MUST BE POORER THAN WE THOUGHT!
NOW LET'S SEE WHAT KIND OF FIGHTER YOU ARE!
WHISH!
WHISH!
WHOOSH!
RIP!
ZWIP!
CRASH!
9.

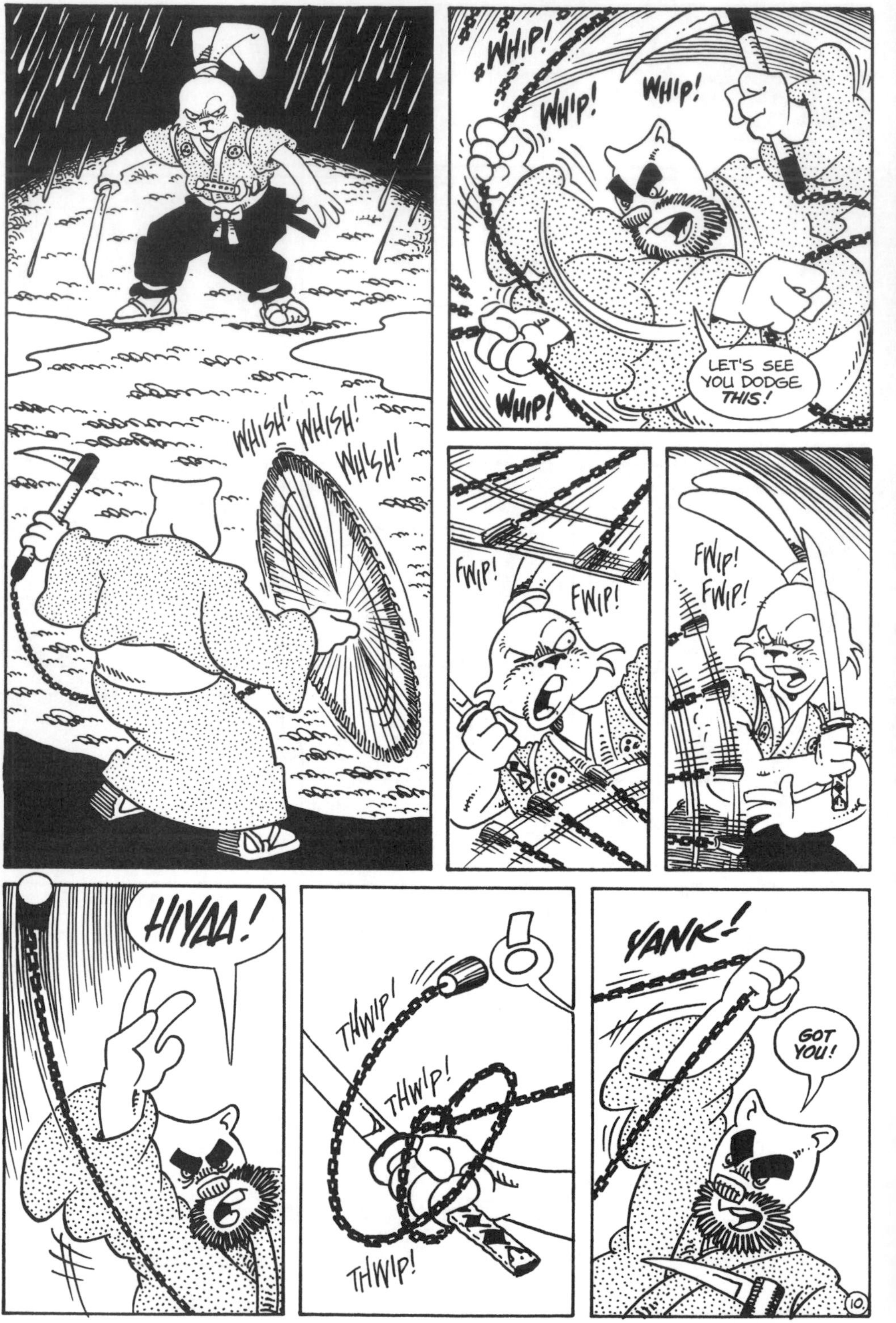
WHISH! WHISH! WHISH!
WHIP! WHIP! WHIP! WHIP!
LET'S SEE YOU DODGE THIS!
FWIP! FWIP!
FWIP! FWIP!
HIYAA!
THWIP! THWIP! THWIP!
!
YANK!
GOT YOU!
10

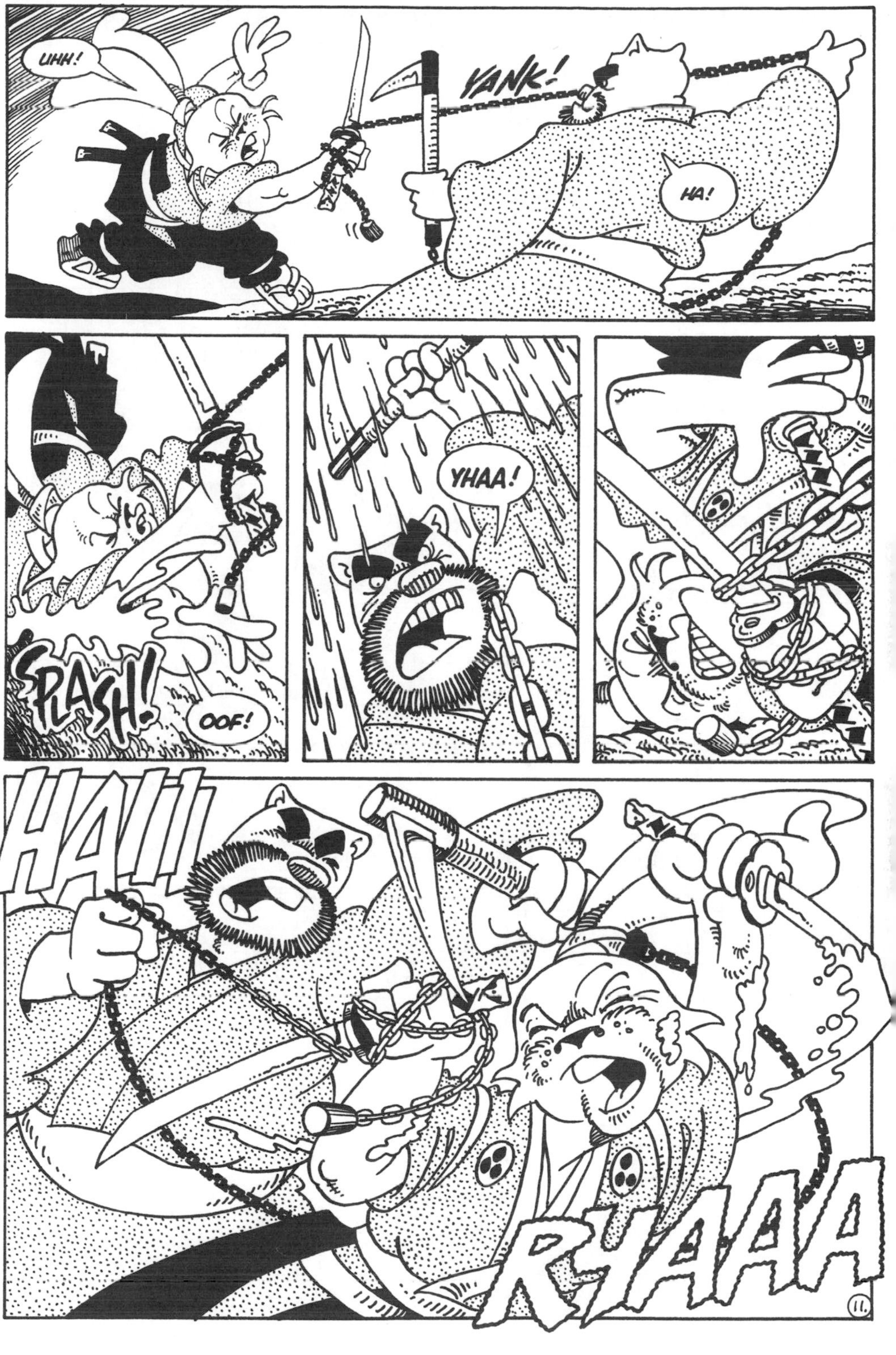
UHH!
YANK!
HA!
SPLASH!
OOF!
YHAA!
HAI!
RYAAA
11.

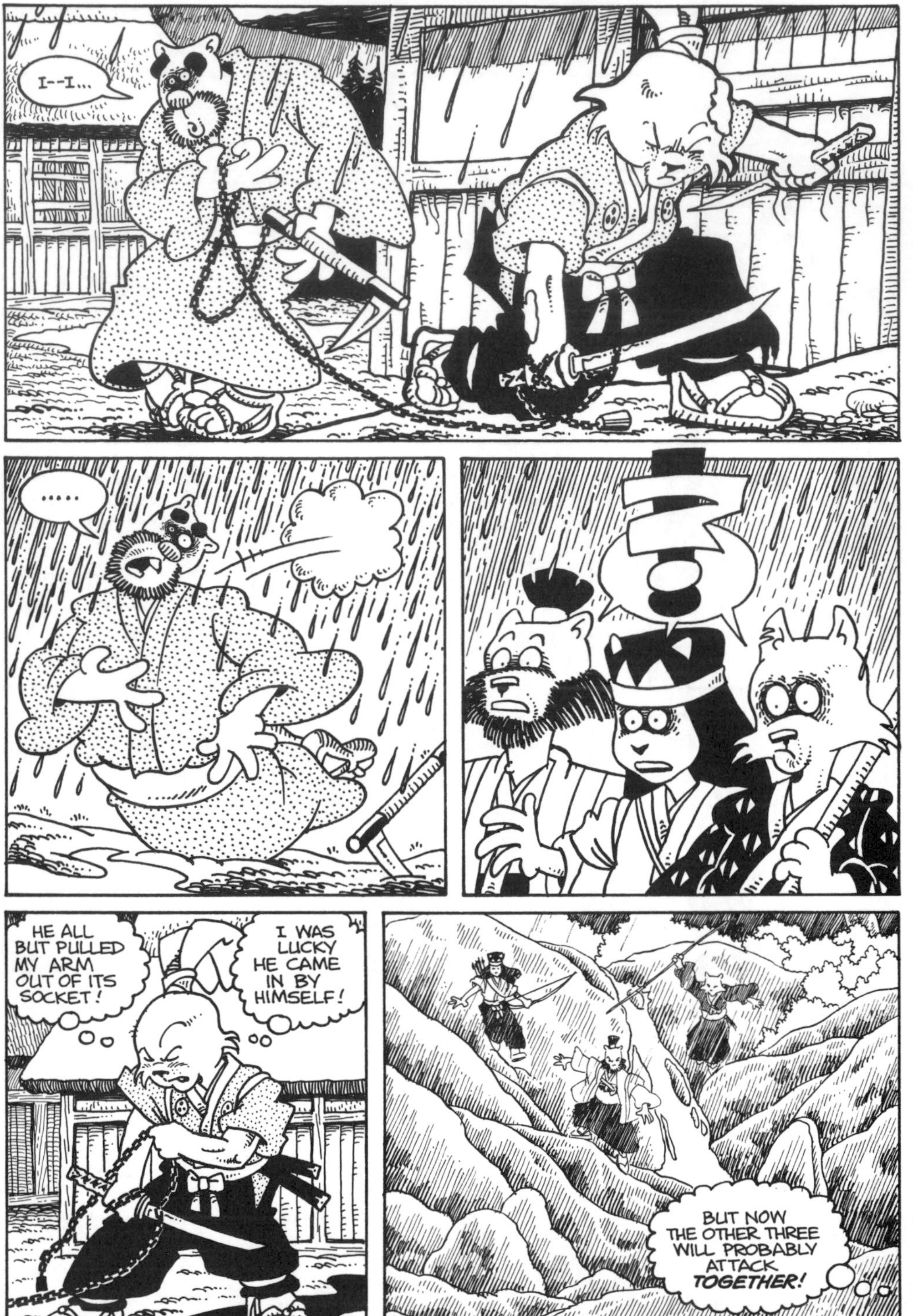
I--I...
.....
HE ALL BUT PULLED MY ARM OUT OF ITS SOCKET!
I WAS LUCKY HE CAME IN BY HIMSELF!
BUT NOW THE OTHER THREE WILL PROBABLY ATTACK *TOGETHER!*
12.

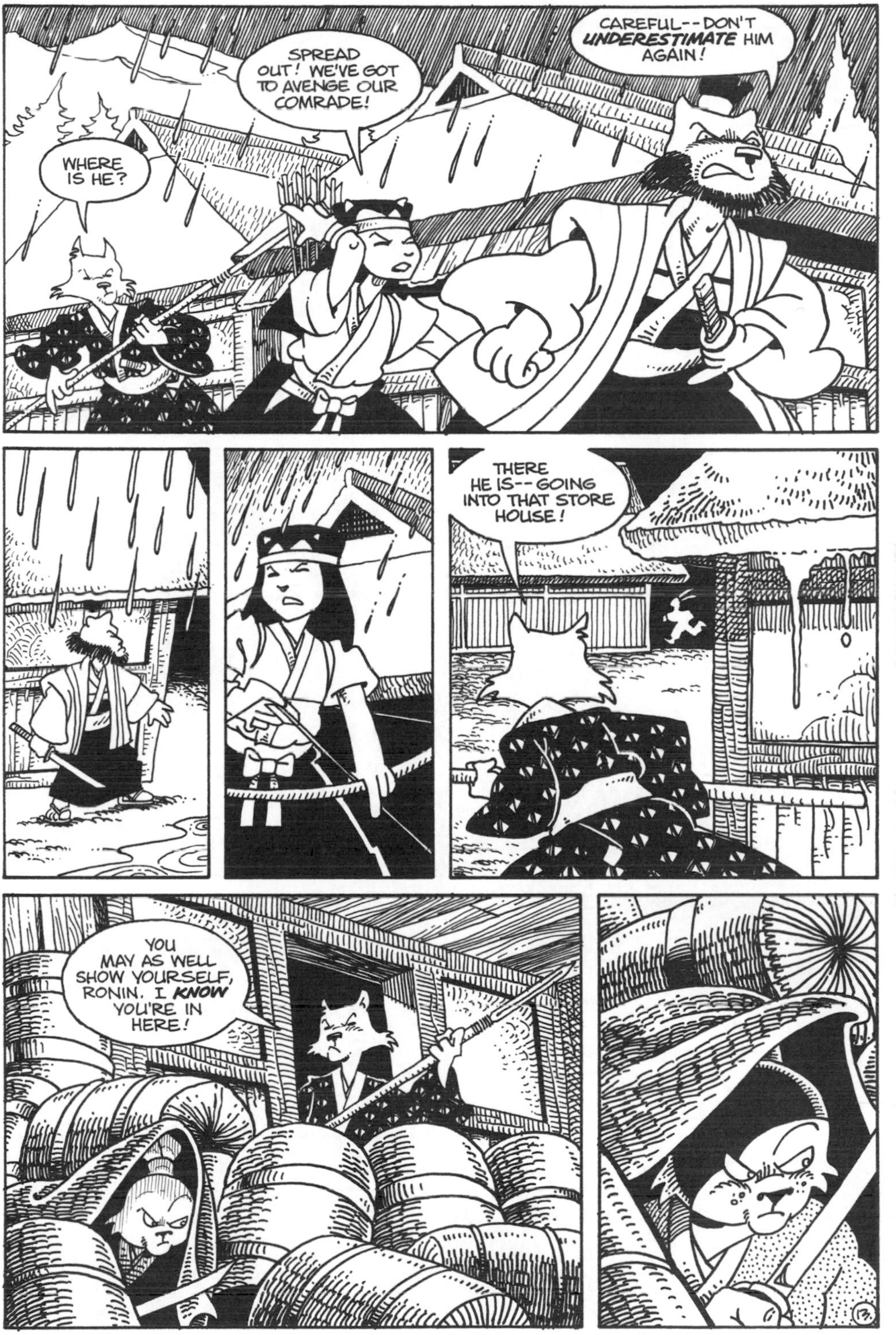
WHERE IS HE?
SPREAD OUT! WE'VE GOT TO AVENGE OUR COMRADE!
CAREFUL--DON'T **UNDERESTIMATE** HIM AGAIN!
THERE HE IS--GOING INTO THAT STORE HOUSE!
YOU MAY AS WELL SHOW YOURSELF, RONIN. I **KNOW** YOU'RE IN HERE!
13.

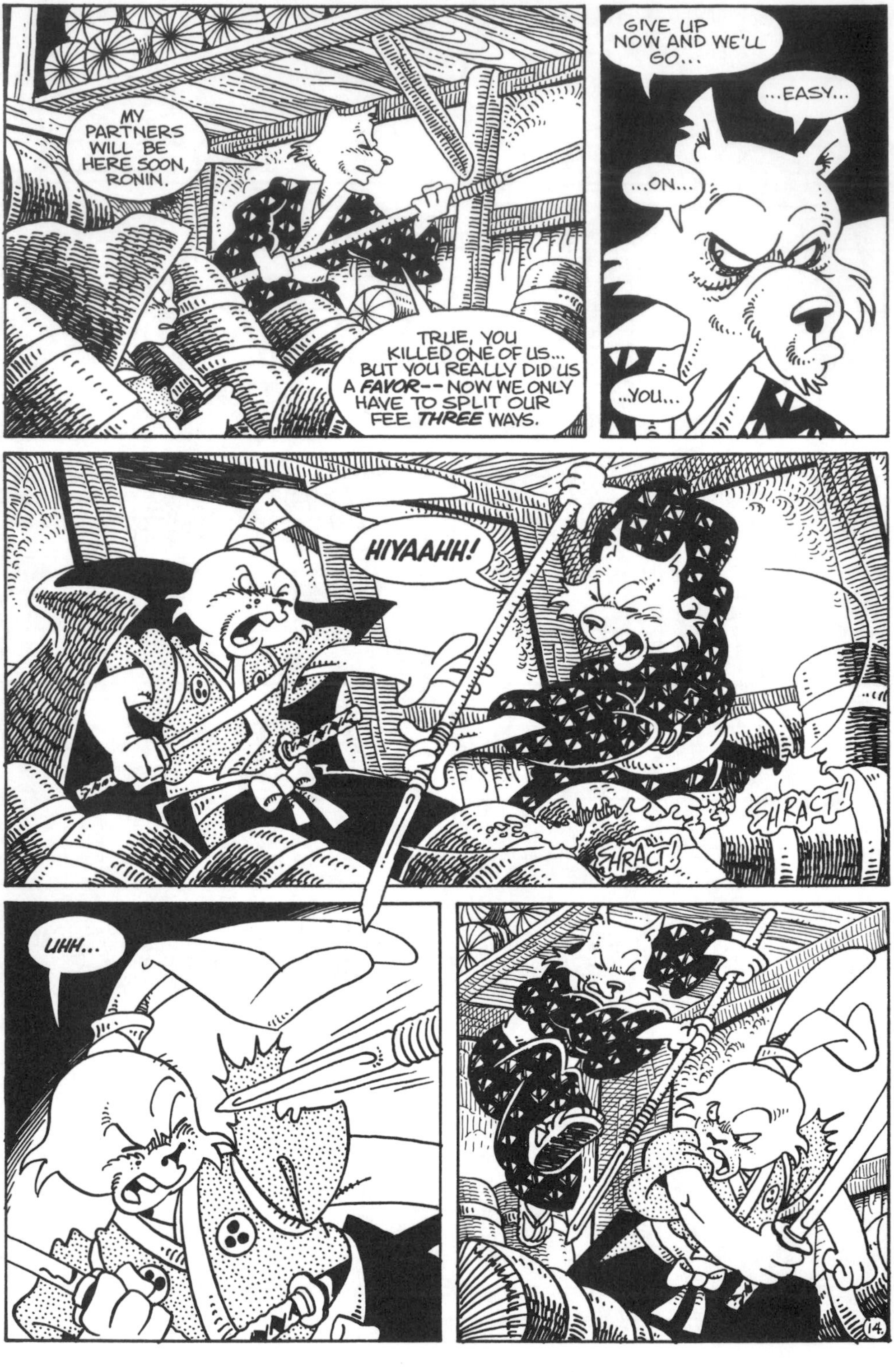
MY PARTNERS WILL BE HERE SOON, RONIN.
TRUE, YOU KILLED ONE OF US... BUT YOU REALLY DID US A **FAVOR**-- NOW WE ONLY HAVE TO SPLIT OUR FEE **THREE** WAYS.
GIVE UP NOW AND WE'LL GO...
...EASY...
...ON...
...YOU...
HIYAAHH!
SHRACT!
SHRACT!
UHH...
14.

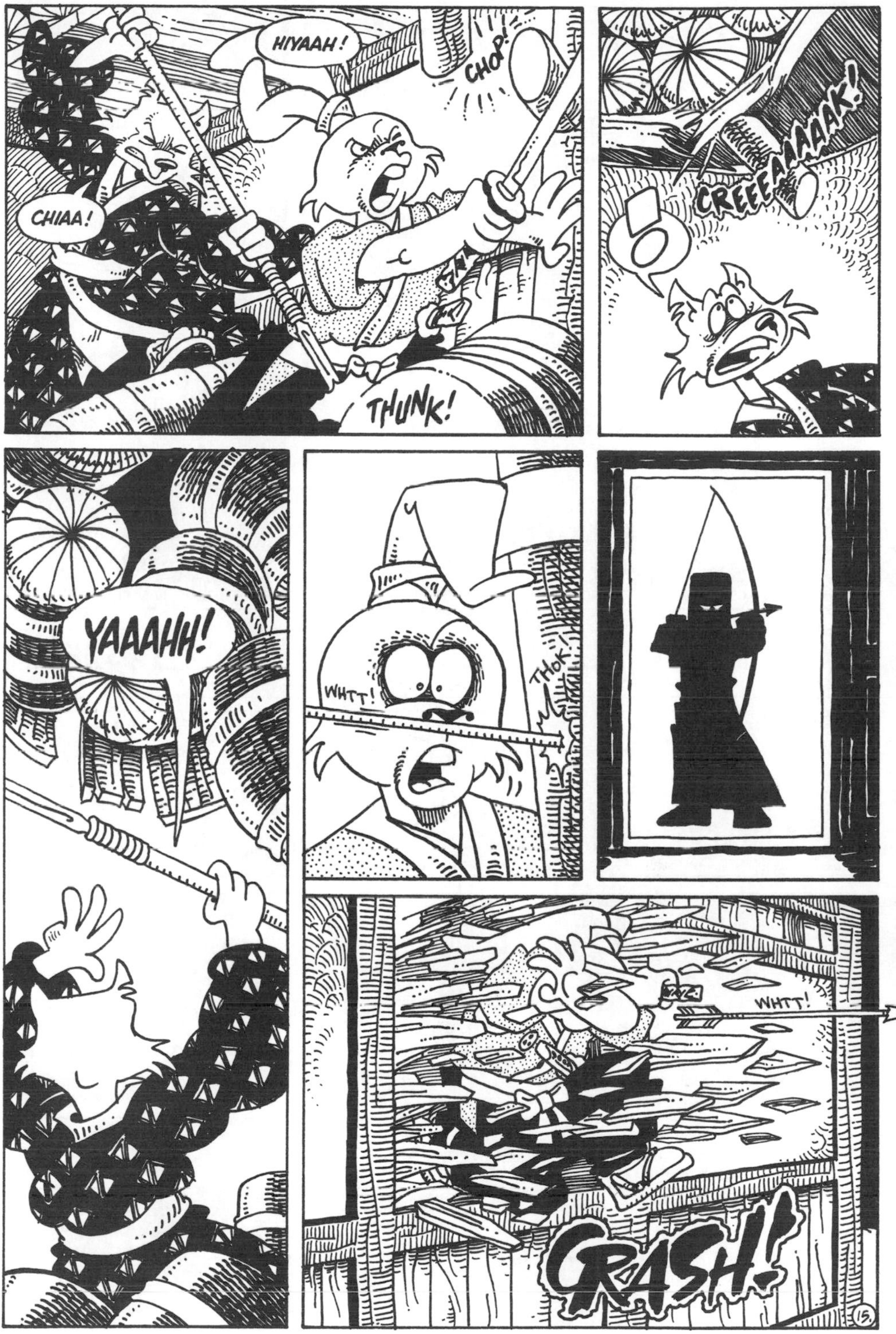
HIYAAH!
CHOP!
CHIAA!
THUNK!
CREEEAAAAAK!
YAAAHH!
WHTT!
THOK
WHTT!
CRASH!
15

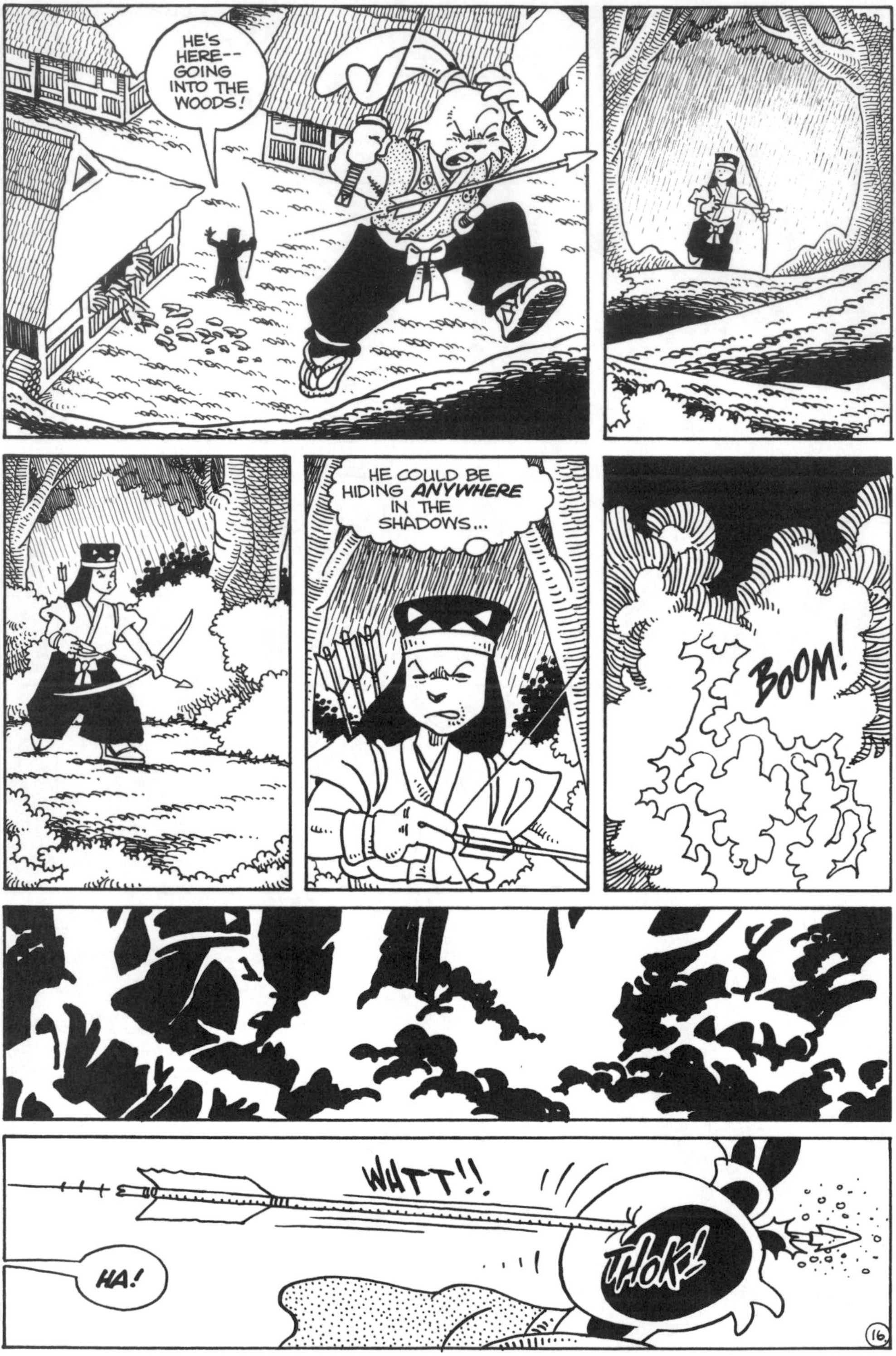
HE'S HERE-- GOING INTO THE WOODS!
HE COULD BE HIDING ANYWHERE IN THE SHADOWS...
BOOM!
WHTT!!
HA!
THOK!
16.

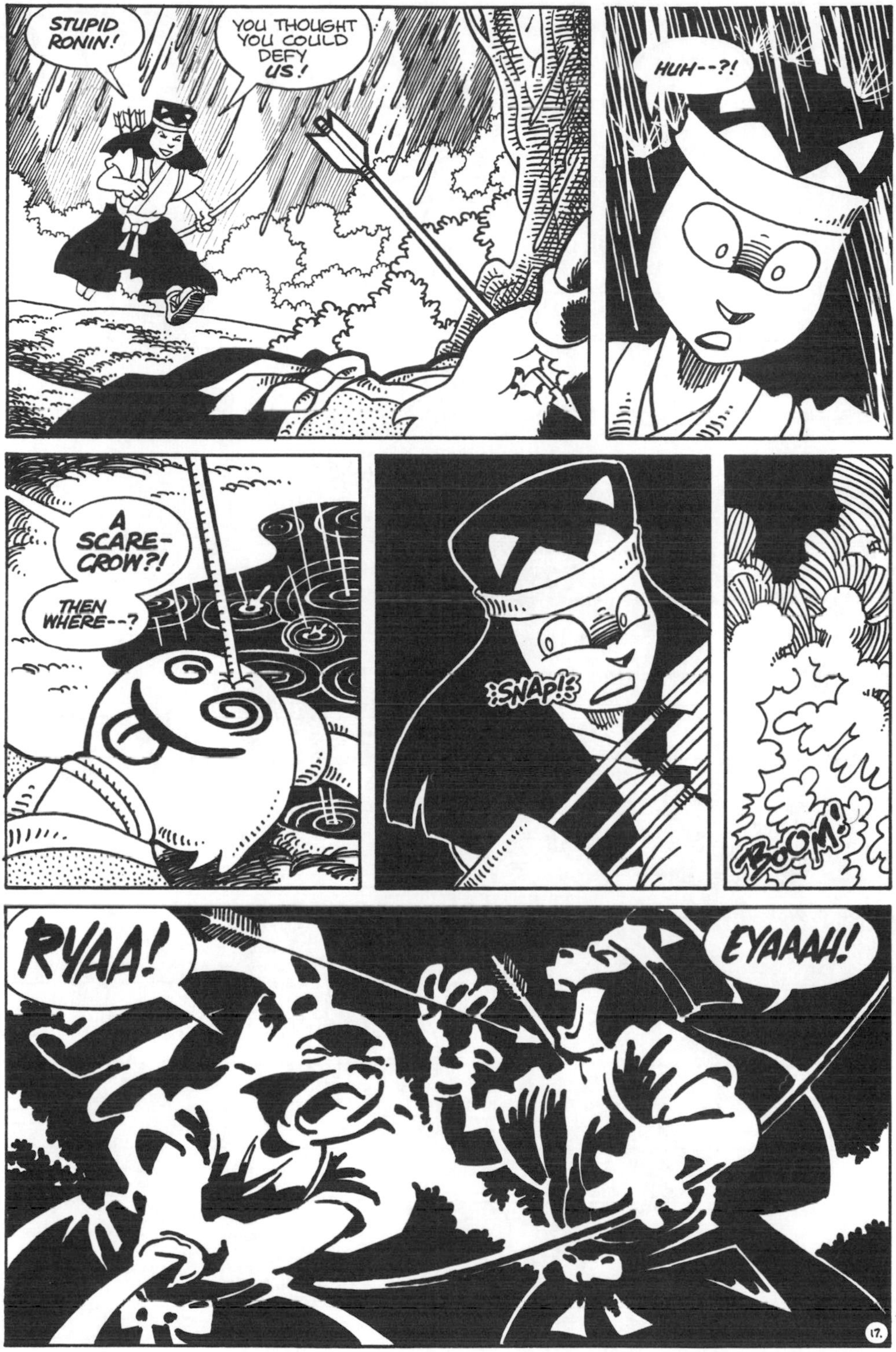
STUPID RONIN!
YOU THOUGHT YOU COULD DEFY US!
HUH--?!
A SCARE-CROW?!
THEN WHERE--?
SNAP!
BOOM!
RYAA!
EYAAAH!
17.

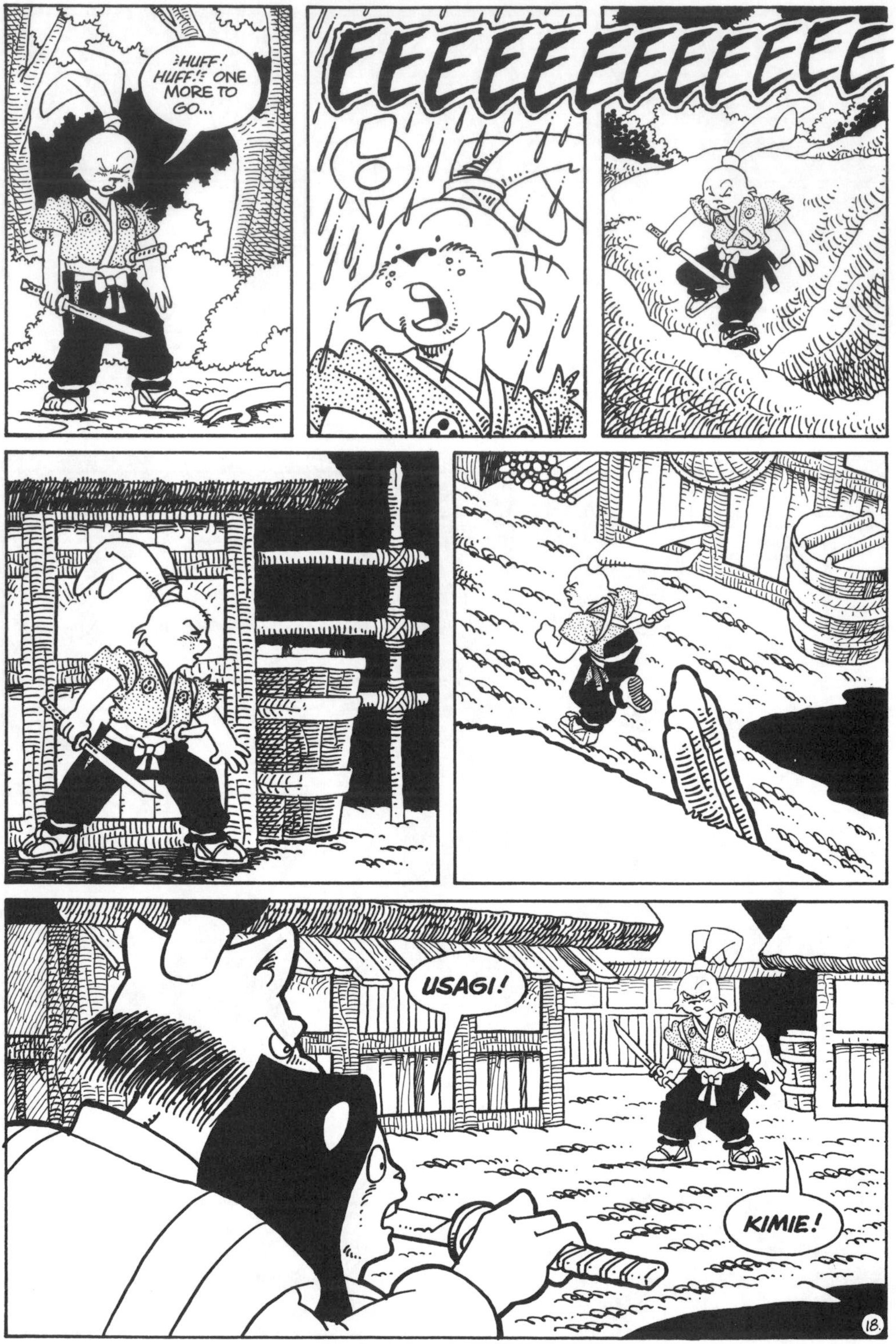

HUFF! HUFF! ONE MORE TO GO...
EEEEEEEEEEEEE
!
USAGI!
KIMIE!
18.

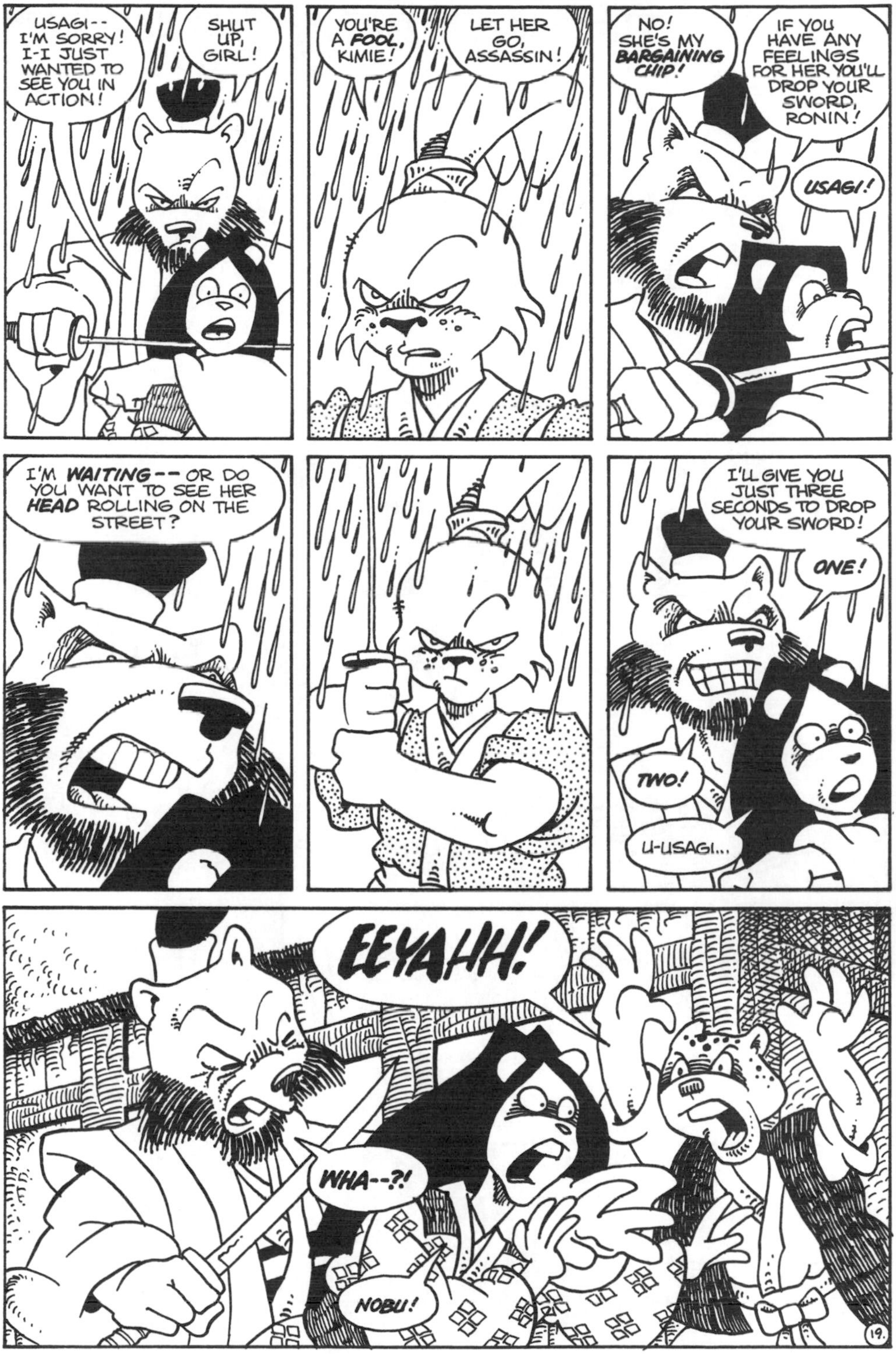
USAGI-- I'M SORRY! I-I JUST WANTED TO SEE YOU IN ACTION!
SHUT UP, GIRL!
YOU'RE A FOOL, KIMIE!
LET HER GO, ASSASSIN!
NO! SHE'S MY BARGAINING CHIP!
IF YOU HAVE ANY FEELINGS FOR HER YOU'LL DROP YOUR SWORD, RONIN!
USAGI!
I'M WAITING-- OR DO YOU WANT TO SEE HER HEAD ROLLING ON THE STREET?
I'LL GIVE YOU JUST THREE SECONDS TO DROP YOUR SWORD!
ONE!
TWO!
U-USAGI...
EEYAHH!
WHA--?!
NOBU!
19.

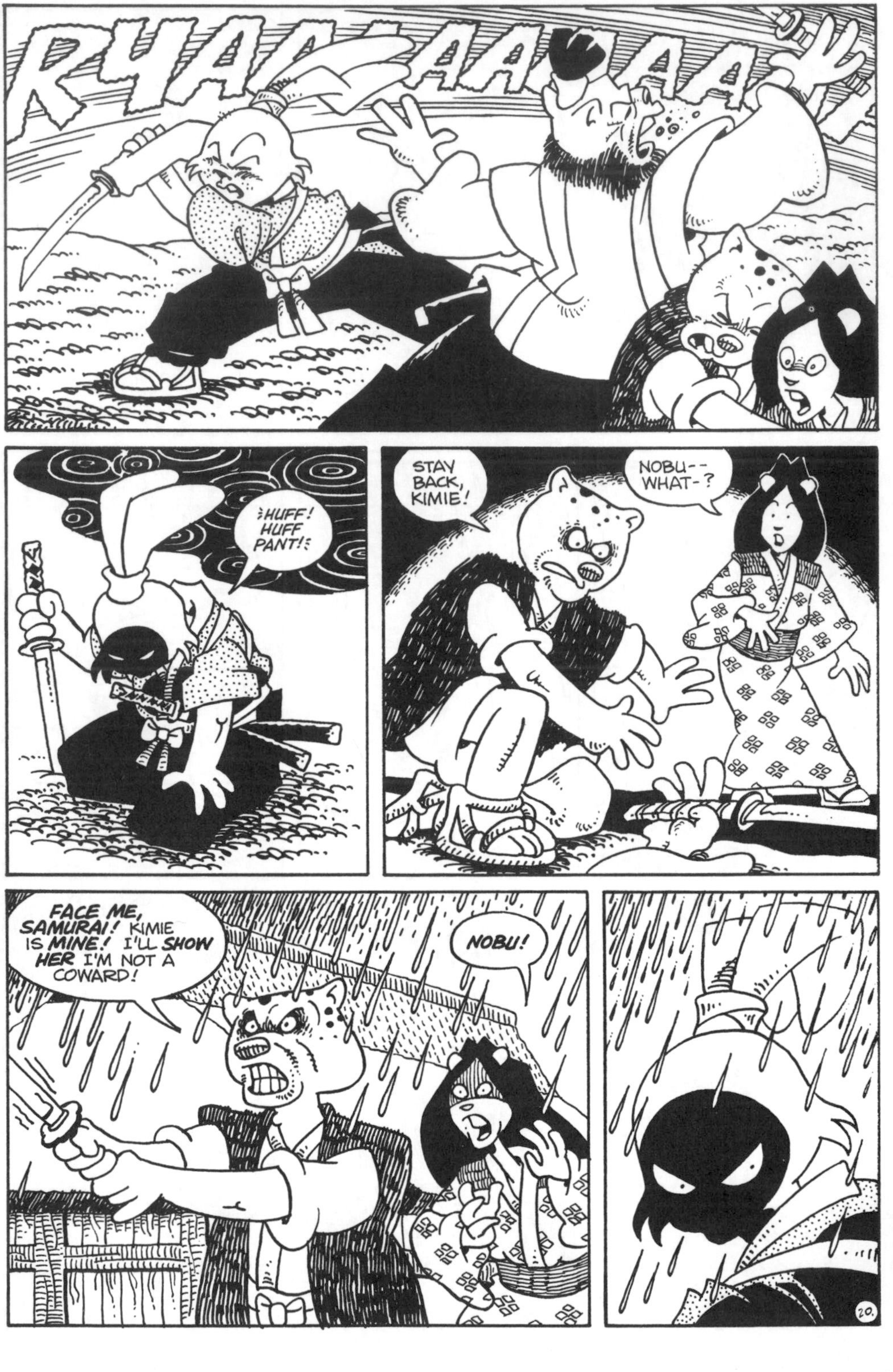
RYAAAAAAAAAAA
HUFF! HUFF PANT!
STAY BACK, KIMIE!
NOBU-- WHAT-?
FACE ME, SAMURAI! KIMIE IS MINE! I'LL SHOW HER I'M NOT A COWARD!
NOBU!
20.

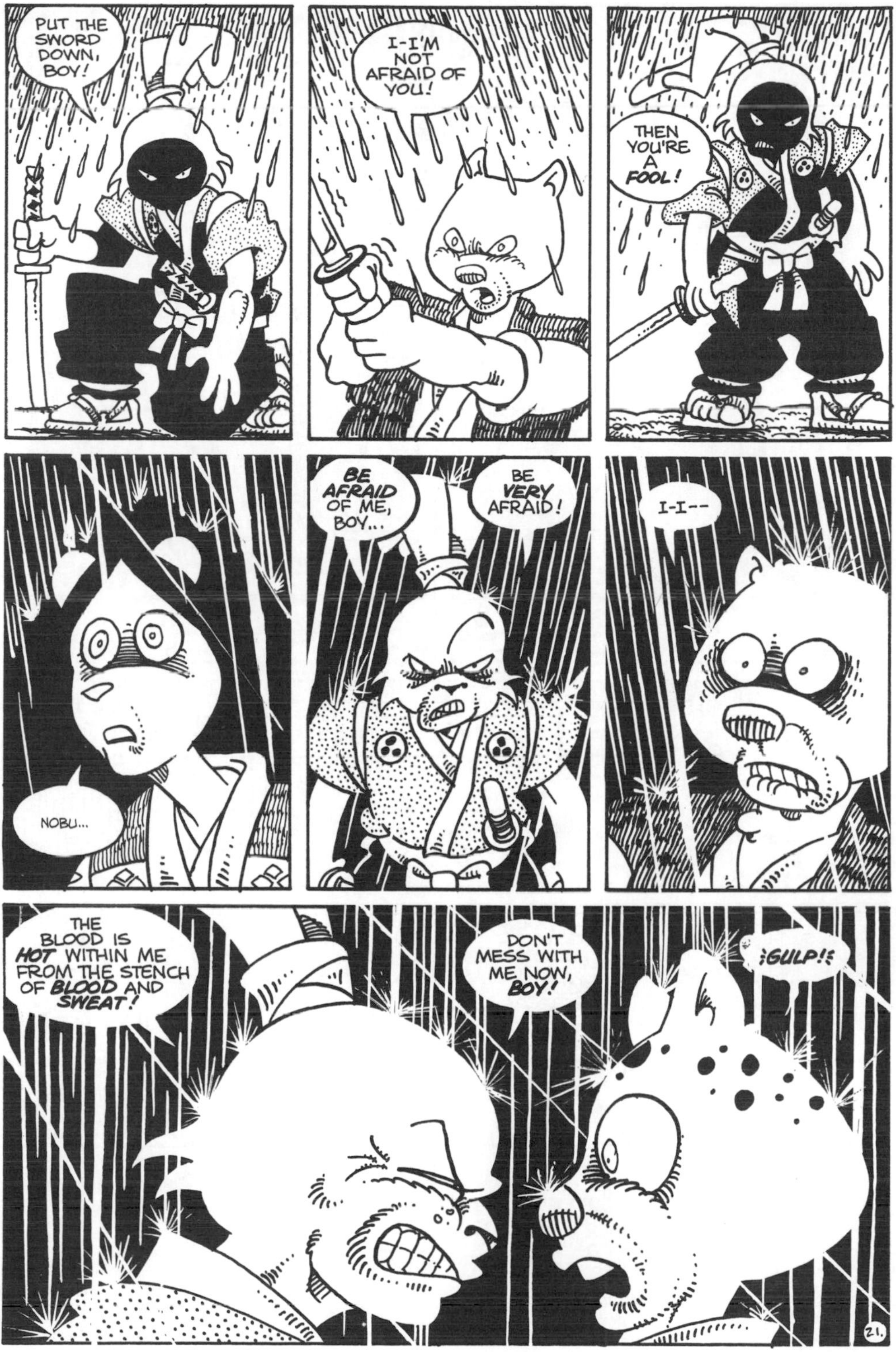
PUT THE SWORD DOWN, BOY!
I-I'M NOT AFRAID OF YOU!
THEN YOU'RE A FOOL!
NOBU...
BE AFRAID OF ME, BOY...
BE VERY AFRAID!
I-I--
THE BLOOD IS HOT WITHIN ME FROM THE STENCH OF BLOOD AND SWEAT!
DON'T MESS WITH ME NOW, BOY!
¡GULP!¡
21.

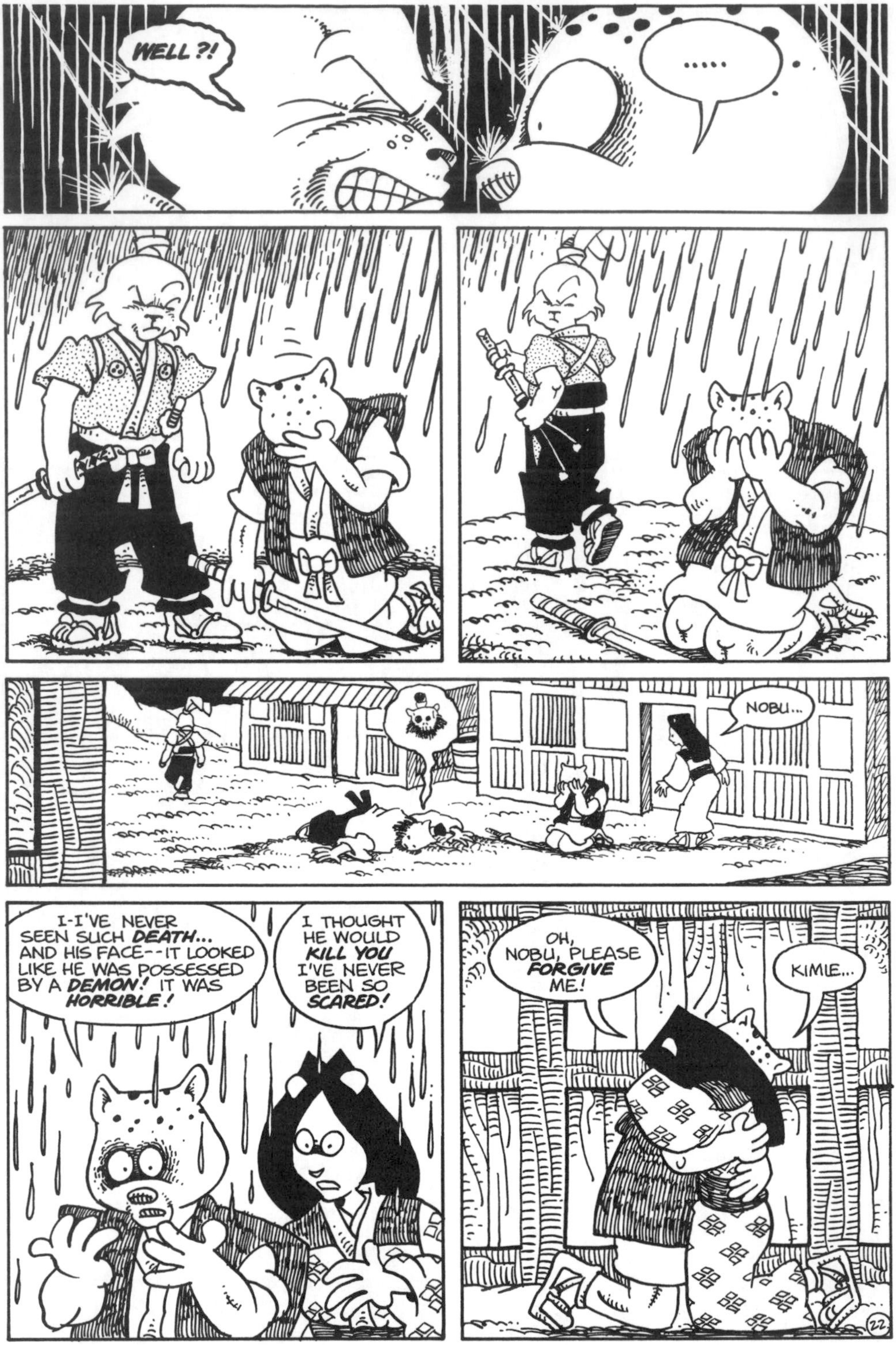
WELL?!
.....
NOBU...
I-I'VE NEVER SEEN SUCH DEATH... AND HIS FACE--IT LOOKED LIKE HE WAS POSSESSED BY A DEMON! IT WAS HORRIBLE!
I THOUGHT HE WOULD KILL YOU I'VE NEVER BEEN SO SCARED!
OH, NOBU, PLEASE FORGIVE ME!
KIMIE...
22

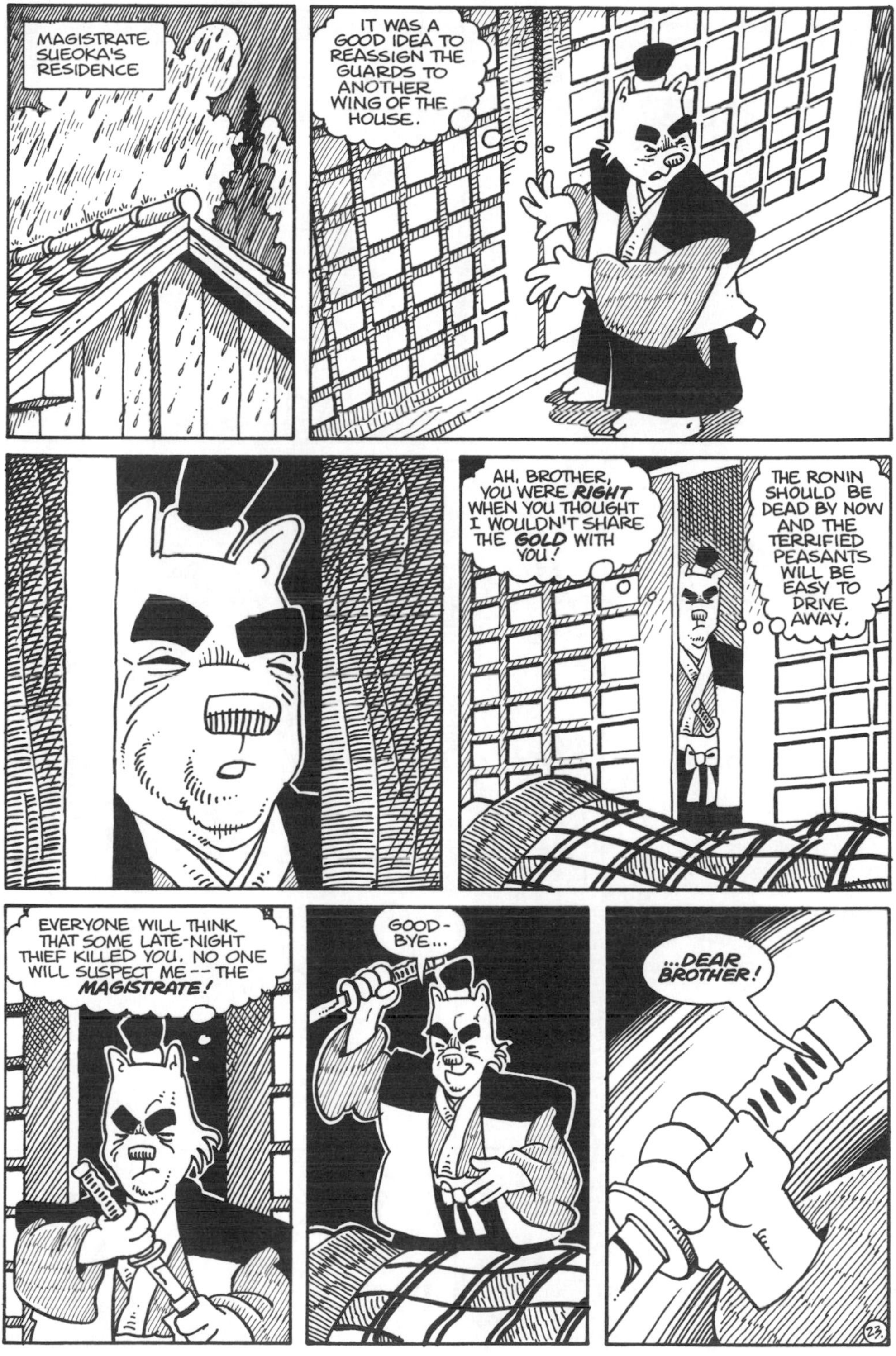
MAGISTRATE SUEOKA'S RESIDENCE
IT WAS A GOOD IDEA TO REASSIGN THE GUARDS TO ANOTHER WING OF THE HOUSE.
AH, BROTHER, YOU WERE **RIGHT** WHEN YOU THOUGHT I WOULDN'T SHARE THE **GOLD** WITH YOU!
THE RONIN SHOULD BE DEAD BY NOW AND THE TERRIFIED PEASANTS WILL BE EASY TO DRIVE AWAY.
EVERYONE WILL THINK THAT SOME LATE-NIGHT THIEF KILLED YOU. NO ONE WILL SUSPECT ME -- THE ***MAGISTRATE!***
GOOD-BYE...
...**DEAR BROTHER!**
23

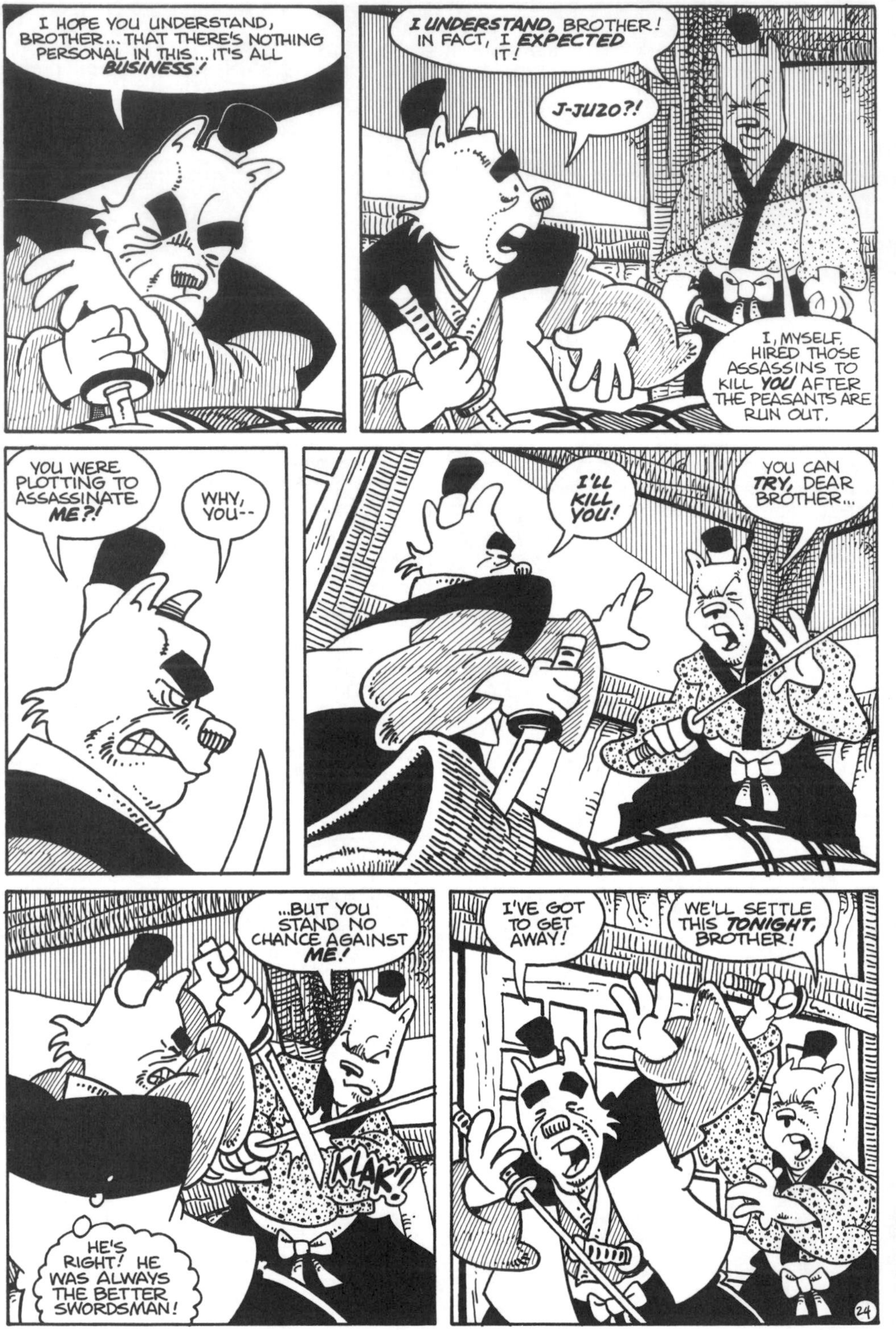
I HOPE YOU UNDERSTAND, BROTHER... THAT THERE'S NOTHING PERSONAL IN THIS... IT'S ALL BUSINESS!
I UNDERSTAND, BROTHER! IN FACT, I EXPECTED IT!
J-JUZO?!
I, MYSELF, HIRED THOSE ASSASSINS TO KILL YOU AFTER THE PEASANTS ARE RUN OUT.
YOU WERE PLOTTING TO ASSASSINATE ME?!
WHY, YOU--
I'LL KILL YOU!
YOU CAN TRY, DEAR BROTHER...
...BUT YOU STAND NO CHANCE AGAINST ME!
KLAK!
HE'S RIGHT! HE WAS ALWAYS THE BETTER SWORDSMAN!
I'VE GOT TO GET AWAY!
WE'LL SETTLE THIS TONIGHT, BROTHER!
24

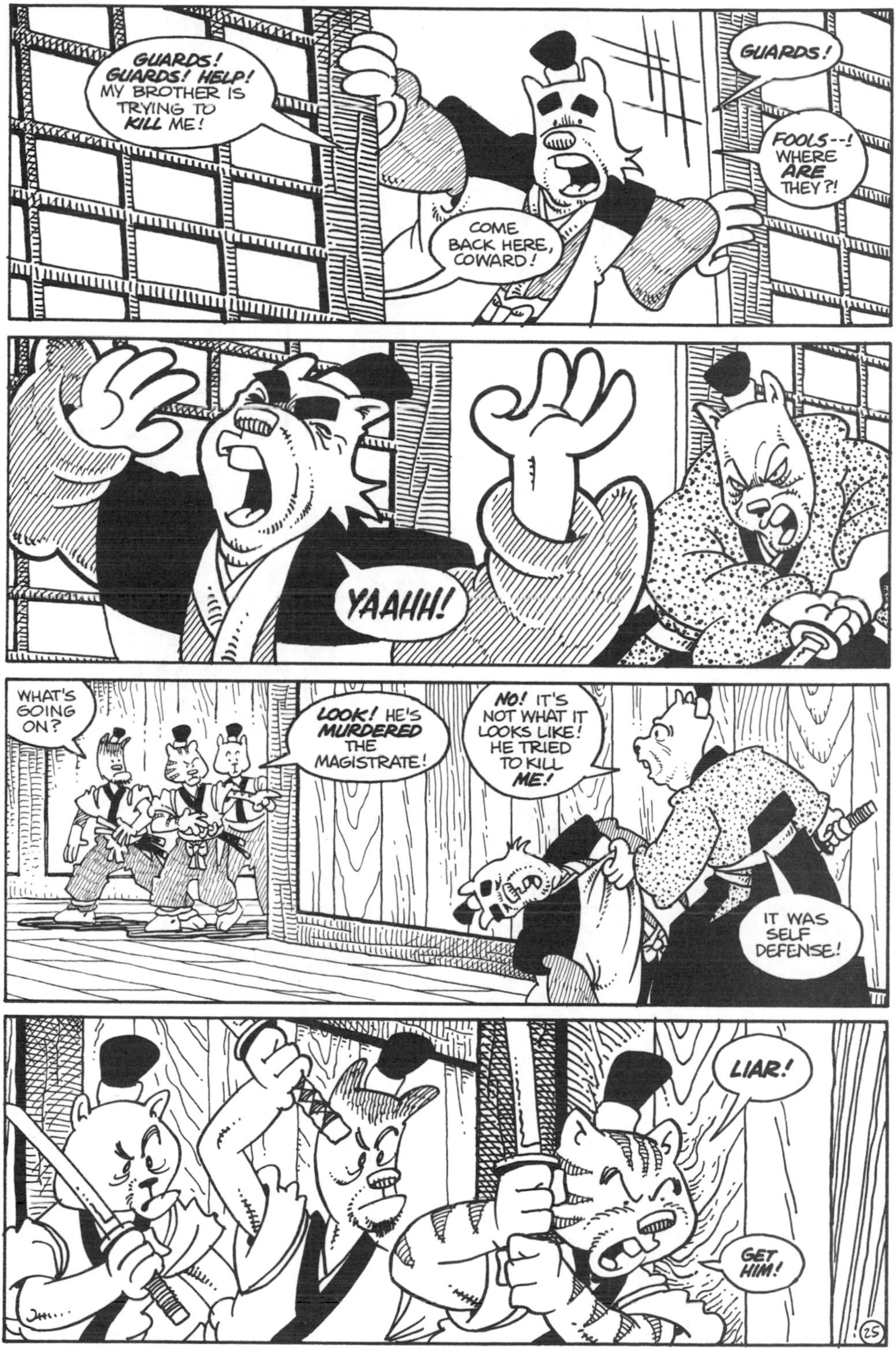
GUARDS! GUARDS! HELP! MY BROTHER IS TRYING TO KILL ME!
GUARDS!
FOOLS--! WHERE ARE THEY?!
COME BACK HERE, COWARD!
YAAHH!
WHAT'S GOING ON?
LOOK! HE'S MURDERED THE MAGISTRATE!
NO! IT'S NOT WHAT IT LOOKS LIKE! HE TRIED TO KILL ME!
IT WAS SELF DEFENSE!
LIAR!
GET HIM!
25

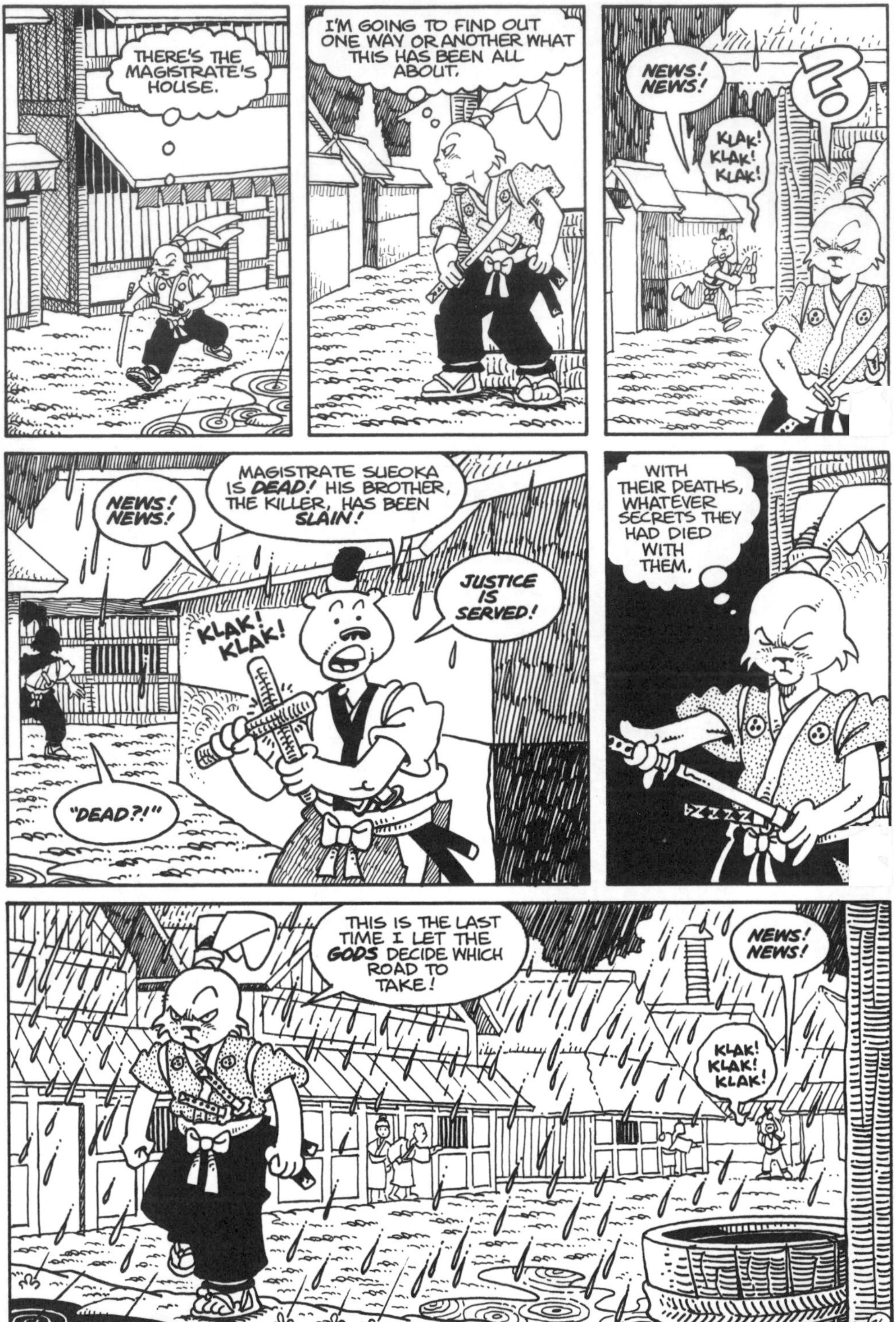
THERE'S THE MAGISTRATE'S HOUSE.
I'M GOING TO FIND OUT ONE WAY OR ANOTHER WHAT THIS HAS BEEN ALL ABOUT.
NEWS! NEWS!
KLAK! KLAK! KLAK!
?
NEWS! NEWS!
MAGISTRATE SUEOKA IS DEAD! HIS BROTHER, THE KILLER, HAS BEEN SLAIN!
KLAK! KLAK!
JUSTICE IS SERVED!
"DEAD?!"
WITH THEIR DEATHS, WHATEVER SECRETS THEY HAD DIED WITH THEM.
ZZZZZ
THIS IS THE LAST TIME I LET THE GODS DECIDE WHICH ROAD TO TAKE!
NEWS! NEWS!
KLAK! KLAK! KLAK!
26

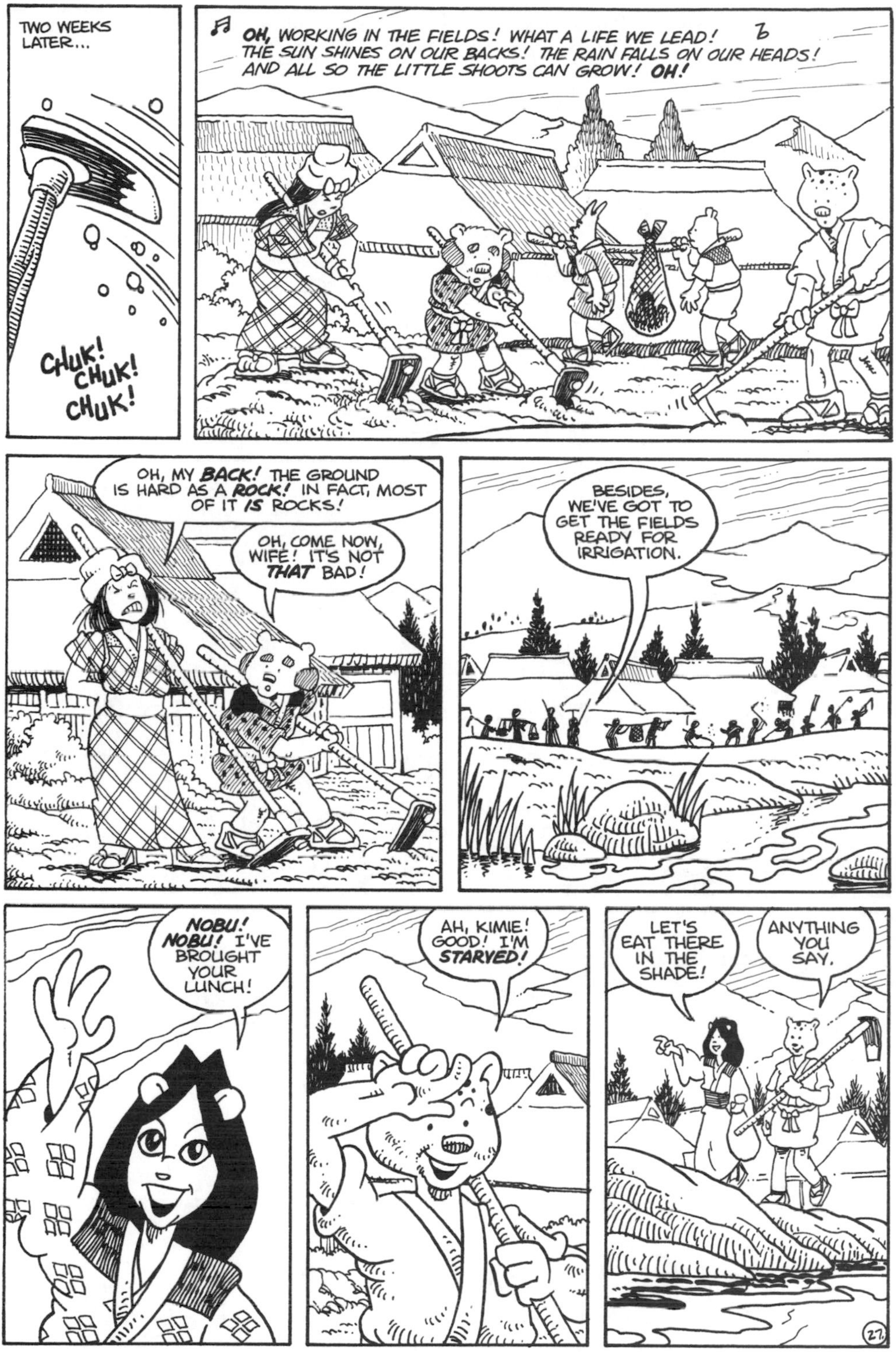
TWO WEEKS LATER...
CHUK! CHUK! CHUK!
OH, WORKING IN THE FIELDS! WHAT A LIFE WE LEAD! THE SUN SHINES ON OUR BACKS! THE RAIN FALLS ON OUR HEADS! AND ALL SO THE LITTLE SHOOTS CAN GROW! OH!
OH, MY BACK! THE GROUND IS HARD AS A ROCK! IN FACT, MOST OF IT IS ROCKS!
OH, COME NOW, WIFE! IT'S NOT THAT BAD!
BESIDES, WE'VE GOT TO GET THE FIELDS READY FOR IRRIGATION.
NOBU! NOBU! I'VE BROUGHT YOUR LUNCH!
AH, KIMIE! GOOD! I'M STARVED!
LET'S EAT THERE IN THE SHADE!
ANYTHING YOU SAY.
27

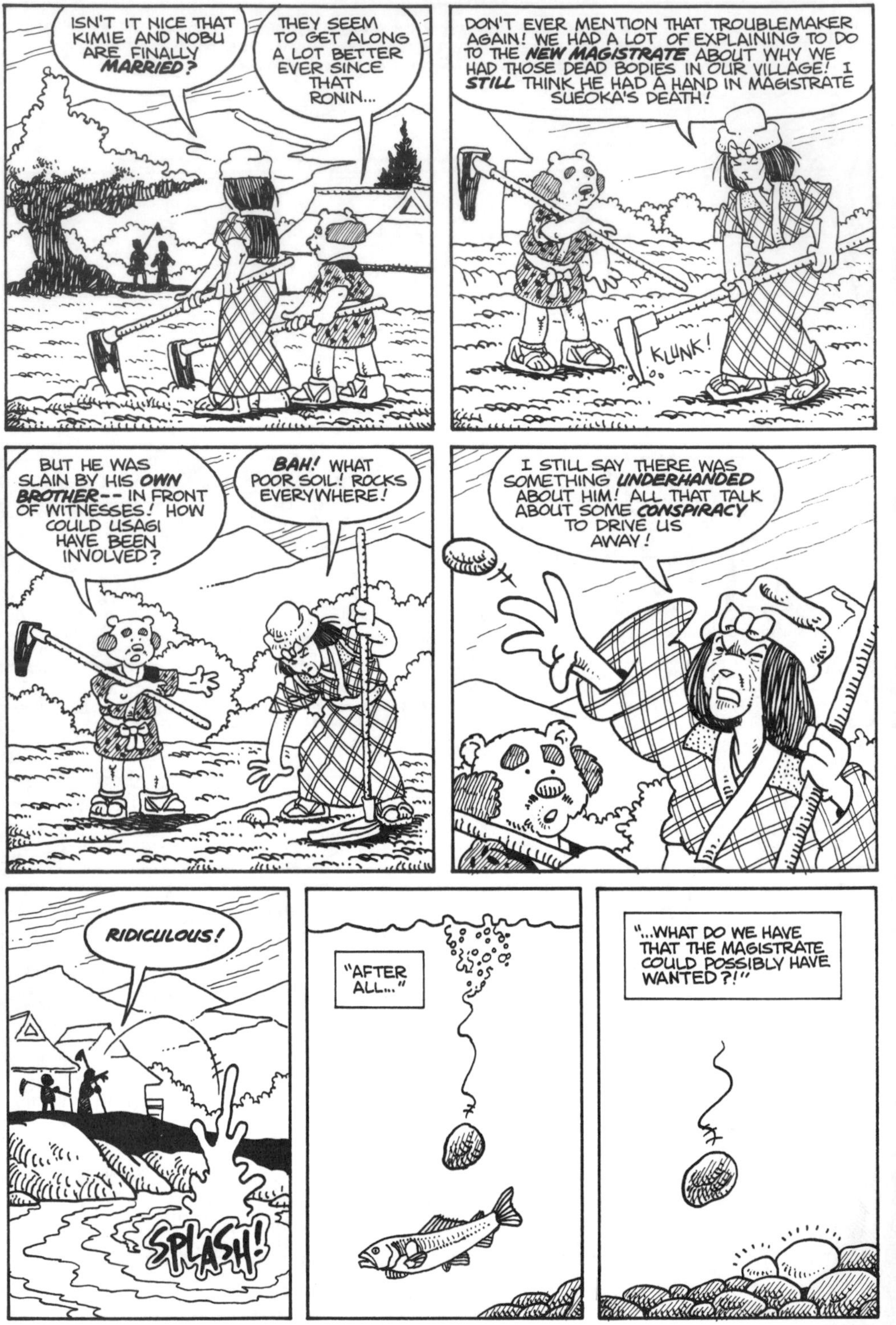
ISN'T IT NICE THAT KIMIE AND NOBU ARE FINALLY MARRIED?
THEY SEEM TO GET ALONG A LOT BETTER EVER SINCE THAT RONIN...
DON'T EVER MENTION THAT TROUBLEMAKER AGAIN! WE HAD A LOT OF EXPLAINING TO DO TO THE NEW MAGISTRATE ABOUT WHY WE HAD THOSE DEAD BODIES IN OUR VILLAGE! I STILL THINK HE HAD A HAND IN MAGISTRATE SUEOKA'S DEATH!
KLUNK!
BUT HE WAS SLAIN BY HIS OWN BROTHER-- IN FRONT OF WITNESSES! HOW COULD USAGI HAVE BEEN INVOLVED?
BAH! WHAT POOR SOIL! ROCKS EVERYWHERE!
I STILL SAY THERE WAS SOMETHING UNDERHANDED ABOUT HIM! ALL THAT TALK ABOUT SOME CONSPIRACY TO DRIVE US AWAY!
RIDICULOUS!
SPLASH!
"AFTER ALL..."
"...WHAT DO WE HAVE THAT THE MAGISTRATE COULD POSSIBLY HAVE WANTED?!"
END.

THE LIZARDS' TALE

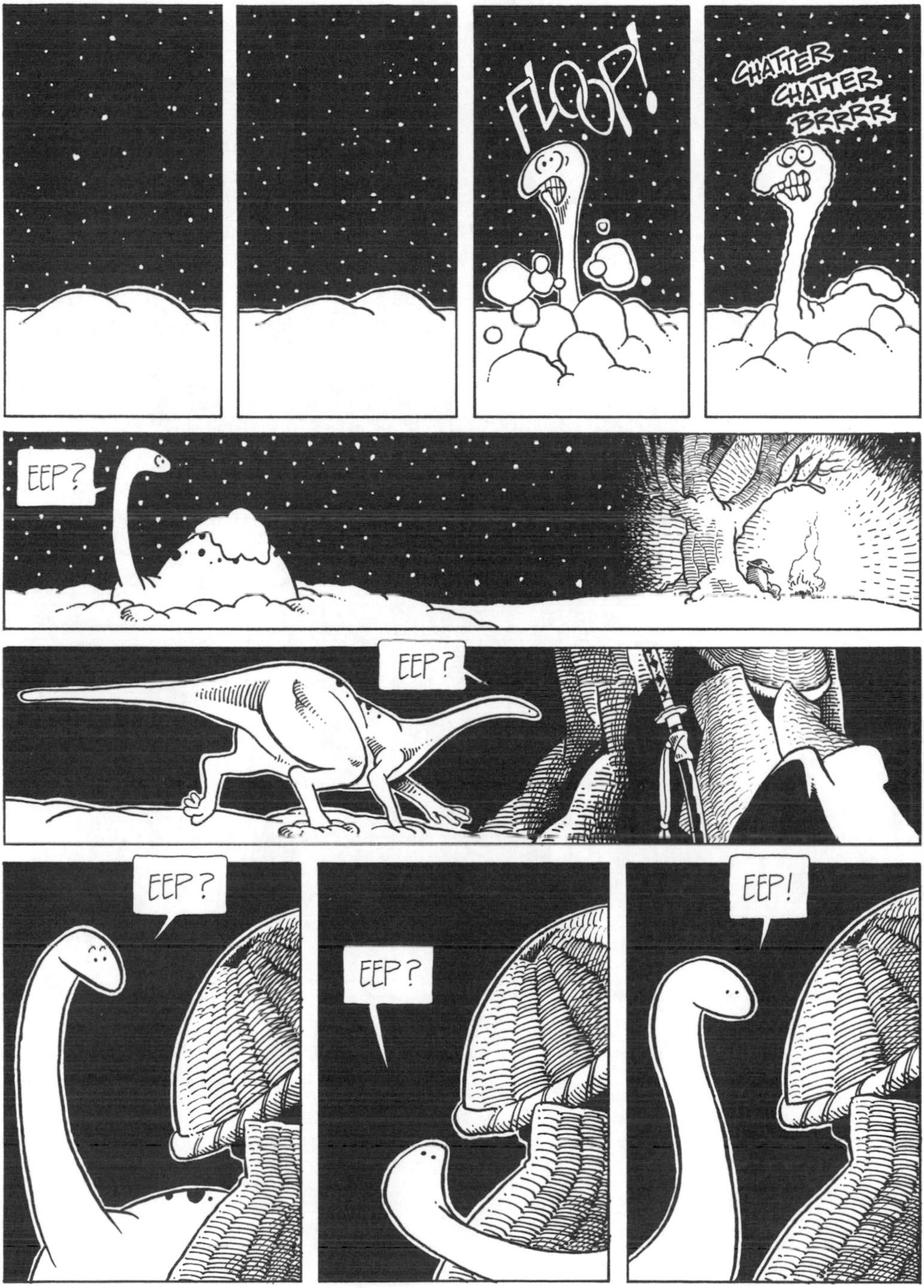
FLOOP!
CHATTER CHATTER BRRRR
EEP?
EEP?
EEP?
EEP?
EEP!

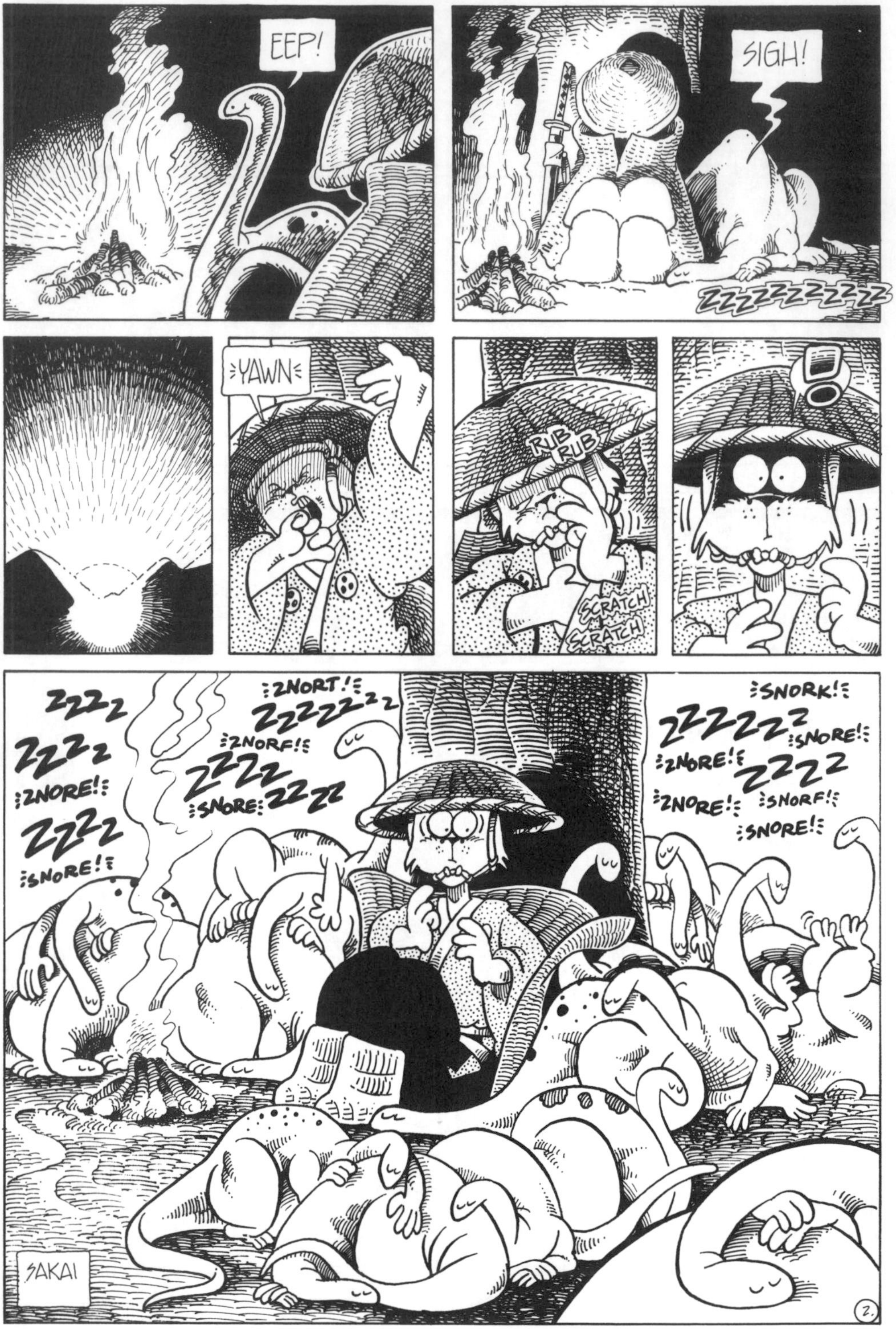

EEP!
SIGH!
ZZZZZZZZZZZ
YAWN
RUB RUB
SCRATCH SCRATCH
ZZZZ
ZZZZ
ZNORE!
ZZZZ
SNORE!
ZNORT!
ZZZZZZZZ
ZNORF!
ZZZZ
SNORE ZZZZ
SNORK!
ZZZZZZZ
SNORE!
ZNORE!
ZZZZ
ZNORE!
SNORF!
SNORE!
SAKAI
2.

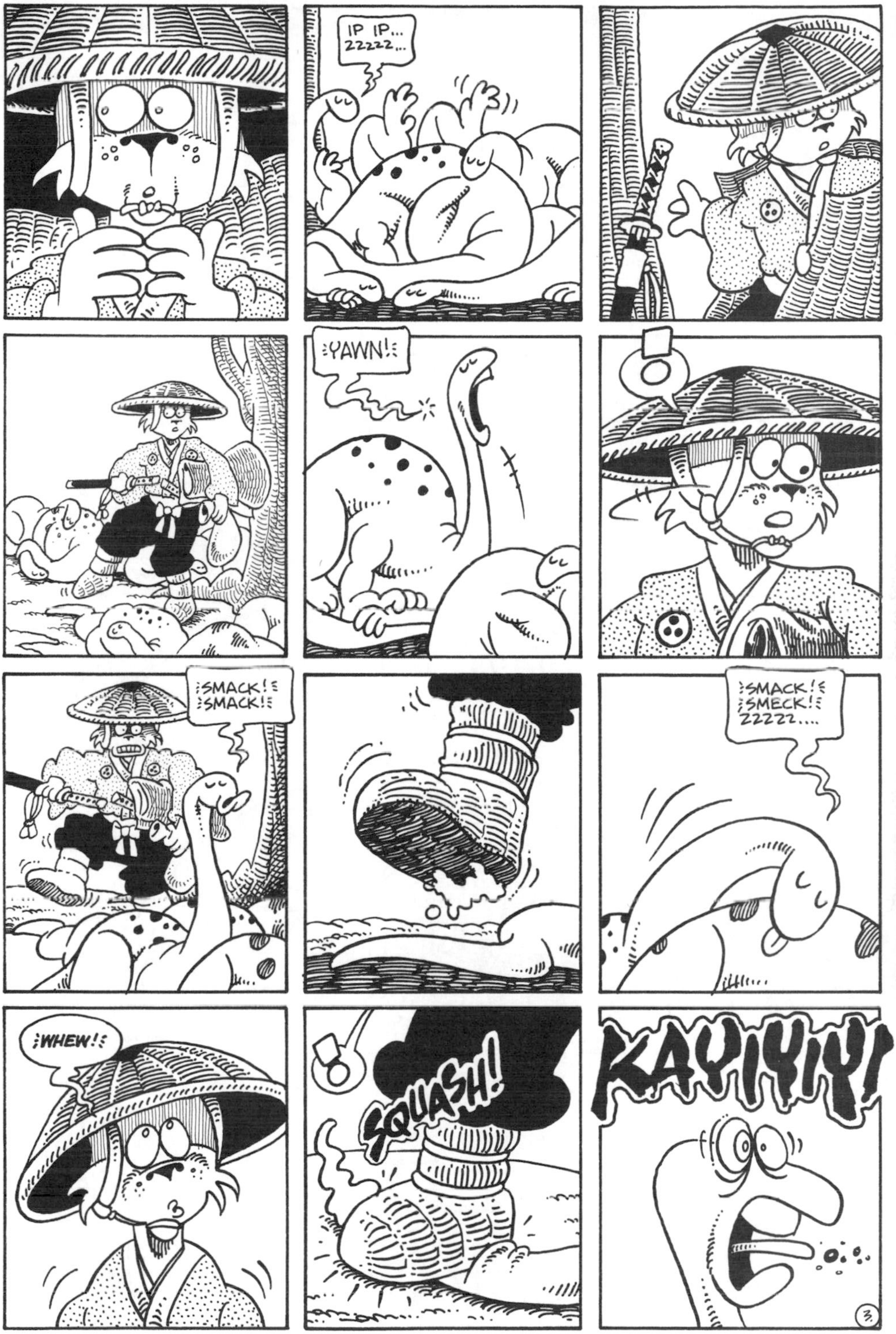
IP IP...
ZZZZZ...
YAWN!
SMACK!
SMACK!
SMACK!
SMECK!
ZZZZZ....
WHEW!
SQUASH!
KAYIYIYI!
3

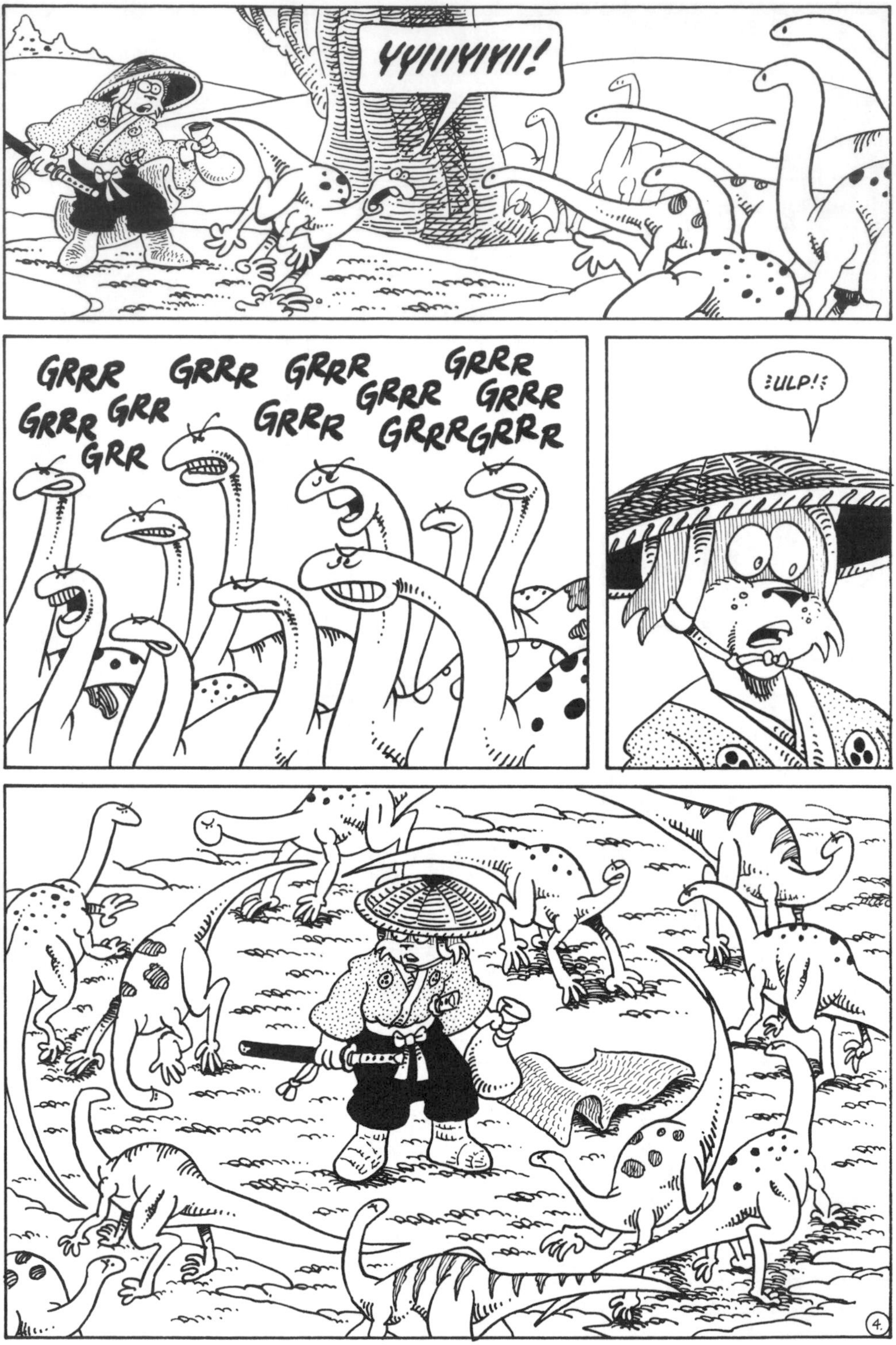
YYIIIYIYII!
GRRR
GRRR
GRRR
GRRR
GRR
GRR
GRRR
GRRR
GRRR
GRRR
GRRRGRRR
:ULP!:
4.

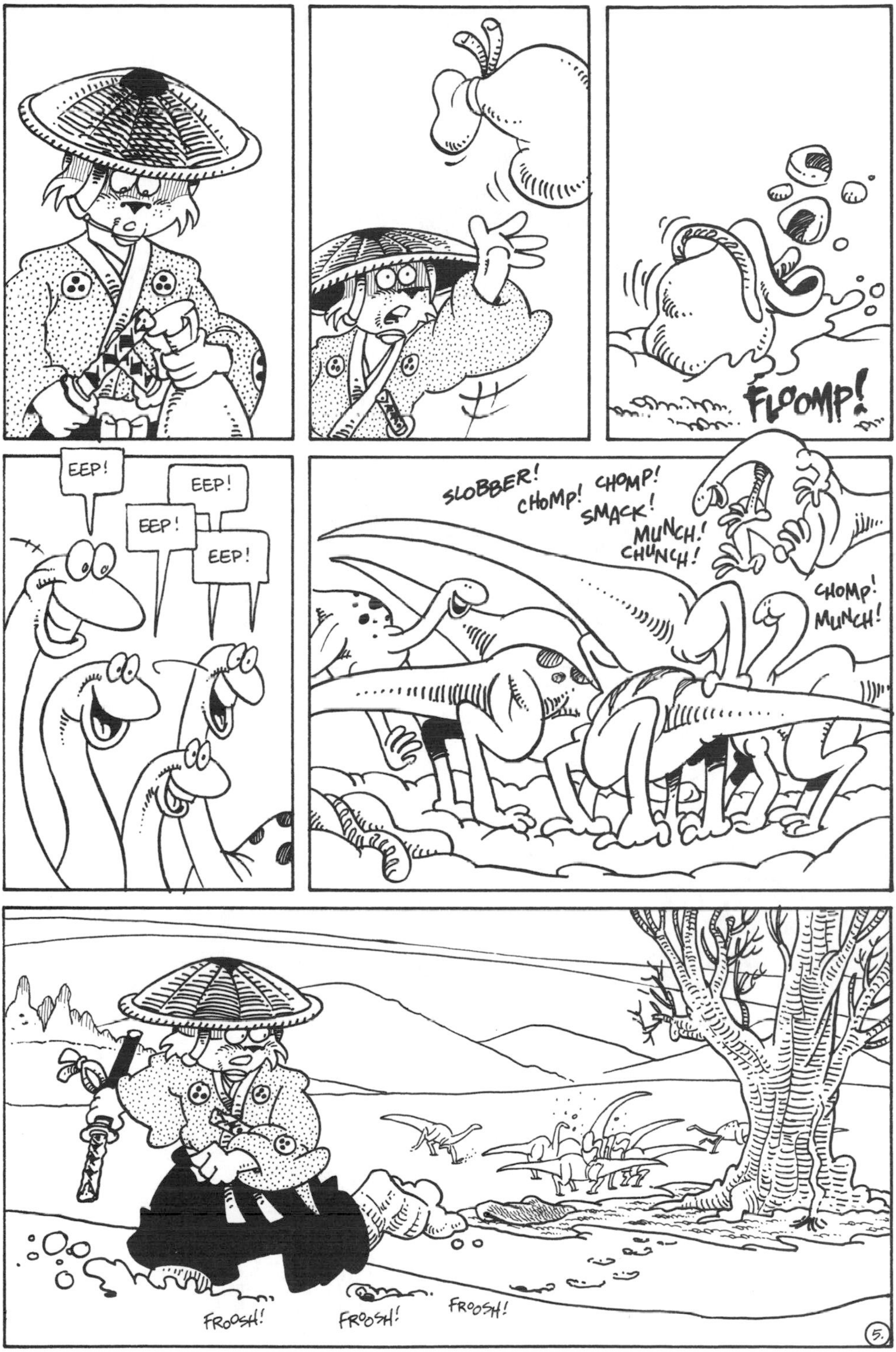
FLOOMP!
EEP!
EEP!
EEP!
EEP!
SLOBBER!
CHOMP! CHOMP!
SMACK!
MUNCH!
CHUNCH!
CHOMP!
MUNCH!
FROOSH!
FROOSH!
FROOSH!
5.

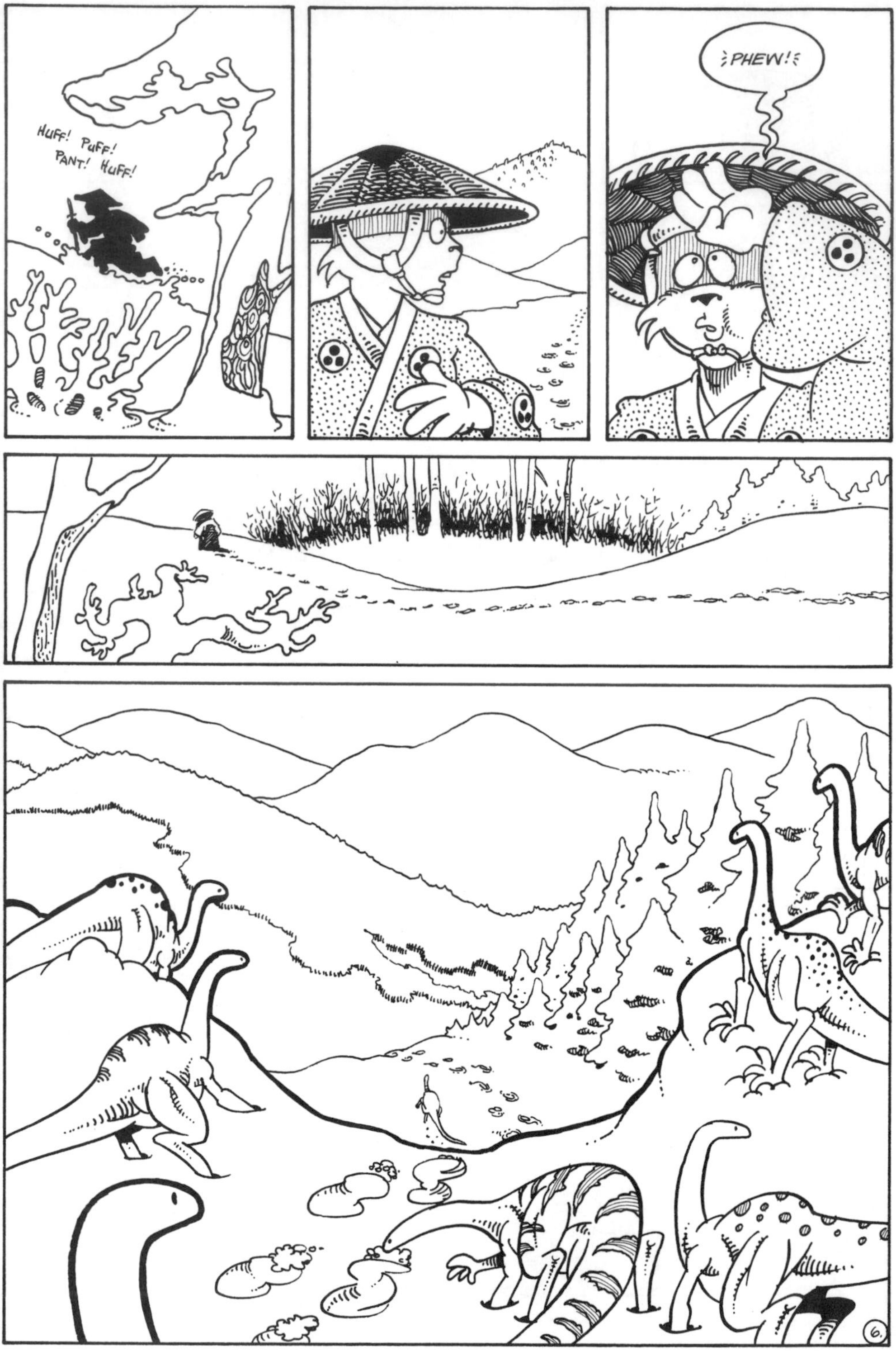
HUFF! PUFF!
PANT! HUFF!
PHEW!
6.

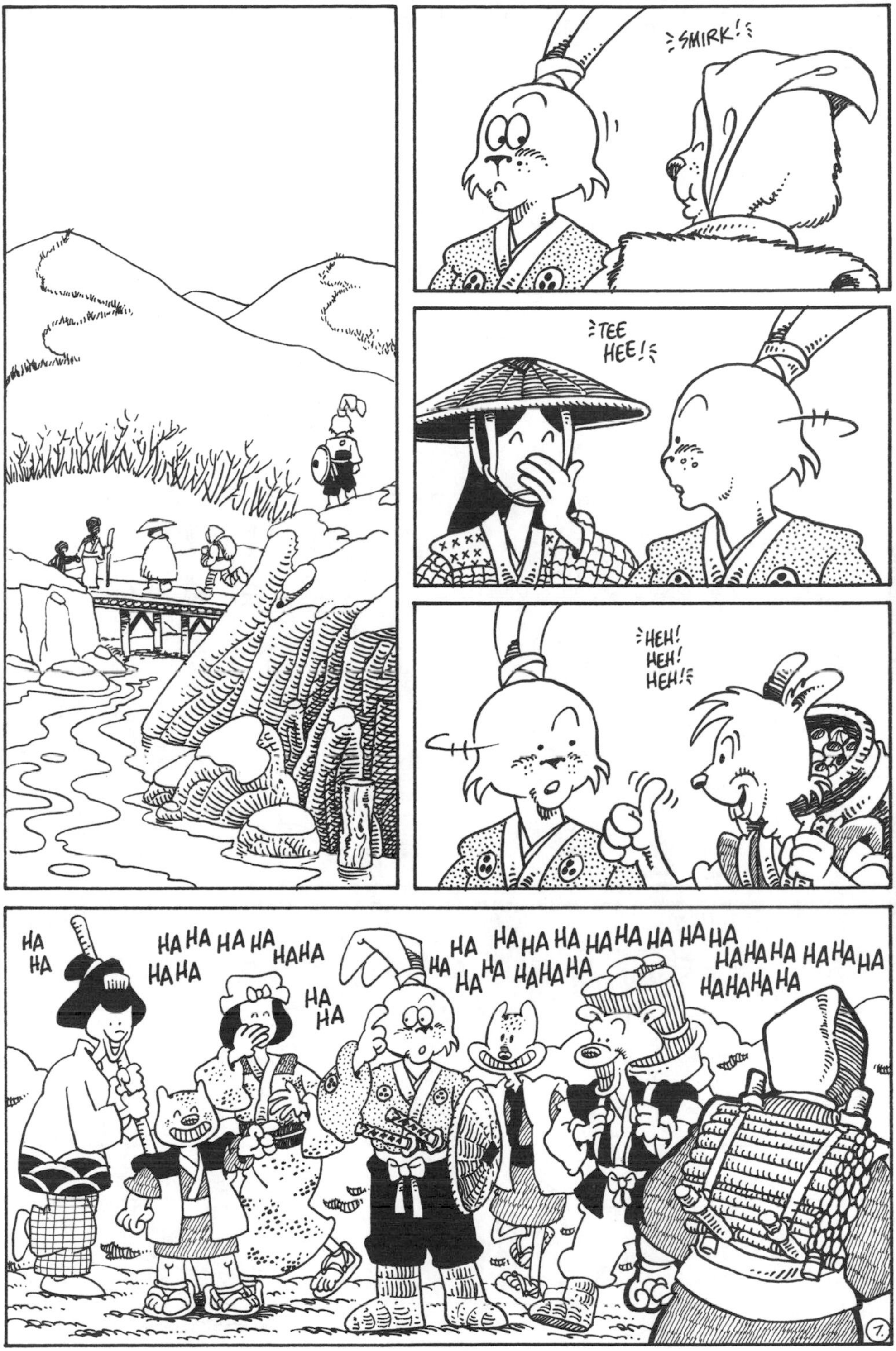
SMIRK!
TEE HEE!
HEH! HEH! HEH!
HA HA
HA HA HA HA HAHA HAHA
HA HA
HA HA HA HA HA HA HA HA HA HA HA HA HA HA HA HA HA HA HA HA HA
HA HA HA HA HA HA HA HA HA HA HA HA HA
7.

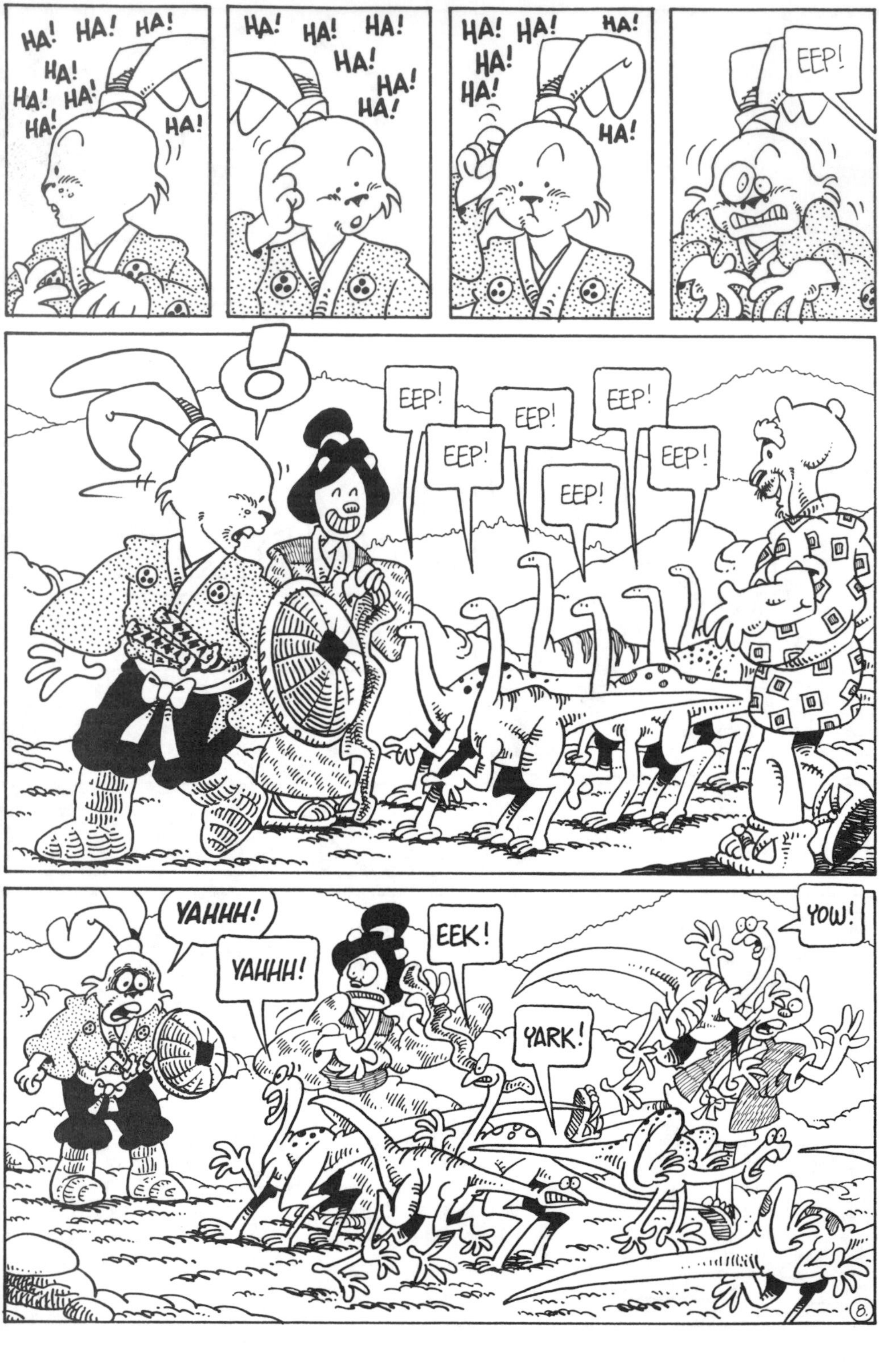
HA! HA! HA!
HA!
HA! HA!
HA!
HA!
HA! HA! HA!
HA!
HA!
HA!
HA! HA! HA!
HA!
HA!
HA!
EEP!
!
EEP!
EEP!
EEP!
EEP!
EEP!
EEP!
YAHHH!
YAHHH!
EEK!
YARK!
YOW!
8.

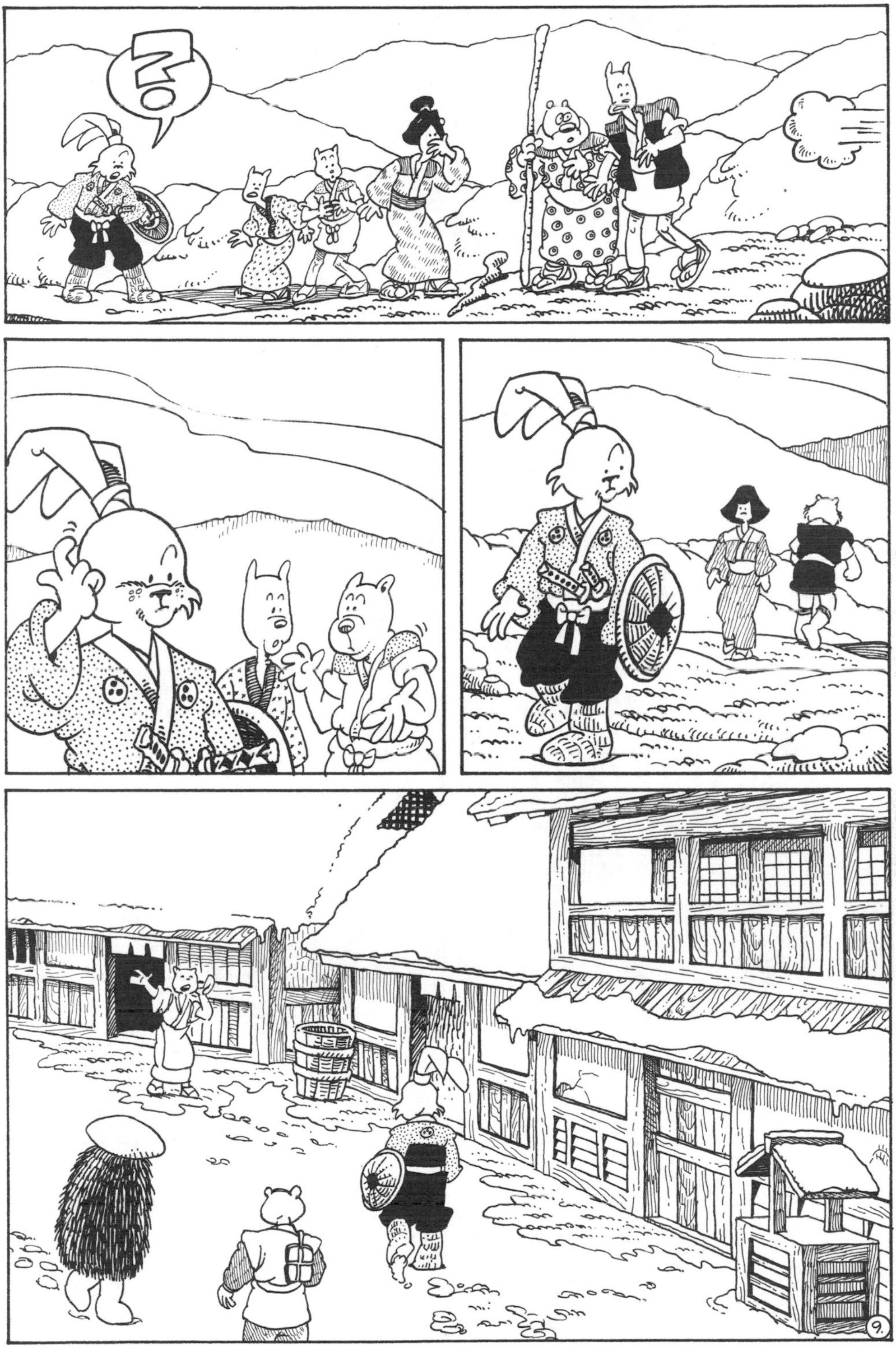
?
9.

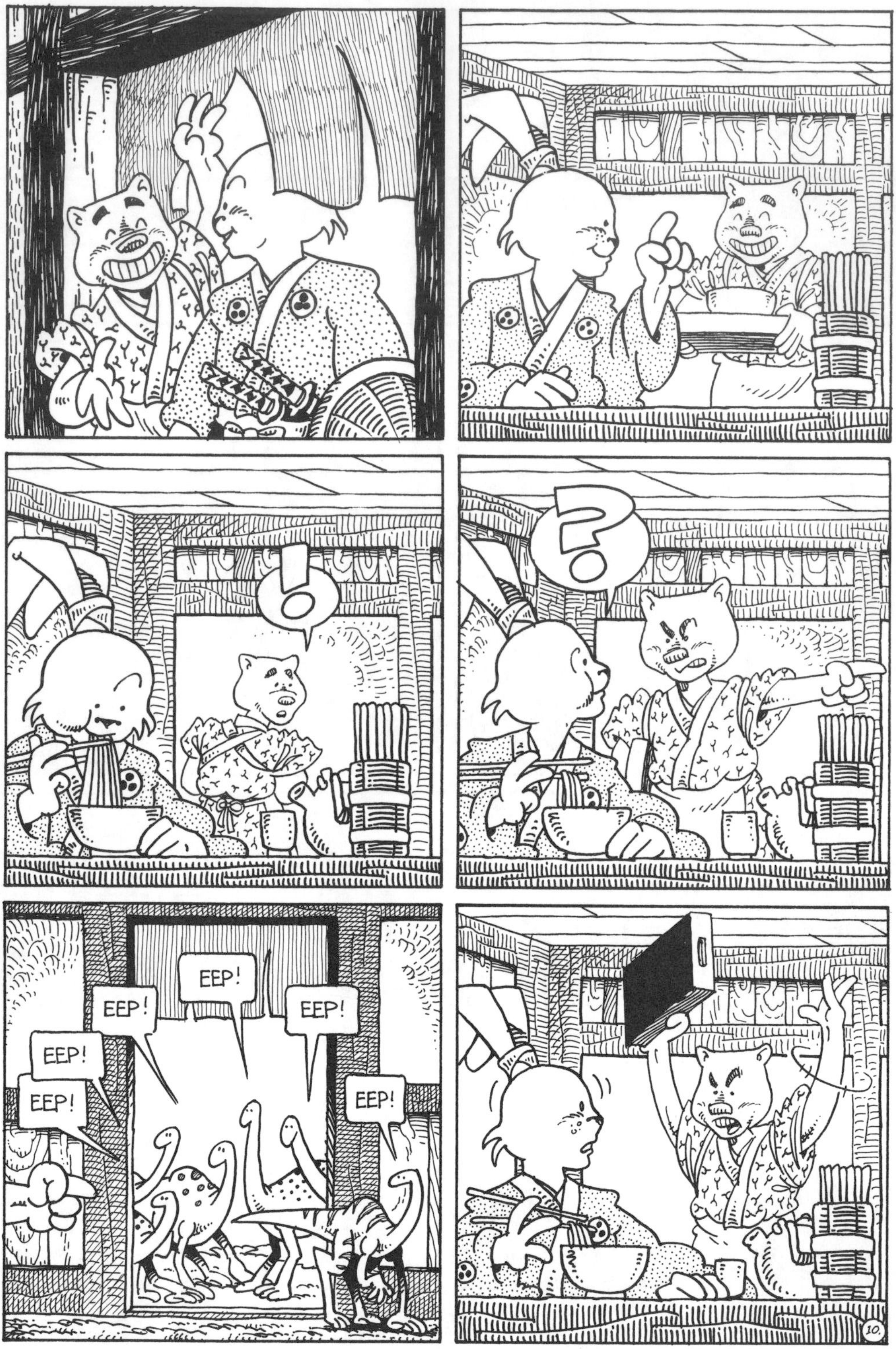
?
!
EEP!
EEP!
EEP!
EEP!
EEP!
EEP!
10.

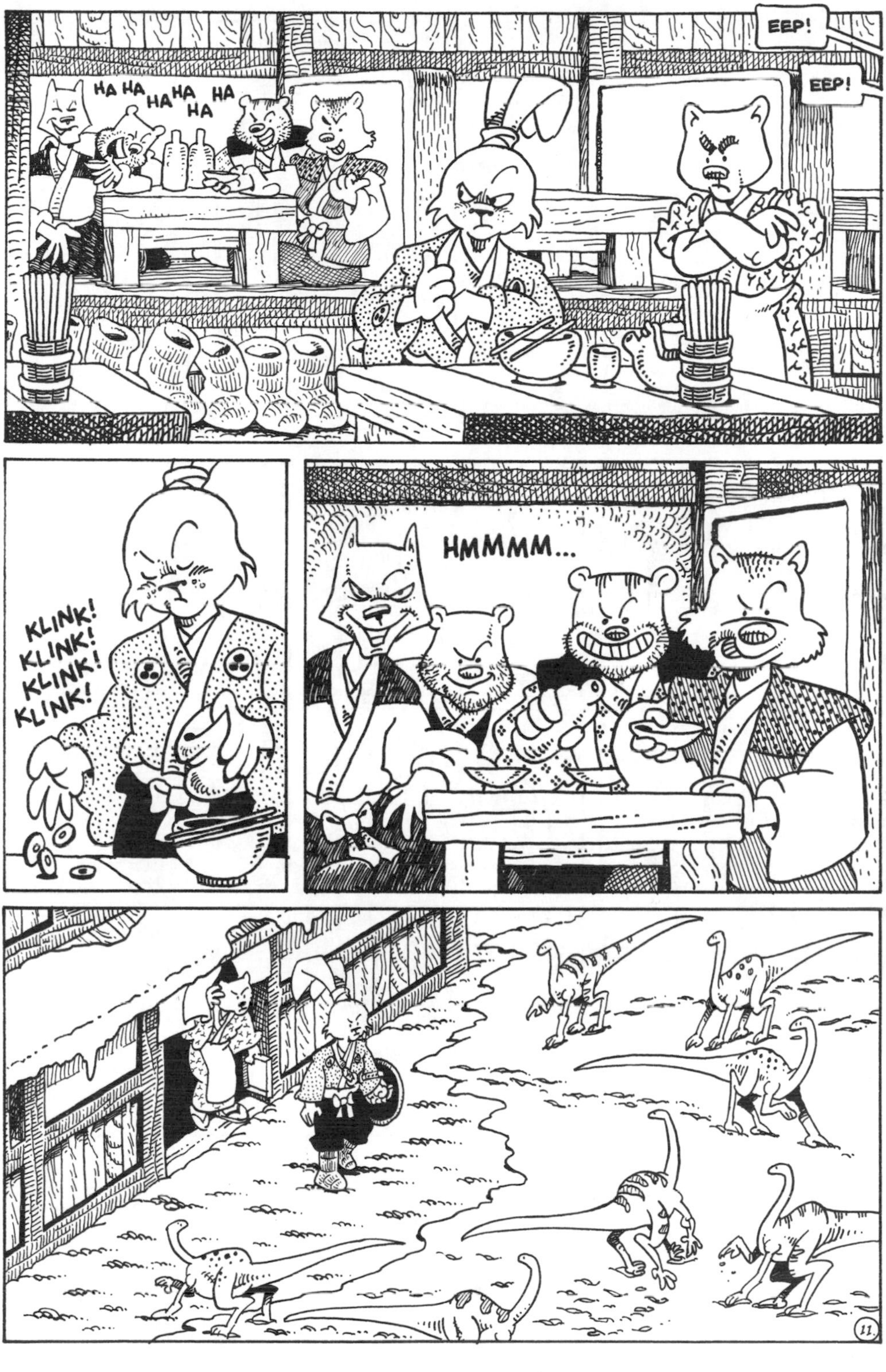
HA HA HA HA HA HA
EEP!
EEP!
KLINK!
KLINK!
KLINK!
KLINK!
HMMMM...
11.

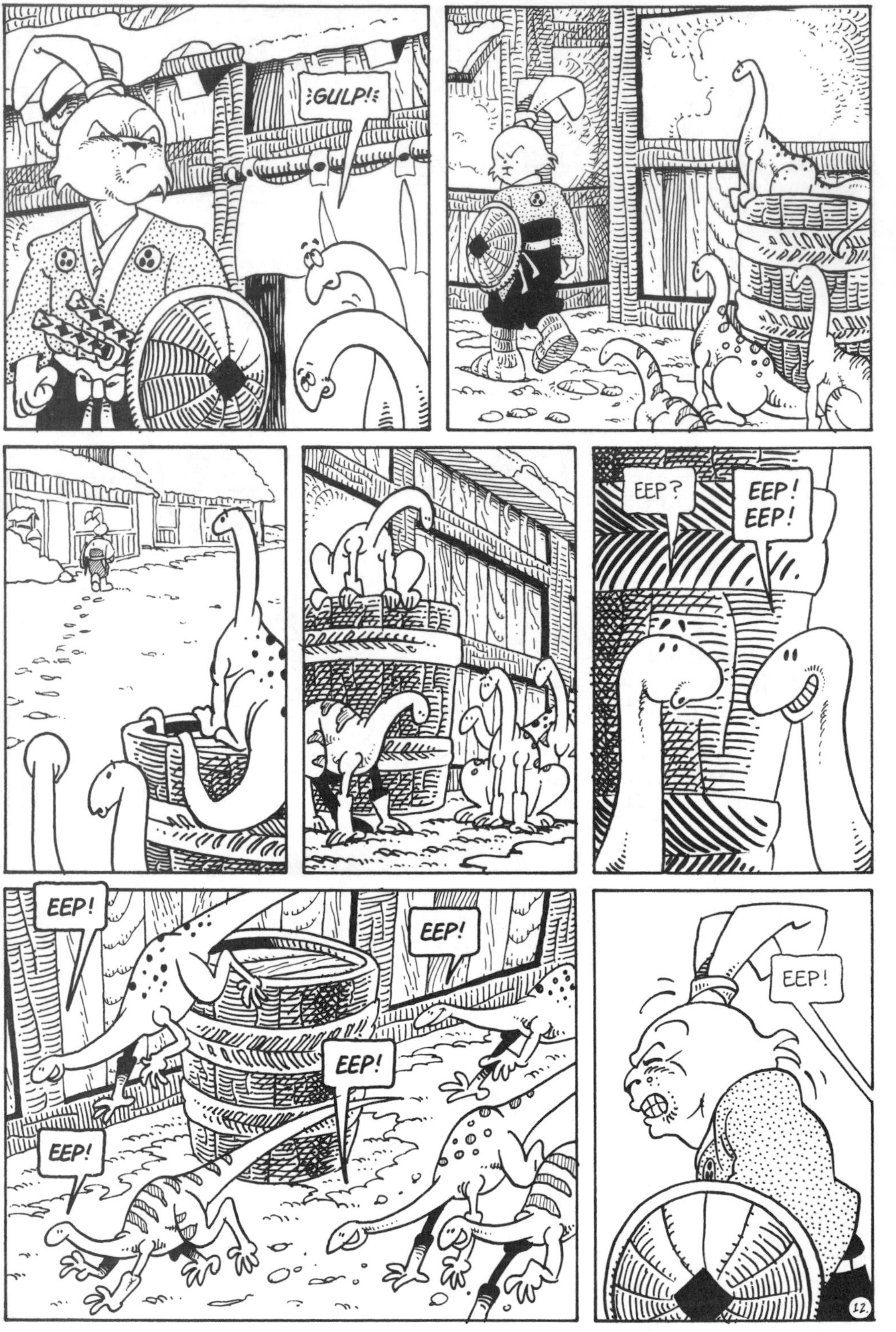
GULP!
EEP?
EEP! EEP!
EEP!
EEP!
EEP!
EEP!
EEP!
12.

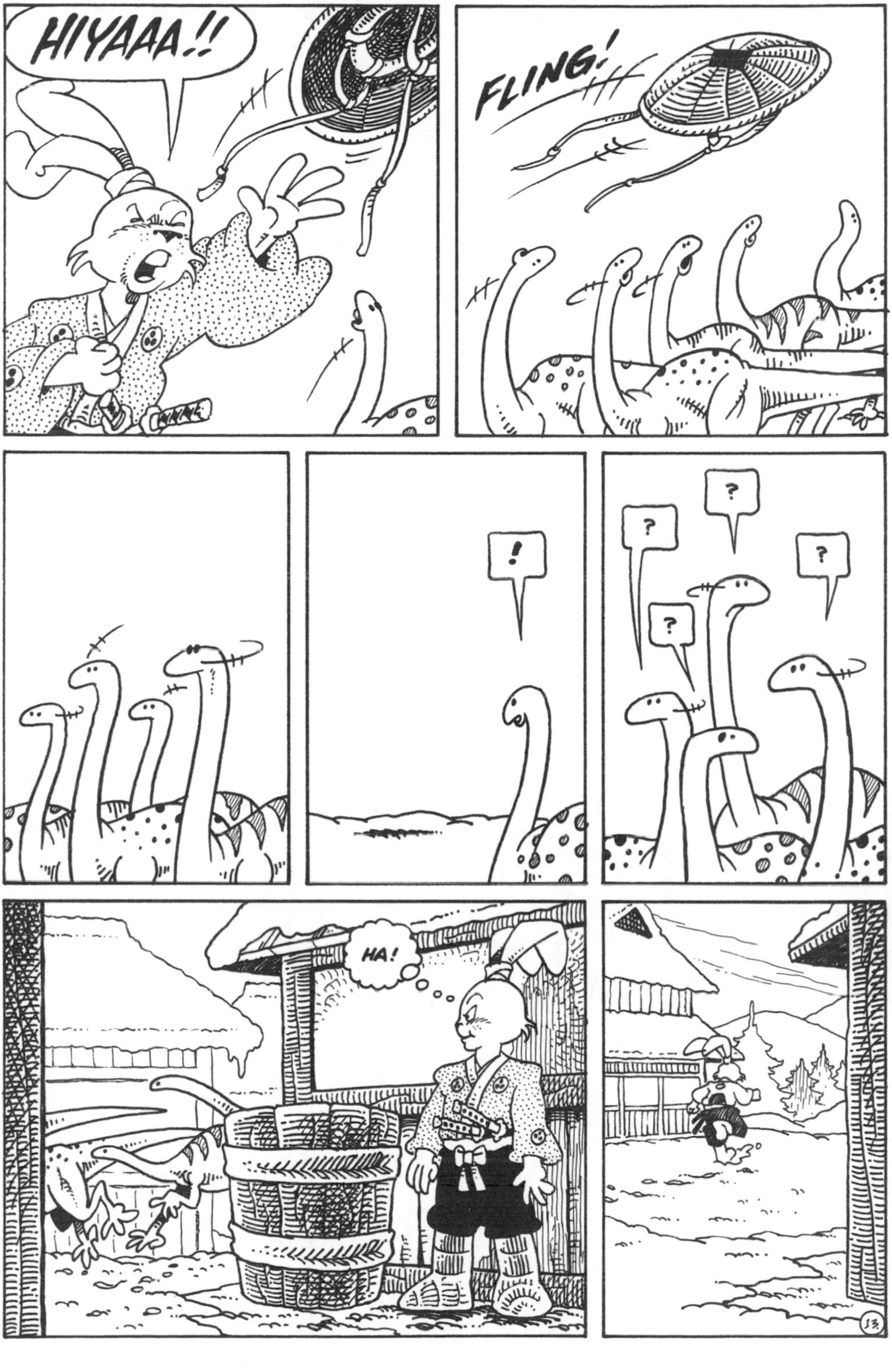
HIYAAA!!
FLING!
!
?
?
?
?
HA!
13

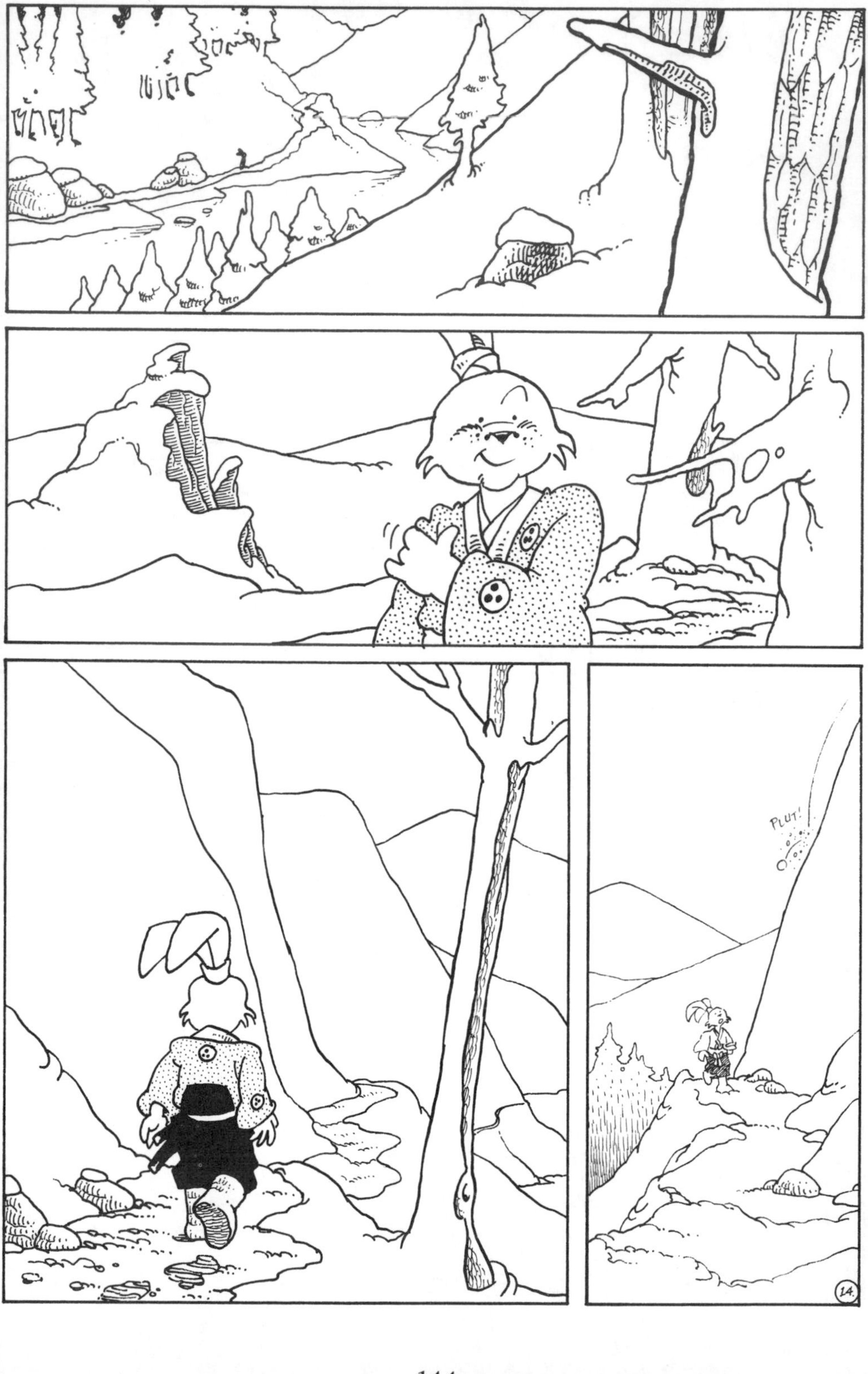
PLUT!
14.

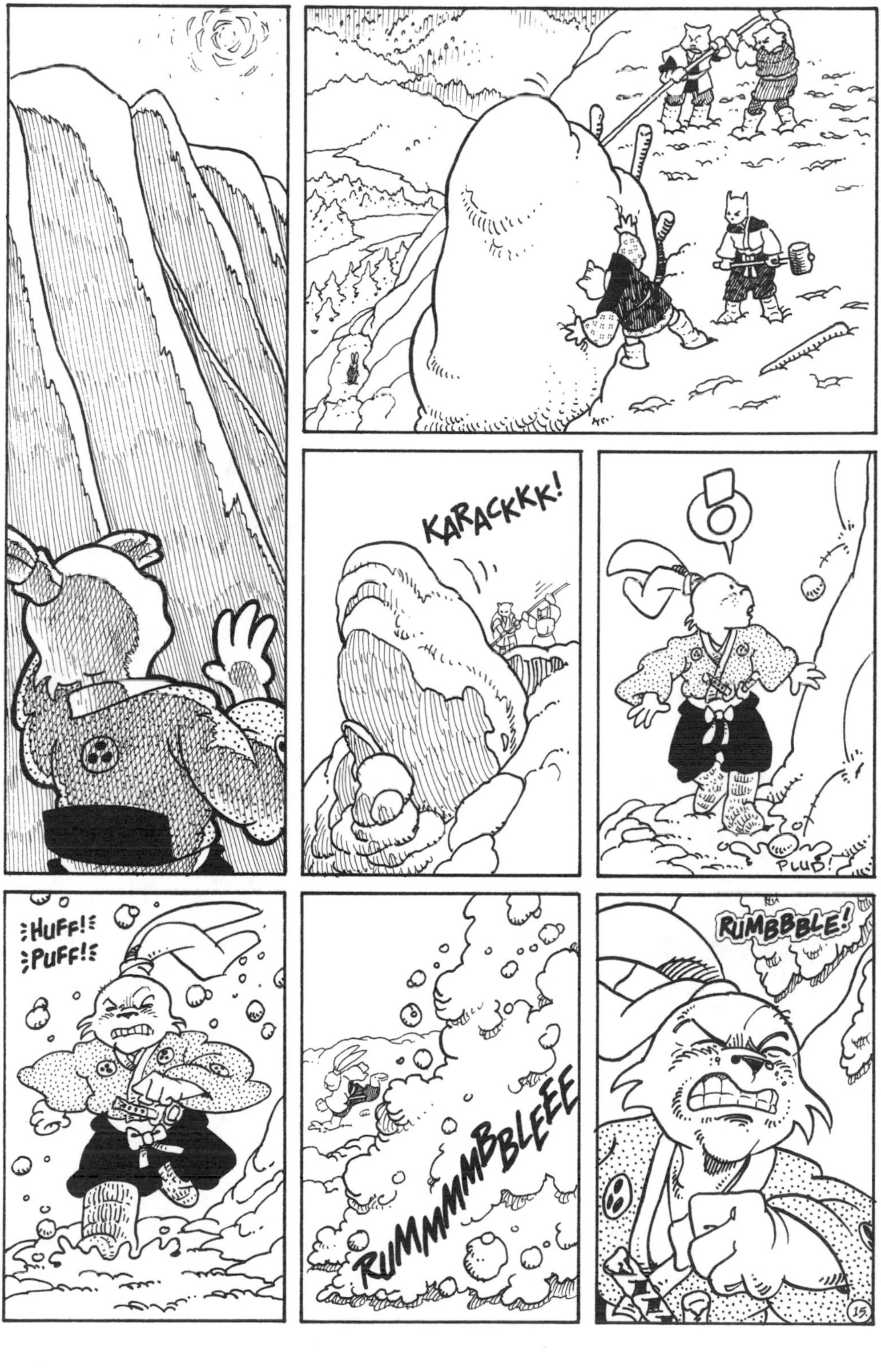
KARACKKK!
!
PLUD!
HUFF!
PUFF!
RUMMMMBBLEEE
RUMBBBLE!
15.

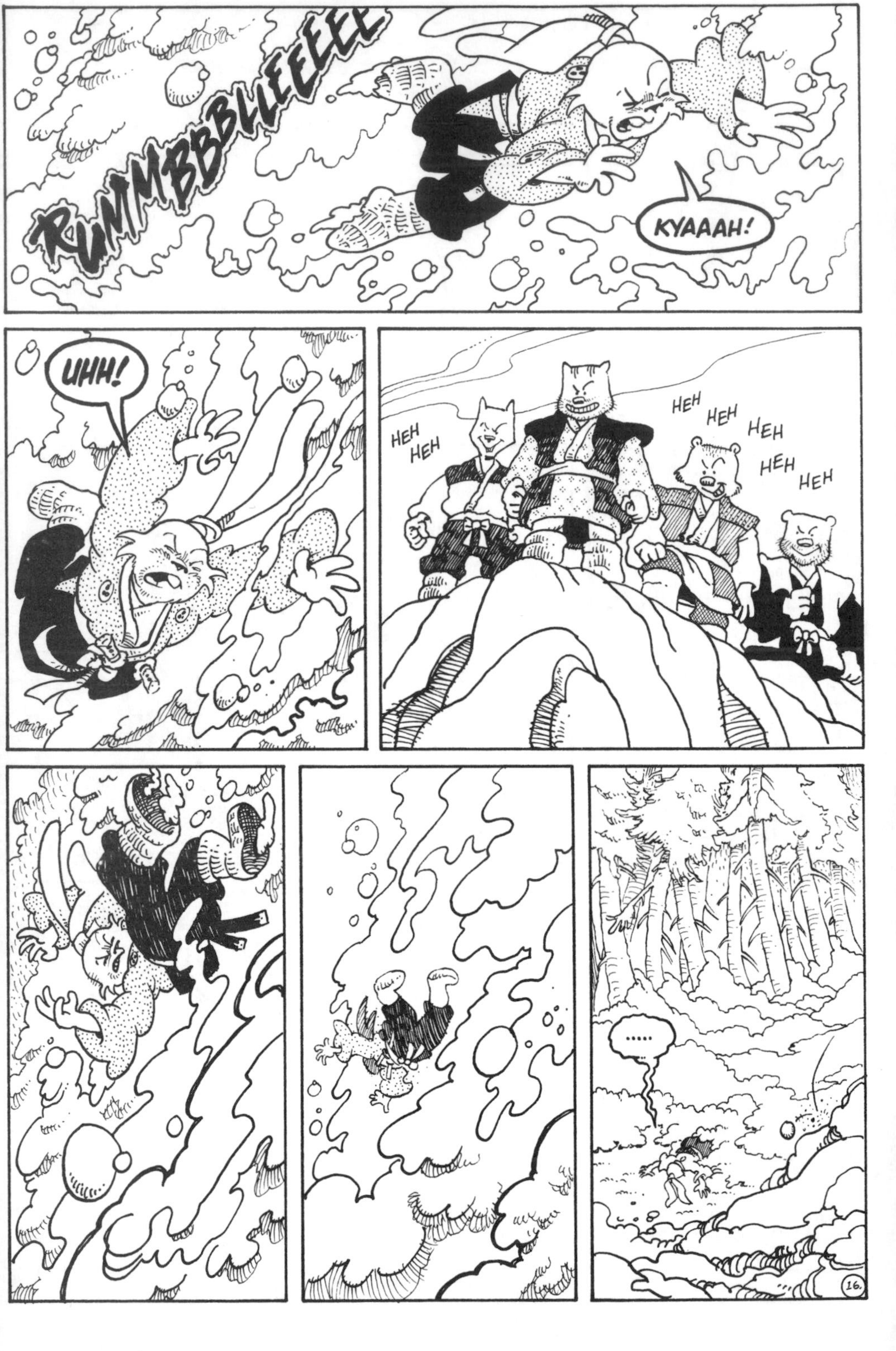
RUMMBBBLLEEEEE
KYAAAH!
UHH!
HEH HEH
HEH HEH HEH HEH HEH
......
16.

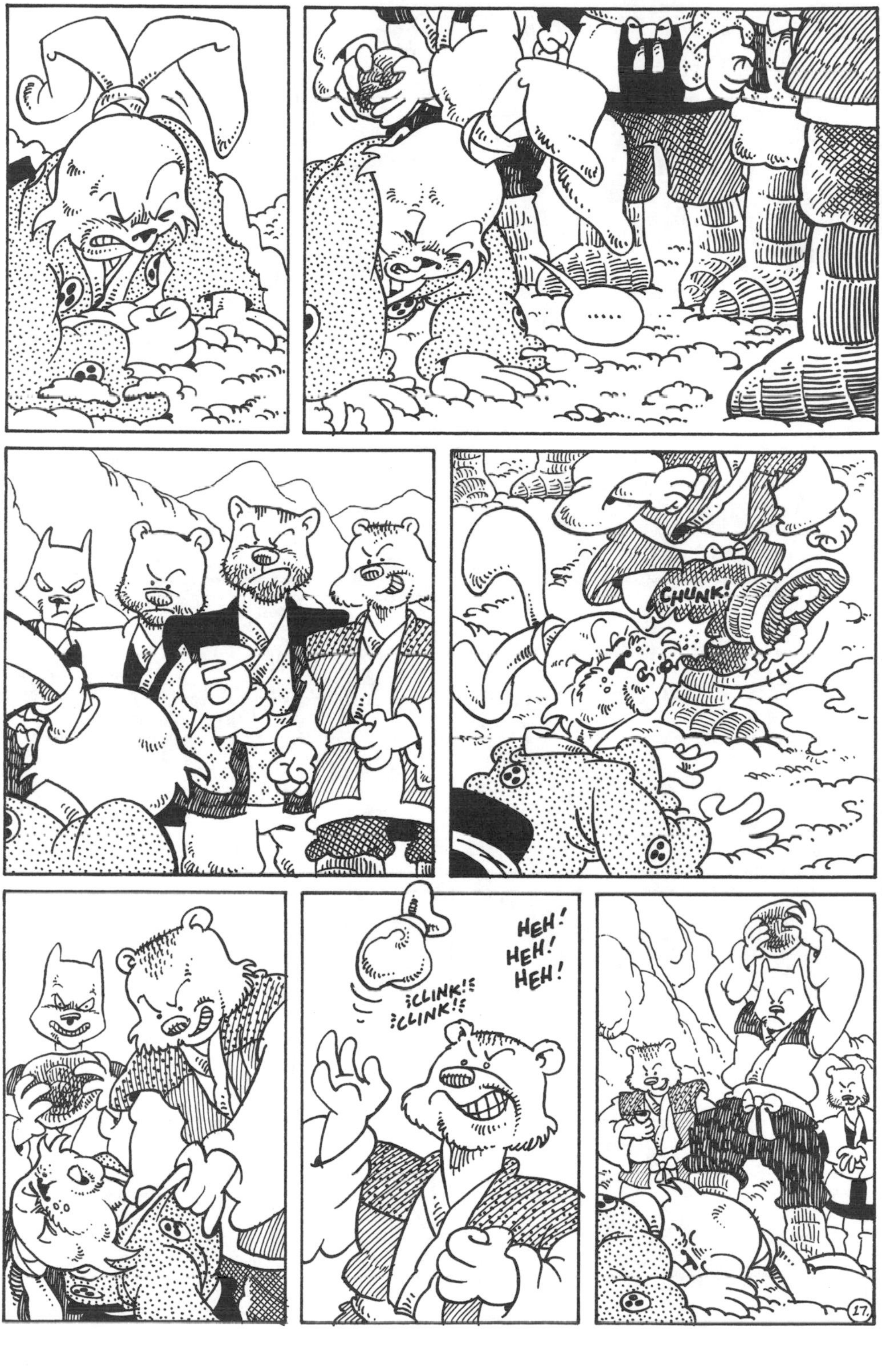
......
CHUNK!
CLINK! CLINK!
HEH! HEH! HEH!
17

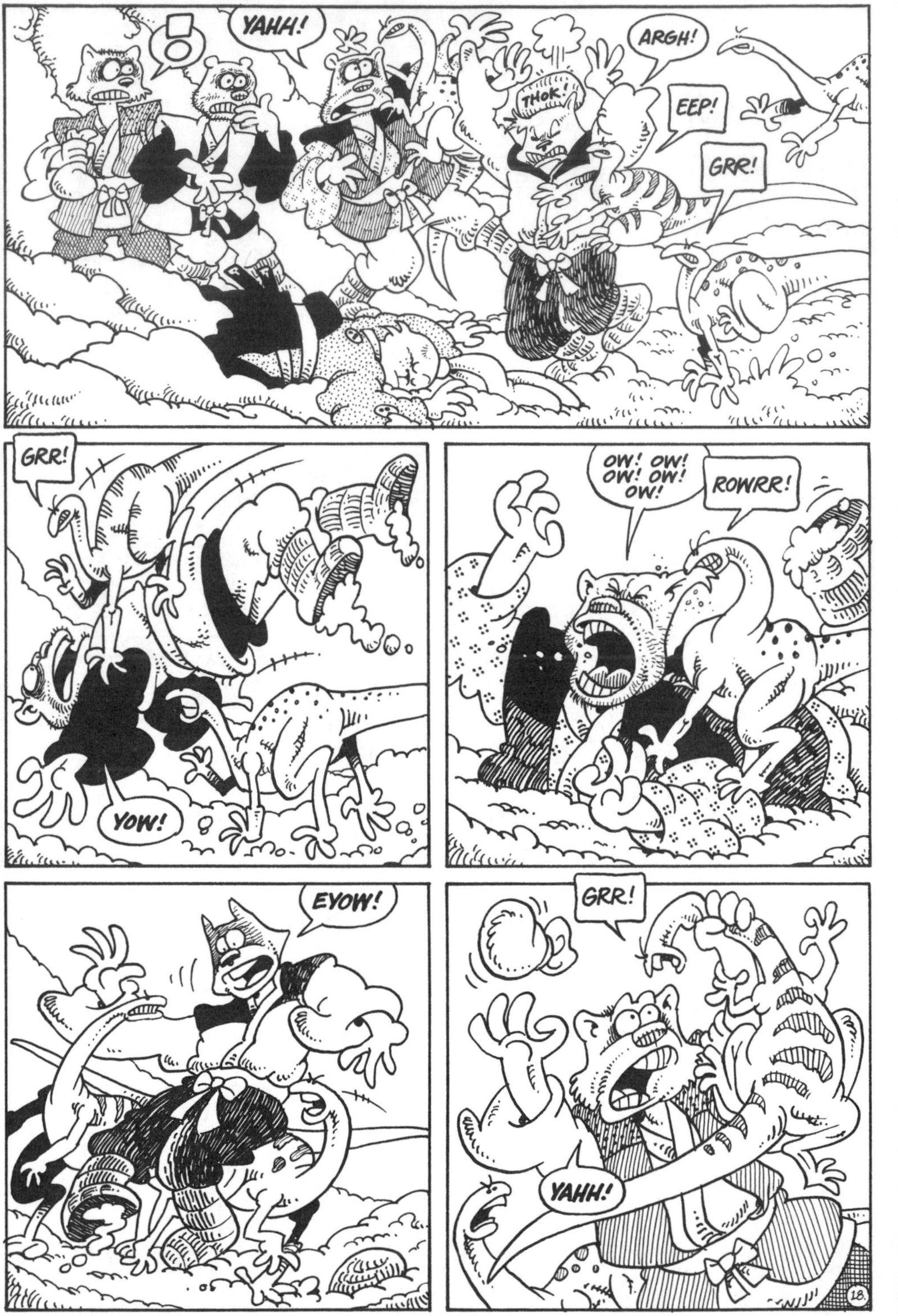
!
YAHH!
ARGH!
THOK
EEP!
GRR!
GRR!
YOW!
OW! OW!
OW! OW!
OW!
ROWRR!
EYOW!
GRR!
YAHH!
18.

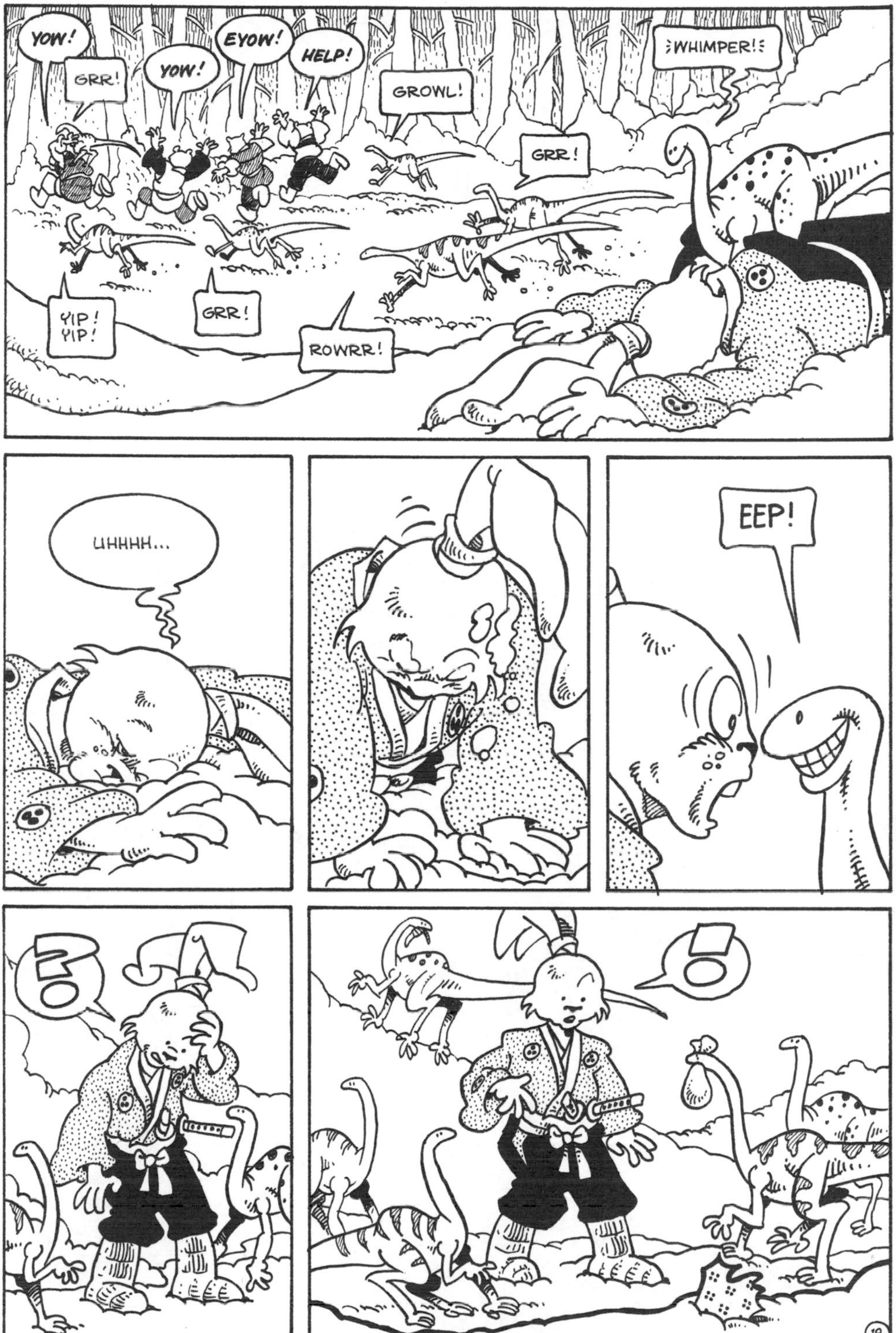
YOW!
GRR!
YOW!
EYOW!
HELP!
GROWL!
WHIMPER!
GRR!
YIP! YIP!
GRR!
ROWRR!
UHHHH...
EEP!
?
!
19.

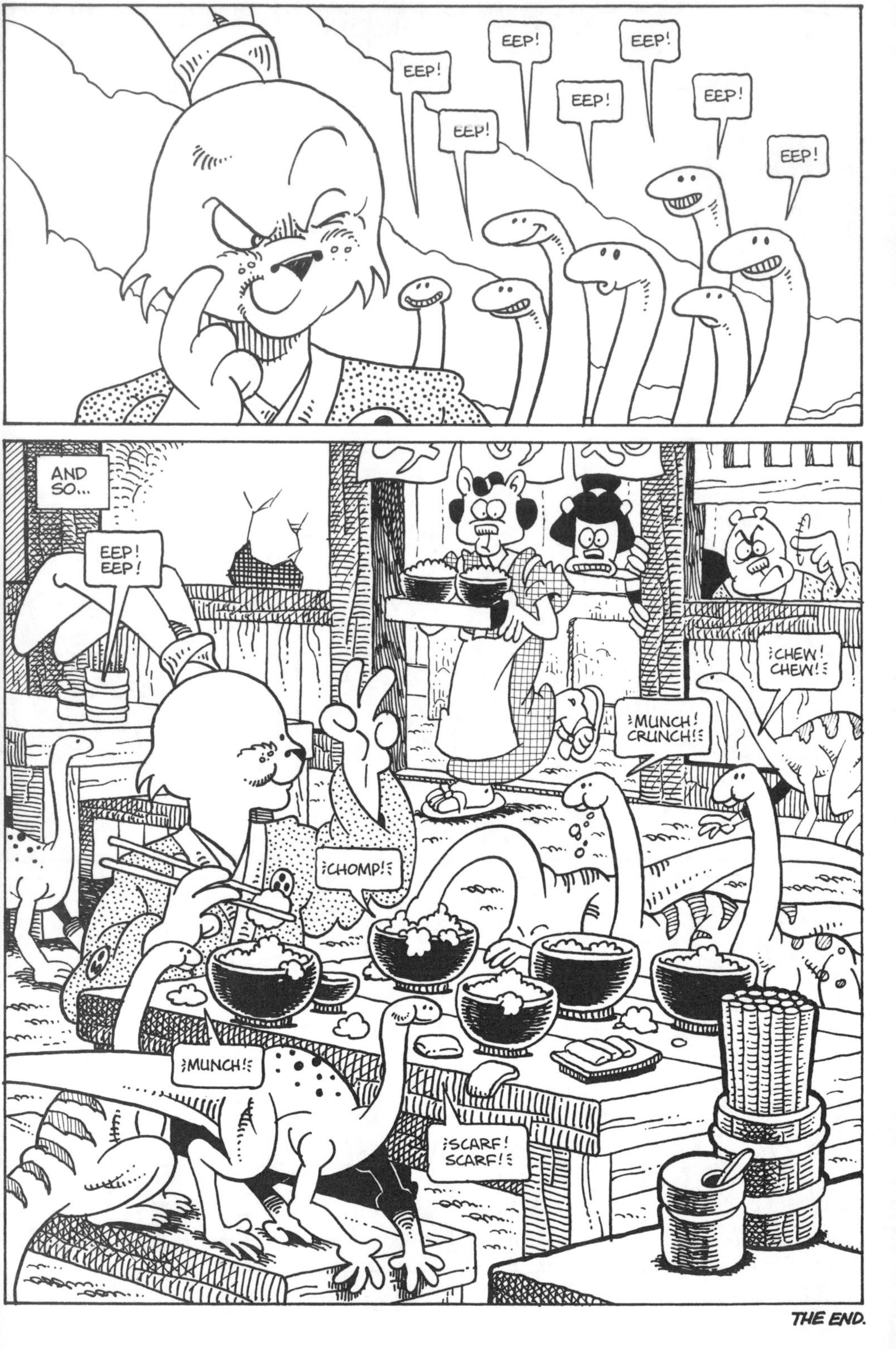
EEP!
EEP!
EEP!
EEP!
EEP!
EEP!
EEP!
EEP!
AND SO...
EEP! EEP!
CHEW! CHEW!
MUNCH! CRUNCH!
CHOMP!
MUNCH!
SCARF! SCARF!

THE END.

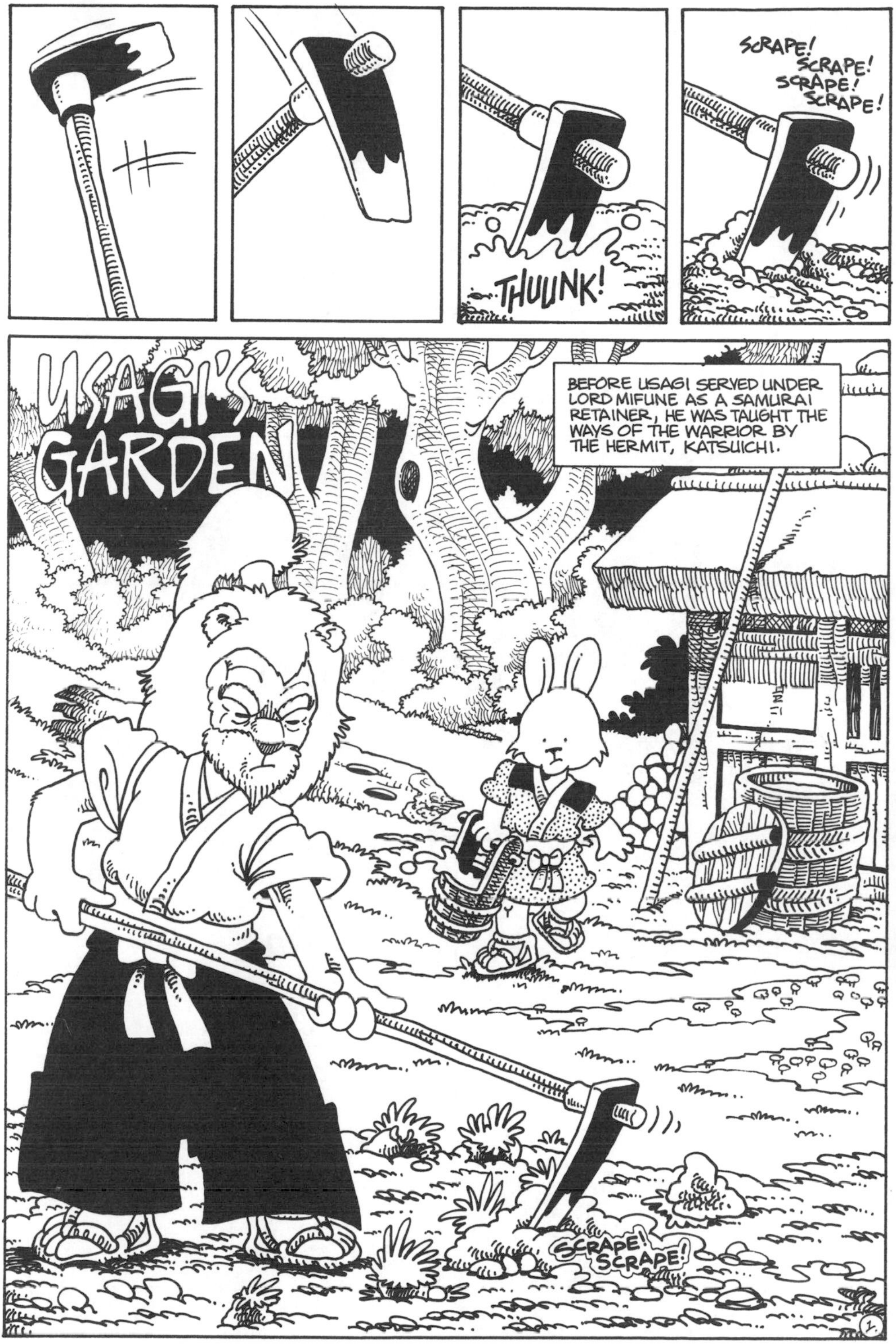
THUUNK!
SCRAPE! SCRAPE! SCRAPE! SCRAPE!
USAGI'S GARDEN
BEFORE USAGI SERVED UNDER LORD MIFUNE AS A SAMURAI RETAINER, HE WAS TAUGHT THE WAYS OF THE WARRIOR BY THE HERMIT, KATSUICHI.
SCRAPE! SCRAPE!
2.

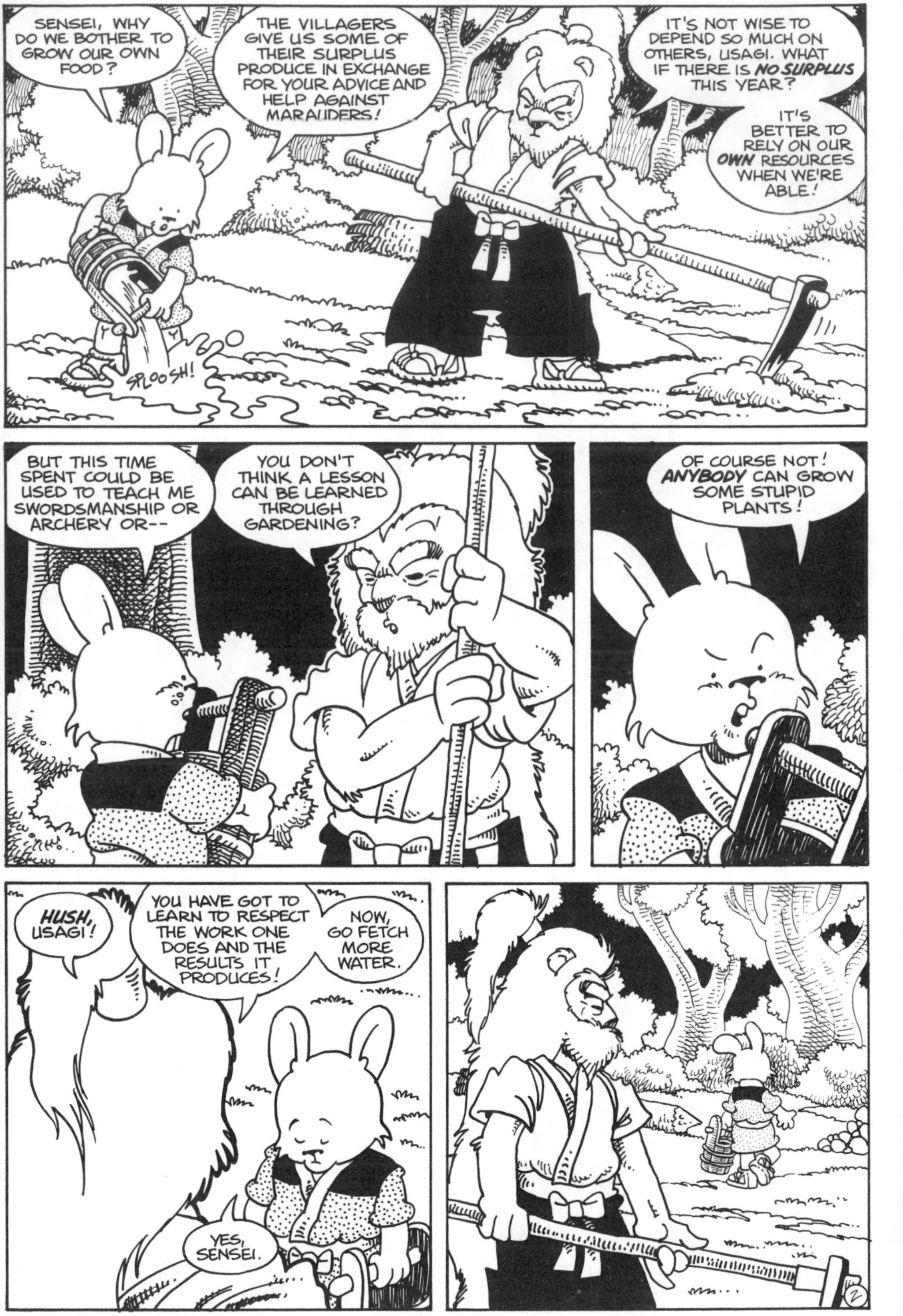
SENSEI, WHY DO WE BOTHER TO GROW OUR OWN FOOD?
THE VILLAGERS GIVE US SOME OF THEIR SURPLUS PRODUCE IN EXCHANGE FOR YOUR ADVICE AND HELP AGAINST MARAUDERS!
IT'S NOT WISE TO DEPEND SO MUCH ON OTHERS, USAGI. WHAT IF THERE IS **NO SURPLUS** THIS YEAR?
IT'S BETTER TO RELY ON OUR **OWN** RESOURCES WHEN WE'RE ABLE!
SPLOOSH!
BUT THIS TIME SPENT COULD BE USED TO TEACH ME SWORDSMANSHIP OR ARCHERY OR--
YOU DON'T THINK A LESSON CAN BE LEARNED THROUGH GARDENING?
OF COURSE NOT! **ANYBODY** CAN GROW SOME STUPID PLANTS!
HUSH, USAGI!
YOU HAVE GOT TO LEARN TO RESPECT THE WORK ONE DOES AND THE RESULTS IT PRODUCES!
NOW, GO FETCH MORE WATER.
YES, SENSEI.
2

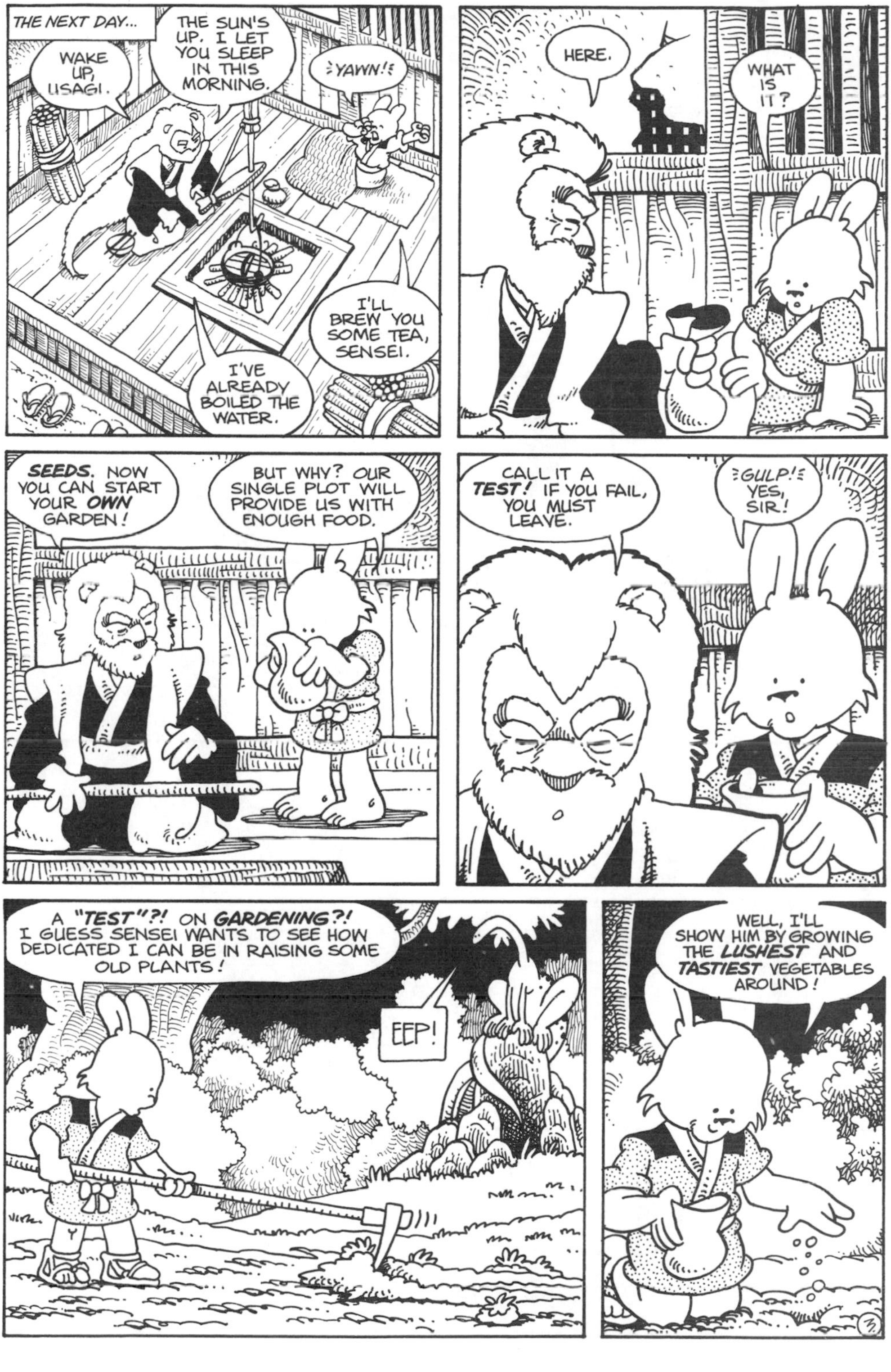
THE NEXT DAY...
WAKE UP, USAGI.
THE SUN'S UP. I LET YOU SLEEP IN THIS MORNING.
YAWN!
I'LL BREW YOU SOME TEA, SENSEI.
I'VE ALREADY BOILED THE WATER.
HERE.
WHAT IS IT?
SEEDS. NOW YOU CAN START YOUR OWN GARDEN!
BUT WHY? OUR SINGLE PLOT WILL PROVIDE US WITH ENOUGH FOOD.
CALL IT A TEST! IF YOU FAIL, YOU MUST LEAVE.
GULP! YES, SIR!
A "TEST"?! ON GARDENING?! I GUESS SENSEI WANTS TO SEE HOW DEDICATED I CAN BE IN RAISING SOME OLD PLANTS!
EEP!
WELL, I'LL SHOW HIM BY GROWING THE LUSHEST AND TASTIEST VEGETABLES AROUND!
3

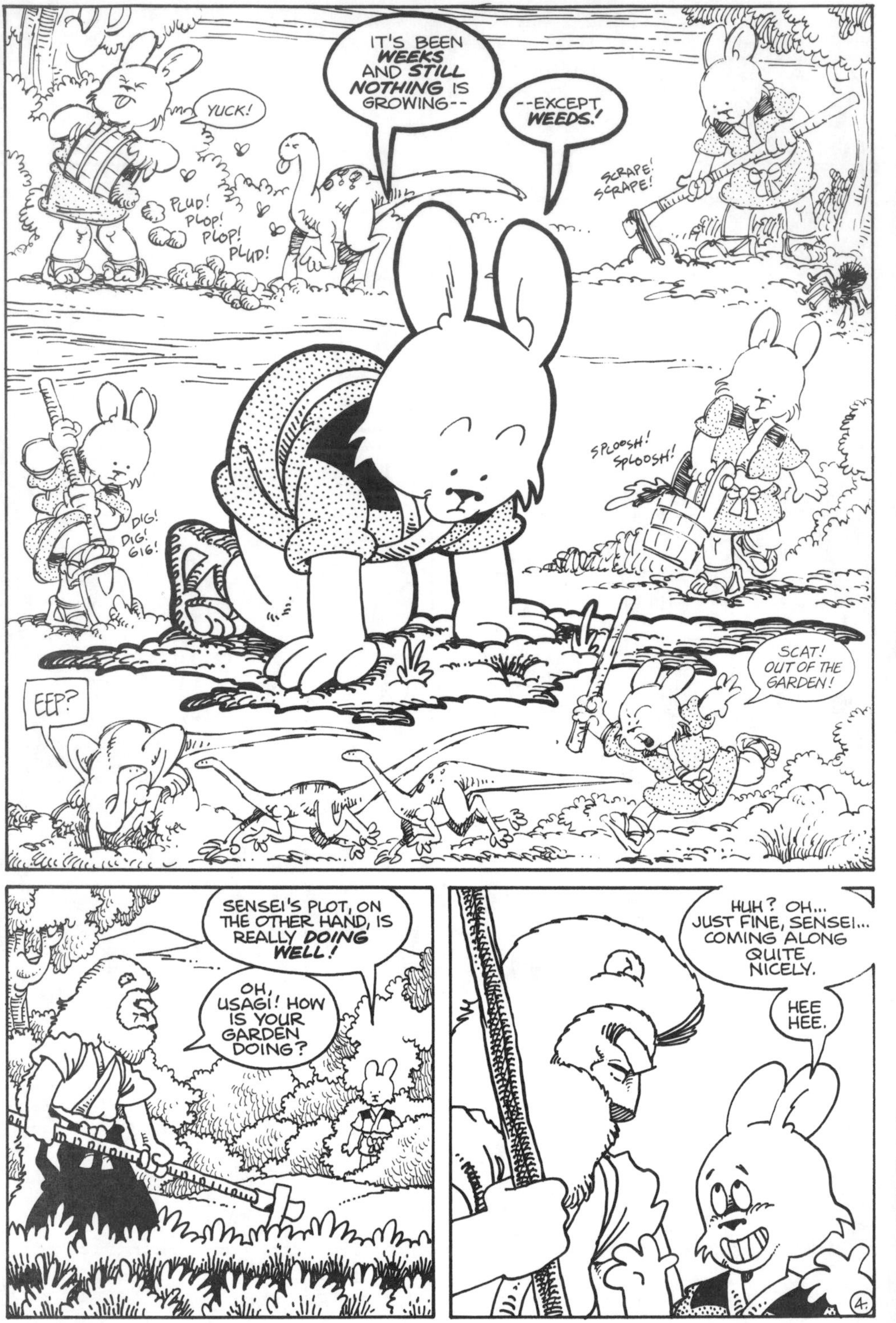
YUCK!
PLUD! PLOP! PLOP! PLUD!
IT'S BEEN WEEKS AND STILL NOTHING IS GROWING--
--EXCEPT WEEDS!
SCRAPE! SCRAPE!
SPLOOSH! SPLOOSH!
DIG! DIG! DIG!
EEP?
SCAT! OUT OF THE GARDEN!
SENSEI'S PLOT, ON THE OTHER HAND, IS REALLY DOING WELL!
OH, USAGI! HOW IS YOUR GARDEN DOING?
HUH? OH... JUST FINE, SENSEI... COMING ALONG QUITE NICELY.
HEE HEE.
4.

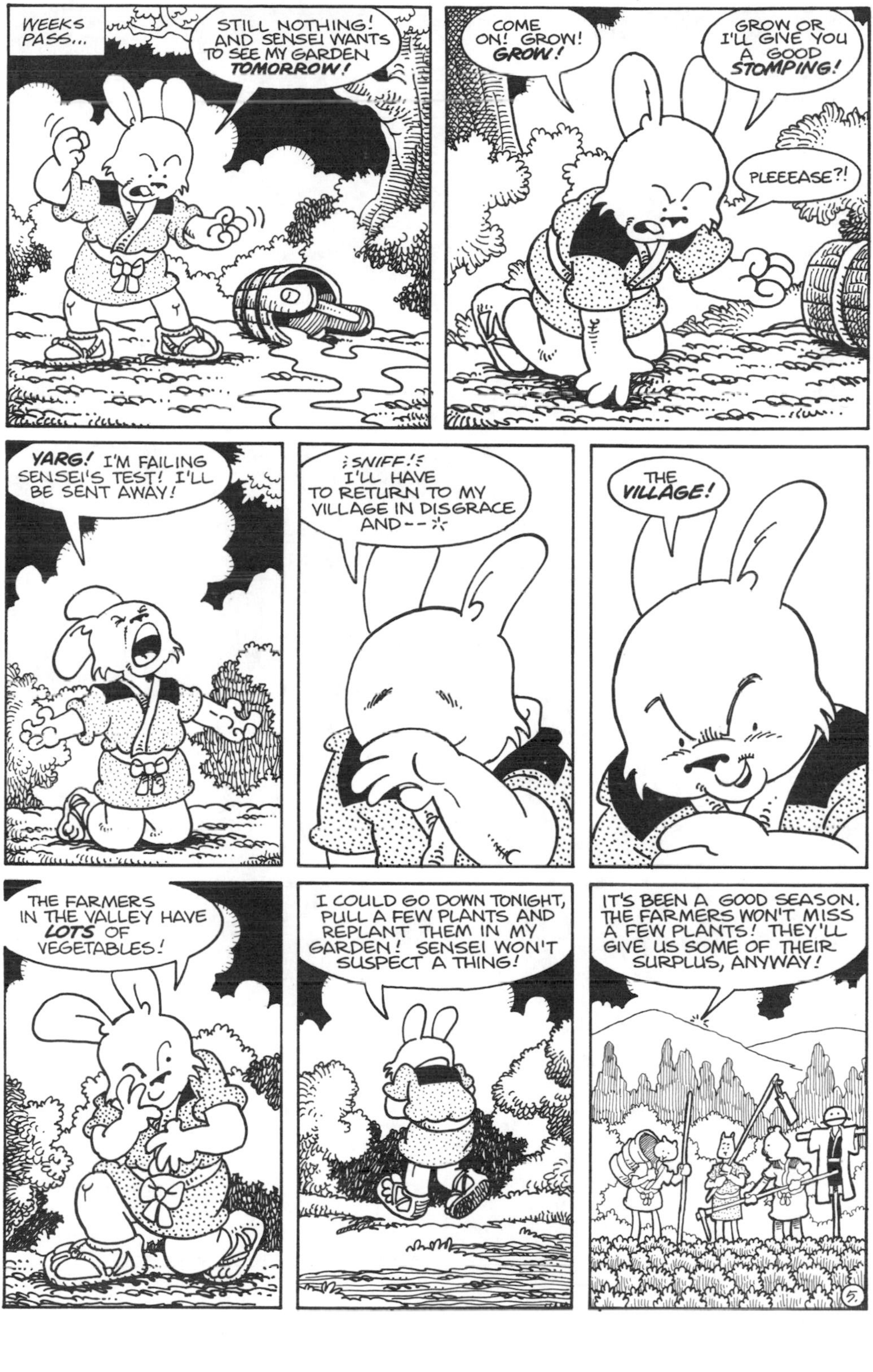
WEEKS PASS...
STILL NOTHING! AND SENSEI WANTS TO SEE MY GARDEN TOMORROW!
COME ON! GROW! GROW!
GROW OR I'LL GIVE YOU A GOOD STOMPING!
PLEEEASE?!
YARG! I'M FAILING SENSEI'S TEST! I'LL BE SENT AWAY!
SNIFF! I'LL HAVE TO RETURN TO MY VILLAGE IN DISGRACE AND--
THE VILLAGE!
THE FARMERS IN THE VALLEY HAVE LOTS OF VEGETABLES!
I COULD GO DOWN TONIGHT, PULL A FEW PLANTS AND REPLANT THEM IN MY GARDEN! SENSEI WON'T SUSPECT A THING!
IT'S BEEN A GOOD SEASON. THE FARMERS WON'T MISS A FEW PLANTS! THEY'LL GIVE US SOME OF THEIR SURPLUS, ANYWAY!
5.

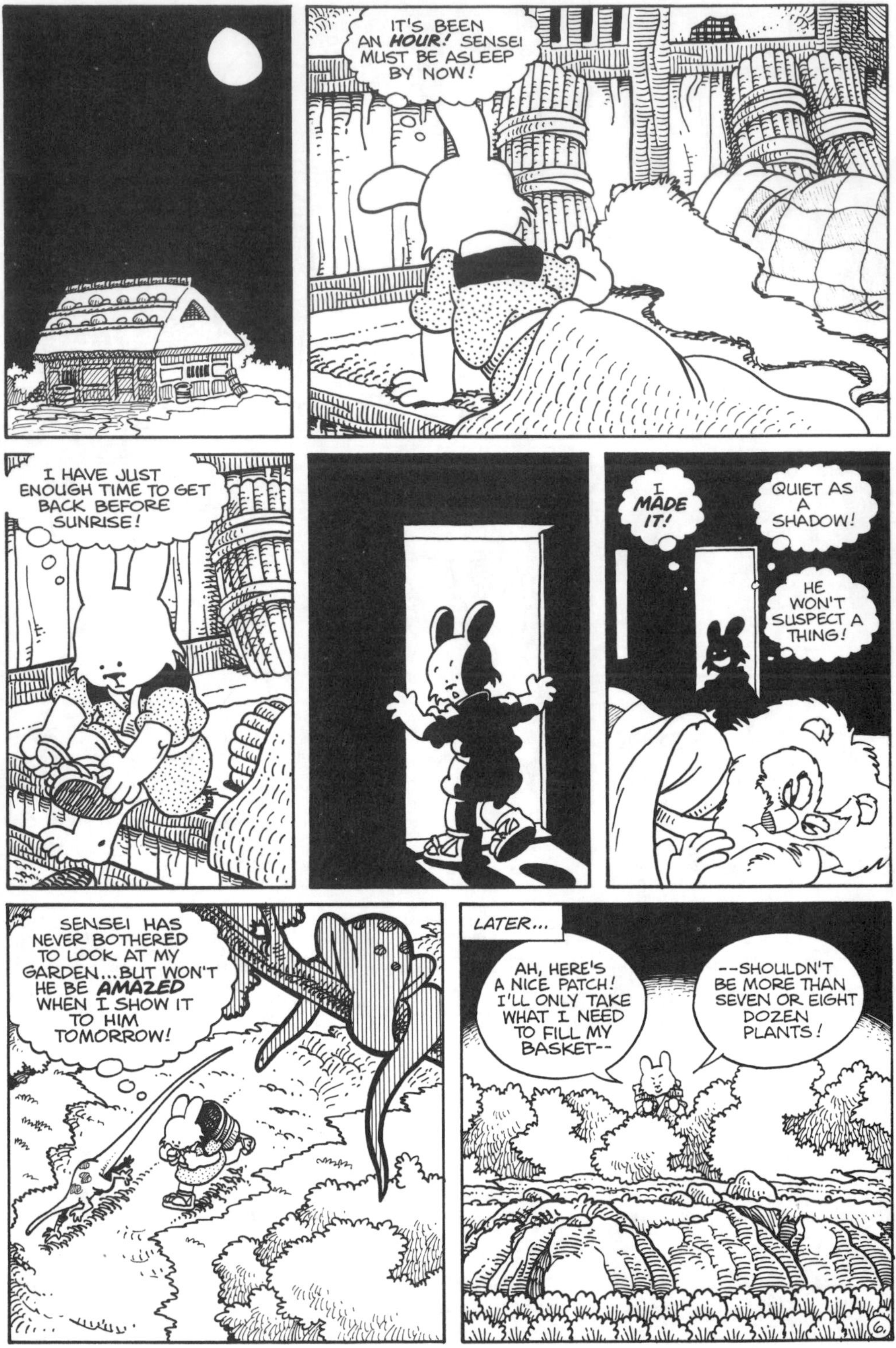
IT'S BEEN AN HOUR! SENSEI MUST BE ASLEEP BY NOW!
I HAVE JUST ENOUGH TIME TO GET BACK BEFORE SUNRISE!
I MADE IT!
QUIET AS A SHADOW!
HE WON'T SUSPECT A THING!
SENSEI HAS NEVER BOTHERED TO LOOK AT MY GARDEN...BUT WON'T HE BE AMAZED WHEN I SHOW IT TO HIM TOMORROW!
LATER...
AH, HERE'S A NICE PATCH! I'LL ONLY TAKE WHAT I NEED TO FILL MY BASKET--
--SHOULDN'T BE MORE THAN SEVEN OR EIGHT DOZEN PLANTS!
6

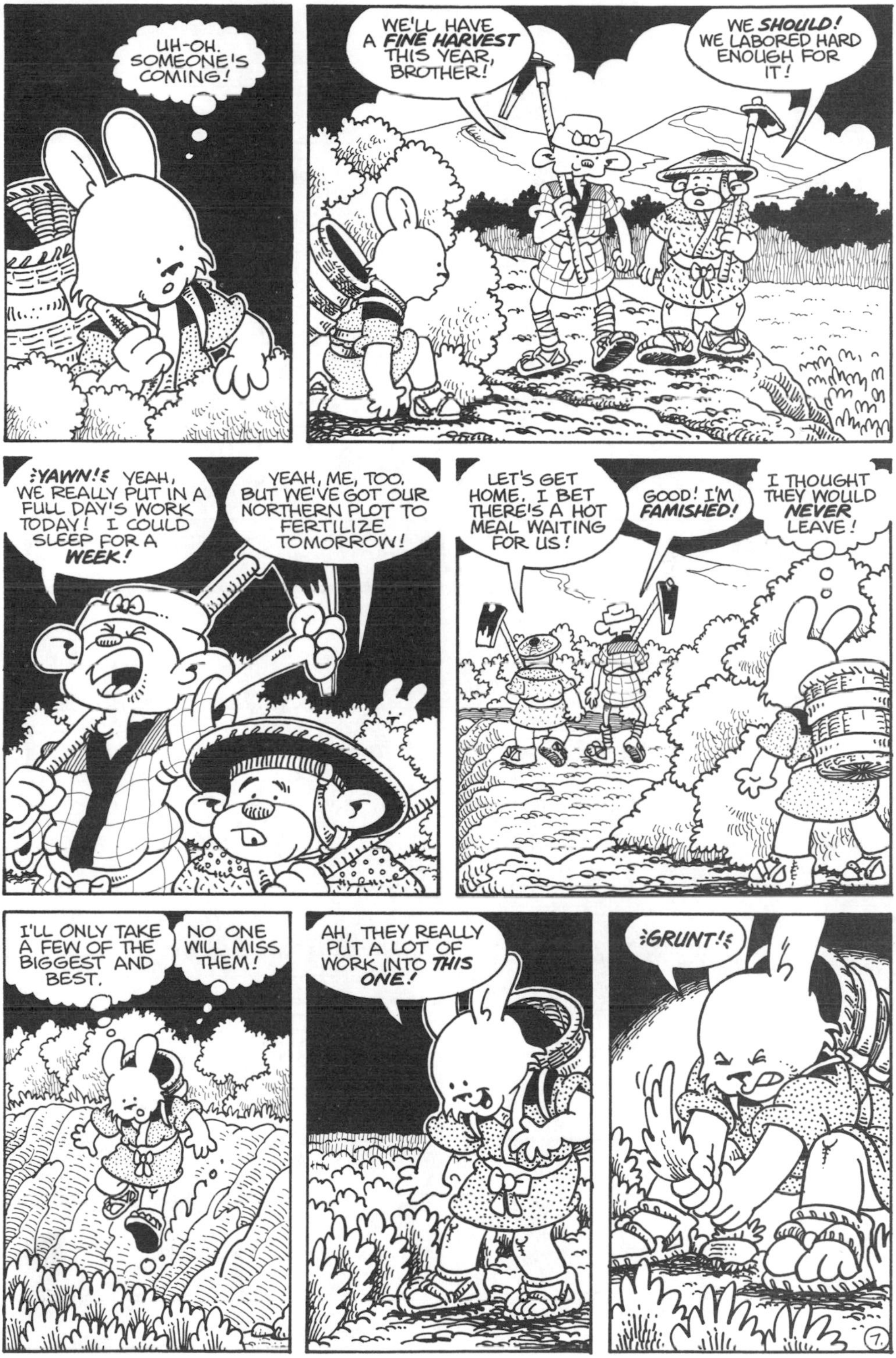
UH-OH. SOMEONE'S COMING!
WE'LL HAVE A FINE HARVEST THIS YEAR, BROTHER!
WE SHOULD! WE LABORED HARD ENOUGH FOR IT!
:YAWN!: YEAH, WE REALLY PUT IN A FULL DAY'S WORK TODAY! I COULD SLEEP FOR A WEEK!
YEAH, ME, TOO, BUT WE'VE GOT OUR NORTHERN PLOT TO FERTILIZE TOMORROW!
LET'S GET HOME. I BET THERE'S A HOT MEAL WAITING FOR US!
GOOD! I'M FAMISHED!
I THOUGHT THEY WOULD NEVER LEAVE!
I'LL ONLY TAKE A FEW OF THE BIGGEST AND BEST.
NO ONE WILL MISS THEM!
AH, THEY REALLY PUT A LOT OF WORK INTO THIS ONE!
:GRUNT!:
7.

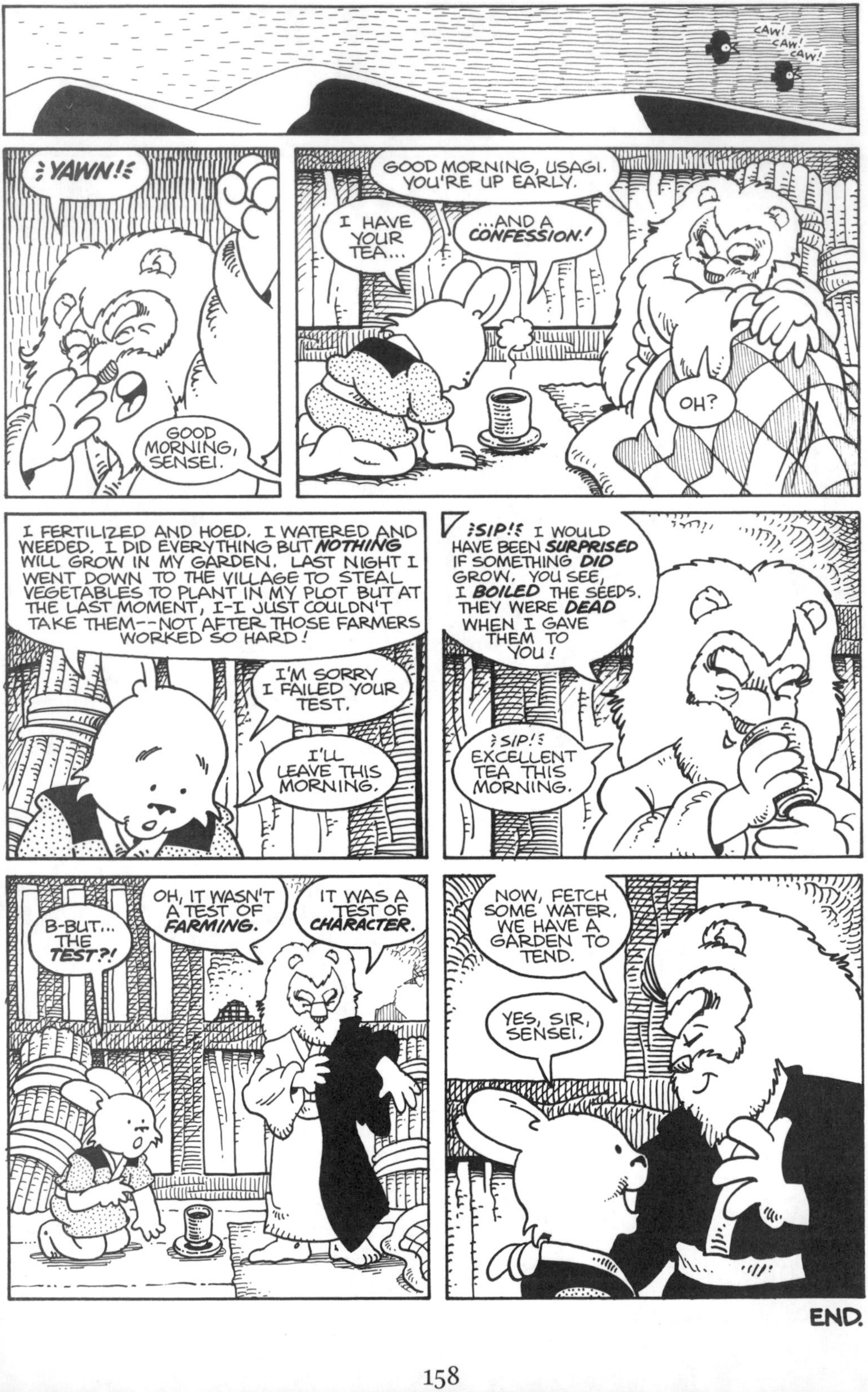
CAW! CAW! CAW!
YAWN!
GOOD MORNING, SENSEI.
GOOD MORNING, USAGI. YOU'RE UP EARLY.
I HAVE YOUR TEA...
...AND A CONFESSION!
OH?
I FERTILIZED AND HOED. I WATERED AND WEEDED. I DID EVERYTHING BUT NOTHING WILL GROW IN MY GARDEN. LAST NIGHT I WENT DOWN TO THE VILLAGE TO STEAL VEGETABLES TO PLANT IN MY PLOT BUT AT THE LAST MOMENT, I-I JUST COULDN'T TAKE THEM--NOT AFTER THOSE FARMERS WORKED SO HARD!
I'M SORRY I FAILED YOUR TEST.
I'LL LEAVE THIS MORNING.
SIP! I WOULD HAVE BEEN SURPRISED IF SOMETHING DID GROW. YOU SEE, I BOILED THE SEEDS. THEY WERE DEAD WHEN I GAVE THEM TO YOU!
SIP! EXCELLENT TEA THIS MORNING.
B-BUT... THE TEST?!
OH, IT WASN'T A TEST OF FARMING.
IT WAS A TEST OF CHARACTER.
NOW, FETCH SOME WATER. WE HAVE A GARDEN TO TEND.
YES, SIR, SENSEI.
END.

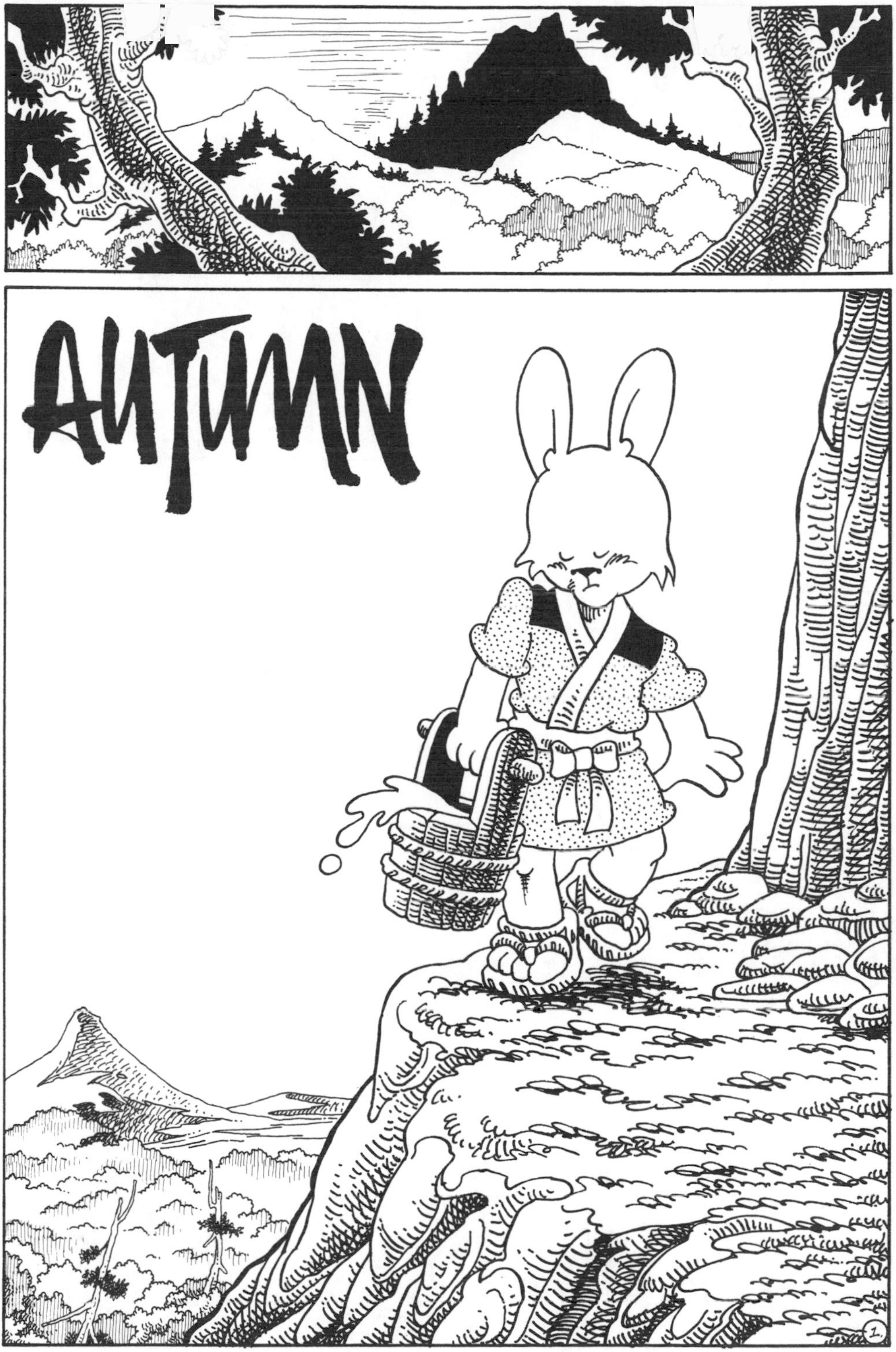
AUTUMN
1.

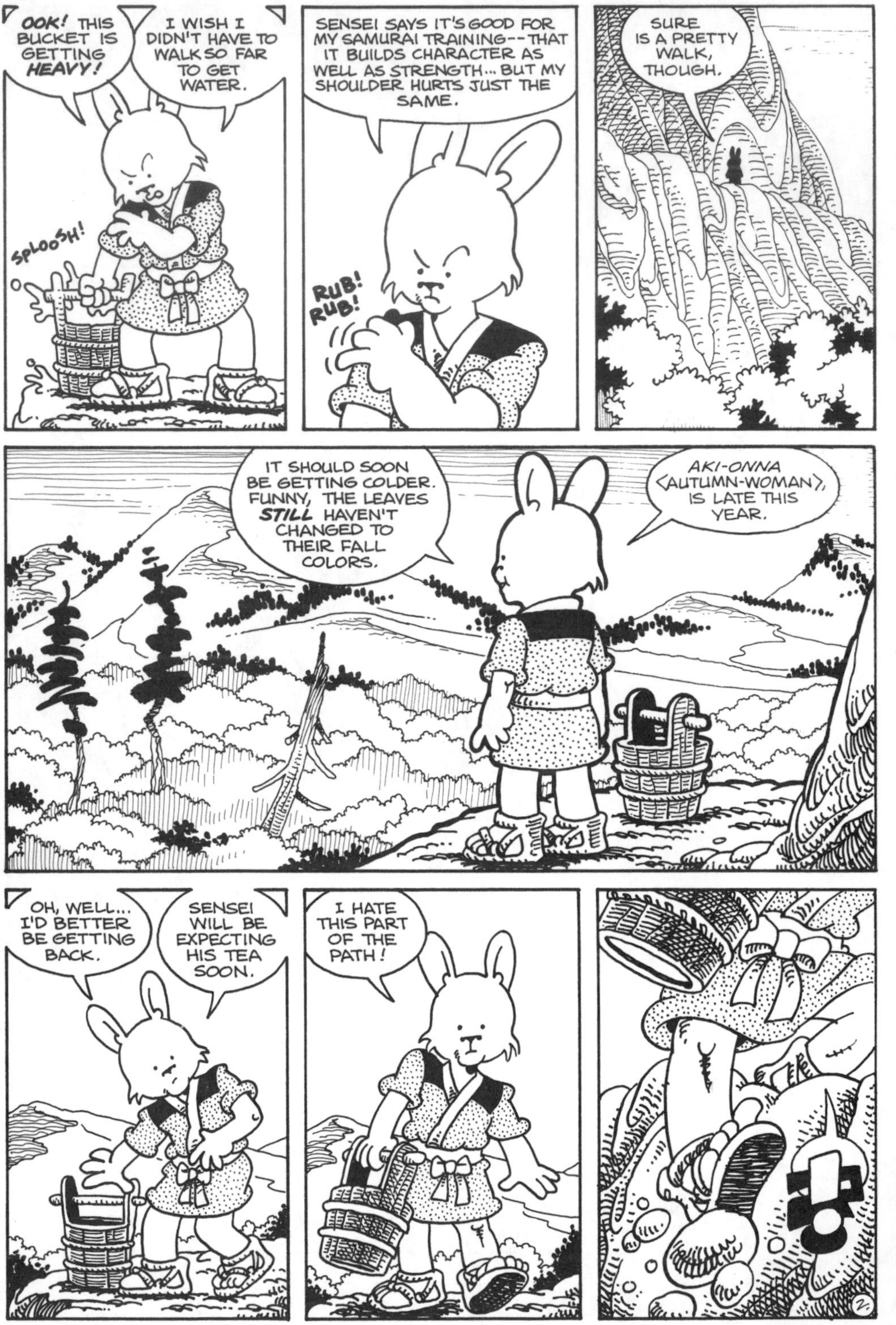

OOK! THIS BUCKET IS GETTING HEAVY!
I WISH I DIDN'T HAVE TO WALK SO FAR TO GET WATER.
SPLOOSH!
SENSEI SAYS IT'S GOOD FOR MY SAMURAI TRAINING--THAT IT BUILDS CHARACTER AS WELL AS STRENGTH... BUT MY SHOULDER HURTS JUST THE SAME.
RUB! RUB!
SURE IS A PRETTY WALK, THOUGH.
IT SHOULD SOON BE GETTING COLDER. FUNNY, THE LEAVES STILL HAVEN'T CHANGED TO THEIR FALL COLORS.
AKI-ONNA <AUTUMN-WOMAN>, IS LATE THIS YEAR.
OH, WELL... I'D BETTER BE GETTING BACK.
SENSEI WILL BE EXPECTING HIS TEA SOON.
I HATE THIS PART OF THE PATH!
2.

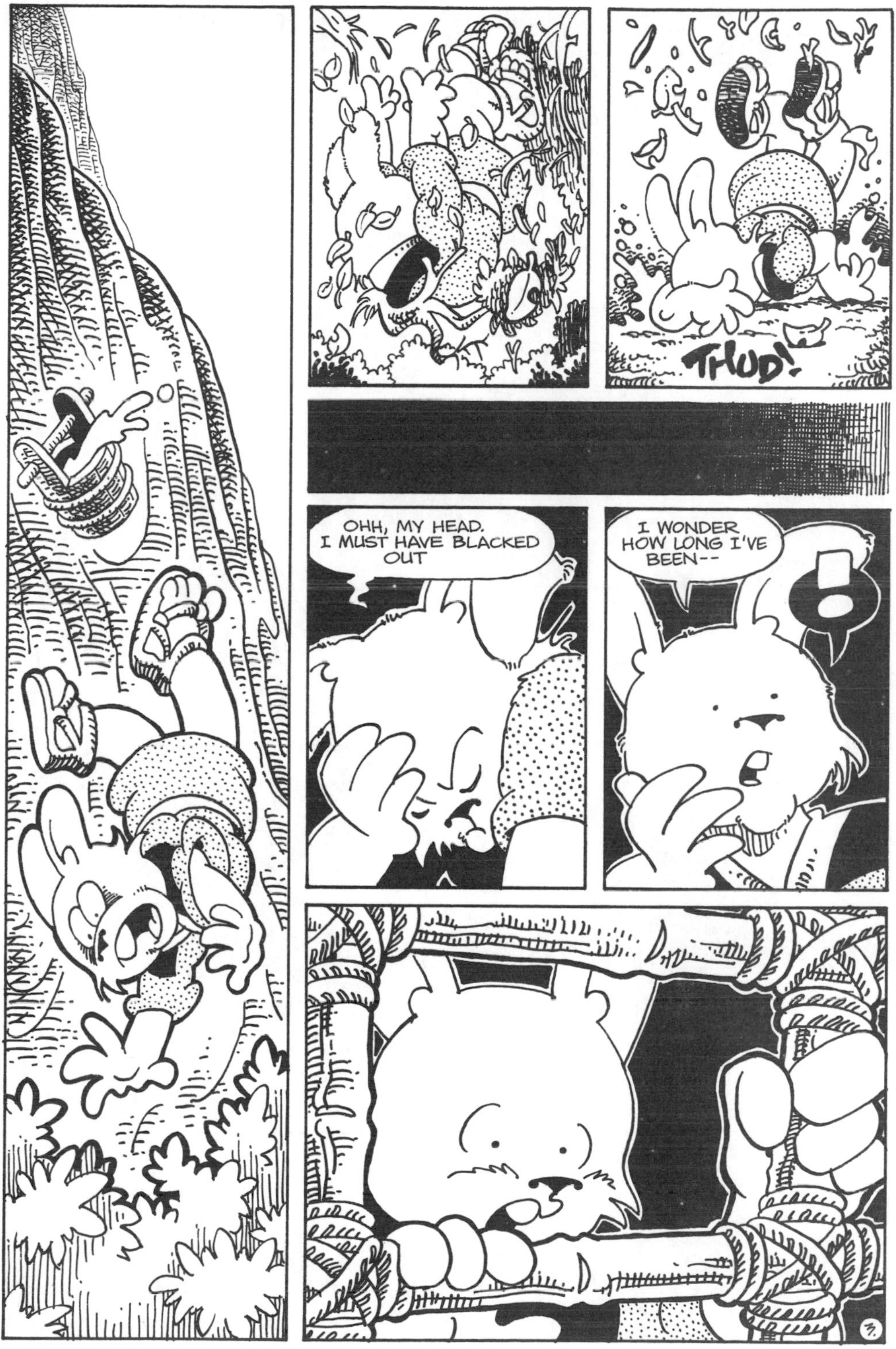
THUD!
OHH, MY HEAD. I MUST HAVE BLACKED OUT
I WONDER HOW LONG I'VE BEEN--
!
3.

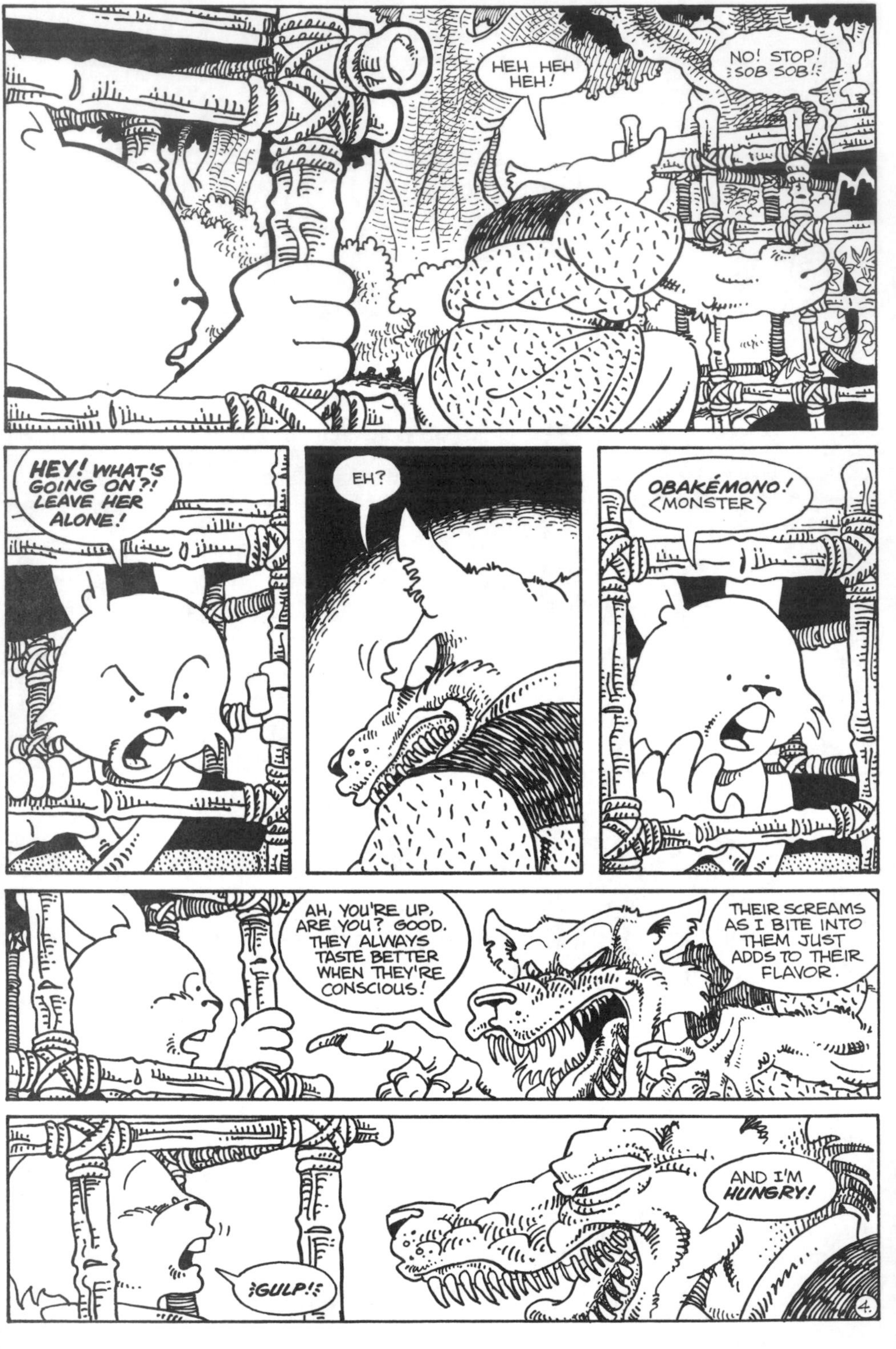
HEH HEH HEH!
NO! STOP! SOB SOB!
HEY! WHAT'S GOING ON?! LEAVE HER ALONE!
EH?
OBAKÉMONO! <MONSTER>
AH, YOU'RE UP, ARE YOU? GOOD. THEY ALWAYS TASTE BETTER WHEN THEY'RE CONSCIOUS!
THEIR SCREAMS AS I BITE INTO THEM JUST ADDS TO THEIR FLAVOR.
GULP!
AND I'M HUNGRY!
4.

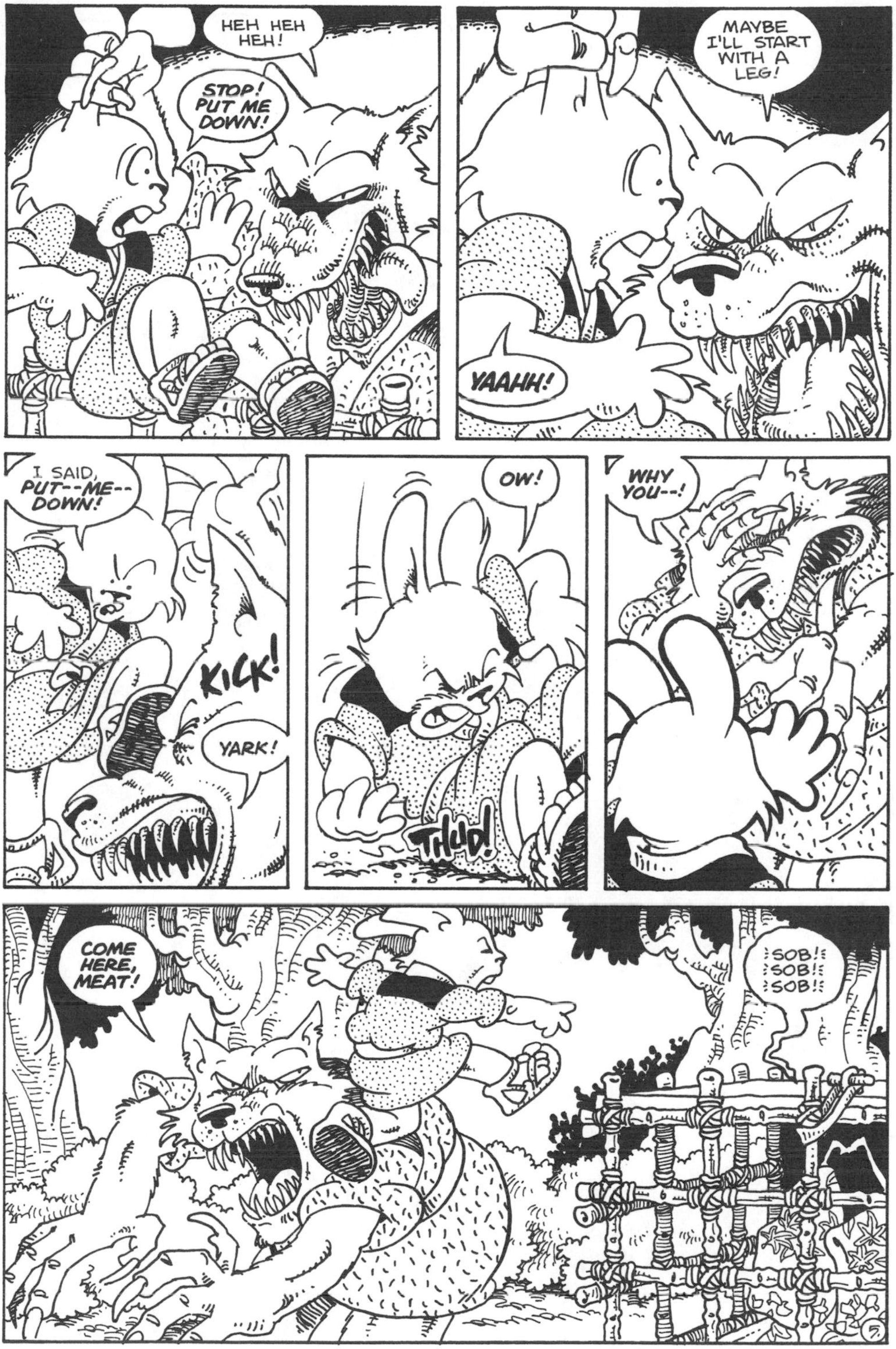
HEH HEH HEH!
STOP! PUT ME DOWN!
MAYBE I'LL START WITH A LEG!
YAAHH!
I SAID, PUT--ME--DOWN!
KICK!
YARK!
OW!
THUD!
WHY YOU--!
COME HERE, MEAT!
SOB! SOB! SOB!

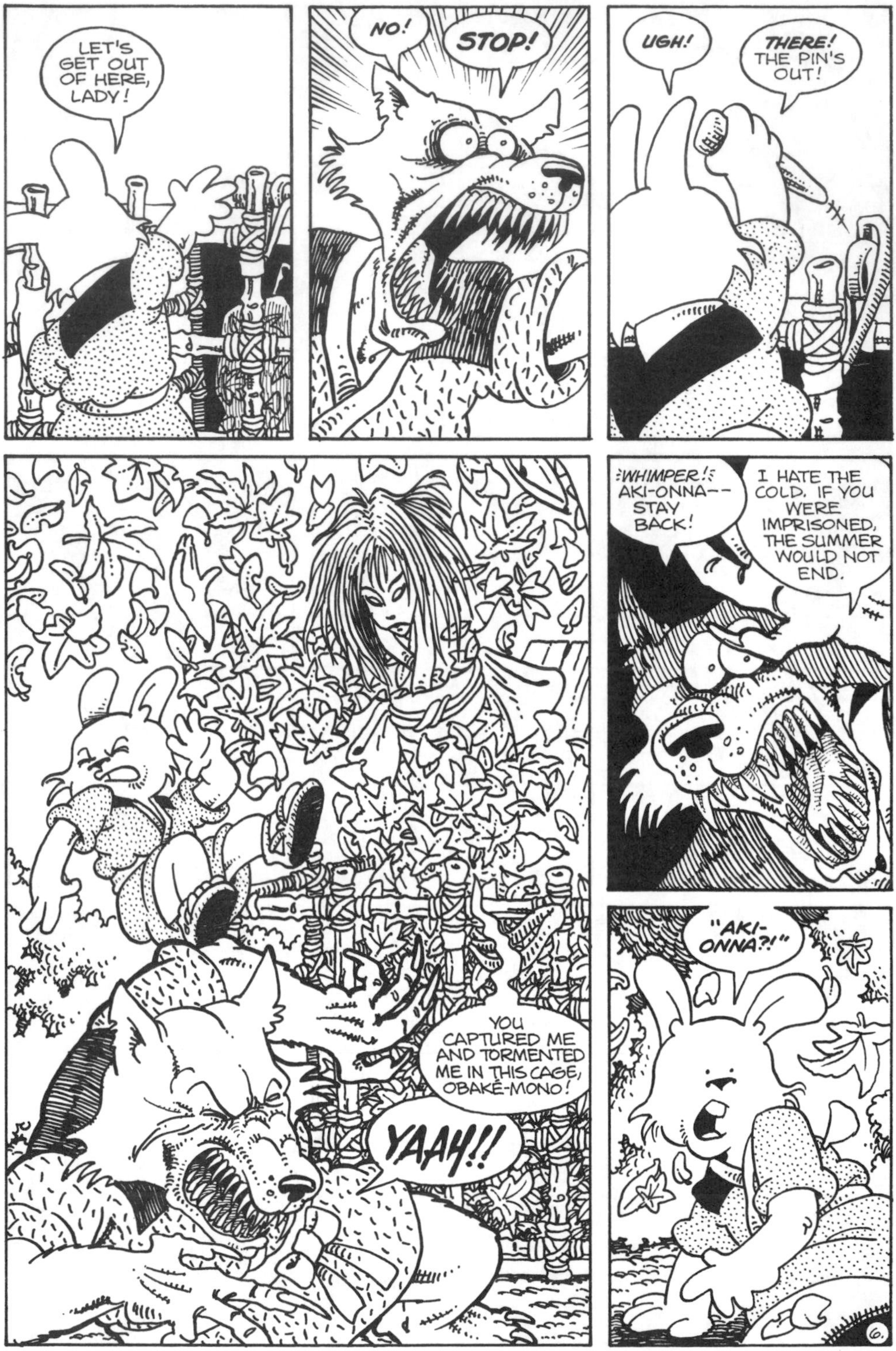
LET'S GET OUT OF HERE, LADY!
NO!
STOP!
UGH!
THERE! THE PIN'S OUT!
YOU CAPTURED ME AND TORMENTED ME IN THIS CAGE, OBAKÉ-MONO!
YAAH!!
:WHIMPER!: AKI-ONNA-- STAY BACK!
I HATE THE COLD. IF YOU WERE IMPRISONED, THE SUMMER WOULD NOT END.
"AKI-ONNA?!"
6.

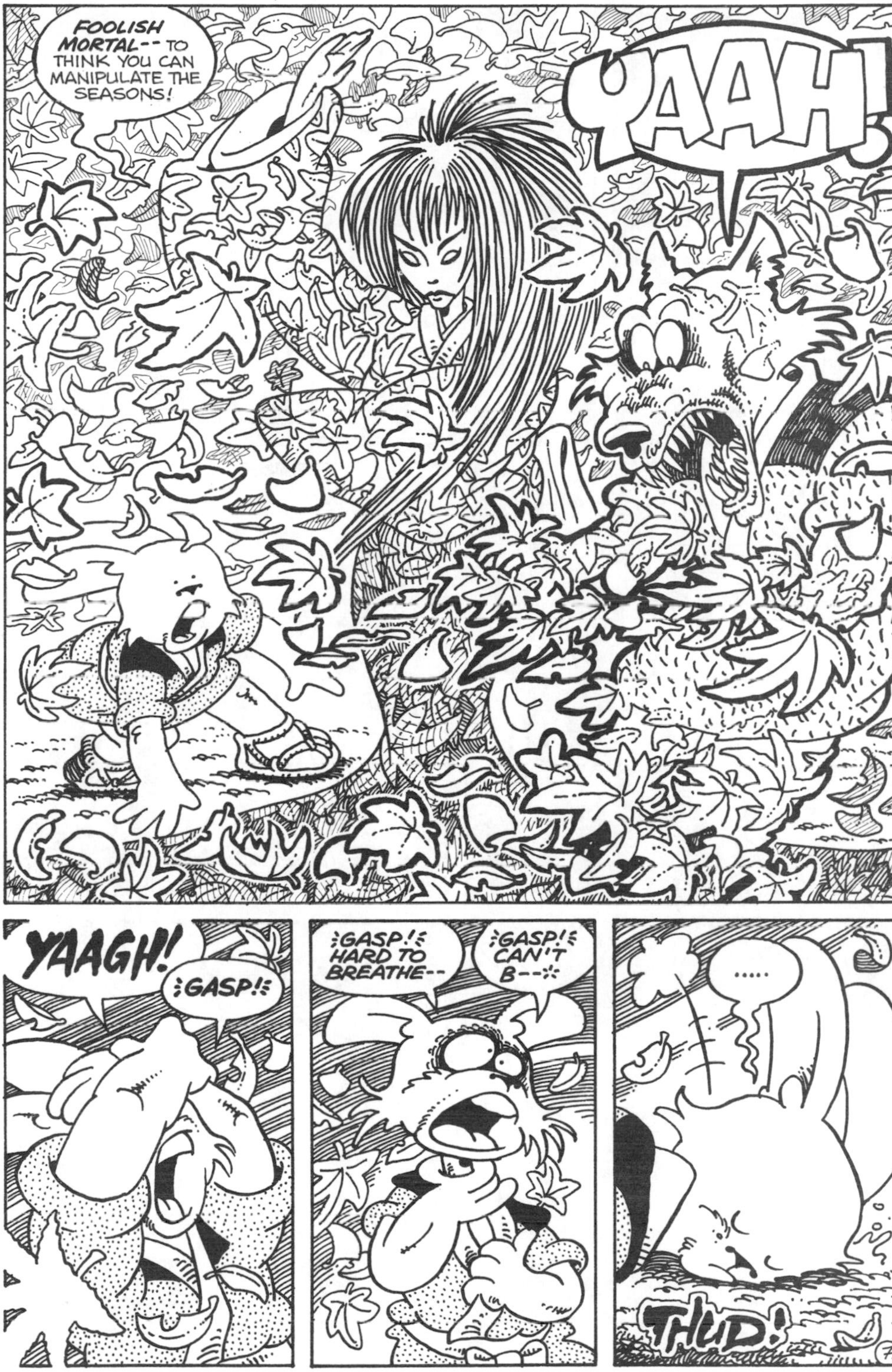
FOOLISH MORTAL-- TO THINK YOU CAN MANIPULATE THE SEASONS!
YAAH!
YAAGH!
GASP!
GASP! HARD TO BREATHE--
GASP! CAN'T B--
.....
THUD!
7.

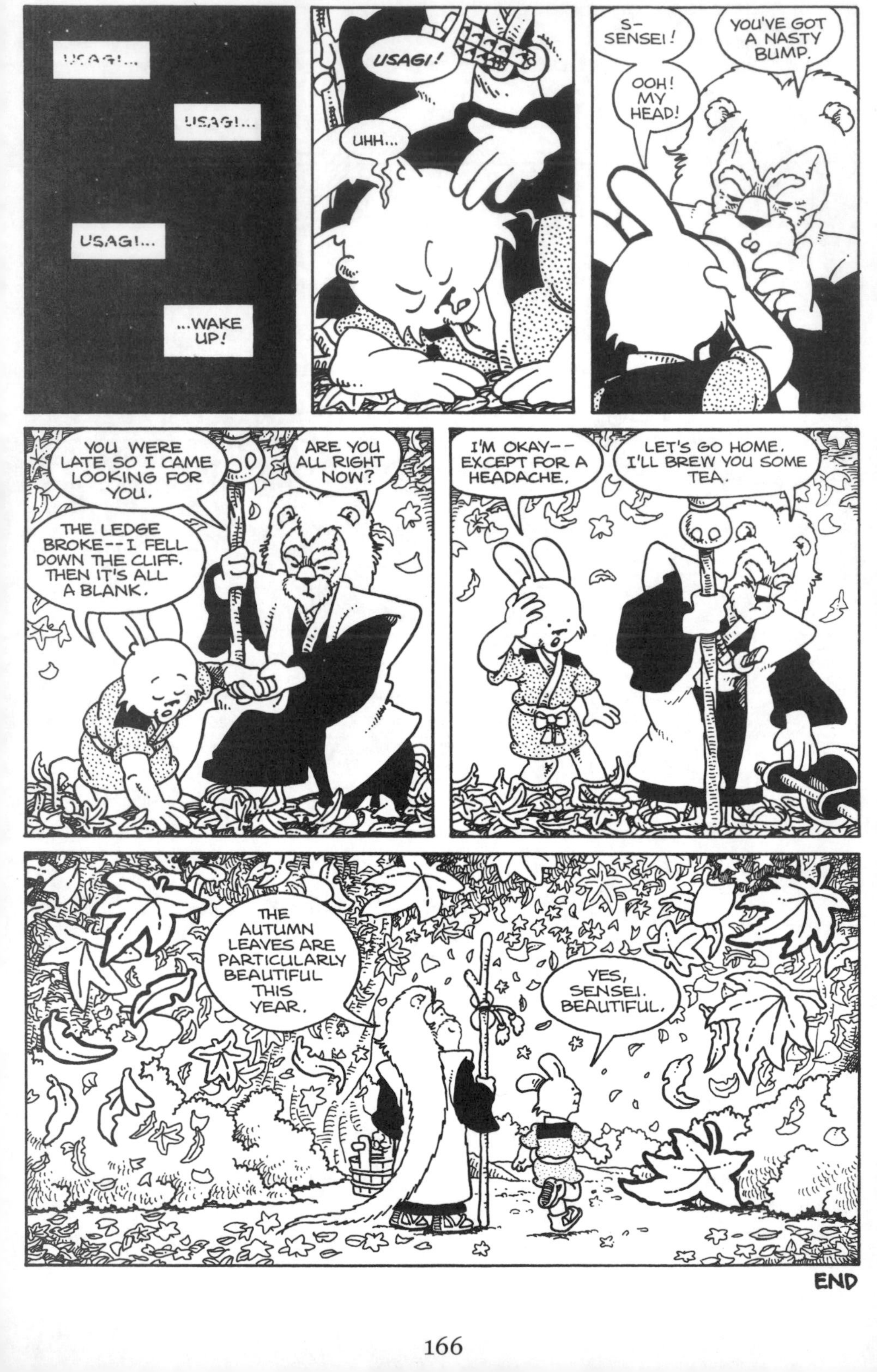
USAGI...
USAGI...
USAGI...
...WAKE UP!
USAGI!
UHH...
S-SENSEI!
OOH! MY HEAD!
YOU'VE GOT A NASTY BUMP.
YOU WERE LATE SO I CAME LOOKING FOR YOU.
ARE YOU ALL RIGHT NOW?
THE LEDGE BROKE--I FELL DOWN THE CLIFF. THEN IT'S ALL A BLANK.
I'M OKAY--EXCEPT FOR A HEADACHE.
LET'S GO HOME. I'LL BREW YOU SOME TEA.
THE AUTUMN LEAVES ARE PARTICULARLY BEAUTIFUL THIS YEAR.
YES, SENSEI. BEAUTIFUL.
END

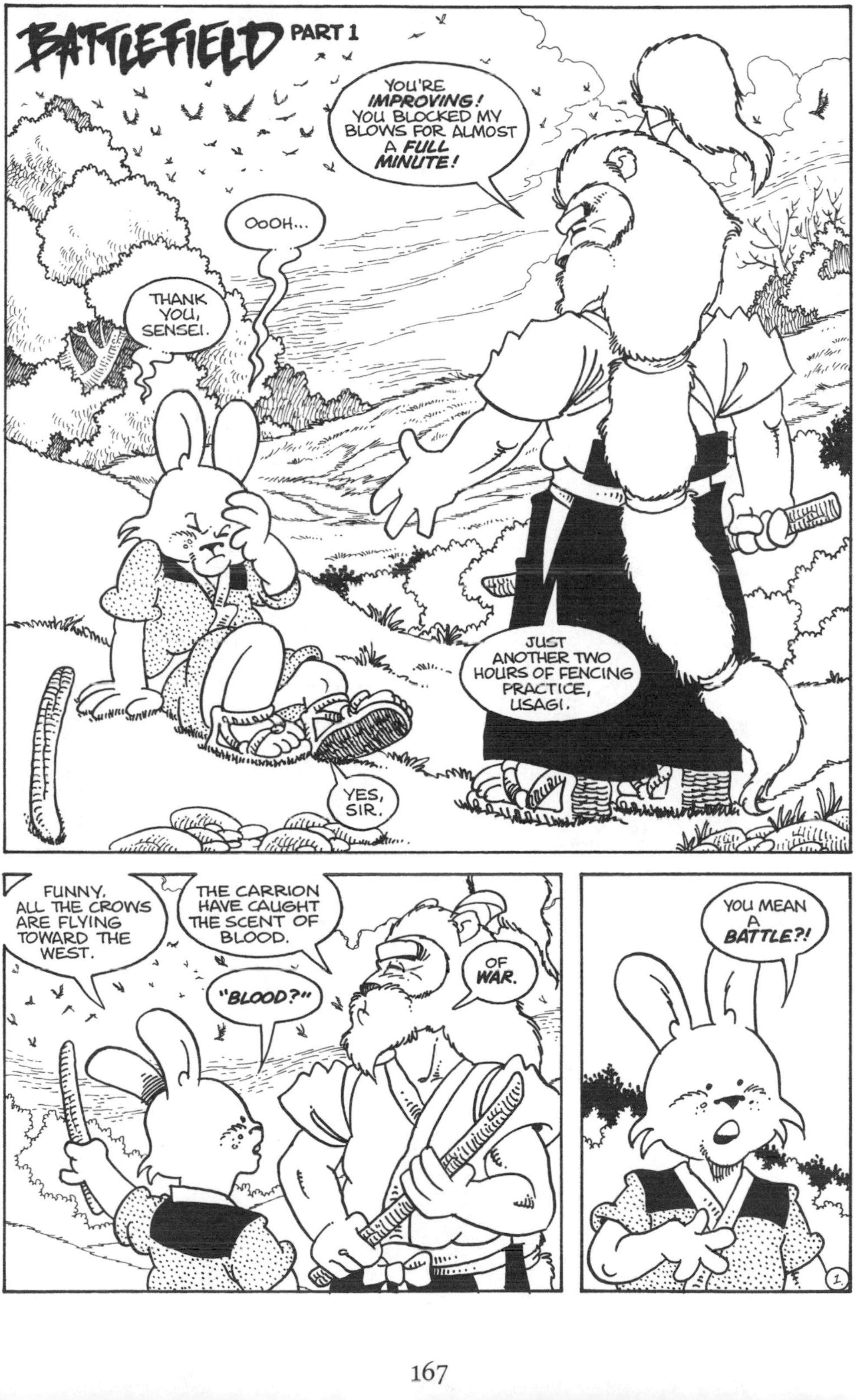
BATTLEFIELD PART 1
YOU'RE IMPROVING! YOU BLOCKED MY BLOWS FOR ALMOST A FULL MINUTE!
OOOH...
THANK YOU, SENSEI.
JUST ANOTHER TWO HOURS OF FENCING PRACTICE, USAGI.
YES, SIR.
FUNNY. ALL THE CROWS ARE FLYING TOWARD THE WEST.
THE CARRION HAVE CAUGHT THE SCENT OF BLOOD.
"BLOOD?"
OF WAR.
YOU MEAN A BATTLE?!
1.

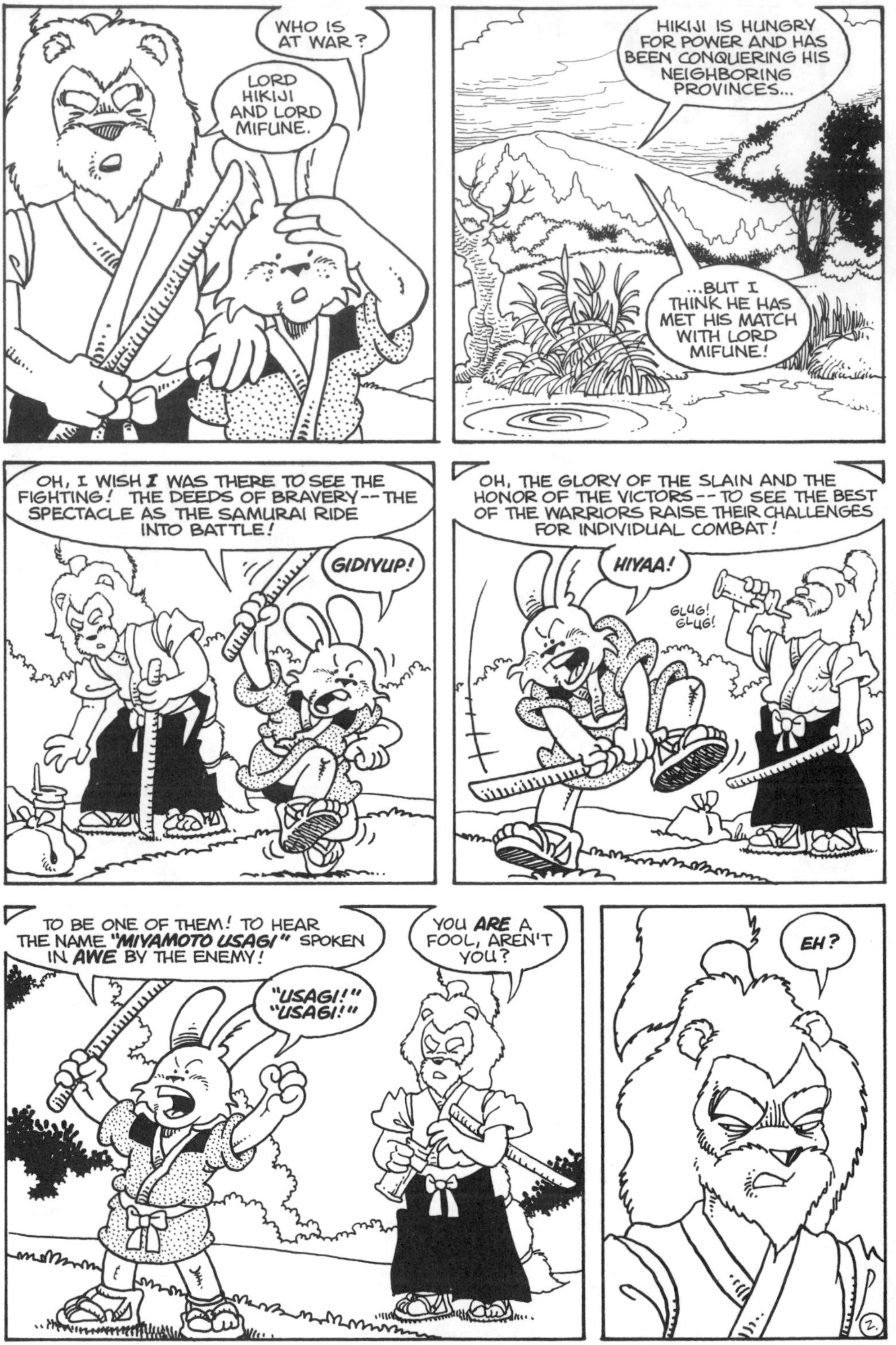
WHO IS AT WAR?
LORD HIKIJI AND LORD MIFUNE.
HIKIJI IS HUNGRY FOR POWER AND HAS BEEN CONQUERING HIS NEIGHBORING PROVINCES...
...BUT I THINK HE HAS MET HIS MATCH WITH LORD MIFUNE!
OH, I WISH *I* WAS THERE TO SEE THE FIGHTING! THE DEEDS OF BRAVERY--THE SPECTACLE AS THE SAMURAI RIDE INTO BATTLE!
GIDIYUP!
OH, THE GLORY OF THE SLAIN AND THE HONOR OF THE VICTORS--TO SEE THE BEST OF THE WARRIORS RAISE THEIR CHALLENGES FOR INDIVIDUAL COMBAT!
HIYAA!
GLUG! GLUG!
TO BE ONE OF THEM! TO HEAR THE NAME "MIYAMOTO USAGI" SPOKEN IN AWE BY THE ENEMY!
"USAGI!" "USAGI!"
YOU ARE A FOOL, AREN'T YOU?
EH?
2.

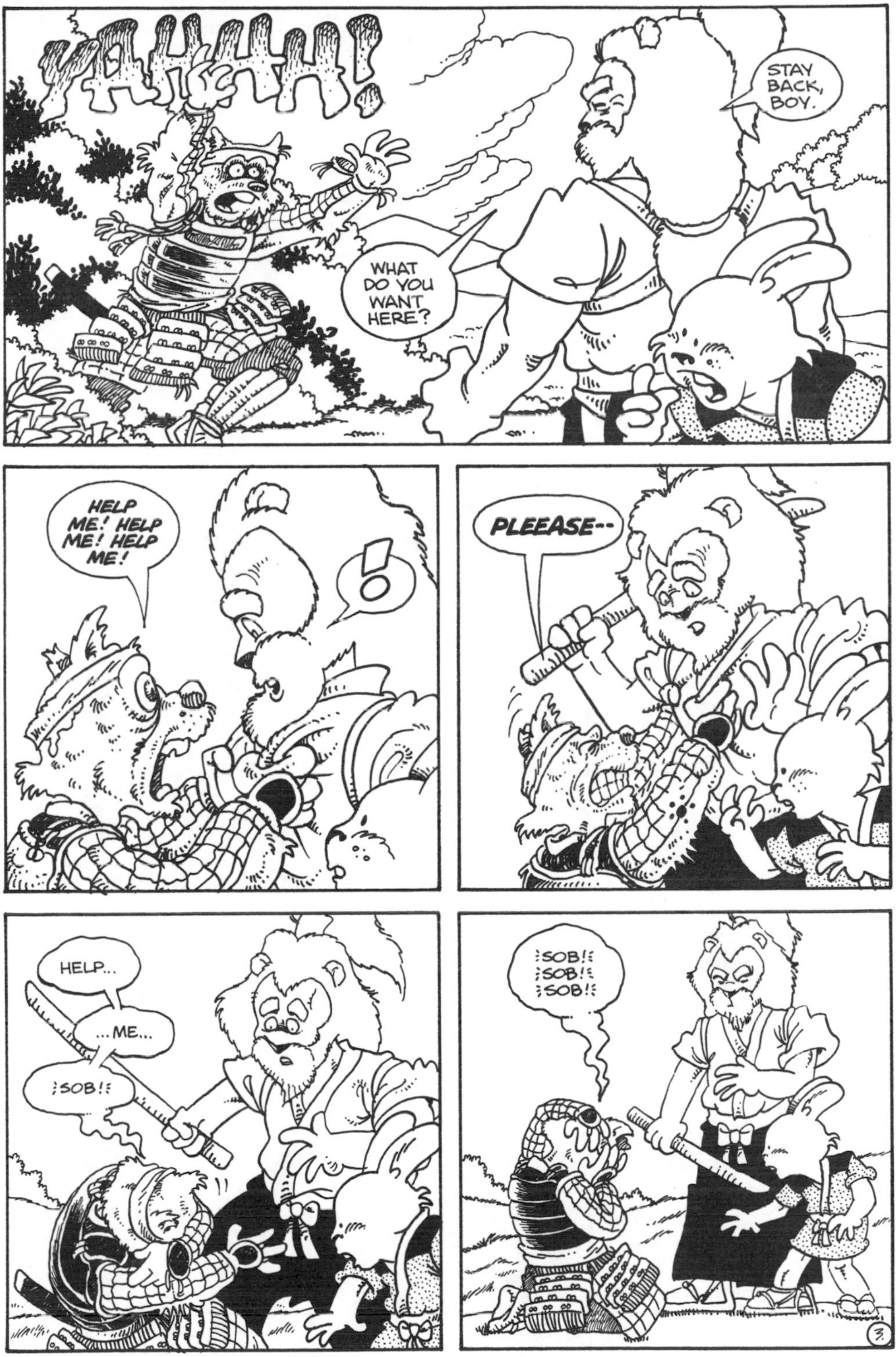
YAHHH!
STAY BACK, BOY.
WHAT DO YOU WANT HERE?
HELP ME! HELP ME! HELP ME!
!
PLEEASE--
HELP...
...ME...
SOB!
SOB! SOB! SOB!
3.

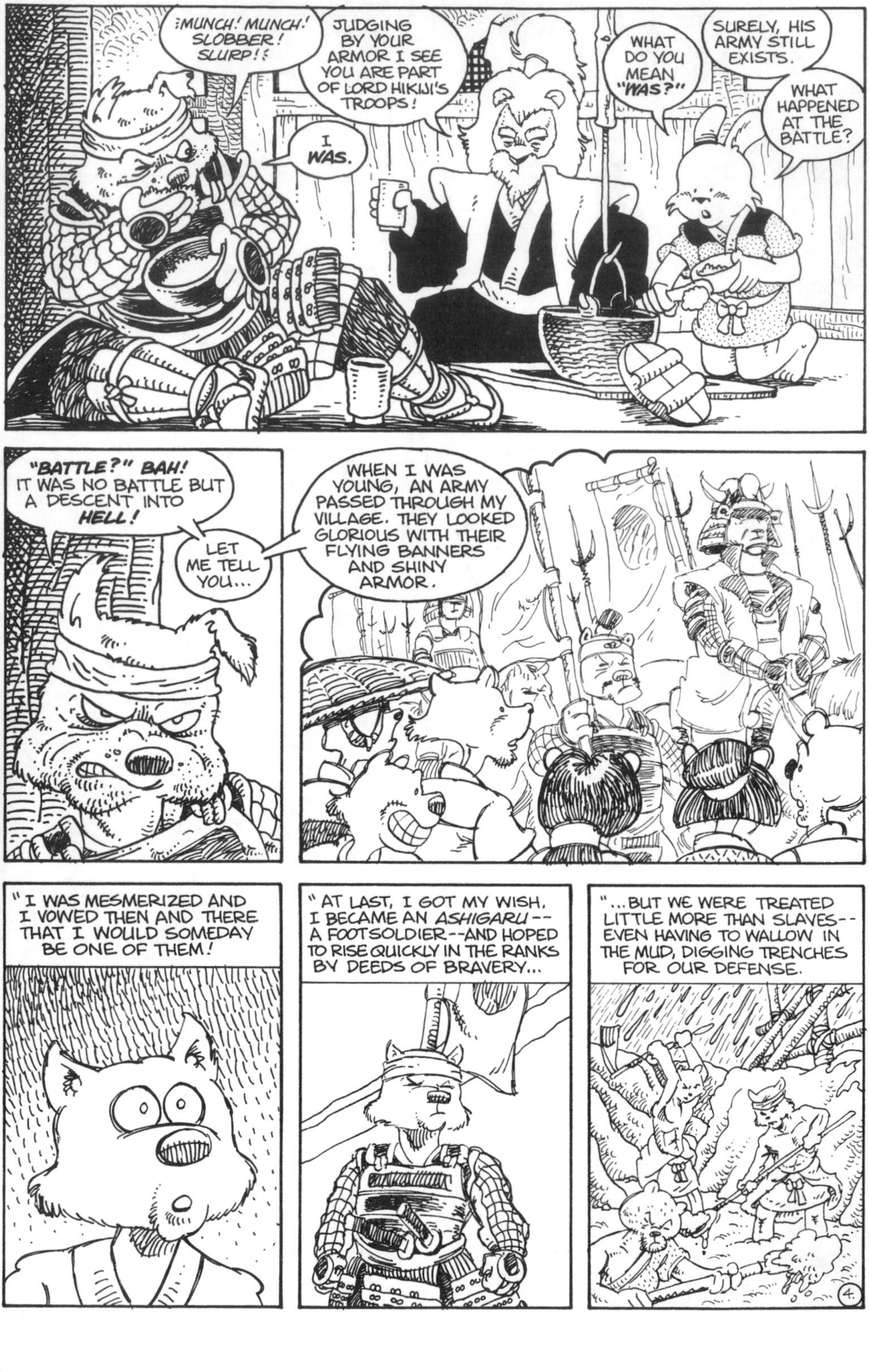
MUNCH! MUNCH! SLOBBER! SLURP!
JUDGING BY YOUR ARMOR I SEE YOU ARE PART OF LORD HIKIJI'S TROOPS!
I WAS.
WHAT DO YOU MEAN "WAS?"
SURELY, HIS ARMY STILL EXISTS.
WHAT HAPPENED AT THE BATTLE?
"BATTLE?" BAH! IT WAS NO BATTLE BUT A DESCENT INTO HELL!
LET ME TELL YOU...
WHEN I WAS YOUNG, AN ARMY PASSED THROUGH MY VILLAGE. THEY LOOKED GLORIOUS WITH THEIR FLYING BANNERS AND SHINY ARMOR.
"I WAS MESMERIZED AND I VOWED THEN AND THERE THAT I WOULD SOMEDAY BE ONE OF THEM!
"AT LAST, I GOT MY WISH. I BECAME AN ASHIGARU-- A FOOTSOLDIER--AND HOPED TO RISE QUICKLY IN THE RANKS BY DEEDS OF BRAVERY...
"...BUT WE WERE TREATED LITTLE MORE THAN SLAVES-- EVEN HAVING TO WALLOW IN THE MUD, DIGGING TRENCHES FOR OUR DEFENSE.
4.

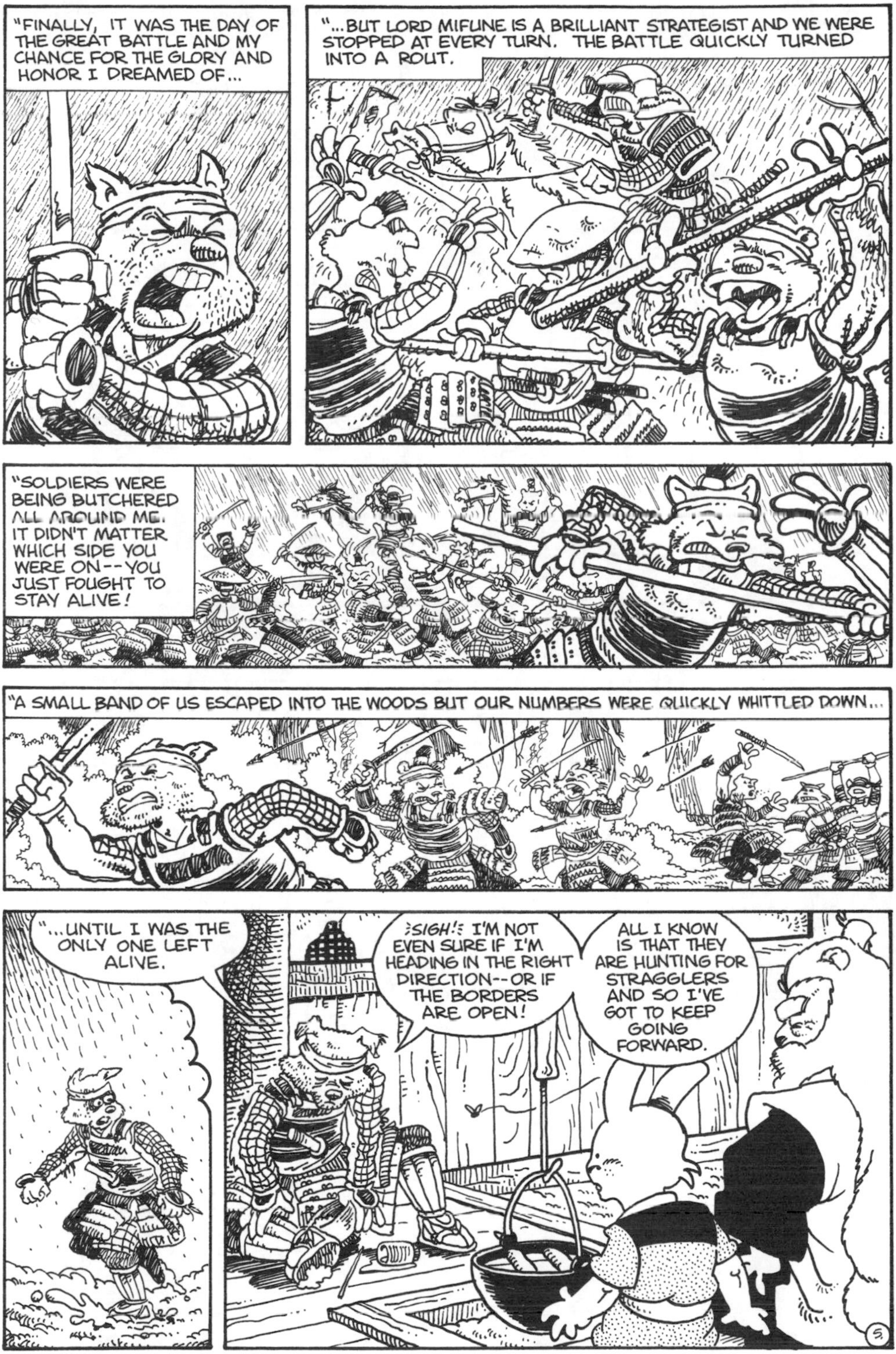
"FINALLY, IT WAS THE DAY OF THE GREAT BATTLE AND MY CHANCE FOR THE GLORY AND HONOR I DREAMED OF...
"...BUT LORD MIFUNE IS A BRILLIANT STRATEGIST AND WE WERE STOPPED AT EVERY TURN. THE BATTLE QUICKLY TURNED INTO A ROUT.
"SOLDIERS WERE BEING BUTCHERED ALL AROUND ME. IT DIDN'T MATTER WHICH SIDE YOU WERE ON--YOU JUST FOUGHT TO STAY ALIVE!
"A SMALL BAND OF US ESCAPED INTO THE WOODS BUT OUR NUMBERS WERE QUICKLY WHITTLED DOWN...
"...UNTIL I WAS THE ONLY ONE LEFT ALIVE.
SIGH! I'M NOT EVEN SURE IF I'M HEADING IN THE RIGHT DIRECTION--OR IF THE BORDERS ARE OPEN!
ALL I KNOW IS THAT THEY ARE HUNTING FOR STRAGGLERS AND SO I'VE GOT TO KEEP GOING FORWARD.
5

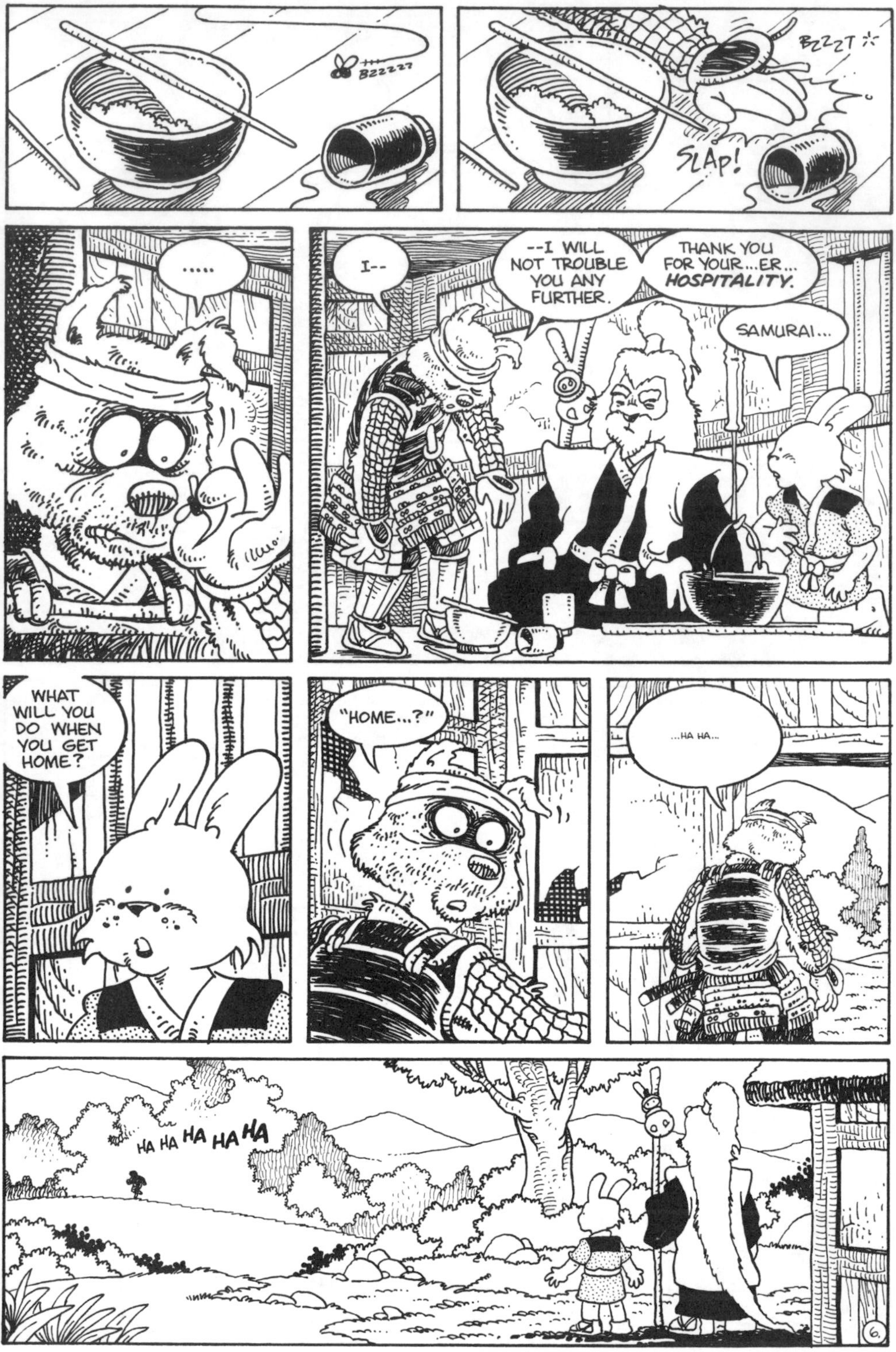
BZZZZZ
BZZZT
SLAP!
.....
I--
--I WILL NOT TROUBLE YOU ANY FURTHER.
THANK YOU FOR YOUR...ER... HOSPITALITY.
SAMURAI...
WHAT WILL YOU DO WHEN YOU GET HOME?
"HOME...?"
...HA HA...
HA HA HA HA HA
6.

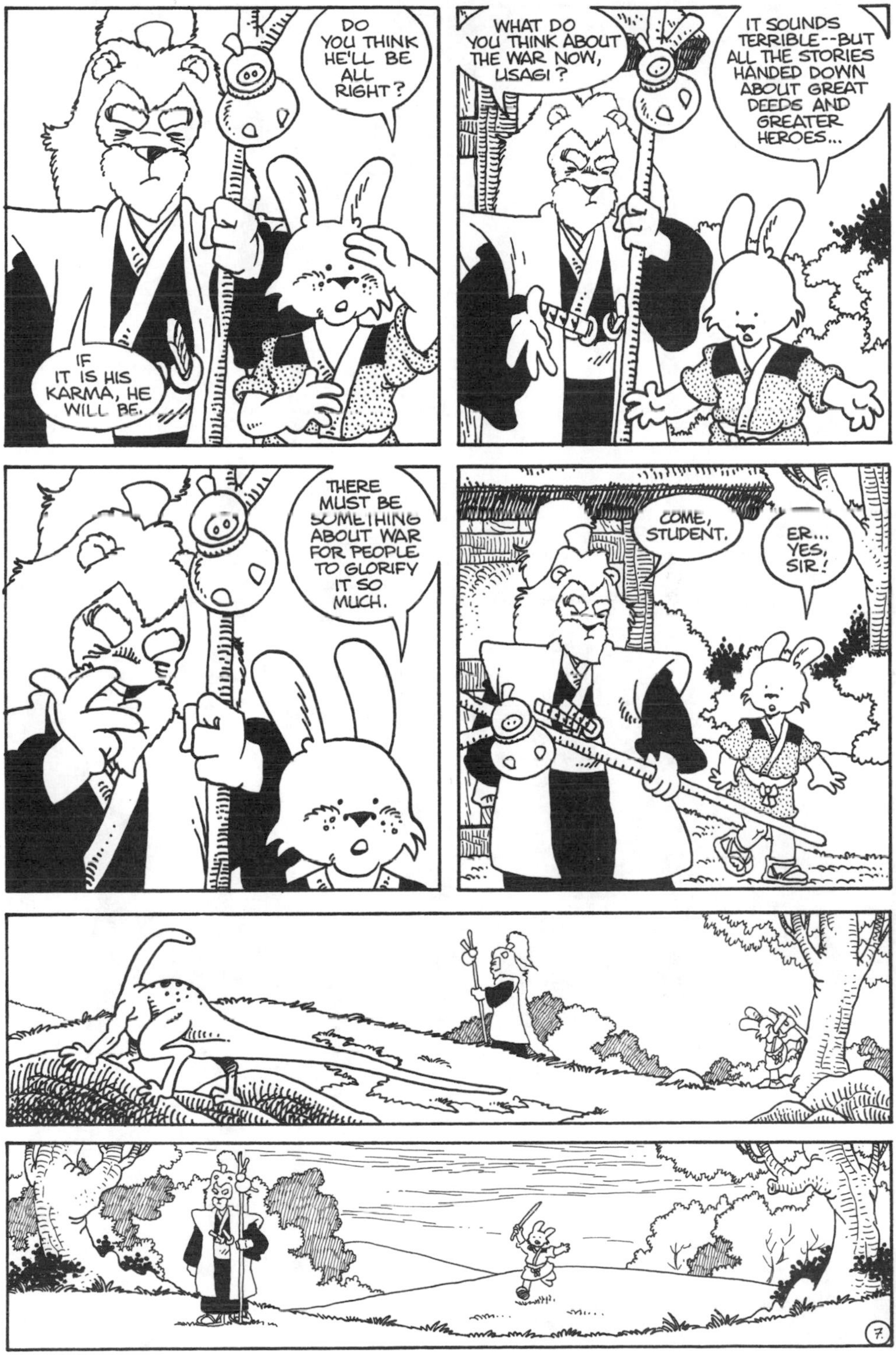
DO YOU THINK HE'LL BE ALL RIGHT?
IF IT IS HIS KARMA, HE WILL BE.
WHAT DO YOU THINK ABOUT THE WAR NOW, USAGI?
IT SOUNDS TERRIBLE--BUT ALL THE STORIES HANDED DOWN ABOUT GREAT DEEDS AND GREATER HEROES...
THERE MUST BE SOMETHING ABOUT WAR FOR PEOPLE TO GLORIFY IT SO MUCH.
COME, STUDENT.
ER... YES, SIR!
7

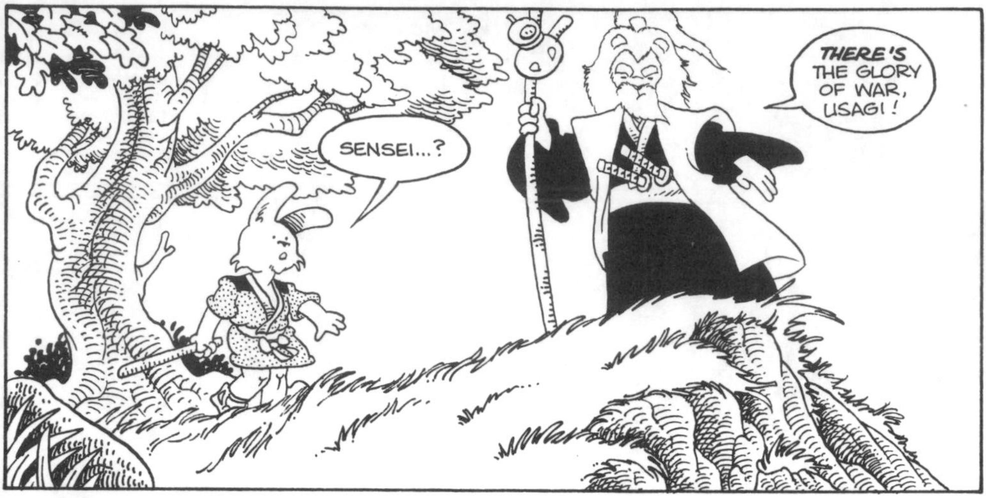
SENSEI...?
THERE'S THE GLORY OF WAR, USAGI!

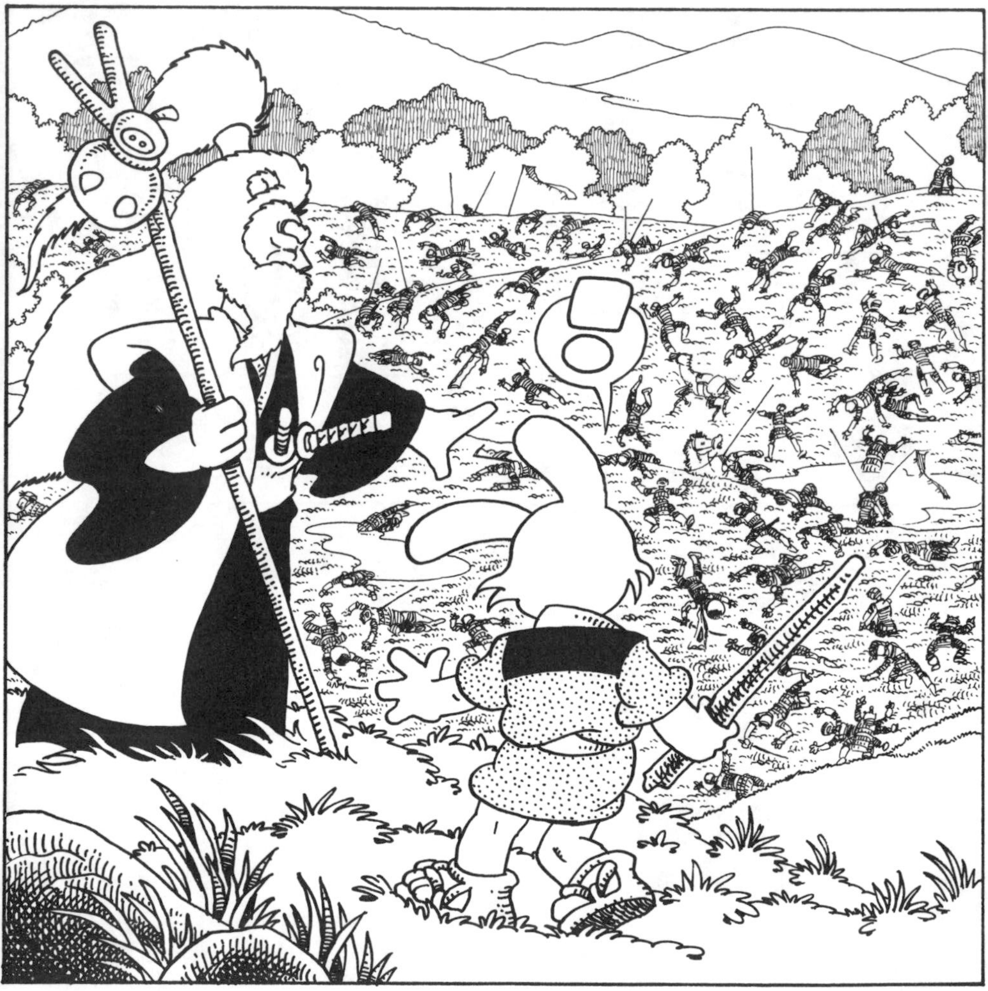

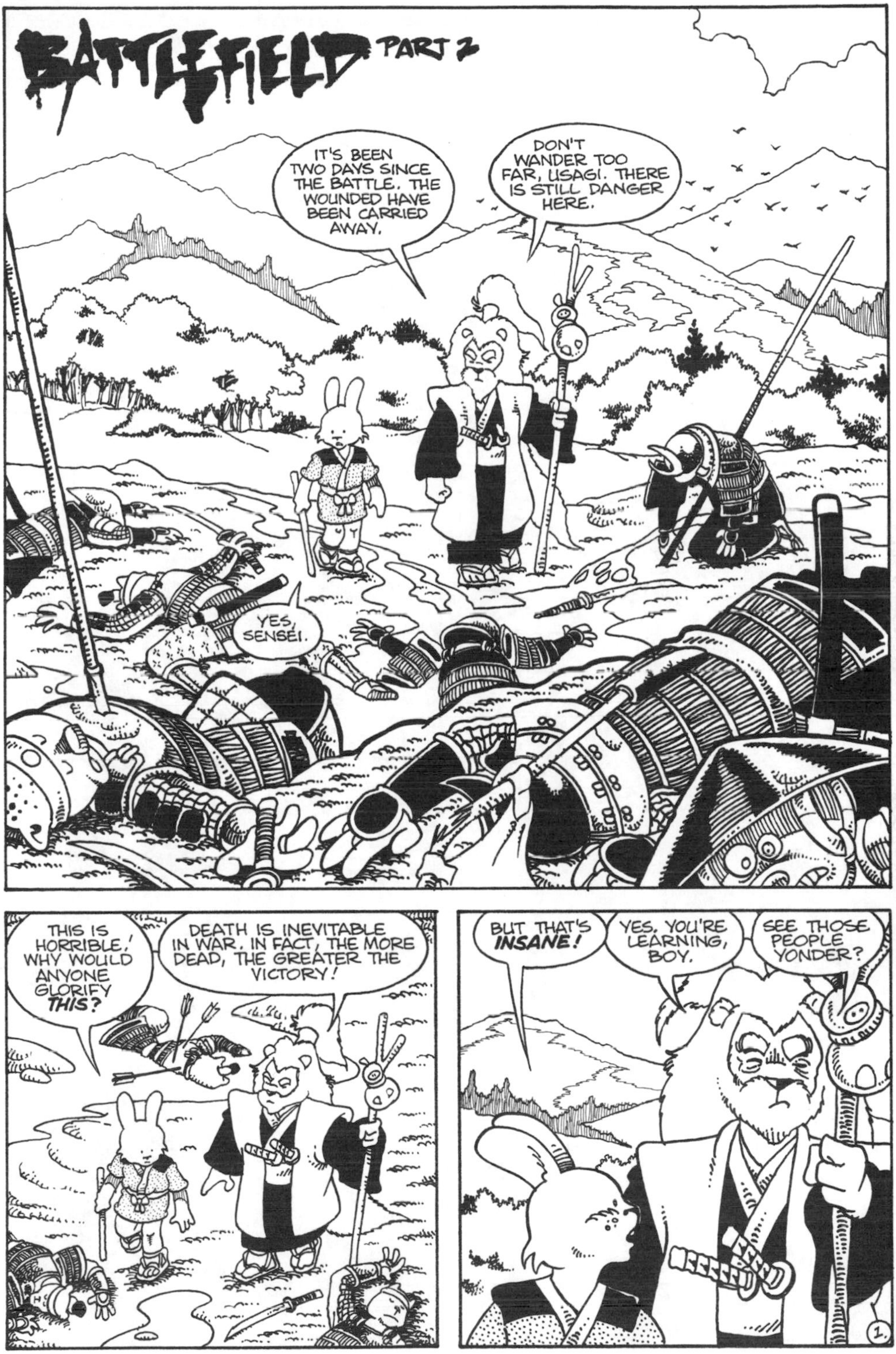
BATTLEFIELD PART 2
IT'S BEEN TWO DAYS SINCE THE BATTLE. THE WOUNDED HAVE BEEN CARRIED AWAY.
DON'T WANDER TOO FAR, USAGI. THERE IS STILL DANGER HERE.
YES, SENSEI.
THIS IS HORRIBLE! WHY WOULD ANYONE GLORIFY THIS?
DEATH IS INEVITABLE IN WAR. IN FACT, THE MORE DEAD, THE GREATER THE VICTORY!
BUT THAT'S INSANE!
YES. YOU'RE LEARNING, BOY.
SEE THOSE PEOPLE YONDER?
1.

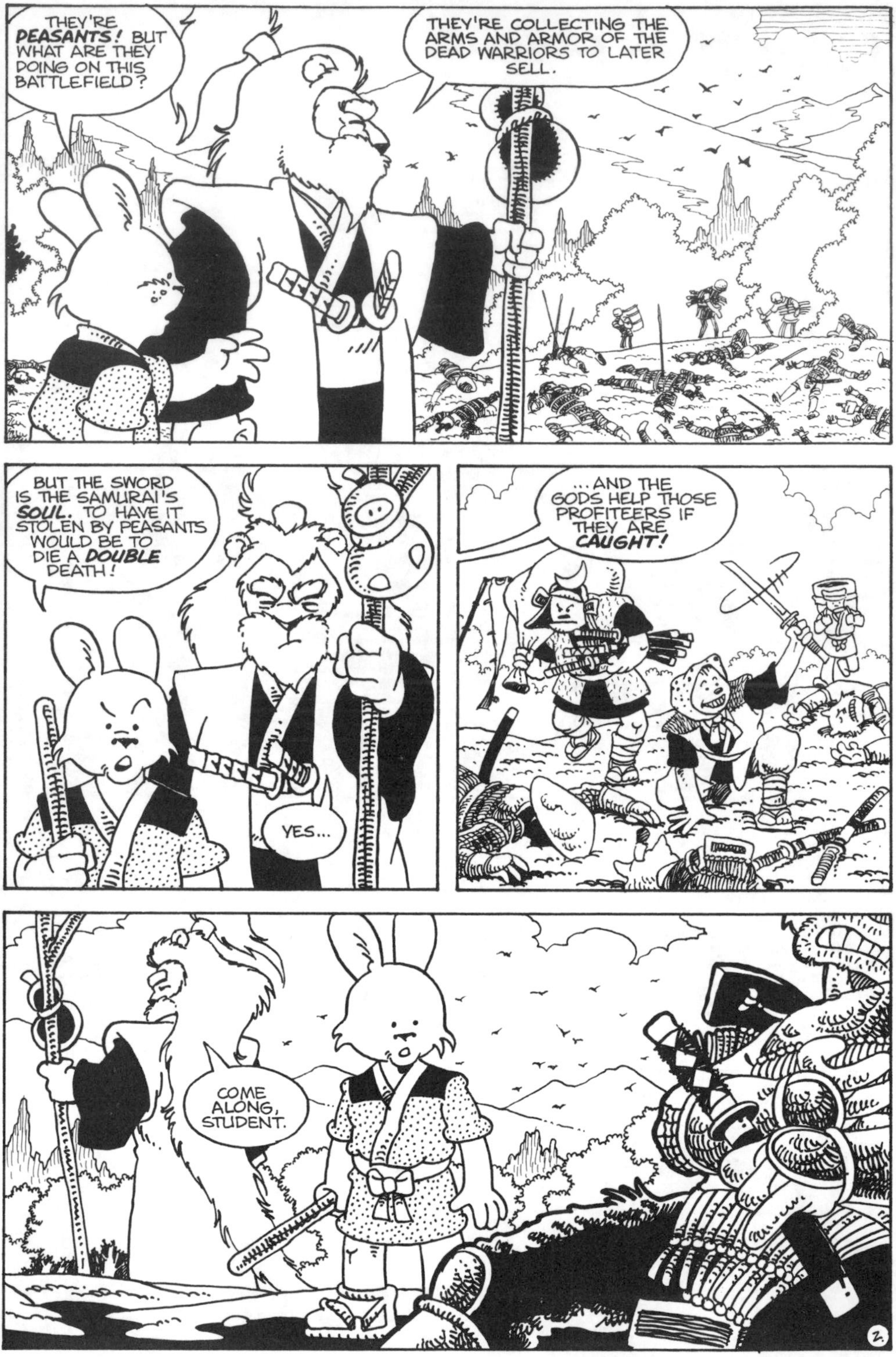
THEY'RE **PEASANTS!** BUT WHAT ARE THEY DOING ON THIS BATTLEFIELD?
THEY'RE COLLECTING THE ARMS AND ARMOR OF THE DEAD WARRIORS TO LATER SELL.
BUT THE SWORD IS THE SAMURAI'S **SOUL.** TO HAVE IT STOLEN BY PEASANTS WOULD BE TO DIE A **DOUBLE** DEATH!
YES...
...AND THE GODS HELP THOSE PROFITEERS IF THEY ARE **CAUGHT!**
COME ALONG, STUDENT.
2.

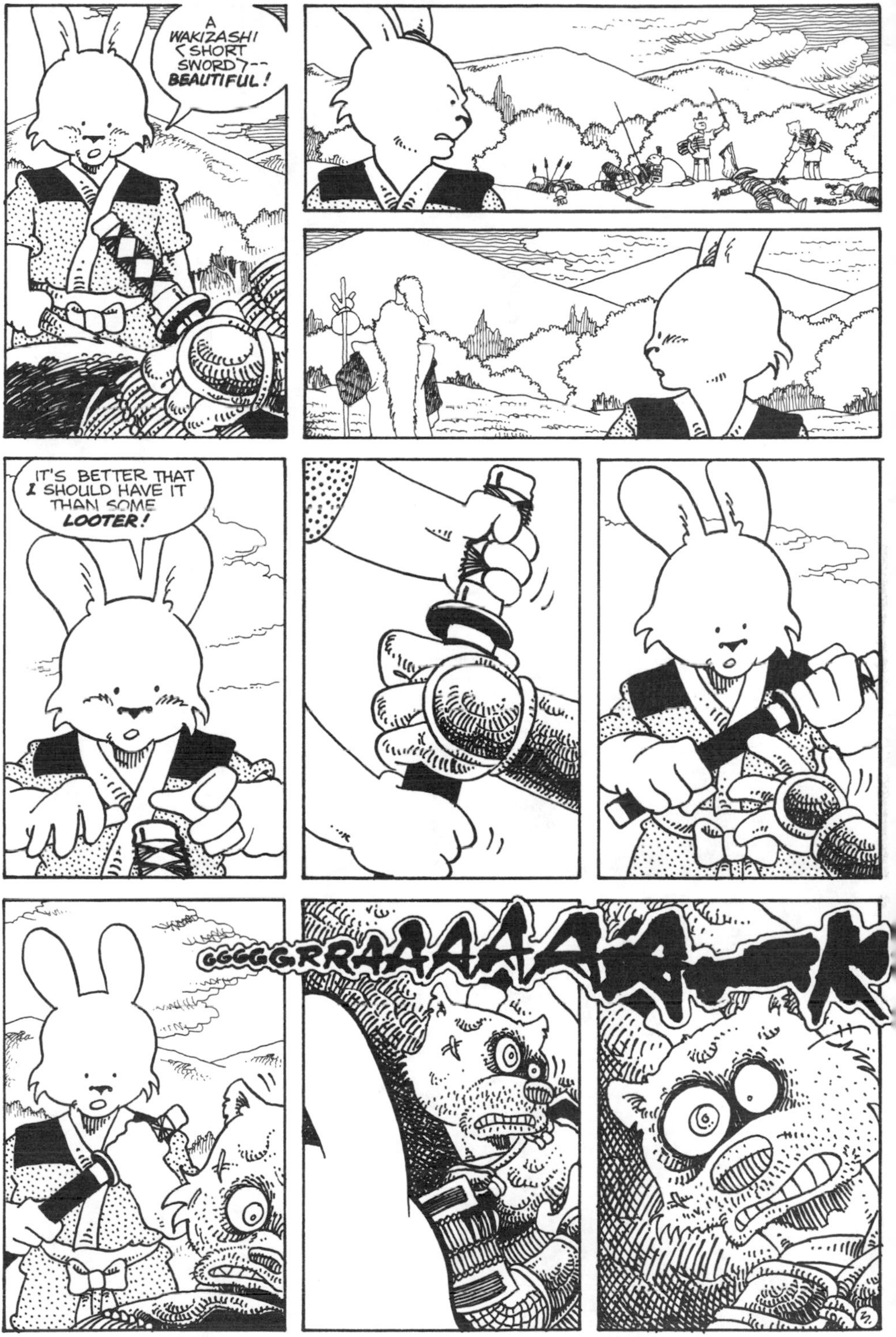
A WAKIZASHI <SHORT SWORD>-- BEAUTIFUL!
IT'S BETTER THAT I SHOULD HAVE IT THAN SOME LOOTER!
GGGGGRRAAAAAAA--K

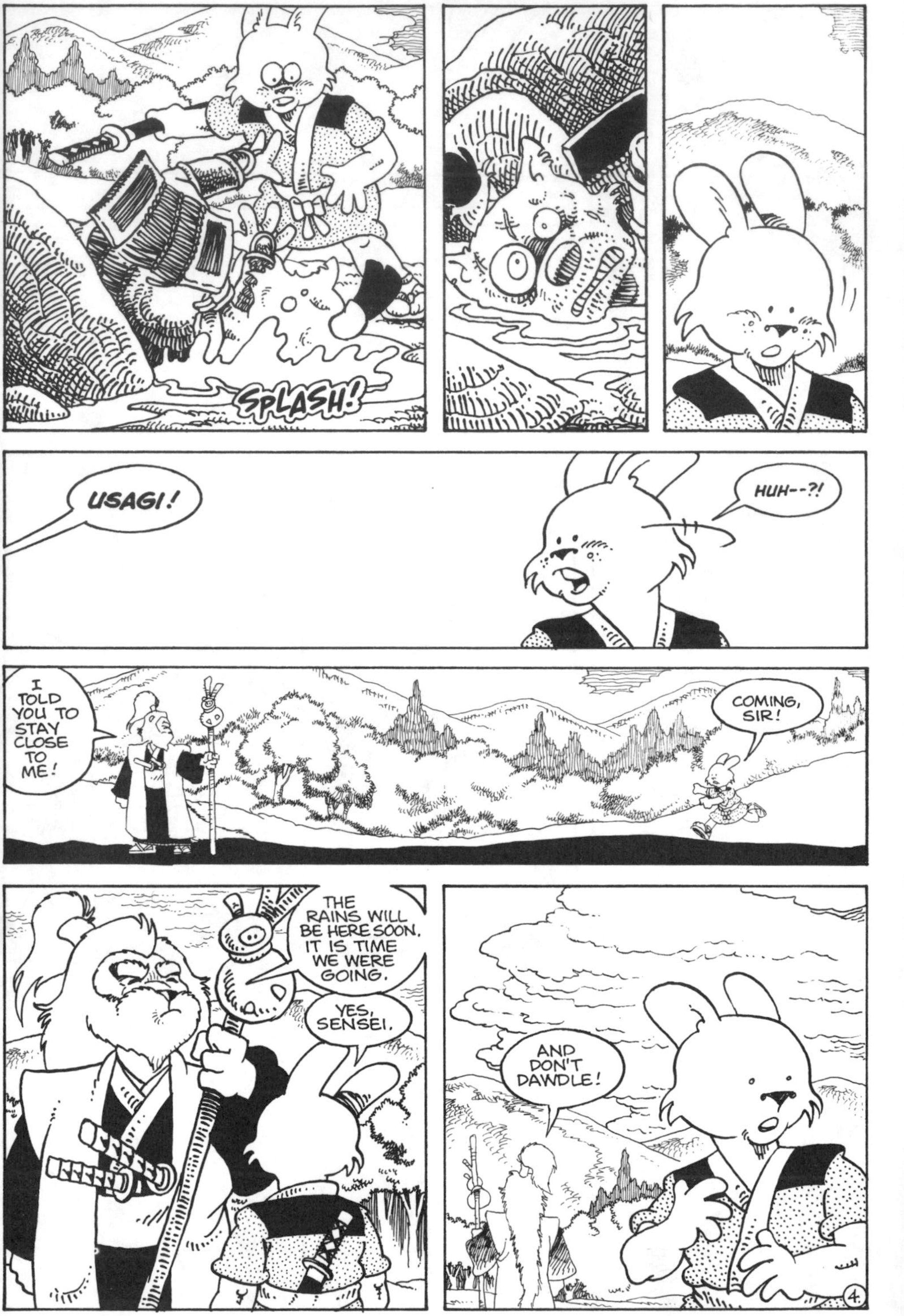
SPLASH!
USAGI!
HUH--?!
I TOLD YOU TO STAY CLOSE TO ME!
COMING, SIR!
THE RAINS WILL BE HERE SOON. IT IS TIME WE WERE GOING.
YES, SENSEI.
AND DON'T DAWDLE!
4.

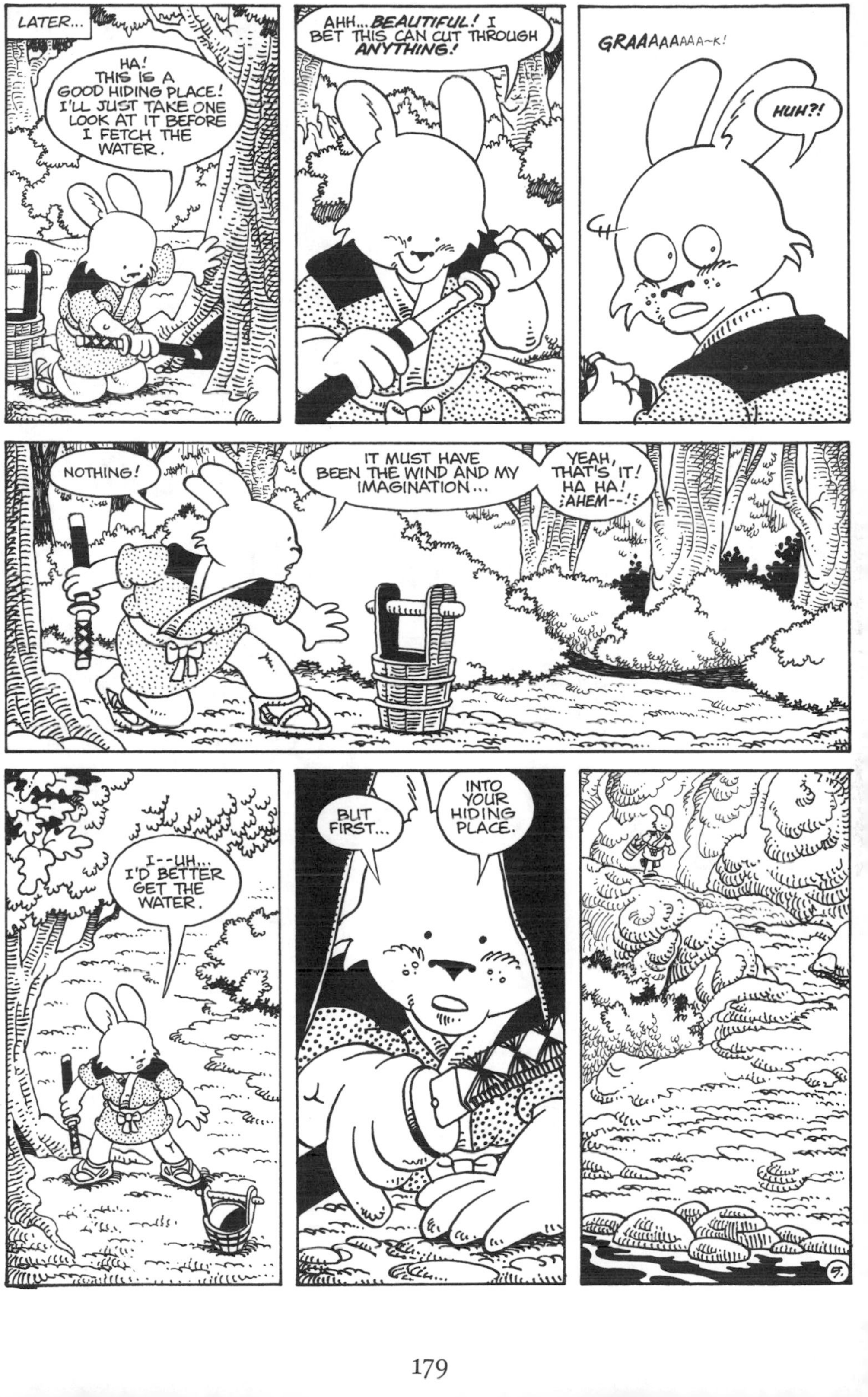

LATER...
HA! THIS IS A GOOD HIDING PLACE! I'LL JUST TAKE ONE LOOK AT IT BEFORE I FETCH THE WATER.
AHH...BEAUTIFUL! I BET THIS CAN CUT THROUGH ANYTHING!
GRAAAAAAAA~K!
HUH?!
NOTHING!
IT MUST HAVE BEEN THE WIND AND MY IMAGINATION...
YEAH, THAT'S IT! HA HA! ;AHEM--!;
I--UH... I'D BETTER GET THE WATER.
BUT FIRST...
INTO YOUR HIDING PLACE.
5.

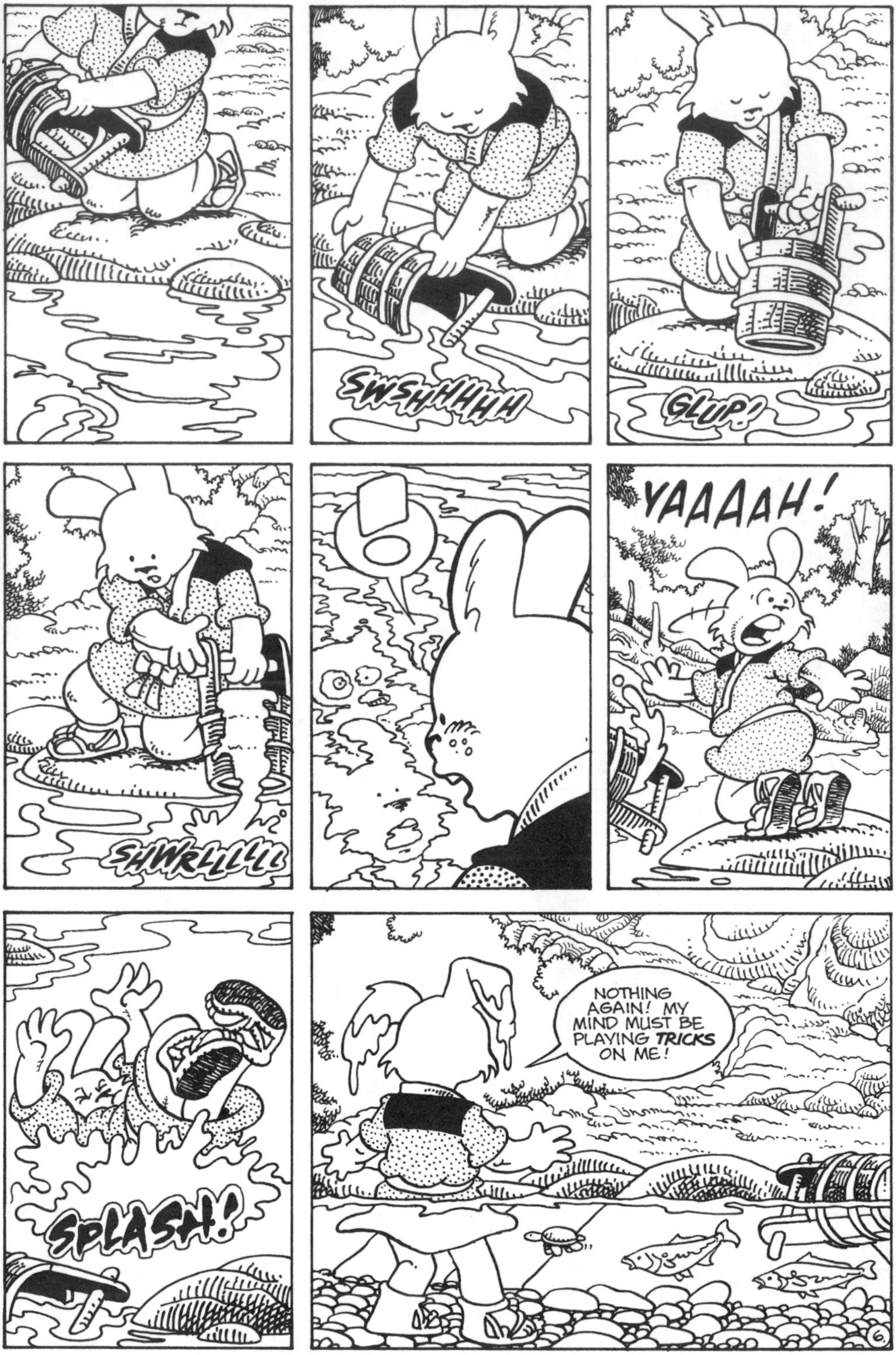
SWSHHHHH
GLUP!
SHWRLLLLLL
YAAAAH!
SPLASH!
NOTHING AGAIN! MY MIND MUST BE PLAYING **TRICKS** ON ME!
6

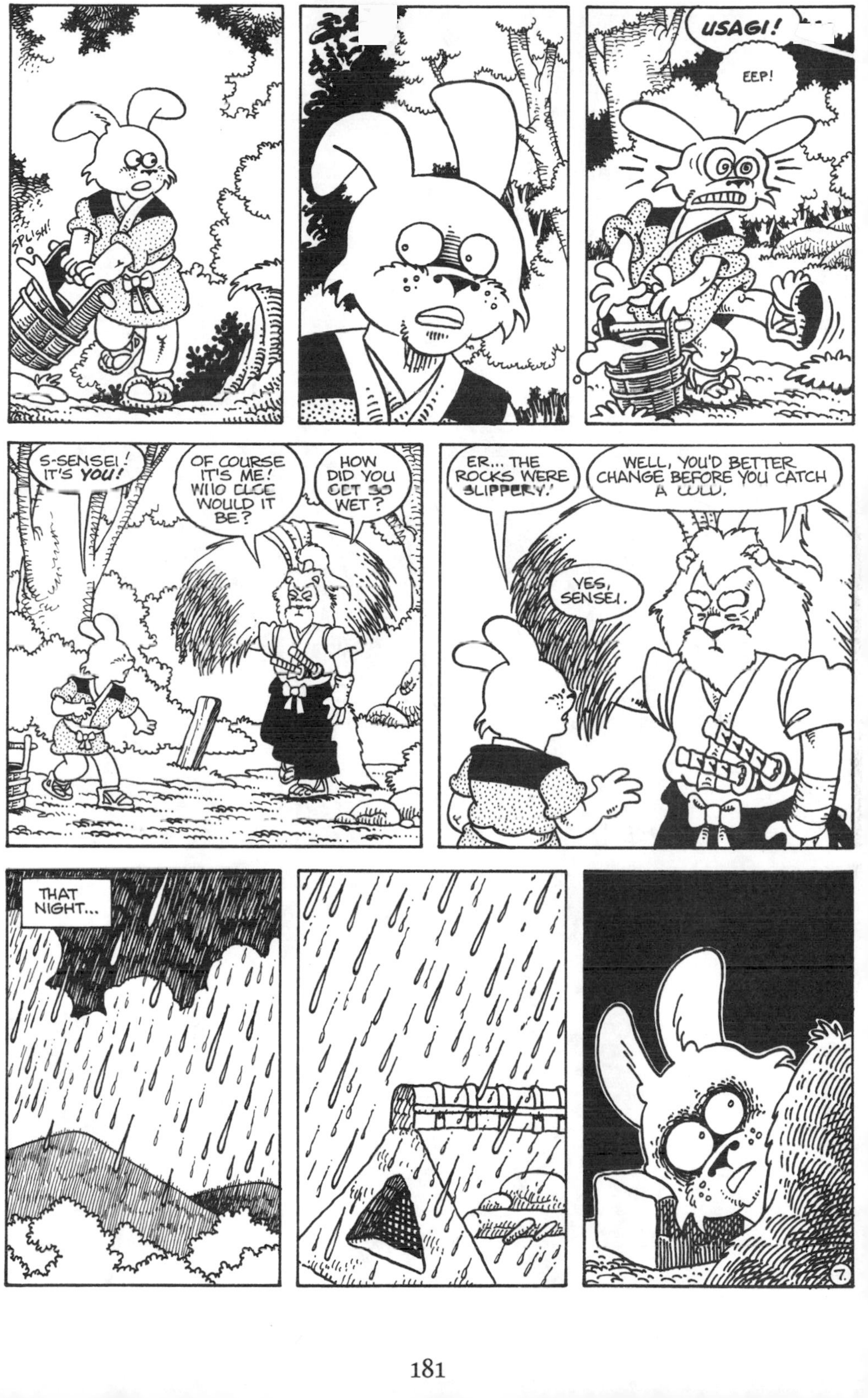
SPLISH!
USAGI!
EEP!
S-SENSEI! IT'S YOU!
OF COURSE IT'S ME! WHO ELSE WOULD IT BE?
HOW DID YOU GET SO WET?
ER... THE ROCKS WERE SLIPPERY.
WELL, YOU'D BETTER CHANGE BEFORE YOU CATCH A COLD.
YES, SENSEI.
THAT NIGHT...
7.

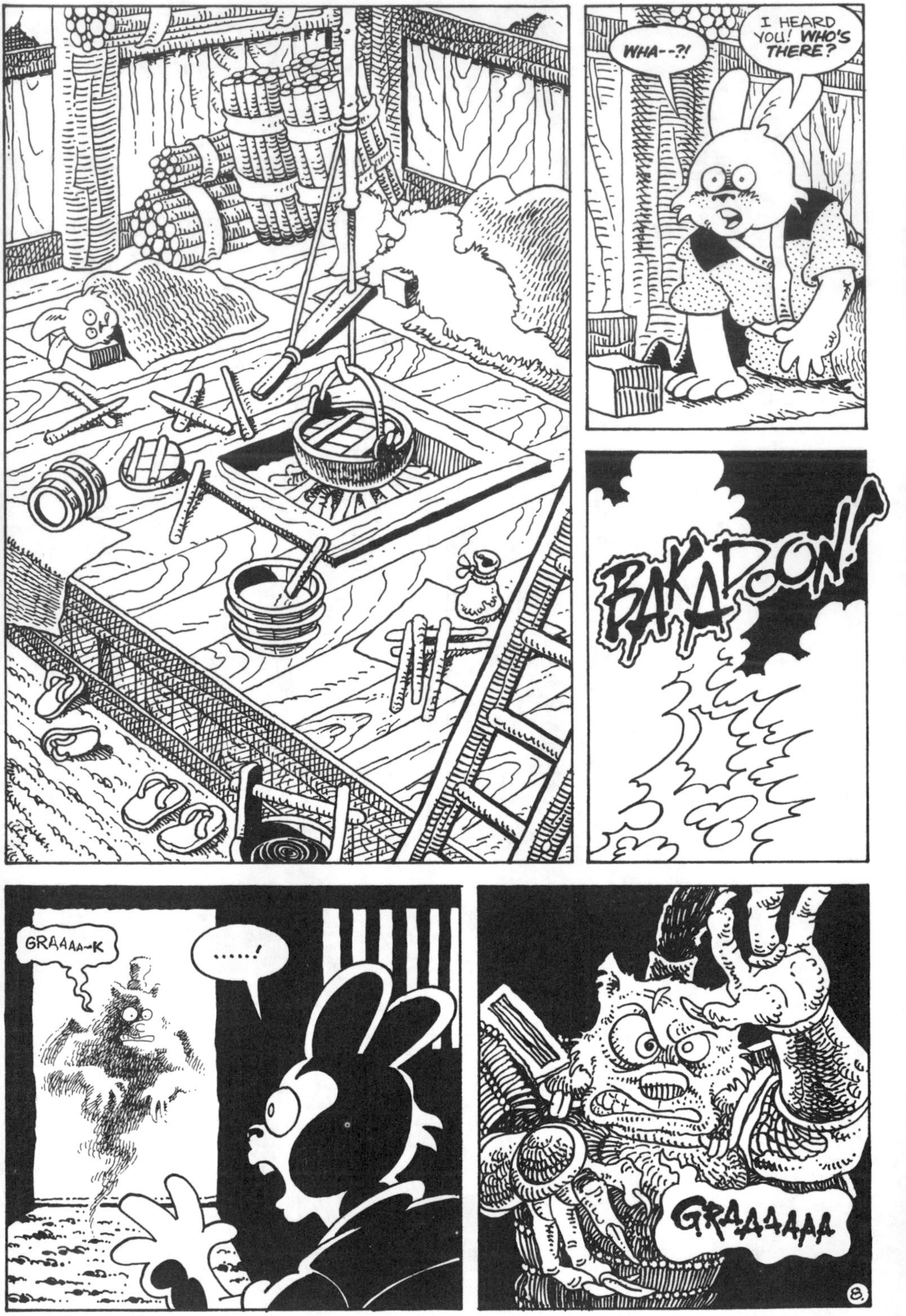
WHA--?!
I HEARD YOU! WHO'S THERE?
BAKADOON!
GRAAAA-K
......!
GRAAAAAA
8.

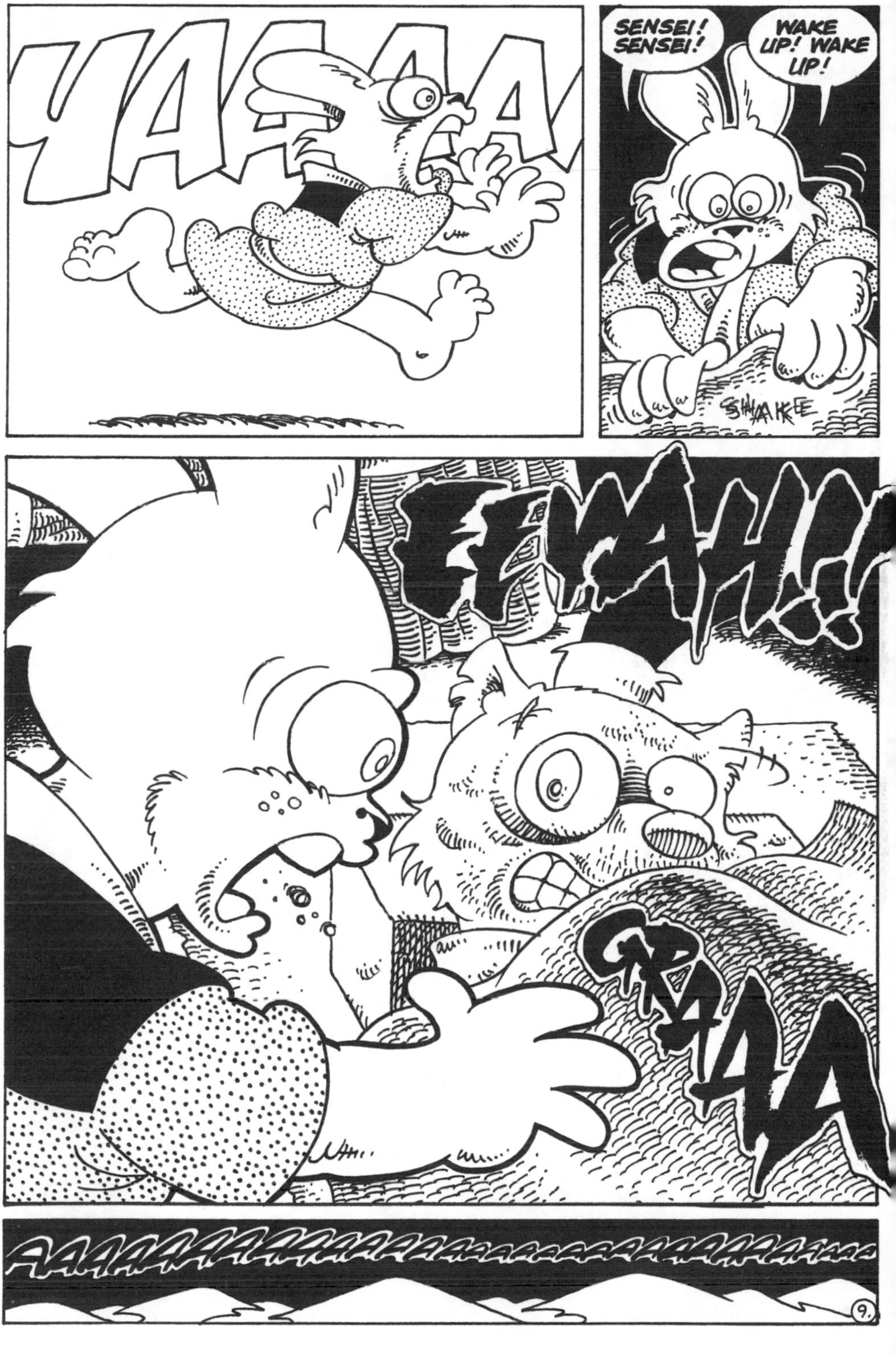
YAAAAA
SENSEI! SENSEI!
WAKE UP! WAKE UP!
SHAKE
EEYAAH!!
GRAAAA
AAAAAAAAAAAAAAAAAAAAAAAAAAAAAAA
9.

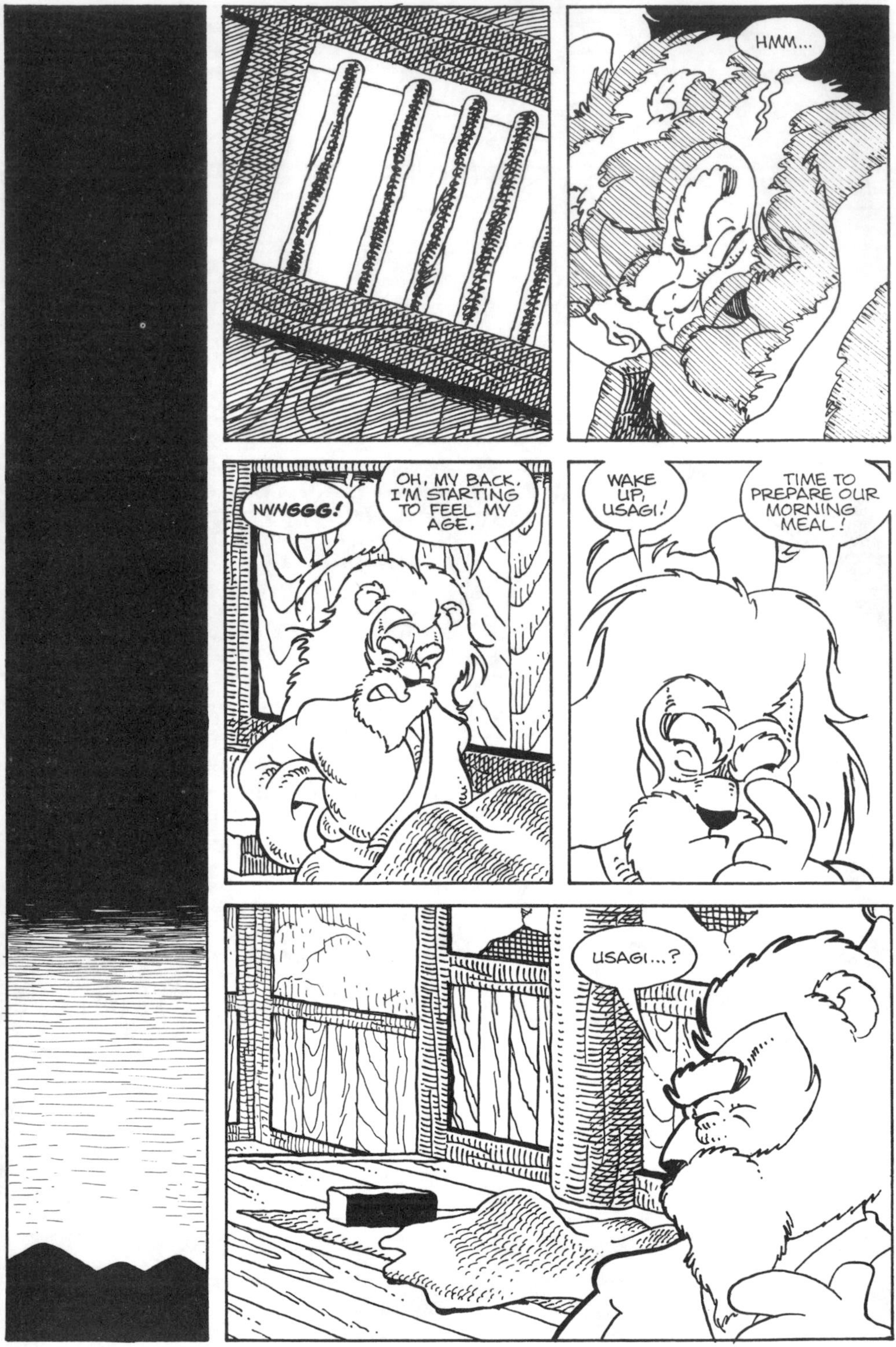
HMM...
NNNGGG!
OH, MY BACK. I'M STARTING TO FEEL MY AGE.
WAKE UP, USAGI!
TIME TO PREPARE OUR MORNING MEAL!
USAGI...?

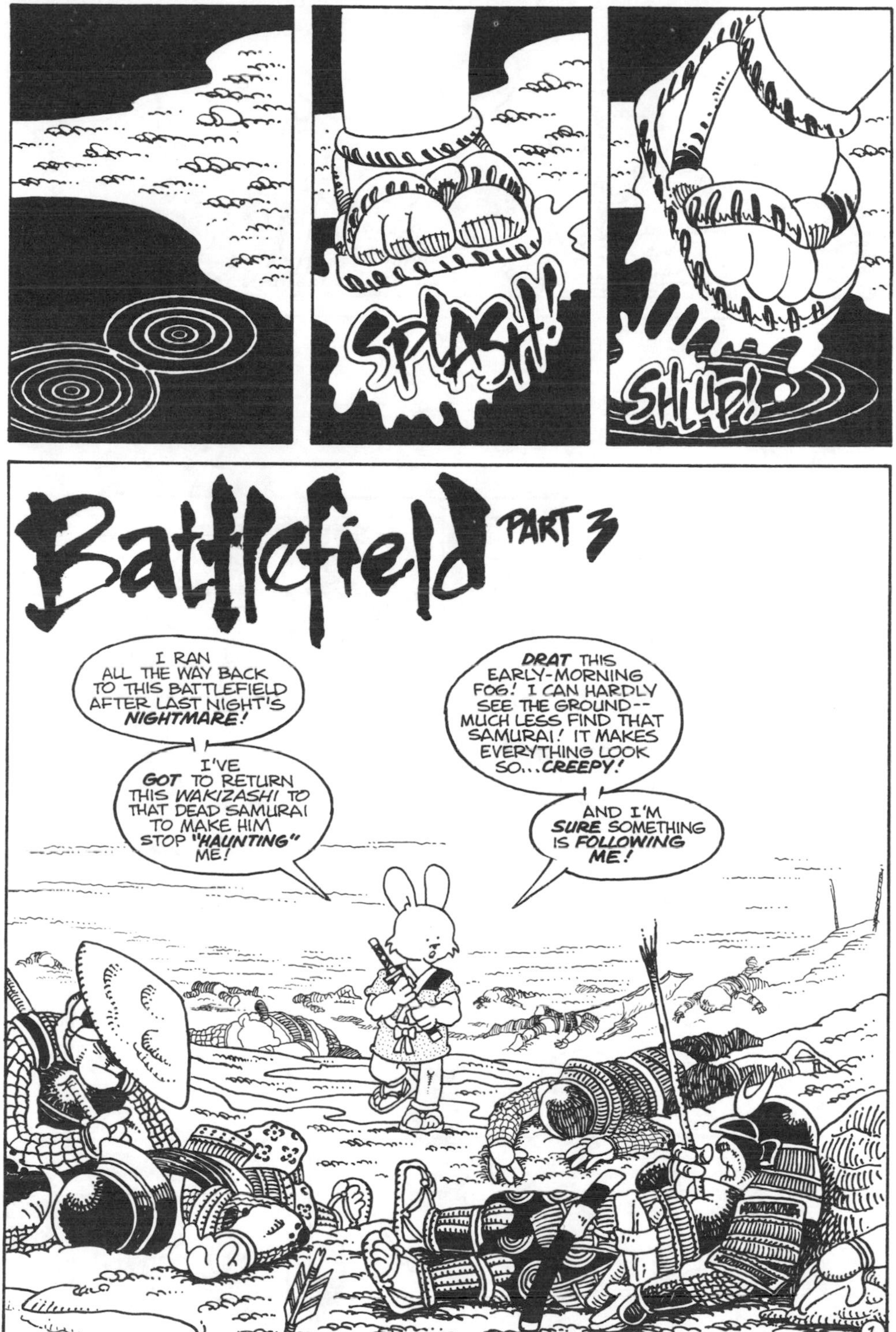
SPLASH!
SHLUP!
Battlefield PART 3
I RAN ALL THE WAY BACK TO THIS BATTLEFIELD AFTER LAST NIGHT'S NIGHTMARE!
I'VE GOT TO RETURN THIS WAKIZASHI TO THAT DEAD SAMURAI TO MAKE HIM STOP "HAUNTING" ME!
DRAT THIS EARLY-MORNING FOG! I CAN HARDLY SEE THE GROUND-- MUCH LESS FIND THAT SAMURAI! IT MAKES EVERYTHING LOOK SO...CREEPY!
AND I'M SURE SOMETHING IS FOLLOWING ME!
1.

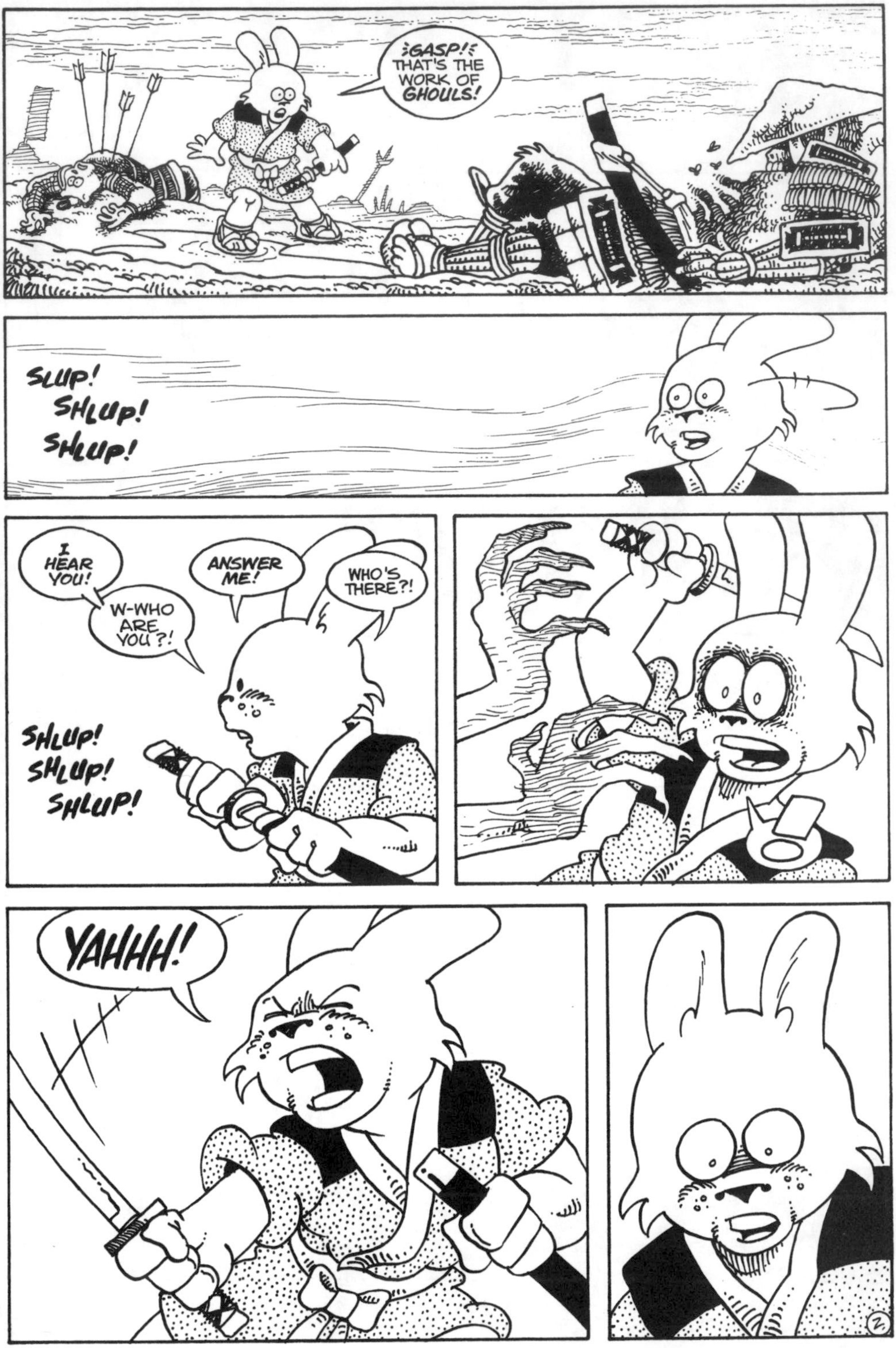
GASP! THAT'S THE WORK OF GHOULS!
SLUP! SHLUP! SHLUP!
I HEAR YOU!
W-WHO ARE YOU?!
ANSWER ME!
WHO'S THERE?!
SHLUP! SHLUP! SHLUP!
YAHHH!

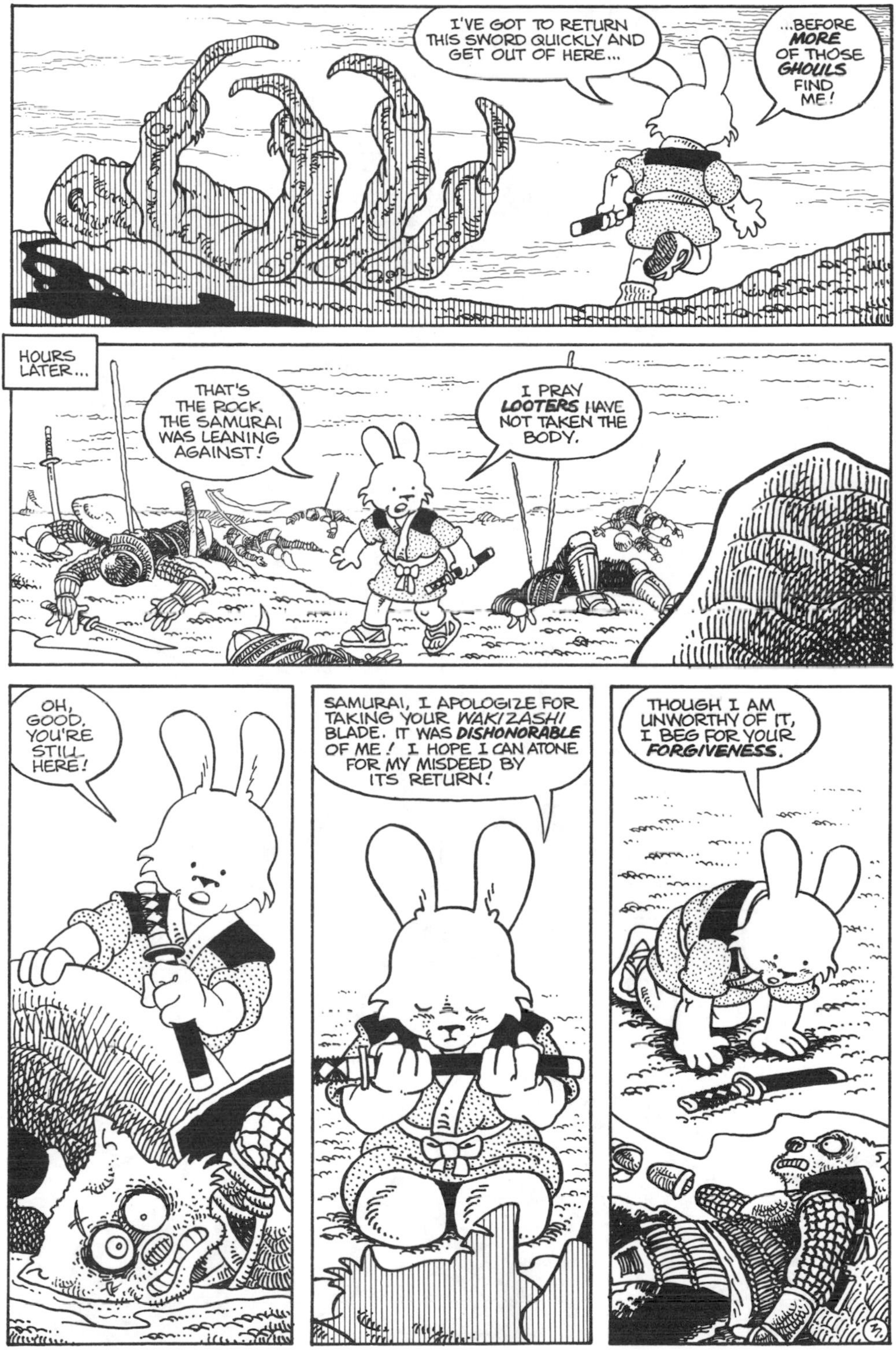
I'VE GOT TO RETURN THIS SWORD QUICKLY AND GET OUT OF HERE...
...BEFORE MORE OF THOSE GHOULS FIND ME!
HOURS LATER...
THAT'S THE ROCK. THE SAMURAI WAS LEANING AGAINST!
I PRAY LOOTERS HAVE NOT TAKEN THE BODY.
OH, GOOD. YOU'RE STILL HERE!
SAMURAI, I APOLOGIZE FOR TAKING YOUR WAKIZASHI BLADE. IT WAS DISHONORABLE OF ME! I HOPE I CAN ATONE FOR MY MISDEED BY ITS RETURN!
THOUGH I AM UNWORTHY OF IT, I BEG FOR YOUR FORGIVENESS.

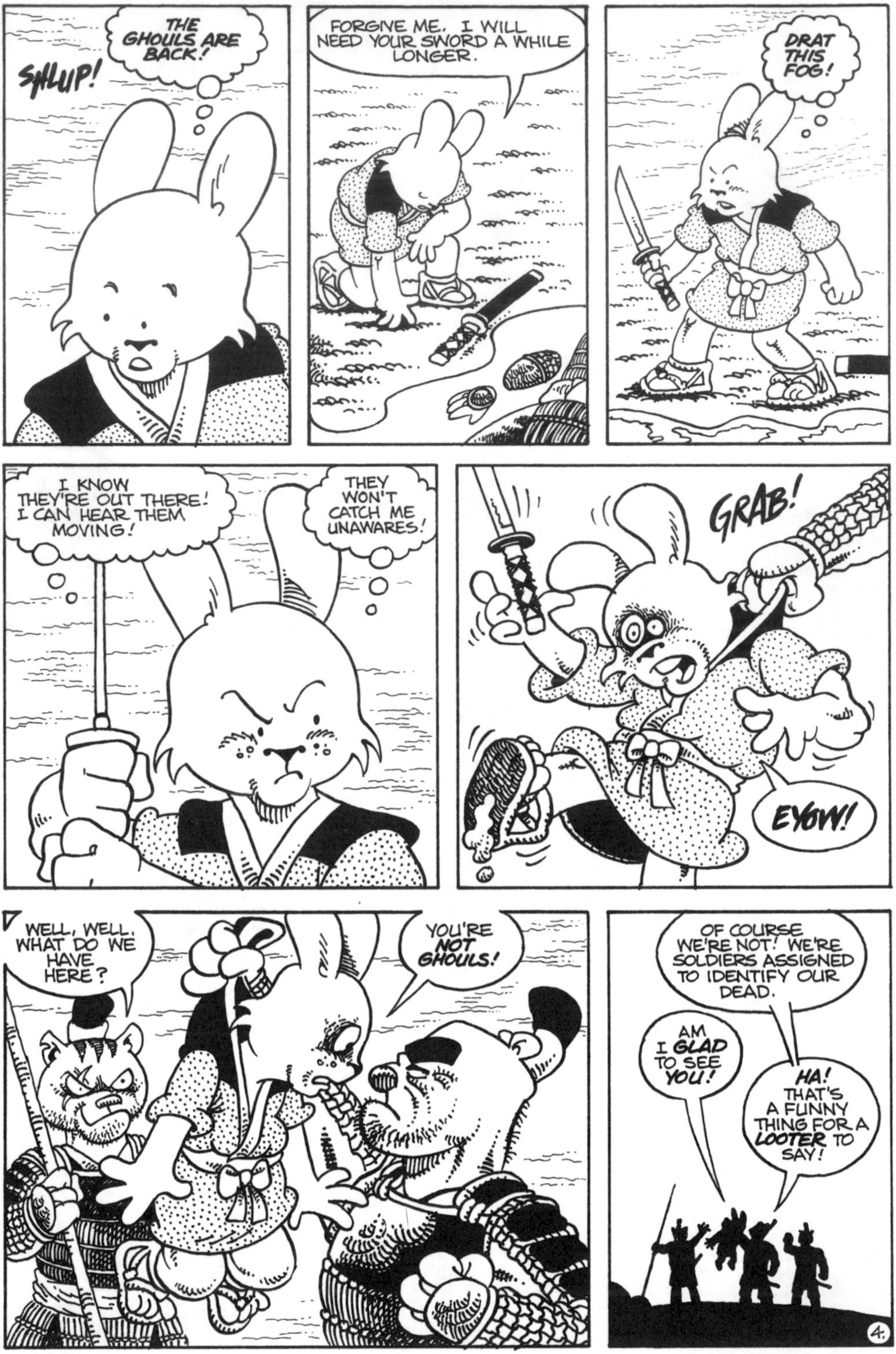
THE GHOULS ARE BACK!
SHLUP!
FORGIVE ME. I WILL NEED YOUR SWORD A WHILE LONGER.
DRAT THIS FOG!
I KNOW THEY'RE OUT THERE! I CAN HEAR THEM MOVING!
THEY WON'T CATCH ME UNAWARES!
GRAB!
EYOW!
WELL, WELL. WHAT DO WE HAVE HERE?
YOU'RE NOT GHOULS!
OF COURSE WE'RE NOT! WE'RE SOLDIERS ASSIGNED TO IDENTIFY OUR DEAD.
AM I GLAD TO SEE YOU!
HA! THAT'S A FUNNY THING FOR A LOOTER TO SAY!
4.

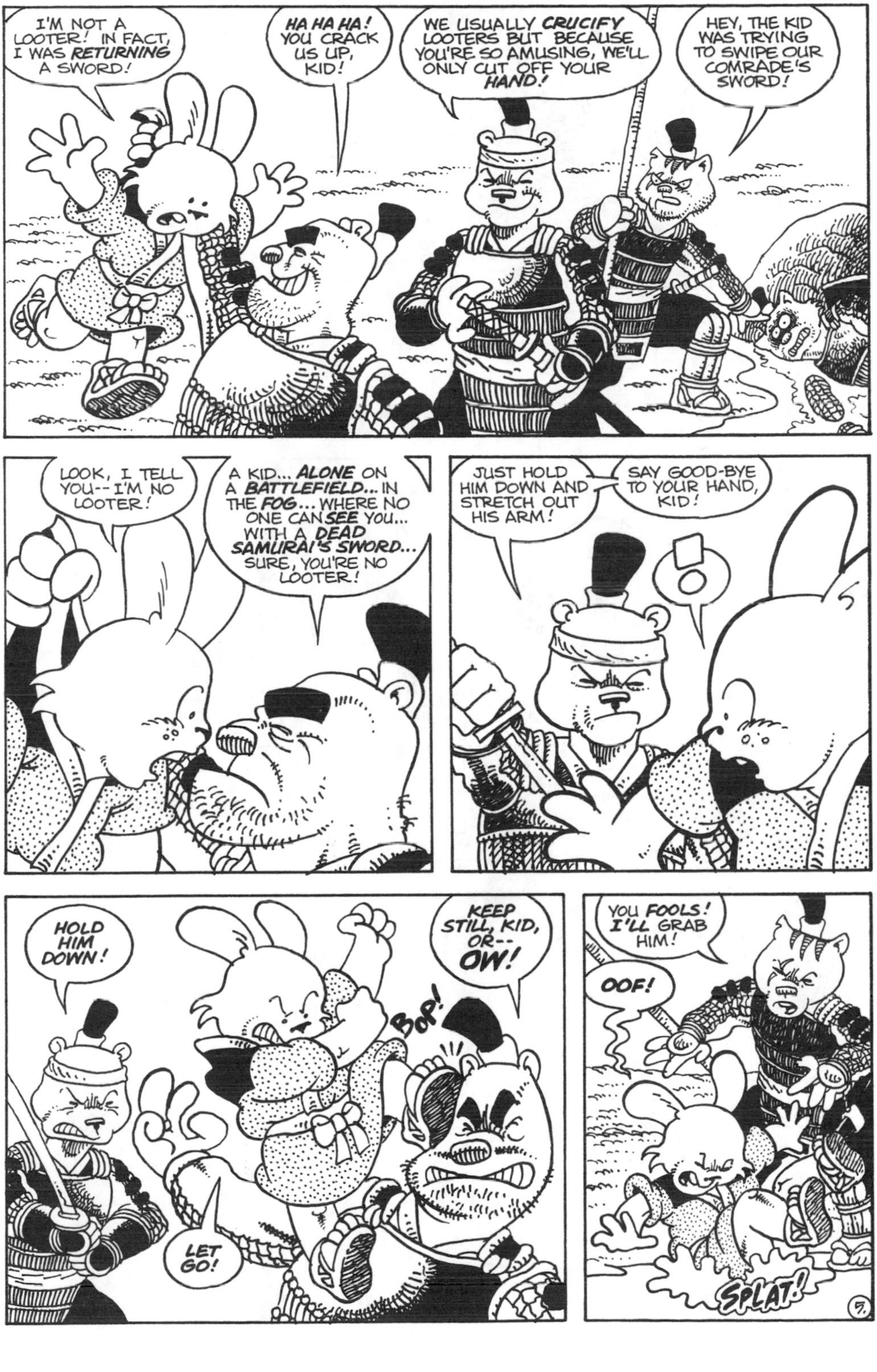
I'M NOT A LOOTER! IN FACT, I WAS RETURNING A SWORD!
HA HA HA! YOU CRACK US UP, KID!
WE USUALLY CRUCIFY LOOTERS BUT BECAUSE YOU'RE SO AMUSING, WE'LL ONLY CUT OFF YOUR HAND!
HEY, THE KID WAS TRYING TO SWIPE OUR COMRADE'S SWORD!
LOOK, I TELL YOU-- I'M NO LOOTER!
A KID... ALONE ON A BATTLEFIELD... IN THE FOG... WHERE NO ONE CAN SEE YOU... WITH A DEAD SAMURAI'S SWORD... SURE, YOU'RE NO LOOTER!
JUST HOLD HIM DOWN AND STRETCH OUT HIS ARM!
SAY GOOD-BYE TO YOUR HAND, KID!
!
HOLD HIM DOWN!
KEEP STILL, KID, OR-- OW!
BOP!
LET GO!
YOU FOOLS! I'LL GRAB HIM!
OOF!
SPLAT!
5.

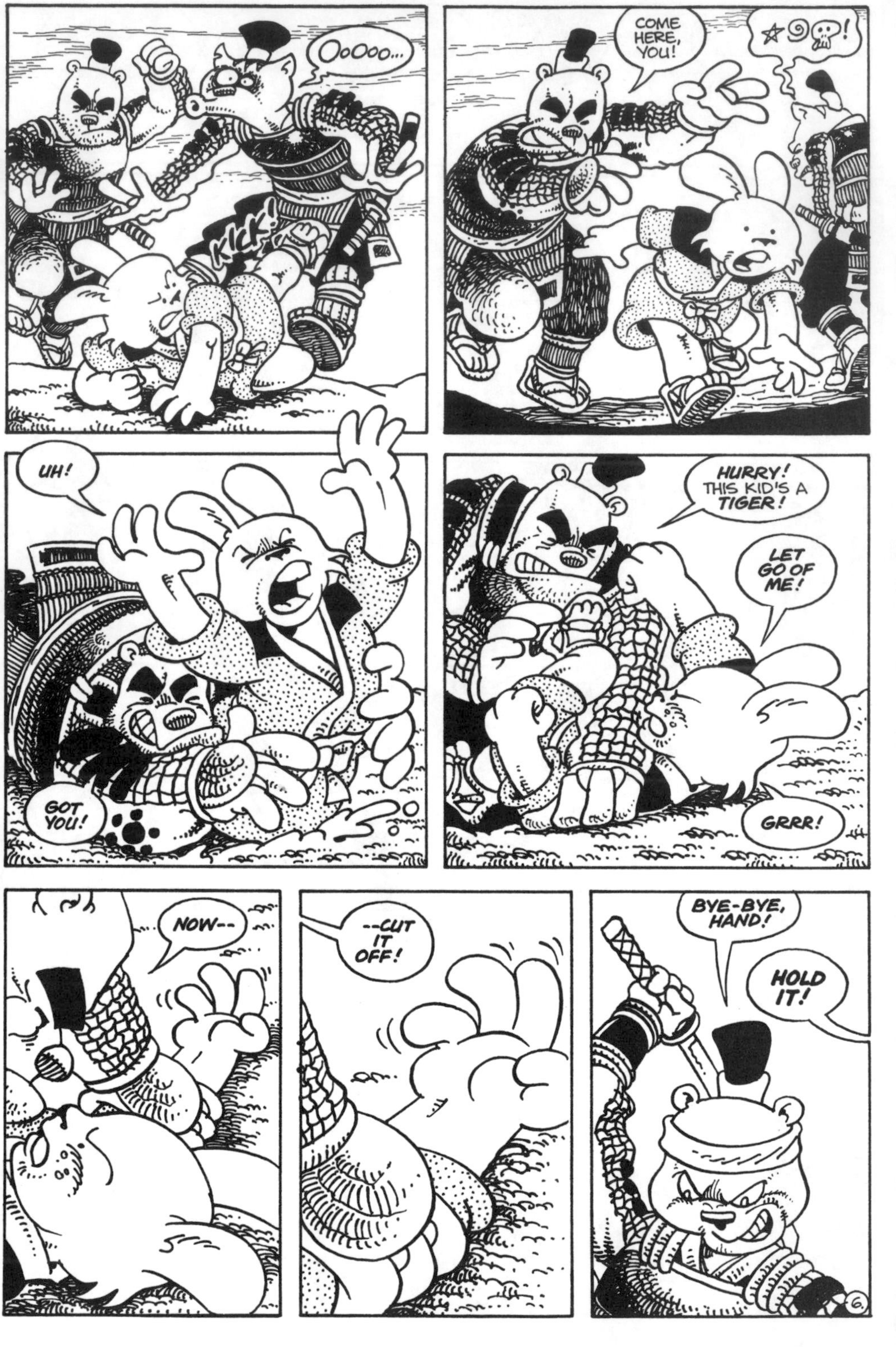
OOOOO...
KICK!
COME HERE, YOU!
☆๑☠!
UH!
GOT YOU!
HURRY! THIS KID'S A TIGER!
LET GO OF ME!
GRRR!
NOW--
--CUT IT OFF!
BYE-BYE, HAND!
HOLD IT!
6.

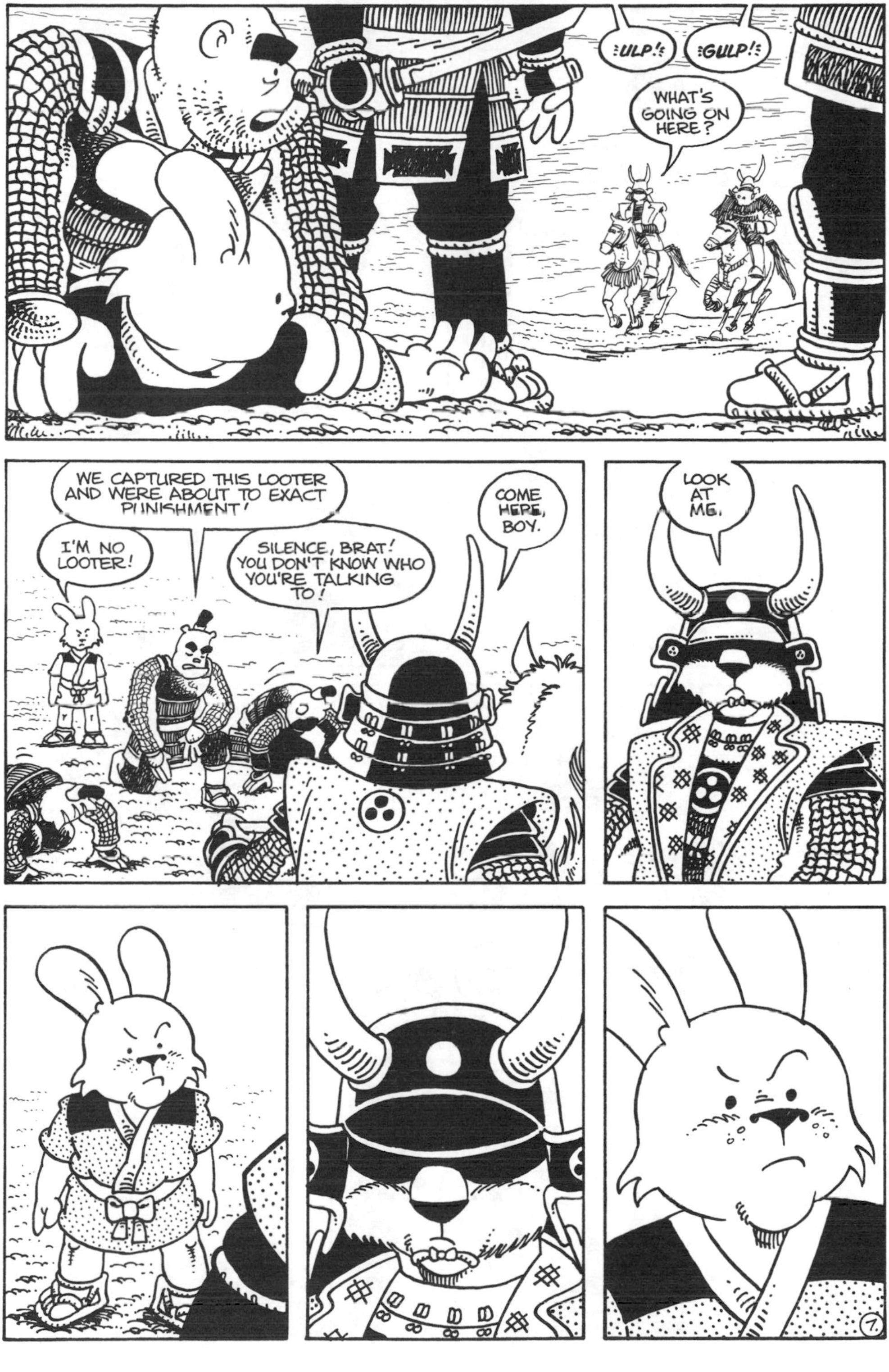
ULP!
GULP!
WHAT'S GOING ON HERE?
WE CAPTURED THIS LOOTER AND WERE ABOUT TO EXACT PUNISHMENT!
I'M NO LOOTER!
SILENCE, BRAT! YOU DON'T KNOW WHO YOU'RE TALKING TO!
COME HERE, BOY.
LOOK AT ME.
7.

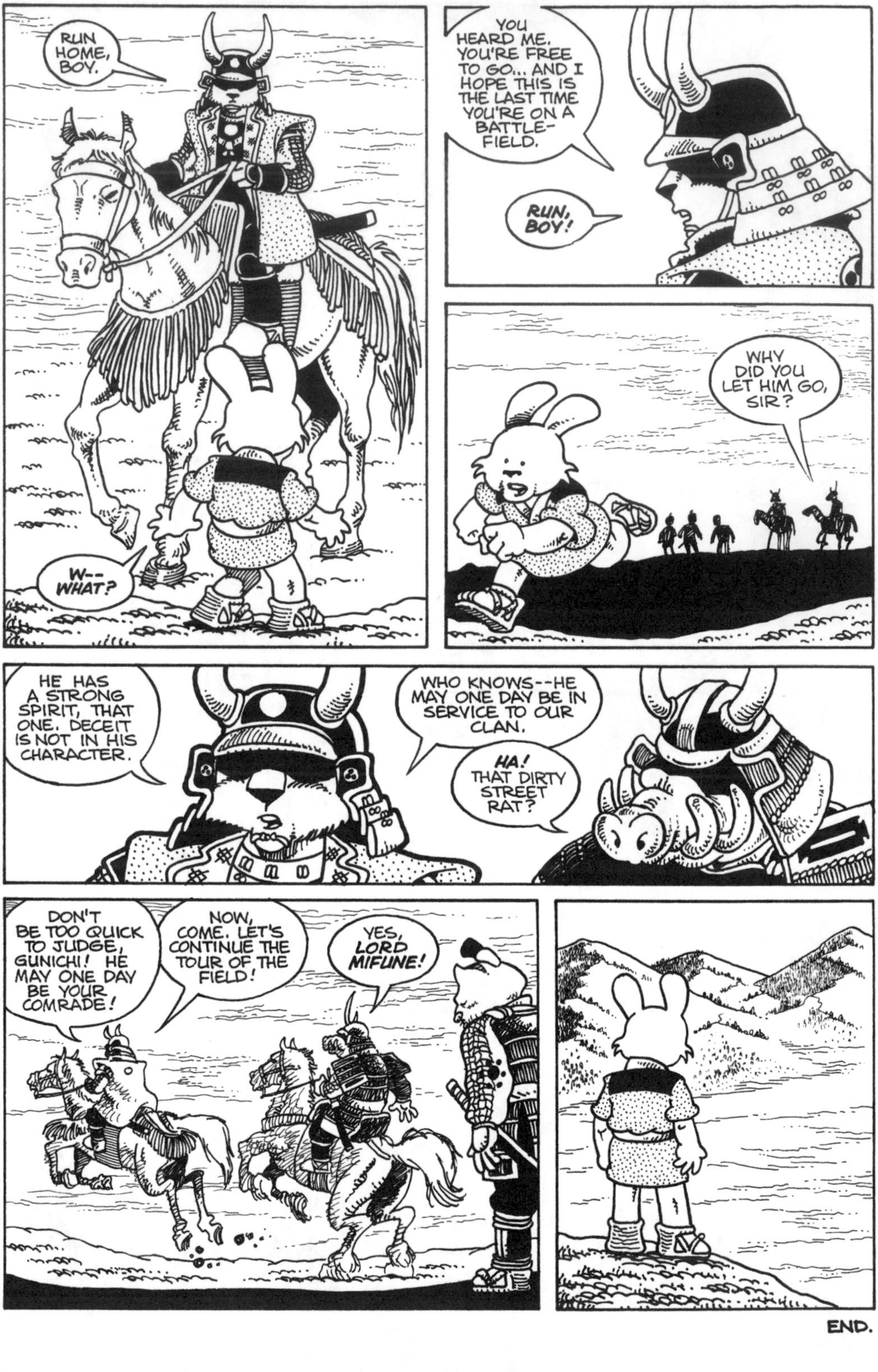
RUN HOME, BOY.
W-- WHAT?
YOU HEARD ME. YOU'RE FREE TO GO... AND I HOPE THIS IS THE LAST TIME YOU'RE ON A BATTLE-FIELD.
RUN, BOY!
WHY DID YOU LET HIM GO, SIR?
HE HAS A STRONG SPIRIT, THAT ONE. DECEIT IS NOT IN HIS CHARACTER.
WHO KNOWS--HE MAY ONE DAY BE IN SERVICE TO OUR CLAN.
HA! THAT DIRTY STREET RAT?
DON'T BE TOO QUICK TO JUDGE, GUNICHI! HE MAY ONE DAY BE YOUR COMRADE!
NOW, COME. LET'S CONTINUE THE TOUR OF THE FIELD!
YES, LORD MIFUNE!
END.

GALLERY

The following are Stan Sakai's covers from issues one through six of Mirage's Usagi Yojimbo™ Volume Two *series.*

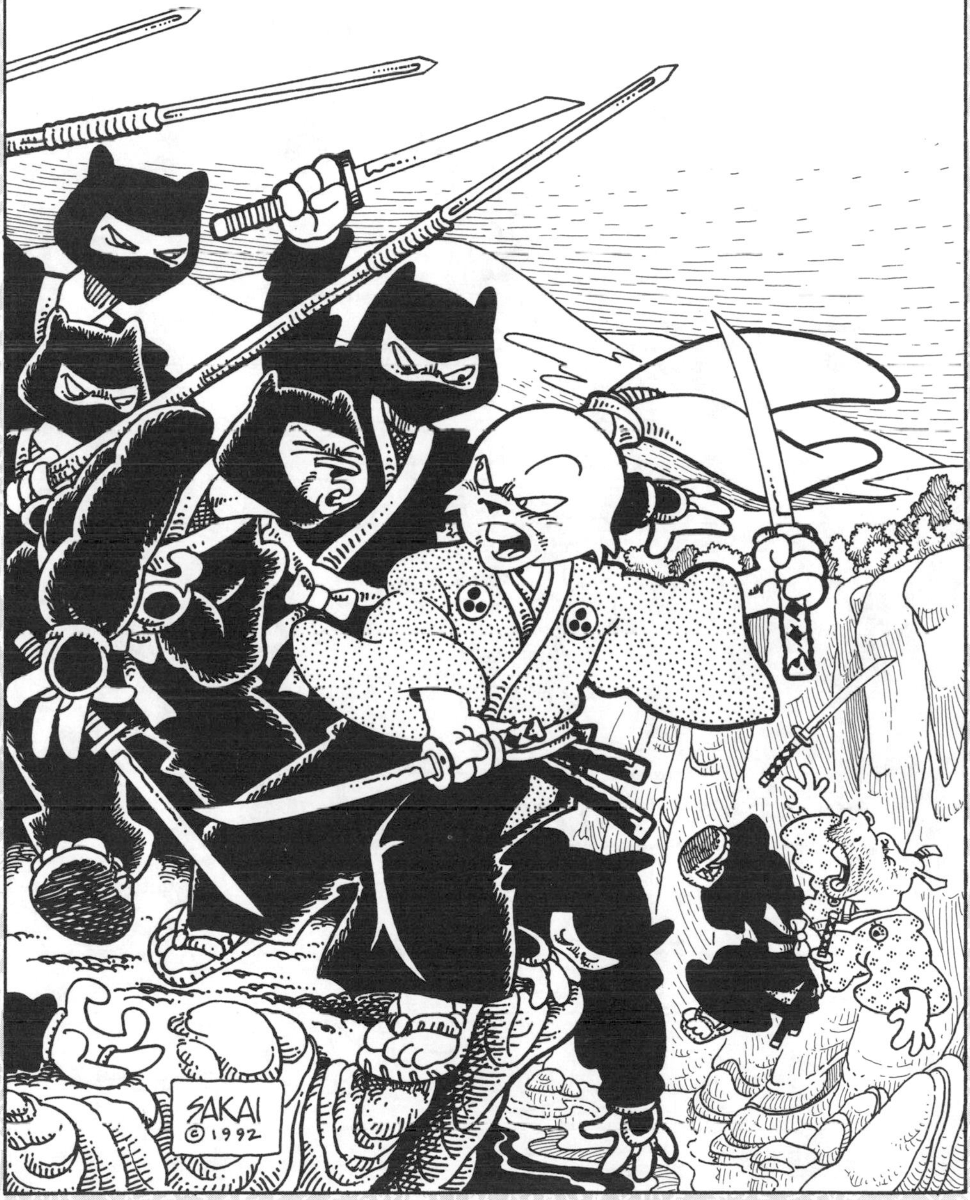
SAKAI
©1992

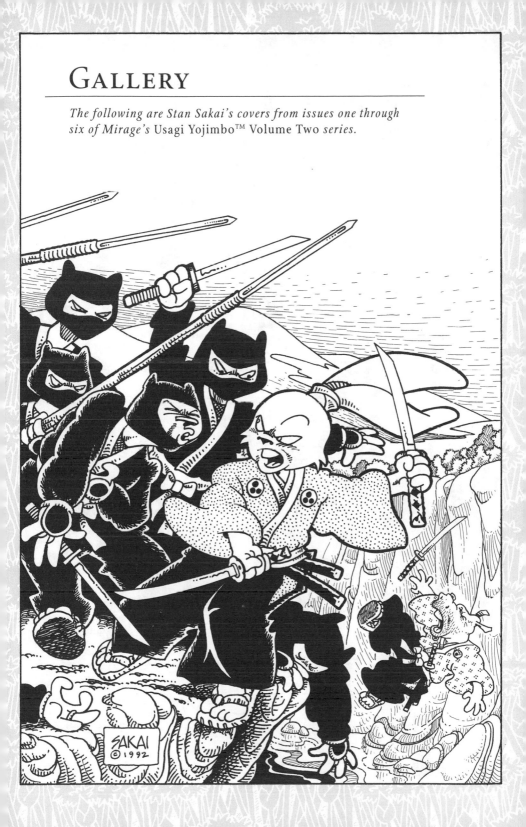

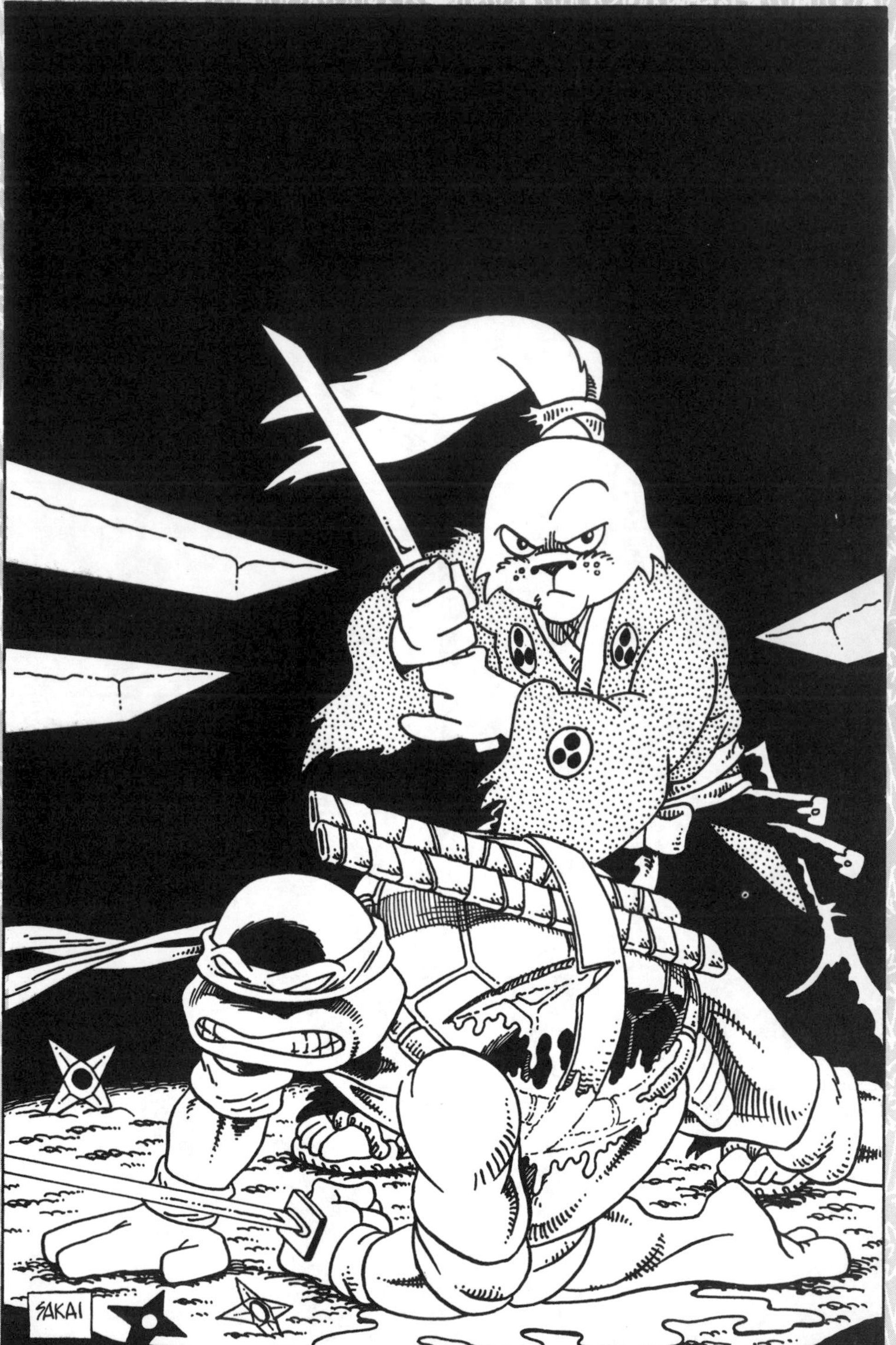
SAKAI

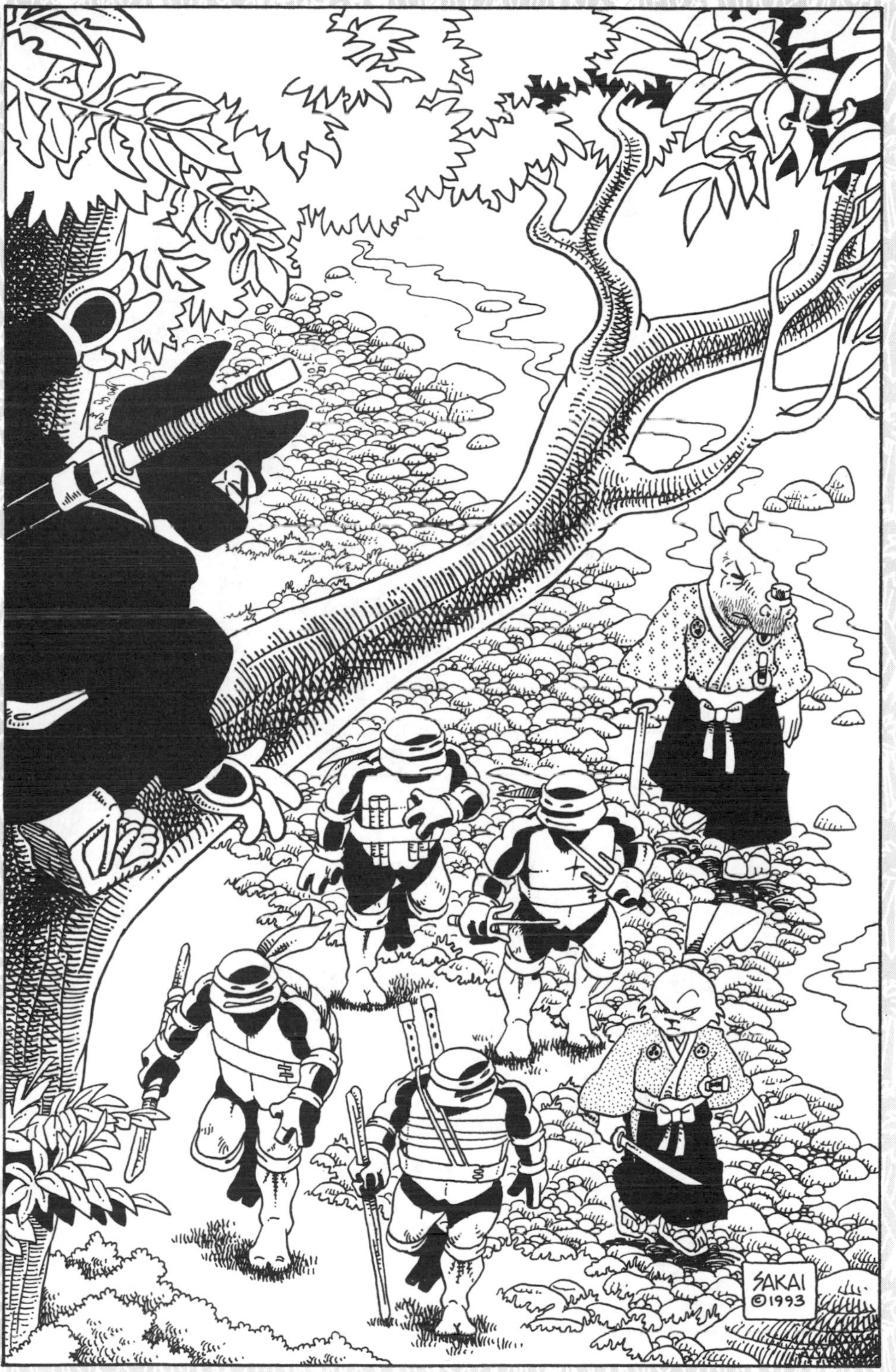
SAKAI
©1993

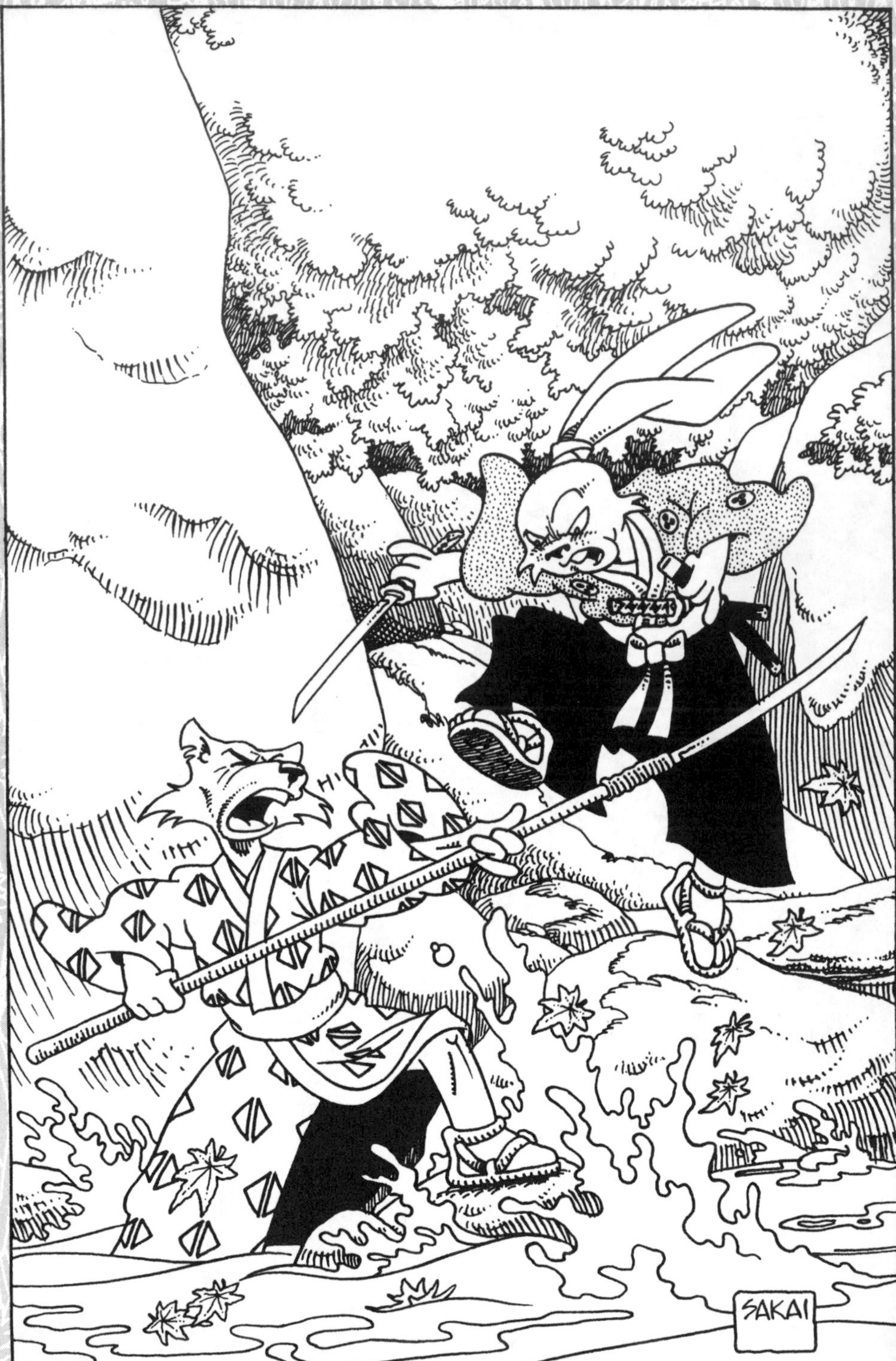
SAKAI

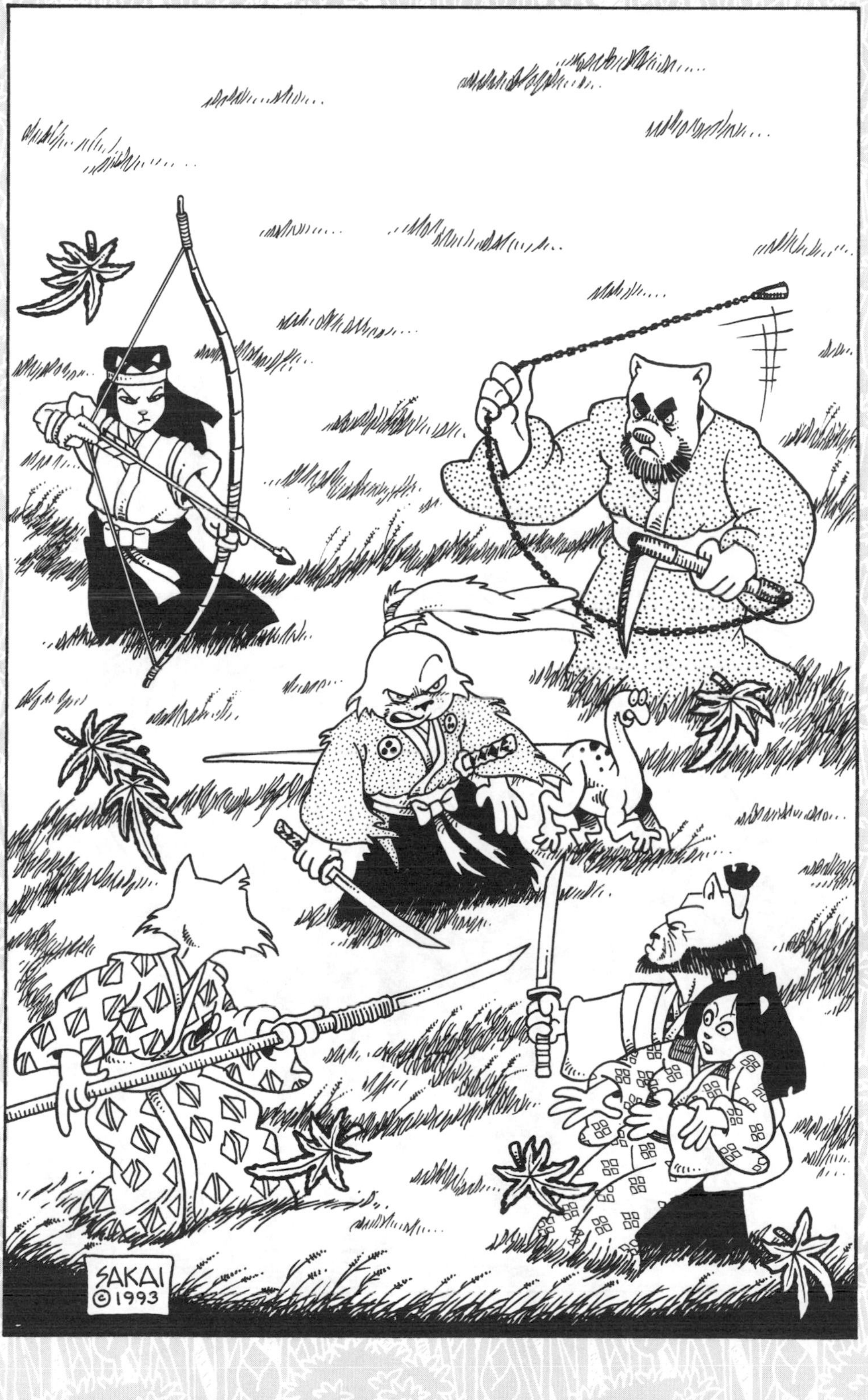
SAKAI
©1993

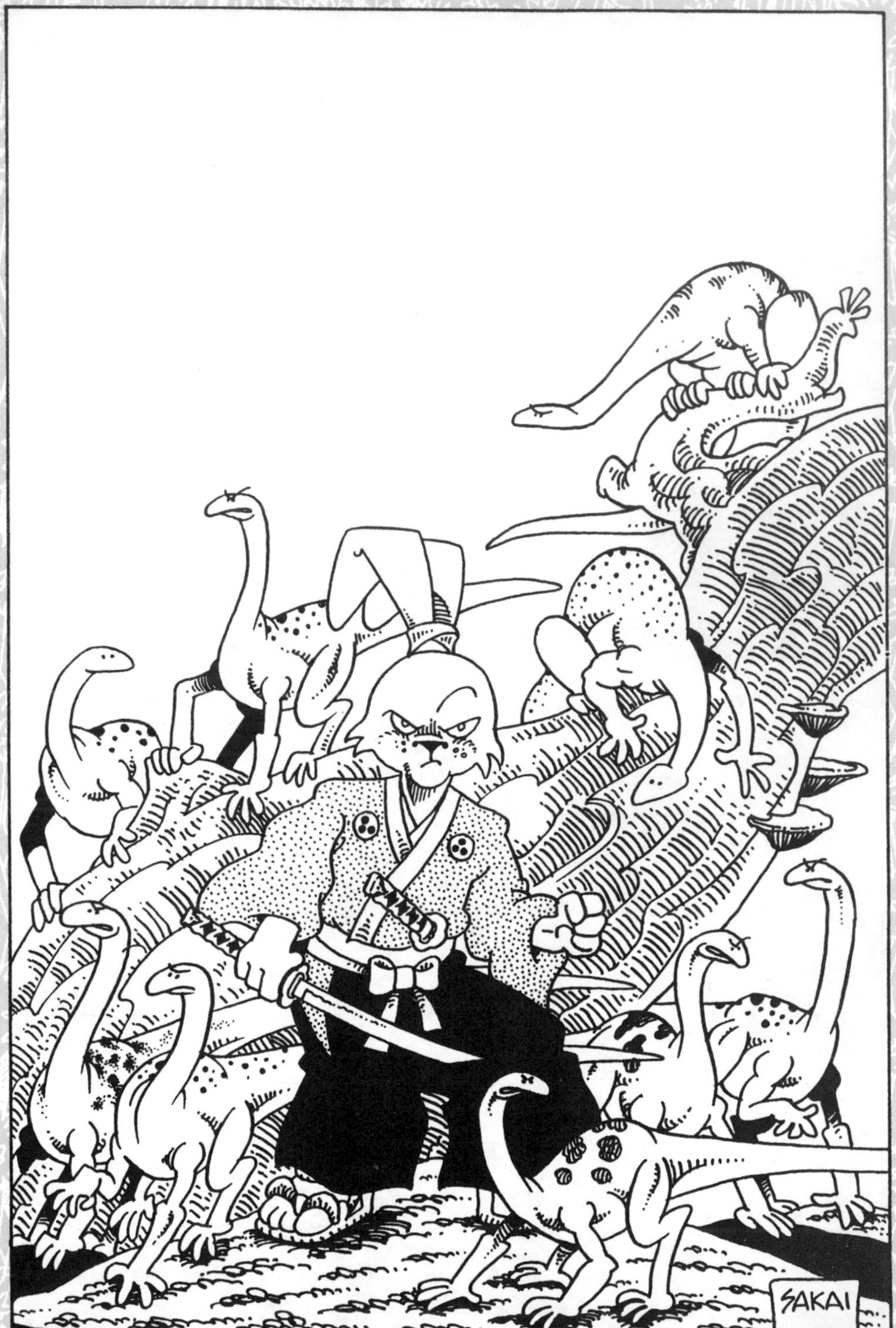
SAKAI

BIOGRAPHY
Stan Sakai

Photo by Greg Preston

STAN SAKAI WAS BORN in Kyoto, Japan, grew up in Hawaii, and now lives in California with his wife, Sharon, and children, Hannah and Matthew. He received a Fine Arts degree from the University of Hawaii and furthered his studies at Art Center College of Design in Pasadena, California.

His creation, Usagi Yojimbo, first appeared in comics in 1984. Since then, Usagi has been on television as a guest of the Teenage Mutant Ninja Turtles and has been made into toys, seen on clothing, and featured in a series of trade-paperback collections.

In 1991, Stan created *Space Usagi*, a series about the adventures of a descendant of the original Usagi that dealt with samurai in a futuristic setting.

Stan is also an award-winning letterer for his work on Sergio Aragonés' *Groo the Wanderer*, the "Spider-man" Sunday newspaper strips, and *Usagi Yojimbo*.

Stan is a recipient of a Parents' Choice Award, an Inkpot Award, and multiple Eisner Awards.

Usagi Yojimbo

Paperback and limited-edition hardcover collections and other merchandise available from Dark Horse Comics

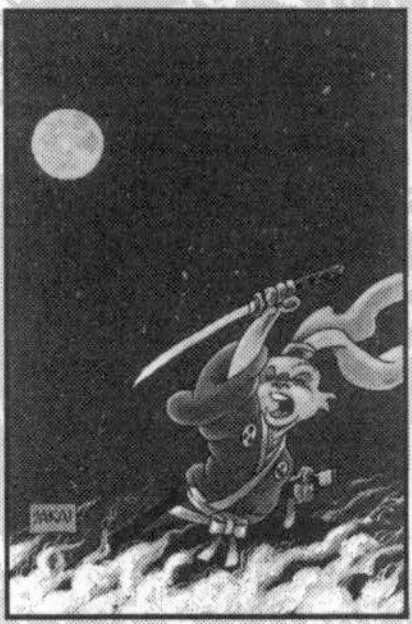

Shades of Death
ISBN: 1-56971-259-X $14.95

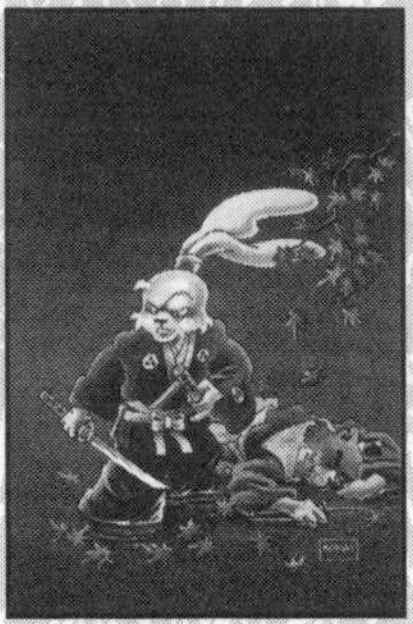

Daisho
ISBN: 1-56971-292-1 $14.95
limited-edition hardcover
ISBN: 1-56971-293-X $49.95

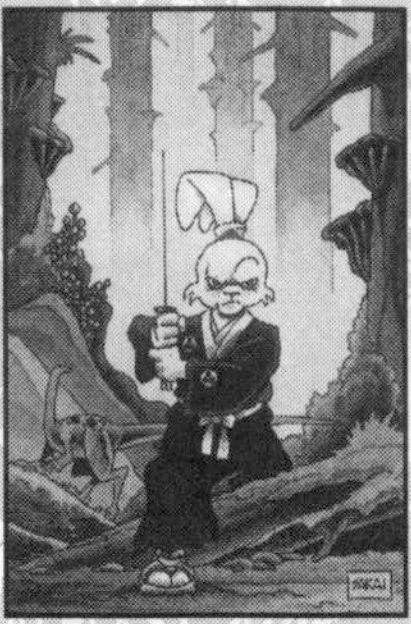

The Brink of Life and Death
ISBN: 1-56971-297-2 $14.95
limited-edition hardcover
ISBN: 1-56971-298-0 $55.00

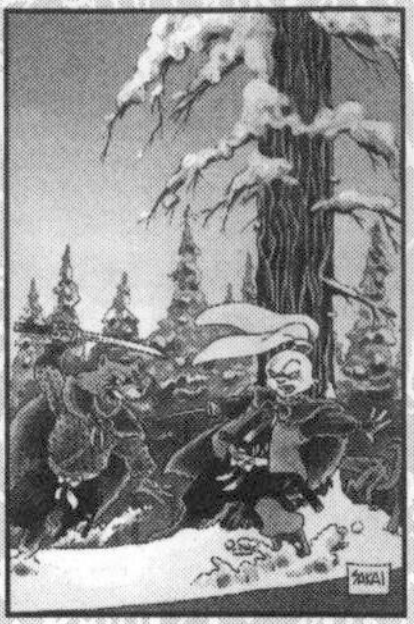

Seasons
ISBN: 1-56971-375-8 $14.95
limited-edition hardcover
ISBN: 1-56971-376-6 $55.00

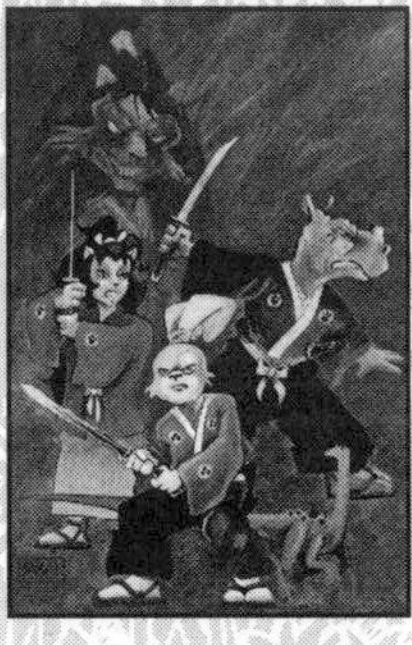

Grasscutter
ISBN: 1-56971-413-4 $16.95

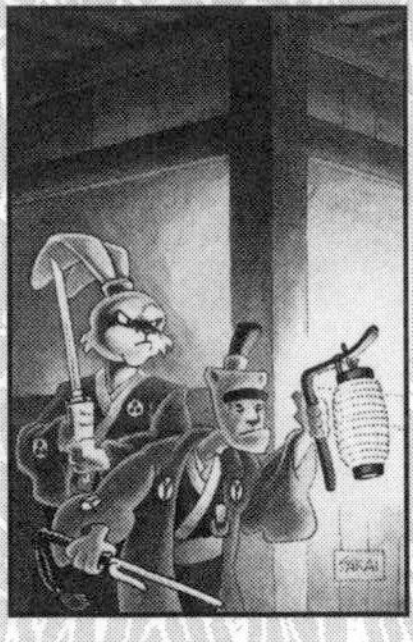

Grey Shadows
ISBN: 1-56971-459-2 $14.95

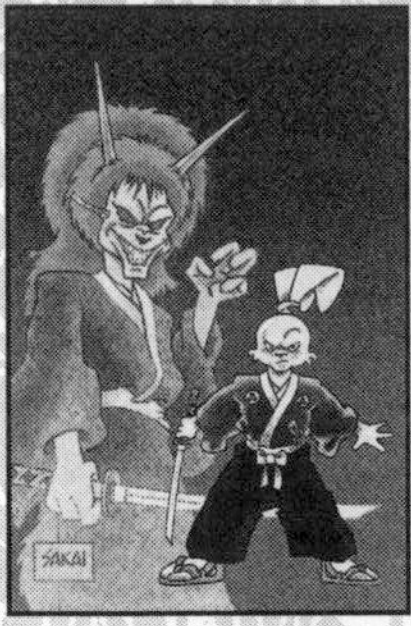

Demon Mask
ISBN: 1-56971-523-8 $15.95
limited-edition hardcover
ISBN: 1-56971-524-6 $56.95

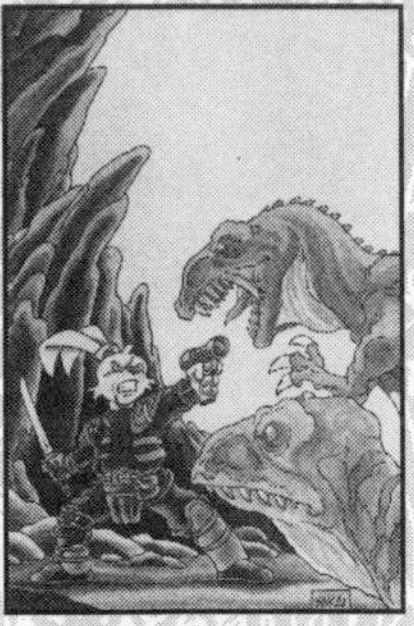

Space Usagi
ISBN: 1-56971-290-5 $17.95
limited-edition hardcover
ISBN: 1-56971-291-3 $59.95

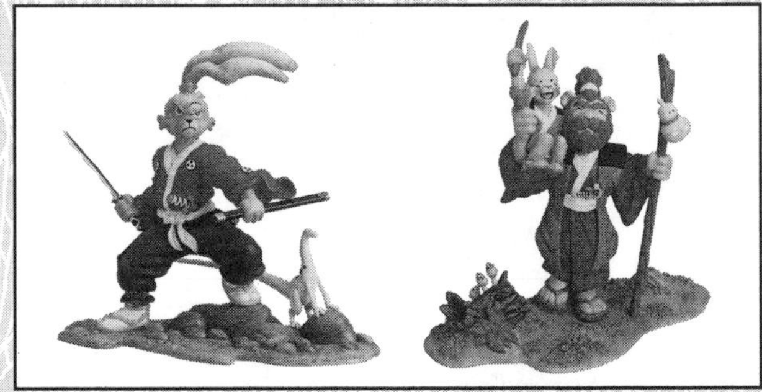

Usagi Yojimbo Cold-Cast Resin Statues
Each statue stands 8" tall, fully painted. Includes a mini-sketchbook and nine exclusive Usagi trading cards; one signed by Stan Sakai.
Usagi Yojimbo #19-179 $79.95 • Young Usagi & Katsuichi #19-289 $79.95

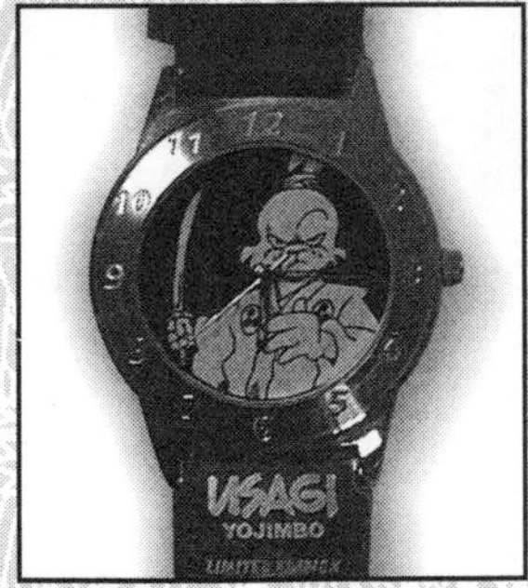
USAGI
YOJIMBO

Usagi Yojimbo Wristwatch
Limited edition of 1,000. Packaged in a collectible wooden box. Includes certificate of authenticity.
#10-011 $49.99

AVAILABLE AT YOUR LOCAL COMICS SHOP OR BOOKSTORE.

To find a comics shop in your area, call 1-888-266-4226. For more information or to order direct: E-MAIL: mailorder@darkhorse.com ON THE WEB: www.darkhorse.com

PHONE: 1-800-862-0052 or (503) 652-9701 Mon.-Sat. 9 A.M. to 5 P.M. Pacific Time

* Prices and availability subject to change without notice.